SCHOOL OF ORIENTAL AND AFRICAN STUDIES
University of London

Please return this book on or before the last date shown

Long loans and One Week loans may be renewed up to 10 times
Short loans & CDs cannot be renewed
Fines are charged on all overdue items

Online: http://lib.soas.ac.uk/patroninfo
Phone: 020-7898 4197 (answerphone)

PRAISE FOR *CROSSROADS*

"This is a passionate diagnosis of the economic threats the world now confronts – and from a highly original perspective and writer. His most important book yet. Read it."

– Will Hutton, Executive Vice Chair, The Work Foundation and author of *The Writing on the Wall: China and the West in the 21st Century*

"Nolan puts his finger on one of the great contradictions of globalization – collectivism in theory but self-interest and localization in practice. Resolving this paradox is a key challenge for the post-crisis world."

– Stephen Roach, Chairman, Morgan Stanley Asia

"Here is an urgent and lucid text about turbulence at the beginning of the 21st century. Started shortly before the major credit crisis when Professor Nolan was already writing about the dangers ahead, he now focuses on planetary complexities and challenges faced particularly by the leading economies. Taking the reader beyond 'wild capitalism,' the author avoids being a predictor or catastrophist, and skilfully directs our attention to solutions and tensions derived from conflict or co-operation, whether political, social, geographical or religious in origin. The tensions are of our own making but will we be clever enough, and fast enough, to discover solutions? Definitely a book to devour."

– Sir Brian Heap, Vice-President, European Academies Science Advisory Council

"For many years now, Professor Nolan has been prophetic about the structure of the global political economy, about the dangers and fate of the global financial system, and about the role of the world's powers in this system. Crossroads continues in that tradition and it is both bold and brilliant. Professor Nolan brings together a deep knowledge of the global political economy and remarkable analytical insight into the inner workings of the key players. Placing America, the exporter of 'wild capitalism,' at the centre of the discussion, he analyzes the role of America in the rise of the current political economic system and then turns to America's relation to China on the one hand and the Islamic world on the other. It is quite simply a tour de force."

– Doug Guthrie, Professor of Management, Stern School of Business, New York University

Crossroads:
The End of Wild Capitalism

Peter Nolan

Marshall Cavendish
Business

Copyright © 2009 Peter Nolan

First published in 2009 by

Marshall Cavendish Limited
Fifth Floor
32–38 Saffron Hill
London EC1N 8FH
United Kingdom
T: +44 (0)20 7421 8120
F: +44 (0)20 7421 8121
sales@marshallcavendish.co.uk
www.marshallcavendish.co.uk

Marshall Cavendish is a trademark of Times Publishing Limited

Other Marshall Cavendish offices: Marshall Cavendish International (Asia) Private Limited, 1 New
Industrial Road, Singapore 536196 • Marshall Cavendish Corporation. 99 White Plains Road,
Tarrytown NY 10591-9001, USA • Marshall Cavendish International (Thailand) Co Ltd. 253 Asoke,
12th Floor, Sukhumvit 21 Road, Klongtoey Nua, Wattana, Bangkok 10110, Thailand • Marshall
Cavendish (Malaysia) Sdn Bhd, Times Subang, Lot 46, Subang Hi-Tech Industrial Park, Batu Tiga,
40000 Shah Alam, Selangor Darul Ehsan, Malaysia

The right of Peter Nolan to be identified as the author of this work has been asserted by him in
accordance with the Copyright, Designs and Patents Act 1988.

A CIP record for this book is available from the British Library

ISBN 978-0-462-09968-2 (Hardback)
ISBN 978-0-462-09972-9 (Trade Paperback)

Project managed by Cambridge Publishing Management Ltd

Printed and bound in Great Britain by
TJ International Ltd, Padstow, Cornwall

For Dermot and Maeve,
and their cousins
Anna, Paul, Brendan, and Tristan,
Peter, Sinead, Maoise, and Conor,
Alice and Molly

Contents

Preface   IX

Introduction: Humanity at the crossroads   1

Part 1: The two-edged sword of capitalist globalization   8

1.1 Capitalist rationality in the era of the global business revolution   10
- What is globalization?   10
- Capitalism and coordination   14
- Finance and development   19
- Competition, industrial concentration, and technological
  progress   23
- Expanding human freedom   29

*1.2 The contradictions of capitalism in the era of the global
business revolution*   41
- Ecology, energy, and the environment   42
- The global business revolution   53
- Class structure   61
- Finance   70
- Conclusion   96

Part 2: Groping for a way forward: Conflict or cooperation?   100

Introduction   103

2.1 America   104
- America's domination of globalization   104
- America's Social Darwinist ideology   105
- America's globalization challenge   107

2.2 America and China   *120*

- Embryonic capitalism in China   124
- China's rise   130
- China's globalization challenge   133
- Resolving the contradictions: conflict or cooperation?   149
- Conclusion   186

2.3 America and Islam   *188*

- Capitalism, development, and Islam   190
- Islam and the West   215
- Conclusion   246

Conclusion: Beyond wild capitalism   252

Epilogue   267

Notes   271

Index   273

Preface

THIS book grew out of two closely related books. The first, *China at the Crossroads* (Polity Press, 2004); Chinese edition *Zhongguo chu zai shizi lukou* (Dafeng Chubanshe, 2007), was written mainly with a Chinese audience in mind. The second, *Capitalism and Freedom* (Anthem Press, 2007), was written mainly with an international audience in mind. I am grateful to both John Thompson of Polity Press and Tej Sood of Anthem Press who were immensely helpful during the process of publishing these books. Having listened to the opinion of a number of friends, I decided that it would be useful to write a book that addressed these issues in relation to an American audience. Moreover, since the publication of *Capitalism and Freedom* in mid-2007, the impending global crisis that formed the central focus of that book has, indeed, come to pass. The main body of this book was written between late 2007 and late 2008. It was completed in mid-January 2009. The global financial crisis was beginning to penetrate the global economy deeply. Israel was in the midst of its violent attack upon Gaza. President Obama was poised to take office on January 20, 2009.

The idea of writing a book of this type arose from discussions with John Cornwell. I am extremely grateful to him for his suggestion and for his unfailing enthusiasm for this project.

I am deeply grateful to Charles Curwen for meticulously reading the first draft of this book. He saved me from serious errors of both fact and interpretation, as well as making invaluable comments on detailed issues of style and language. I have benefited from his sage advice ever since he attempted to improve my Chinese language skills in the early 1970s.

I am grateful also to Brendan Kelly for his meticulous reading of the whole text, and innumerable helpful suggestions relating to both style and substance.

I have been helped greatly by innumerable discussions with Liu Chunhang and Zhang Jin on the topics analyzed in this book.

I am grateful also to Wang Xiaoqiang for the discussion of these topics over two decades.

I am grateful to Tim Clissold and Alistair Michie for their careful reading of earlier drafts of this book. Their numerous comments and suggestions were immensely helpful. I greatly appreciate their enthusiasm for this book and for its purpose.

I am grateful to Paul Westlake and Robert Wilkinson for innumerable discussions over five decades; to John Sender for many discussions and helpful suggestions on the topics covered in this book; to Sidney Rittenberg for sharing with me his experiences and his view of the world; to Maha Abdelrahman for her comments on the Muslim world; and to Teodor Shanin for sharing his views on Zionism.

I am most grateful to Martin Liu both for his enthusiasm and for his invaluable comments.

I am grateful to Patrick Walsh for his comments and suggestions.

I have benefited greatly from the feedback from the students in the M.Phil in Development Studies in the University of Cambridge who have taken my paper on Globalization over many years.

Despite the best efforts of the above-mentioned people, there are certain to be errors of fact and interpretation that remain in this book. These are entirely my responsibility.

There are numerous books that predict "the end" of something or other, including the "end of ideology," "the end of history," or, even, the "end of accountancy." Few, if any, of these predictions come to pass. This book does not make predictions. Instead, it records a fact that is now widely accepted, especially since the eruption of the global financial crisis: namely, that the era of "wild capitalism" is over. What follows next is an open question. Humanity stands at a crossroads. One path, the "road less traveled by," leads to cooperation. The other path, well-trodden throughout human history, leads to conflict.

Two roads diverged in a yellow wood,
And sorry I could not travel both
And be one traveler, long I stood
And looked down one as far as I could
To where it bent in the undergrowth;

Then took the other, as just as fair,
And having perhaps the better claim,
Because it was grassy and wanted wear;
Though as for that, the passing there
Had worn them really about the same,

And both that morning equally lay
In leaves no step had trodden black.
Oh, I kept the first for another day!
Yet knowing how way leads on to way,
I doubted if I should ever come back.

I shall be telling this with a sigh
Somewhere ages and ages hence:
Two roads diverged in a wood, and I—
I took the one less traveled by,
And that has made all the difference.

Robert Frost, *The Road Not Taken*

Introduction: humanity at the crossroads

No man is an island, entire of itself; every man is a piece of the continent, a part of the main. If a clod be washed away by the sea, Europe is the less, as well as if a promontory were, as well as if a manor of thy friend's or of thine own were. Any man's death diminishes me, because I am involved in mankind; and therefore never send to know for whom the bell tolls; it tolls for thee.

John Donne, Meditation XVII, *Devotions upon Emergent Occasions*

It's lovely to live on a raft. We had the sky, up there, all sparkled with stars, and we used to lay on our backs and look at them, and discuss whether they was made or only just happened—Jim, he allowed they was made, but I allowed they happened... [I]t would have been a miserable business to have any unfriendliness on a raft; for what you want, above all things on a raft, is for everybody to be satisfied and feel right and kind toward the other.

Mark Twain, *Huckleberry Finn*

Ultimately, every man's path is every other's. There are no separate journeys for there are no separate men to make them. All men are one and there is no other tale to tell.

Cormac McCarthy, *The Crossing*

A MERICA sits at the center of the global system of political economy. Since the 1970s it has been the central force in the spread of free market capitalism across the globe. That system now faces fundamental challenges, which threaten the very existence of the human species. The way in which America responds to those challenges will determine the fate of the whole human race.

Within America from the 1960s onward, Social Darwinist policies based on individualism and the lightly regulated free market have once again occupied the mainstream of politics, just as they did in the late nineteenth and early twentieth century. America has been the unchallenged world leader during the recent period of capitalist globalization. It has used its hegemonic position to promote a privatized free market economy in which the constraints that regulated the market economy in previous decades have been progressively dismantled. This ushered in an era of "wild capitalism." It was widely thought in America that this era would witness the "end of history" and the worldwide dominance of American values and institutions.

The force of self-interest in the pursuit of profit exercised through the market mechanism has been centrally important for progress over several millennia of settled human civilization. Not far from Cambridge in Britain there are 3,000-year-old mine workings, called Grime's Graves. The site extends over almost 100 acres. It contains around 400 mine shafts, which extend to a depth of up to twelve meters in order to reach buried flints. The mines each have numerous galleries extending off the main shaft. The flints were worked through chipping, in order to produce cutting tools, axe-heads, arrow heads and agricultural implements. It is estimated that the site produced as many as 28 million pieces of worked flint. These were traded over long distances across Britain and northern Europe.

As capitalism broadened its scope in the era of globalization under American leadership, so the benefits increased. Removal of the constraints on the operation of global markets allowed capitalism's competitive force, and its unique power to disseminate information, to liberate human beings to an even greater degree than before from the tyranny of nature, from poverty, and from war. The era of capitalist globalization witnessed an unprecedented pace of technological progress. It witnessed an ever-deeper intermeshing of national economies, drawn together by the bonds of trade and, even more, by cross-border investment by international firms. It widened the scope for individual freedom from control by others over people's lives, and provided the foundation for democratic institutions. It witnessed the construction of a global culture, facilitated by the amazing advances in information technology. It contributed to peace among nations thanks to the market's function of nurturing contacts and trust across national boundaries. The advances achieved by the globalization of capitalism appeared all the more striking when set against the failure of non-capitalist systems of economic organization.

However, capitalist freedom is a two-edged sword. The market mechanism is a force that human beings themselves have created unconsciously, but which contains its own fundamental contradictions. Those who have recognized the contradictions inherent within the capitalist system include not only Marx and Engels, but also other intellectual giants, such as Adam Smith and John Stuart Mill, who both admired its dynamism, but feared its anarchic character. They both deplored the fact that it unleashed and nourished the selfish, materialistic, non-benevolent aspects of human nature.

The past three decades of capitalist development have intensified the contradictions latent within the capitalist system. Due to the dramatic widening of the geographical scope of the capitalist system, its contradictions have become, for the first time, global in scope. As human beings took to new heights their ability to free themselves from fundamental constraints through the market mechanism, so they also reached new depths in terms of the uncontrollability of the structures they created. Unrestrained global capitalism has created intense threats to the very existence of the human species at the same time that it has liberated humanity more than ever before from fundamental constraints over their lives.

The unrestrained force of wild capitalist globalization comprehensively threatens the global natural environment, with the possibility that many complex ecological problems are already irreversible. A ferocious international struggle is under way, comparable to a struggle between neighboring colonies of insects, to secure access to scarce exhaustible resources. Capitalist globalization has resulted in an unprecedented concentration of business power, not only among the leading "systems integrator" firms within each industrial sector, but also far down into the value chain. It has led to intensified global inequality within both rich and poor countries, and between the internationalized global power elite and the mass of citizens rooted within their respective nations. It has produced extreme financial instability. Financial markets are more closely interconnected than ever before. The global financial crisis which began in 2007 is shaking the global economic system to its foundations.

As wild capitalist globalization unfolded, the contradictions produced by the free play of market forces, including ecology, exhaustible resources, the role of the large global firm, increased inequality in income and wealth, and financial system risk, became ever more clearly visible. This led to intensified concern from a widening circle of scholars, politicians, novelists, film-makers, and ordinary citizens. Taken together, this amounts to a broad consensus about the necessity for human beings to assert their control over the market mechanism. The explosion of the global financial crisis has deeply reinforced such feelings. Across the world, human beings' sense of insecurity has greatly increased. Only collective action to face the multiple crises can provide the sense of personal security that people crave. The unconstrained global free market has failed. The era of wild capitalist globalization is over.

Ecologists such as Harvard's Edward Wilson warn that mankind confronts an "Age of Loneliness" unless radical action is taken to prevent an unprecedented rate of species destruction. The leading scientists from all countries in the Intergovernmental Panel on Climate Change have reached a consensus that without radical international intervention, the world faces an environmental disaster. Most of the staunchest opponents of this view have been forced by the evidence to change their minds. In both America and in developing countries, economists and politicians lament the drastic increase in inequality and injustice in the distribution of income, wealth and life chances that have characterized the era of globalization. There is no plausible ethical defense for the fact that the richest two percent of the world adult population hold more than one-half of total global wealth, while the entire bottom half owns barely one percent of the total. The idea that there is a "global level playing field" and that the "world is flat" is unsustainable in the face of the mounting evidence that the basic tendency of unregulated capitalism is toward intense concentration of business power, not only at the apex of the global business system, but also far down in the value chain, hidden from the view of most observers. In April 2008, Paul Volcker, former chairman of the Federal Reserve, concluded: "The bright new financial system—for all its talented participants, for all its rich rewards—has failed the test of the marketplace." The dramatic events in the months that followed this showed how accurate Volcker's judgment was.

If mankind is to survive the twenty-first century, there is no choice but to move toward cooperative institutions that regulate global capitalism, which is the most dynamic force in human history, in the collective interest of all human beings. In order to achieve sustainable human development, the world has no choice but to move into a new era of global market regulation, covering many areas including ecology, energy use, the distribution of income and wealth, and the operation of financial markets. For the first time in the history of capitalism, its contradictions threaten the whole world. No longer can an individual nation, however powerful and large its military expenditure, isolate itself from the negative impact of the unconstrained free market. No country, however big, is decoupled in the era of capitalist globalization. It is a delusion for any country to imagine that it is invulnerable.

The new forms of regulation can already be perceived in embryo. They are being discussed in all key areas of socio-economic life in response to widespread human feelings about the undesirable consequences of the anarchy of capitalist markets in the era of globalization. This amounts to a comprehensive transformation of the global socio-economic system. It does not seek to obliterate the market economy. It is global in character. It is emerging from the widespread sentiments expressed by people in response to the different types of contradictions that are inherent in the capitalist system.

However, there are enormous difficulties facing the achievement of the required collective action. Despite the deep interpenetration of national economies achieved by capitalist globalization, the main focus of political life and economic system regulation remains the nation state, to which most people are bound by the accident of their birth. Nation states have different interests, due to the fact that they are at different levels of development, and have different belief systems and histories. The central actors on the global stage, who will determine whether this critical phase of capitalist globalization is sustainable, are, on the one hand, America, which is still the world's hegemonic power, and, on the other hand, the rising force of China, with a population of 1.3 billion people, and the transnational force of the Muslim world, also with a population of 1.3 billion people. Between them Chinese and Muslims comprise two-fifths of the world's population, each contained within a relatively unified cultural environment. Any attempt to regulate the global free market in the collective interest of all human beings would be profoundly significant ethically. Ethics is the Pole Star that guides humanity on its journey through time. It is time to turn back to reflect on what great thinkers from each of these cultures, Western, Muslim, and Chinese, have had to say about the ethics of unconstrained free markets since the dawn of capitalism.

The world's dominant economic, political, and cultural power, America, led the global drive toward unrestrained free market capitalism. It benefited in numerous ways from capitalist globalization. American firms sit at the center of capitalist globalization. American shareholders and pension funds benefited from the global success of American firms and the dominant position of American technology. American consumers benefited from the surge in low-priced imports from "emerging markets." However, capitalist globalization is a two-edged sword for

America, which feels threatened by the ecological consequences of rapid growth in developing countries. Its citizens feel threatened by low-wage employees in developing countries. They feel threatened by the fact that American firms are decreasingly reliant on the American home market, and the leaders of these firms identify less and less with American national interests. Americans feel threatened by the financial turmoil that has grown out of the global free market in money. They feel threatened by the rise of a giant new political-economic force, China. They feel threatened and puzzled by the deep hostility from much of the Muslim world. The world feels very different from the way that most Americans imagined it would be at the start of this era.

According to a poll by the *Wall Street Journal* and NBC, in 1997 48 percent of Americans thought globalization was good, and 42 percent thought it was bad. By 2007, the proportion who thought globalization was good had shrunk to just 28 percent, while the proportion who thought it was bad had swelled to 58 percent. In the midst of the global financial crisis it is almost certain that the proportion of Americans who think globalization is bad has risen still further.

From the perspective of the developing countries, including both China and the countries of the Muslim world, capitalist globalization also presents great challenges. The ecology of these countries is deteriorating fast, as they pass from being "poor and clean" to being "large and dirty." Integration into the capitalist global system has been accompanied by a widespread and large increase in internal inequality of income, wealth, and life chances. Large swathes of their economies are dominated by giant global firms from the high-income countries. As they liberalized their financial systems, they faced surging bubbles in property, stock markets, and commodity prices, and the prospect of the chaotic unwinding of these asset bubbles. Their deep integration with the capitalist trade system greatly increased their vulnerability to downturns in demand for their exports. The Asian financial crisis undermined confidence in the free market policies of the US-led Washington Consensus. The global financial crisis destroyed any remaining illusions that the global free market would work naturally and spontaneously to their benefit.

Capitalist globalization has the potential to generate intense conflict between America and China on the one hand, and America and the Muslim world on the other. Conflict might arise from the deterioration of the global ecology; the struggle over scarce resources, especially energy; the changing nature of the large company and its relationship to the nation state; or from perceptions of the causes of changes in the distribution of income and wealth, and of the causes of financial instability. The financial crisis which rapidly penetrated the real economy in America in late 2008 could quite conceivably lead to a social crisis, and, even, to a political and international relations crisis. In the face of the perceived threats, the American government spends around two billion dollars per day on the armed forces. It refuses to dismantle its vast stock of nuclear arms, sufficient to obliterate global civilization in the blink of an eye. It is even possible to imagine a variety of scenarios that might lead to the disaster of large-scale military conflict between America and those it perceives to be its enemies.

The future of the world hangs in the balance. Is America capable of interacting constructively with China and the Muslim world, in order to produce a peaceful cooperative solution to the common problems that confront humanity at this critical stage in the evolution of the human species? Will America be able to engage constructively with both China and the Muslim world to devise cooperative solutions to the inherent contradictions of wild capitalist globalization, which threaten the very survival of humanity?

These challenges raise fundamental questions about human nature. Are people basically aggressive, competitive, masculine, and violent, or are they basically cooperative, loving, feminine, and peaceful? Which of these aspects of human nature are most likely to contribute to the solution of the challenges that face the world—and especially America, which sits at the center of these challenges?

The idea that the pursuit of individual self-interest serves the interests of the human species as a whole appeared to receive strong support from Charles Darwin's theory of human evolution, as expounded in *The Descent of Man*, especially in the phrase "the survival of the fittest." Social Darwinists argue that aggression is the key instinct of all animals, including human beings, and view intra-species competition as a fundamental driver of evolution. They consider that one of the strongest and most creative instincts known to man is the attempt by individuals to promote their own interests. They consider that the exercise of these instincts through the market has been the central force in human progress.

In fact, Social Darwinists use the term "survival of the fittest" in a somewhat different way from Darwin himself. Darwin insisted upon the term "natural selection" being taken in its "large and metaphorical sense, including dependence of one being on another, and including (which is more important) not only the life of the individual, but success of the progeny." In *The Descent of Man* Darwin paid close attention to the evolution in human beings of moral qualities that have enabled them to survive as a species: "[O]f all the differences between man and lower animals," he wrote, "the moral sense is by far the most important." Darwin ranged widely in exploring these human instincts, under which he included love, mutual love, "the all-important emotion of sympathy," sympathetic feelings, instinctive sympathy, sympathetic kindness to others, mutual aid, fidelity, and benevolent actions. He uses the word "love" more than 90 times in *The Descent of Man*.

Philosophers have debated endlessly about the essential features of human nature, and the relationship of these features to the market economy. From ancient times to the present day, they have sought to find a middle way, or mean, between competing extremes as the ethical foundation for the good society. The human species cannot survive without a sustainable ethic, but neither extreme negative nor extreme positive freedom offers the solution. Human beings must find common ethical ground from across the different world civilizations, "using the past to serve the present" in order to form a common ethic for global survival, which answers people's fundamental spiritual needs and which forms the basis for a simple rational philosophy that everyone can understand. They must learn to tame and civilize the market economy in a new way in the context of global capitalism, to serve the collective social purpose on a global scale. The solution to sustainable development lies neither in the utopia of a purely benevolent, selfless, non-competitive world, nor in the anarchy of an unconstrained, individualistic, competitive global capitalism.

Human beings cannot avoid the duality that is at the center of their being, the struggle between cooperative, loving instincts and destructive death instincts. They have no choice but to live with this duality. They must cooperate and love, while living with their fears and instincts to behave aggressively. In *Civilisation and its Discontents* Sigmund Freud posed the struggle facing mankind: "[T]he meaning of the evolution of civilisation is no longer obscure to us. It must present the struggle between Eros and Death, between the instinct of life and the instinct of destruction, as it works itself out in the human species. This struggle is what all life essentially consists of, and the evolution of civilisation may therefore be simply described as the struggle for life of the human species."

As the world moves into the new millennium, humanity stands at a crossroads. The era of wild capitalist globalization is at an end, its demise hastened by the global financial crisis. The contradictions of capitalism in the early twenty-first century are, for the first time, global in nature. In the search for solutions to the multiple threats to the sustainability of life for the human species, there is no alternative other than to work together across national frontiers, cultures, and levels of development, to find a pragmatic, non-ideological, cooperative way to overcome these threats. The threats derive from the nature of capitalist globalization itself, and the solutions too are inherent within the universal tendencies of capitalism. The path taken by America, at this crossroads in its own history and in that of the human race, will determine the outcome for the whole human species.

The challenges that are faced by human beings are the product of people's own purposive activities, expressed mainly through the economic system. It is within their collective power to resolve these contradictions. The very depth of the challenges they now face may shock them into the collective action necessary to ensure the survival of the species. Alongside human beings' competitive and destructive instincts are their instincts for species survival through cooperation. However great the challenge may be, human beings have the capability to solve the contradictions that are of their own making. It may only be the approaching "final hour" which finally forces human beings to grope their way toward globally cooperative solutions that ensure the survival of the species.

America cannot avoid a central role in this drama. It stands at a crossroads in its own history. The choice it takes will determine the fate of the world.

Part 1

The two-edged sword of capitalist globalization

It was the best of times, it was the worst of times, it was the age of wisdom, it was the age of foolishness, it was the epoch of belief, it was the epoch of incredulity, it was the season of Light, it was the season of Darkness, it was the spring of hope, it was the winter of despair, we had everything before us, we had nothing before us ...

Charles Dickens, *A Tale of Two Cities*

1.1 CAPITALIST RATIONALITY IN THE ERA OF THE GLOBAL BUSINESS REVOLUTION

For over two thousand years, capitalism, through the mechanism of marketplace competition in the pursuit of profit, has been the key force propelling forward human ingenuity to increase productivity and improve material well-being. Financial institutions and mechanisms have been centrally important to the growth of capitalism. Since the 1970s, in the era of globalization, the forces of capitalist competition have operated with a new intensity as capitalism has penetrated ever more deeply into the four corners of the globe. This period has witnessed an unprecedented advance in technological progress, achieved mainly through research and development undertaken by large oligopolistic firms. The period of capitalist globalization has witnessed a comprehensive expansion of the realm of individual freedom from the numerous forces that constrain the lives of ordinary people.

WHAT IS GLOBALIZATION?

THE recent dramatic changes in the world business system constitute a surge forward of capitalism to a global scale. However, despite the dramatic advance of capitalism, it constitutes only the most recent stage in a process that has been under way since human beings' early history. Capitalism, in the sense of production for profit for the market, stimulated by the incentive to "truck and barter," has been a central part of the history of the world since ancient times. For several thousand years, human history has been organized around an ever-increasing division of labor, extension of the market, and pursuit of profit. This force has been the central factor in technological progress, which has transformed the lives of human beings as they have gained ever greater mastery over the forces of nature. Until the early modern period, the main consequence of technological progress was to enable population growth and output more or less to keep pace with each other, advancing together in a complex symbiotic relationship. However, around 200 years ago, population growth and income per person began an unprecedented, simultaneous acceleration. This period of unprecedented global population growth is likely to end in the final decades of this century.

The evolution of capitalism in early modern Western Europe, within the overall feudal socio-economic structure, has been studied closely. However, large parts of the world outside Europe also contained significant pockets of capitalism within overall non-capitalist socio-economic structures. These involved urban trading centers and specialist production for both local and distant markets. There is now a rich historical literature on the extensive pockets of capitalism in East and South Asia, as well as in the Middle East. Large parts of the pre-modern world were linked by long-distance international trade in products with high value/weight ratios, from China through South and Southeast Asia, the Middle East, coastal Africa, and Europe.

Industrial production in the pre-modern world was widely dispersed, including specialized industries such as food processing, metallurgy, mining, textiles, carpets, pottery, shipbuilding, salt, sugar, and tea, as well as the construction of canals, ports, roads, bridges, and buildings. These often involved relatively large-scale enterprises, amid a myriad of small-scale "proto-industrial" production. It is estimated that in 1750, China accounted for around one-third of total world manufacturing output, and South Asia for around one-quarter, while "the West" still accounted for less than one-fifth. Commercial growth interacted with institutional change, stimulating the evolution of urban-based legal and financial mechanisms to facilitate commerce.

Recent research has shown that technological change in the non-Western world played a far more important role in global pre-modern technological progress than was once thought to be the case. Many of the key technological innovations of the late Middle Ages in Europe either originated in Asia, or were independently invented there. Technological progress occurred mainly through innovations by profit-seeking entrepreneurs who responded to commercial opportunities. The technological advances that had evolved slowly within the capitalist segments of the non-European world made their way to Europe in the Middle Ages. These interacted with indigenously evolving technological progress, and with the fast-evolving capitalist institutions, to produce the European Industrial Revolution. Technological progress accelerated far beyond the rates that had previously been achieved. In the eighteenth century, global markets for British-made goods expanded at a fierce rate, with great fluctuations from one period to another. The search for profits to enable British manufacturers to benefit from this process greatly stimulated the search for innovations in manufacturing and transport technologies.

By the middle of the nineteenth century, industrial capitalism had spread across Europe, and was taking firm root in North America behind high protectionist barriers. By 1900, the share of "the West" in global manufacturing output had risen to over three-quarters, from less than one-fifth a mere 150 years previously. The combined share of China and South Asia had shrunk to less than one-tenth of the world total, from nearly three-fifths in the mid-eighteenth century. From the perspective of Europe and North America in the nineteenth century, the non-Western world increasingly assumed the character of a homogeneously "stagnant" economy and society, "vegetating in the teeth of time."

Large parts of the "non-Western" world were integrated through military conquest into global industrial capitalism. The period witnessed the rapid growth of international trade, facilitated by technological progress in transport, including the railroad, the steamship, and refrigeration. Merchandise exports as a share of GDP for the whole world increased from one percent in 1820 to eight percent in 1914. International movements of capital accelerated, especially in the latter part of the period. Foreign assets as a share of world GDP rose from seven percent in 1870 to 18 percent in 1914. By the end of the nineteenth century, industrial capitalism had enjoyed over a century of high-speed growth, with large parts of the world integrated by relatively open trade systems and the free movement of capital. The integration of global markets reached levels far beyond those of the pre-modern era. The world appeared to be on the threshold of limitless capitalist expansion.

The advance of global capitalism was rudely interrupted in 1914, and a succession of phenomena stifled its growth for much of the twentieth century. These included World Wars I and II, the impact of the Civil War and Anti-Japanese War in China, and the war in the Pacific. In the high-income countries, the searing impact of the Great Depression led to the introduction of "beggar-my-neighbor" policies of high tariff protection in the interwar years, and a sharp decline in the growth of world trade. After 1945 trade protection in the manufacturing sector of the high-income countries was gradually reduced. In the interwar years, exchange controls were applied widely, and capital flows out of the high-income countries slumped, while in the post-war period, high-income countries maintained severe restrictions on international capital flows. In the post-war period most of the western European countries nationalized large swathes of their economies and nurtured national champion firms in both the public and private sectors.

The October Revolution in Russia ushered in a series of communist revolutions, and by 1950 a "sea of communism" extended from the Elbe in the west to China and Vietnam in the east. The communist countries established a non-capitalist economy, from which the anarchy of the market was eliminated. They drastically limited their interaction with global capitalism, which cut off vast swathes of the world, containing around two-fifths of the world's population, from the international economy. Developing countries, which were heavily dependent on primary product exports, were devastated by the impact of the Great Depression and the collapse of primary product prices. Post-war economic policies in developing countries were influenced strongly by this experience. In addition, the Soviet Union appeared to offer an alternative route toward self-reliant development, freed from the disruptive effects of the anarchic international economic system. In the post-war period, throughout the non-communist developing world, economic policies focused on import-substituting industrialization. Most non-communist developing countries heavily protected indigenous manufacturing and established large state-owned enterprises as the core of their manufacturing sectors. It was hoped that the resulting structural transformation would free developing countries from reliance on primary products which have unstable prices and were perceived to suffer from unequal exchange with imports of manufactured goods. It was thought that this would permit accelerated growth through increased indigenous manufactured goods production, which could benefit from economies of scale and technological progress.

From the mid-1970s onward a series of far-reaching changes set the scene for the renewed spread of global capitalism. Like a spring that has been held under pressure, the release was followed by an explosive expansion. In 1974, following the first oil crisis, after decades of restrictions on international capital flows, the high-income countries moved decisively toward floating exchange rates and freedom of international capital movements. In the 1980s and 1990s, most of Europe's vast structure of state-owned enterprises was privatized. By the turn of the century many of these large and technologically powerful firms had been transformed into global business giants. The outward stock of foreign direct investment (FDI) from developed countries rose from $503 billion in 1980 to almost $11 trillion in 2006.[1]

In the communist world, the death of Chairman Mao in 1976 set in motion comprehensive system reform. Reform in China was gradual, "touching stones to cross the river," with steadily expanding penetration of market forces under the leadership of the Chinese Communist Party (CCP). The "Chinese wall" between the domestic and global economies was dismantled slowly, brick by brick. By 2004, China had risen to be the world's third largest exporter and the largest recipient of annual flows of FDI. In the former USSR and Eastern Europe, after a period of experimentation with gradual economic reform, Communist Party rule collapsed. In the 1990s the whole region opened up to international investment and trade.

In the non-communist developing world it was felt widely that import-substituting growth had run its course, and that only comprehensive integration with the international economy would enable output and income growth to accelerate. The conventional wisdom in development thinking shifted profoundly, strongly influenced by the ideas developed in the IMF and World Bank, the so-called "Washington Consensus" institutions. In the 1980s and 1990s, non-communist developing countries carried out comprehensive privatization of state assets, dismantled protectionist barriers, and opened their economies to international investment. As a result, exports of goods and services rose from 13 percent of developing countries' GDP in 1965 to 35 percent of their GDP in 2006. By 2006 total merchandise trade (imports plus exports of goods) amounted to 59 percent of developing countries' GDP.[2] The inward stock of FDI in developing countries rose from $108 billion in 1980 to $3.2 trillion in 2006, while stock market capitalization rose from 19 percent of developing countries' GDP in 1990 to 73 percent in 2006.

The global economy took up from where it had left off before World War I. Once again, private enterprise dominated, international trade was relatively unregulated, and capital could flow freely across national borders. Leading global firms were increasingly international in terms of their markets, employees, and the composition of ownership. The principal difference with the period before 1914 was the migration of people. In the earlier period there were massive international migrations to the "lands of recent settlement," but in the recent period, international migration, especially of poor people, has been severely restricted. However, in most respects the world economy again entered a period of free markets and a "global level playing field" comparable to the late nineteenth century, the previous highpoint of the liberal free market economy.

Developing countries became deeply integrated into the capitalist global economy, with profound effects on daily life. The consumption choices dramatically widened for a significant fraction of the population. The middle class in developing countries could now put their savings into global banks; insure their lives and property with global insurance companies; communicate through global telecoms providers with equipment provided by global companies; travel on planes, in cars, and buses made by global companies; transport their goods in trucks made by global companies; have their sewage and water supply managed by global companies; buy footwear, clothing, and sports goods from global companies; drink beer and soft drinks provided by global companies; eat food in global fast-food restaurants; drink coffee and eat cakes in coffee bars run by global companies; and shop in supermarkets and hypermarkets owned by global companies.

CAPITALISM AND COORDINATION

> *The division of labour, from which so many advantages are derived, is not originally the effect of any human wisdom, which foresees and intends that general opulence to which it gives occasion. It is the necessary, though very slow and gradual, consequence of a certain propensity in human nature which has in view no such extensive utility; the propensity to truck, barter, and exchange one thing for another.*

> Adam Smith, *The Wealth of Nations*

Since the earliest days of the emergence of capitalist markets, the market mechanism has acted as an instrument for coordinating the activities of individual economic agents, each engaged in their own particular function within the overall division of labor. However, the nature of that coordinating mechanism has changed greatly over time, not least in the era of the global business revolution.

The invisible hand

Through the process of the division of labor and exchange, human beings establish complex forms of interdependence and cooperation, even though they may not intend it and may be only dimly aware of it. Economists have long marveled at the independently functioning market, which allows the actions of market participants to be "magically" coordinated, without any apparent guiding hand. Markets were coordinated in this fashion throughout the trading centers of the Muslim world,

South Asia, and China long before the European countries entered their early modern market expansion.

Writing on the eve of the Industrial Revolution, Adam Smith produced the most famous of all analyses of the division of labor and its impact upon cooperation among people. Smith places the division of labor at the heart of his analysis of economic development, making it the first sentence of the first chapter of *The Wealth of Nations*: "The greatest improvement in the productive powers of labour, and the greater part of the skill, dexterity, and judgement with which it is any where directed, or applied, seem to have been the effects of the division of labour." Smith examines closely the variety of objects in the accommodation of "the most common artificer or day-labourer in a civilized and thriving country," and concludes that "the number of people of whose industry a part, though but a small part, has been employed in procuring him this accommodation, exceeds all computation." "If we examine, I say, all these things, and consider what a variety of labour is employed about each of them, we shall be sensible that without the assistance and cooperation of many thousands, the very meanest person in a civilized country could not be provided, even according to what we very falsely imagine, the easy and simple manner in which he is commonly accommodated."

For Smith, the market was not simply a static mechanism for achieving greater output from given resources, it was the essential mechanism for raising the productivity of resources through technological progress. Capital accumulation and the ways in which capital could become more productive through technological progress were central to Smith's economic analysis. He devoted great care to analyzing technological progress, distinguishing between three sources. First, there are technologies that are developed by specialist "philosophers and men of speculation, whose trade it is to observe everything; and who, on that account are often capable of combining together the powers of the most distant and dissimilar objects." These are, in their turn, "subdivided into a great number of different branches." As a result, each individual becomes "more expert in his own peculiar branch, more work is done on the whole, and the quantity of science is considerably increased by it." Secondly, many improvements in machines are made by "the ingenuity of the makers of the machines, when to make them became the business of a particular trade." Thirdly, technological progress is also achieved by "the inventions of common workmen, who, being each of them employed in some very simple operation, naturally turned their thoughts toward finding out easier and readier methods of performing it."

The "invisible hand" of capitalism powerfully affected technological progress in the critically important period of European and, indeed, of world history, namely the period of the Scientific Revolution from the fourteenth to the seventeenth centuries. This period saw the emergence of an increasingly powerful capitalist class in Western Europe. From the fourteenth century to the middle of the eighteenth century, Europe's population more or less doubled. During this long, persistent increase in Europe's population, revolutionary technological advances took place, incorporating a great deal of technological progress from the Muslim world and from China. The revolutionary advances in Europe laid the foundations for the Industrial Revolution, which is best seen as part of a process that began at the start of the European Middle Ages. Technological changes interacted in symbiotic fashion with the extension of the market. The core of technological change has always been in the transformation of capital goods. During this extraordinary period, the widening market provided a steadily expanding source of profit to reward innovation in capital goods, which were increasingly produced by specialist industrial enterprises.

Technological progress by the makers of capital goods revolutionized production processes across almost every sector of the economy. Technological progress in agriculture, for example, could support a larger population, which in turn permitted greater densities of population, thereby reducing transport costs and allowing an increasingly rapid spread of knowledge. Technological progress in paper-making and printing enabled new ideas to spread more rapidly. It enabled knowledge to diffuse more widely, and allowed craftsmen to acquire new technological knowledge more easily. Advances in lens-making and spectacles enabled people to spend more of their time reading. Advances in transport, especially in shipbuilding and navigation, reduced transport costs, thereby increasing the distance over which it was profitable to transport goods. This technological revolution was not driven mainly by the state or by scientific research in universities; the state's direct involvement in production was mainly evident in the manufacture of warships and weapons, though even here much military equipment was purchased from the private sector. The main generators of technological progress were the makers of capital goods, whose principal incentive was to make money by meeting the needs of their customers through the provision of better and cheaper products. Through this mechanism, capitalism in the Middle Ages achieved immense progress; the capitalist market economy was like a giant reciprocating engine in which the parts constantly interacted to mutual benefit.

Through the invisible hand of the market, human beings have over millennia achieved non-zero-sum outcomes from their interactions. In zero-sum games, one party to a transaction can only gain at the expense of the other party, whereas in non-zero-sum games, both parties are better off as a result of the transaction. The more extensive the market, and the lower the transaction costs, which are reduced through advances in transport and communication technologies, the greater the gains from non-zero-sum interactions between the market participants. This has been a fundamental instrument allowing human progress. People are often unaware that they are interacting with each other in a mutually profitable fashion, but "reciprocal altruism" to achieve "beneficial exchange" is deeply built into human behavior. Through market exchange, both parties are better off than they would be in isolation. "Non-zero-sumness" is an important characteristic of human evolution, in which human beings have played "ever larger, and ever more complex non-zero-sum games." Globalization can be viewed as the culmination of this process. Robert Wright argues that through the greatly extended impact of non-zero-sum interactions "a magnificent new social structure—our future home—is being built before our very eyes."

The visible hand [3]

The traditional American and European business firm of the early Industrial Revolution was a single-unit business enterprise. The activities of these small, personally owned and managed enterprises were coordinated and monitored by the "anonymous" market and price mechanisms. In the late nineteenth century, the modern firm emerged in America and Europe. It brought many different units under its control, operating in different locations, and entering different lines of business through vertical and horizontal integration. Complex internal business relationships were now monitored and coordinated by salaried employees rather than by the market mechanism. By the middle of the twentieth century this type of firm had become dominant in all the high-income countries. Such firms employed large numbers of middle and top managers, who supervised the work of tens or hundreds of thousands of employees working in hundreds of different operating units. Salaried managers were increasingly able to control firms without interference from their owners, the shareholders. Within such firms, the boundaries shifted decisively compared with the enterprises of the early Industrial Revolution, as goods and services that had formerly been purchased through anonymous market transactions were instead produced within the firm.

The result was that large areas of business now became subject to the "visible hand" of planned resource allocation within the vertically and horizontally integrated firm. Prior to the 1930s, economists were reluctant even to acknowledge the existence of such firms, and since then they have looked on large-scale business enterprise suspiciously. Even today much economic theory is based on the assumption that most production and distribution is managed by the invisible hand of the market. The anonymous small and medium-sized firm is used as the basis for economic analysis. It is believed that this form of business organization is preferable to the large-scale modern enterprise, which is regarded as "an aberration, and an evil one at that." Its existence is explained mainly by the desire to establish monopoly power rather than by the benefits from economies of scale and scope.

Although the internal mechanism of the large corporation became a form of planned economy governed by a "visible hand," the invisible hand of inter-firm competition operated even more powerfully. Large firms continued to struggle ferociously against each other, battling to achieve technological progress and lower costs of production. Market share and profits changed constantly, which kept oligopolies from becoming stagnant and monopolistic. The large, oligopolistic firm became the central vehicle for technological progress in advanced economies. The modern industrial enterprise played a central role in creating the most technologically advanced, fastest growing industries of their day. They provided the underlying dynamic of modern industrial capitalism.

In the late nineteenth century, the first-mover large firms established themselves as dominant oligopolistic players and became the learning ground for technological, managerial, and organizational knowledge for the entire economy in high-income countries. These firms were primarily in those parts of the manufacturing sector that constituted the Second Industrial Revolution, including such capital-intensive activities as primary metals, petroleum refining, chemicals, electrical products, and transport equipment. Technological advances achieved by large firms in these industries contributed to improved productivity in a wide range of other industries, including transport, communications, and financial services. The Third Industrial Revolution during and after World War II was also dominated by large enterprises. This revolution involved new technologies in chemicals, pharmaceuticals, aerospace, and electronics.

The external firm

In the current capitalist period, key functions of control and coordination have extended across the boundaries of the legally defined firm in a new form of separation of ownership and control. Through the greatly increased planning function undertaken by systems integrator firms, facilitated by recent developments in information technology, the boundaries of the large corporation have not only shifted, so that a wider range of goods and services is procured from outside the firm, but the very boundaries of the firm have become blurred. The core systems integrators across a wide range of sectors have become the coordinators of an extensive array of business activity outside the boundaries of the legal entity in terms of ownership. The relationship extends far beyond the purchase price. In order to develop and maintain their competitive advantage, the systems integrators penetrate the value chain deeply both upstream and downstream, becoming closely involved in business activities ranging from long-term planning to meticulous control of day-to-day production and delivery schedules. Competitive advantage for the systems integrator firm requires that it must consider the interests of the whole value chain in order to minimize costs across the whole system. The core systems integrator interacts intimately with the major segments of the value chain across a wide range of business types, from fast-moving consumer goods to aircraft manufacture. One of the most remarkable features of the global business revolution is the persistence of the invisible hand of inter-firm competition in the form of intense oligopolistic competition between giant global firms, which have sophisticated internal planning systems (the "visible hand") and a vast "external firm" coordinated by them.

FINANCE AND DEVELOPMENT

Short of a major and devastating geopolitical incident undermining, in a significant way, consumer confidence, and hence financial asset valuation, it is hard to see where systemic threats could come from in the short term.

IMF, 2005

Finance has always stood at the center of economic advance. Availability of credit has been central to the growth of trade and investment finance. Wherever capitalism has matured beyond a certain point, sophisticated payment systems, through banking systems that allow the safe carriage of goods over long distances without the need to carry cash, have been critical to the development of long-distance trade. This was true for the world of medieval Islam, South Asia and China, as it was for Europe in the late Middle Ages and in the early modern period. During and after the Industrial Revolution, financial institutions reached new heights of sophistication, facilitating further development of capitalism. In recent decades financial institutions and financial flows took another leap forward in size and sophistication, standing at the heart of capitalist globalization.

Private capital flows

In the past three decades a consensus grew up among the "Washington Consensus" institutions (the World Bank and the IMF), which argues that there are large benefits for both rich and poor countries alike to be gained by liberalization of international capital flows. The size of the financial sector alone, regardless of its sophistication, was thought to have a strong causal relationship with economic performance. Measures which stimulate the growth of national financial systems "enhance productivity and growth by facilitating transactions and improving resource allocation." Allowing free access to international capital markets and financial institutions stimulates "financial deepening" in developing countries, whose financial systems were "repressed" by government intervention, and were much smaller than those of the high-income countries.

The Washington Consensus argues that free financial markets are more efficient and that greater efficiency produces faster economic growth. Capital account liberalization leads to global economic efficiency by allocating savings to those who can use them most productively, and it enables firms to raise capital more cheaply in international markets. Citizens of countries with free capital movements can benefit from diversifying their portfolios, thereby increasing their rate of return. Pressure from global capital markets serves as an important discipline on government economic policies, which improves overall economic performance by rewarding good policies and penalizing bad ones. The removal of restrictions on the international movement of capital encourages developing country governments to reform their financial sectors. It pressures them to break the connections between financial institutions and borrowers, and to establish effective bankruptcy regimes, which helps to protect the property rights of foreign capital. Moreover, capital controls are costly to enforce and are a source of corruption. The Washington Consensus argued that it is beneficial for developing countries to allow free access to international financial firms, in order to benefit from their size, skill, and economies of scale. However, it is argued that the only way to attract such firms is to allow them to repatriate their capital, remit earnings, and have free access to global financial markets. Underlying the Washington Consensus is the ethical argument that being able to freely convert one's personal savings into a foreign currency and move them wherever one chooses is a fundamental human right.

After the 1970s, restraints on the international flow of capital were greatly reduced. Gross private capital flows to developing countries doubled their share of GDP from six percent in 1990 to twelve percent in 2004. The largest and most stable element in these private capital flows has consisted of FDI: the stock of FDI in developing countries rose from $108 billion in 1980 (22 percent of the global total) to $3.2 trillion in 2006 (26 percent of the total). Between them, East Asia, Southeast Asia, and Latin America account for as much as 80 percent of the total stock of FDI in developing countries. In these three regions, local production systems built by multinational firms have grown into critically important parts of the local economy. For example, in Brazil multinational firms account for 14 of the top 25 "Brazilian" firms. In China foreign-funded enterprises account for 60 percent of pharmaceuticals output, 75 percent of medical, precision, and optical instruments output, 88 percent of electronic and telecommunications equipment output, and 96 percent of computer and office equipment output. In China's passenger vehicle industry, joint ventures with global firms occupy 72 percent of the domestic market.

The subsidiaries established by multinational firms in developing countries have a powerful influence on the modern sector of the local economy. They contribute to the spread of global production technologies, management systems, and employee skills. Large manufacturing assembly facilities owned by multinational firms in developing countries stimulate the development of clusters of supplier companies, often encouraging other multinationals to invest to meet the needs of their global customers, thereby contributing to the technological upgrading of the whole supply chain. Multinational firms tend to produce globally standardized products, whether they are final consumer goods for the global middle class or capital goods for other companies, making use of standard global machine tools and components, and adopting the same capital/labor ratios as in high-income countries. Multinationals in developing countries can take advantage of global procurement to lower unit costs of inputs of goods and services. Global oligopolistic firms carry their intense competition into developing countries, whether in the production of consumer goods and services or capital goods for intermediate customers.

In developing countries stock market capitalization increased its share of GDP from 19 percent in 1990 to 73 percent in 2006. Stock markets have numerous benefits. They can stimulate economic growth. They provide a mechanism for shareholders to monitor standards of corporate governance. They stimulate savings and channel them into investment. They facilitate mergers and acquisitions, allowing realization of the benefits from economies of scale. They contribute to social stability by providing pension funds with a channel through which to diversify their investments. The flow of portfolio equity funds to developing countries rose from $3 billion in 1990 to $105 billion in 2006. Standards of corporate governance in developing countries needed to rise in order to attract international capital, and international equity holders now constitute an important fraction of share ownership in many developing countries that were formerly substantially closed to multinational equity investors.

Financial firms

After the 1970s, there were large changes in the conditions affecting financial firms, including the reduction of obstacles to mergers and acquisitions across the boundaries of different segments of the industry, across regions within large countries (especially in America), and across national boundaries. International mergers and acquisitions by large financial firms formed an important part of the international merger and acquisition explosion. The institutional structure of financial firms was strongly affected by the transformation of their customers, both business and private, who increasingly sought global services from financial institutions. The large economies of scale and scope derived from procurement of IT hardware and software act as a powerful driver of institutional change in financial services, as they do in the manufacturing sector. Financial firms benefit also from economies of scale in branding and marketing, and in human resource acquisition.

In this period the banking sector was comprehensively transformed, with high-speed merger and acquisition, and the internationalization of operations. The world's leading banks benefited enormously from deregulation and financial innovation. In less than a decade between 1997 and 2006, the world's top 25 banks increased their share of the total assets of the world's top 1000 banks (the "Global 1000") from 28 percent to 42 percent. A group of ten super-large global banking titans emerged, all from high-income countries, including J.P. Morgan Chase, Citigroup, HSBC Holdings, Deutsche Bank, Bank of America, UBS, Credit Agricole, BNP Paribas, Fortis Bank, and Mizuho Financial Group. By 2005 this group had average revenues of $90 billion, average assets of $1.4 trillion, and average profits of $11 billion. The world's leading international financial institutions almost all have their headquarters in the high-income countries. In the *Fortune 500* in 2006 there was a total of 115 financial firms, of which just nine were from developing countries. In the *FT 500* in 2007 there was a total of 133 financial firms, of which just 11 were from developing countries. In 2006 among the world's top 25 banks ranked by total assets, 24 of the top 25 were from high-income countries.

Following financial liberalization in most developing countries, these giant global financial firms rapidly increased their acquisition activity. By 2001, within Latin America, the share of foreign banks in total bank assets had risen to 90 percent in Mexico, 62 percent in Peru, 61 percent in Argentina and Chile, 59 percent in Venezuela, and 49 percent in Brazil. By 2001, in Eastern Europe the share of foreign banks in total bank assets stood at 99 percent in Estonia, 90 percent in the Czech Republic and Poland, 89 percent in Hungary, 86 percent in Slovakia, 78 percent in Lithuania, and 75 percent in Bulgaria.

The Washington Consensus institutions advanced numerous arguments to support the proposition that global financial firms benefited developing countries. Those "transition economies" that were more willing to cede majority control of their banks to foreign interests enjoyed higher growth rates than their neighbors. Countries with a higher proportion of foreign-owned banks are less prone to financial crises, because foreign banks are better regulated, better managed, and more immune to pressure for imprudent lending. The threat of competition from global banks forces local banks to improve their operating mechanisms. Global banks spread risk across different markets. They have access to vast global assets and possess sophisticated IT systems with which to evaluate risk. They had also established a culture built around strict internal control systems, and have long experience of operating under the sophisticated financial regulations of the high-income countries. Global banks operate according to rigorous and systematic procedures, so that lending tends to be based on strict commercial criteria to a much greater extent than in many developing countries' banking systems. This increases the possibility that loans will be made to firms that are able to employ them effectively. This may lead to more effective use of savings and thereby stimulate growth, as well as tending to reduce the risk of bad loans and of a financial crisis. Financial reforms in developing countries have often found it difficult to break the link between bankers and local political power holders, but the entry of global banks can help to break this link more effectively. By working with global banks, multinational firms can grow faster in developing countries. They can benefit from lower-priced and higher quality services supplied to them on a global basis. Local depositors may also benefit from the presence of global banks, by having greater security for their deposits and more opportunity to benefit from global wealth management. Local pension funds may benefit by having access to the global asset management services of global banks.

Global financial risk

During the three decades of globalization the financial system underwent tremendous change. Across much of the developing world the system "deepened," gradually supplanting the former "repressed" financial structures. Advances in information technology and in financial instruments were widely thought to have greatly improved risk control in commercial banks. New financial instruments distributed risk extensively throughout the economic system. Alan Greenspan, the former Chairman of the American Federal Reserve, argued that there was a "new paradigm" of "active credit management," which made the global financial system far more robust. It was argued that credit derivatives permitted risks to be unbundled and transferred to those players who were best able to absorb them. Hedge funds' arbitrage activity was thought to make markets more efficient and keep the financial system fluid and flexible. The global financial system demonstrated its newly found robustness by surviving a series of crises, including the Mexican "Tequila" crisis, the Asian financial crisis, the Russian and Argentine financial crises, the collapse of the dot.com bubble, and 9/11. Most financial experts agreed with the IMF's view that the global financial system had become so "thick" as to be nearly indestructible.

COMPETITION, INDUSTRIAL CONCENTRATION, AND TECHNOLOGICAL PROGRESS

The explosion of advanced technologies now means that suddenly, knowledge pools and resources have connected all over the planet, leveling the playing field as never before, so that each of us is potentially an equal—and competitor—of each other.

Thomas Friedman, *The World is Flat*

Contrasting views

The mainstream ("neo-classical") view of the competitive process believes that the perfectly competitive model best describes the essence of capitalist competition. Departures from it are viewed as exceptional and typically arising from government intervention, including international protection and nationalization. At the heart of the mainstream view is the self-equilibrating mechanism of market competition. It is believed that the basic driver of the capitalist process, competition, ensures that if any firm enjoys super-normal profits, rivals will soon enter to bid away those profits and undermine any temporary market dominance that the incumbent enjoys. The mainstream approach emphasizes the importance of competition among small firms as the central explanation for the prosperity of the advanced economies. It considers that there is a general bias and tendency to overemphasize the importance of the big firm versus the small one.

Most mainstream economists believe that managerial diseconomies of scale set in after firms reach a certain size. The classic expression of this view was contained in Alfred Marshall's *Principles of Economics*, in which the industrial structure was likened to the "trees in the forest," in a perpetual state of flux, with a powerful tendency toward the decline of trees as they became old: "One tree will last longer in full vigour and attain a greater size than another; but sooner or later age tells on them all. Though the taller ones have a better access to light and air than their rivals, they gradually lose vitality; and one after another they give place to others, which though of less material strength, have on their side the vigour of youth … [I]n almost every trade there is a constant rise and fall of large businesses, at any one moment some firm being in the ascending phase and others in the descending."

Despite the explosive growth of mergers and acquisitions since the 1970s, it is widely argued that global concentration levels did not increase. There is a high rate of disappearance of companies from the *Fortune 500*. Based mainly on the analysis of shareholder returns, mainstream economists believe that mergers and acquisitions mostly fail. Geoff Meeks's influential study of mergers and acquisitions is evocatively entitled *Disappointing Marriage*. The explanation that is usually advanced for mergers and acquisitions is the pursuit of power and wealth by CEOs, who are alleged to pursue their own interests at the expense of those of shareholders.

It is argued that in the era of globalization markets have become so large that it is hard for any firm or small group of firms to dominate a given sector, with limitless opportunities for firms from developing countries to catch up on the vast global level playing field. Advances in information technology have transformed the nature of the firm, as activities that were formerly carried out within the firm can now be performed by networks of small firms connected by the internet. Mainstream economists believe that large firms, particularly in the traditional production industries, have been outperformed by smaller, nimbler competitors. In Thomas Friedman's memorable description, the world has become flat for individuals and firms from developing countries.

From the earliest stages in the development of modern capitalism, there were economists who believed that capitalism contained an inherent tendency toward industrial concentration. Karl Marx argued that there was a "law of centralization of capital," or the "attraction of capital by capital." The driving force of concentration was competition itself, which pressured firms to cut the cost of production by investing ever larger amounts of capital in new means of production and in "the technological application of science," which in turn creates barriers to entry. In the early 1970s, on the eve of the modern era of globalization, Stephen Hymer visualized the possible outcome of the capitalist process if the restrictions on mergers and acquisitions were lifted. He imagined a situation at some point in the near future in which giant multinational corporations (say 300 from America and 200 from Europe and Japan) had established themselves as the dominant form of international enterprise and controlled a significant share of modern industry in every country. The world economy would then resemble more and more the American economy, where large corporations spread over the entire continent, and penetrate almost every nook and cranny.

Edith Penrose's path-breaking book *The Theory of the Growth of the Firm* examined the limits to the growth of the firm. She identified a number of potential advantages that can be enjoyed by the large firm, the most significant of which she termed "managerial economies." Penrose concluded that there are no theoretical limits to the size of the firm.

The succession of studies which purport to show the irrationality of mergers and acquisitions are almost entirely based on the analysis of the consequences for shareholder value in the short term. The much smaller number of studies which analyze the long-term impact of mergers and acquisitions on business survival and growth show a different story. They suggest, rather, that well-selected and well-executed mergers and acquisitions can increase the business capability of the firm concerned. They can strengthen the firm's presence in given geographical markets, increase its access to technologies it did not formerly possess, acquire scarce human resources, add valuable brands to its portfolio, and enable long-term savings through economies of scale and scope in procurement, research and development, and marketing.

The evidence

The end of communist central planning and of inward-looking development strategies in poor countries, together with widespread privatization and liberalization, ushered in the era of globalization. The changes began with China's reform efforts in the late 1970s, after the death of Chairman Mao. The key date was the central party meeting in December 1978. There was a broader movement towards economic reform and liberalization in capitalist developing countries from roughly the same point, but less precise to pinpoint. Reforms in the Soviet Union began in the late 1980s under Gorbachev. The new era was characterized by a drastic reduction in state intervention, with comprehensive privatization, a large reduction in state support for national firms, the removal of protectionist barriers on cross-border mergers and acquisitions, and the extension across the entire globe of markets for most goods and services. Economists have held sharply differing views about the basic determinants of industrial structure under free market conditions. From the late 1970s on, state intervention receded and markets became more and more free, providing an opportunity to put these different views to a scientific test, and to assess the validity of the competing views of the determinants of industrial structure under free market conditions.

The period saw a large change in the nature of business organization, amounting to nothing less than a business revolution. As global markets opened up, multinational companies typically responded by divesting their non-core businesses to focus on a small array of closely related products in which they had global leadership, achieved through the possession of superior brands and technology, and through economies of scale in procurement. Leading global firms increasingly outsourced manufacturing and non-core service functions, to focus on the "brain" functions of design, product development, final assembly, marketing, and financing. They developed skills in systems integration and coordination of their supply chain, and they attracted the best employees in the international battle for talent.

In almost every sector, the period since the 1970s has witnessed an unprecedented number of mergers, acquisitions and divestments, as leading firms have consolidated their position at the center of global markets by achieving focus and scale. Global mergers and acquisitions increased from around $700 billion in 1995 to $3.3 trillion in 2000. After 2000 the level slumped, before rising to a new peak in 2006, when they reached $3.7 trillion. In addition to highly publicized large-scale mergers, there was a continuous process of smaller-scale acquisitions, with leading companies each acquiring numerous small and medium-sized firms annually in order to enhance their leading positions in their respective markets.

Global industrial consolidation advanced unceasingly, affecting almost every sector, from the most sophisticated, high technology capital goods, to the simplest consumer goods. It is was as though a law came into play under which in every sector the top half dozen systems integrator firms, with their superior brands and/or technologies, should account for over one-half of the entire global market in that particular product. Moreover, in different subcategories within each broad product category, levels of industrial concentration are typically even higher. These developments are consistent with the persistence in most sectors of a large number of small and medium-sized firms, which produce mainly non-branded, low technology products, supplying local markets, and which collectively occupy a small share of global markets. These parts of the segmented industrial structure typically supply the lower groups within each country's income distribution. The high-speed advance in industrial consolidation among system integrator firms, in its turn, had an impact on industrial structure. The global industry leaders in each sector used their procurement power to exert intense pressure on their supply chains, which resulted in intense pressure upon supplier firms themselves to merge and acquire, and to divest non-core business, in order to gain scale and focus, enabling them to achieve economies of scale in research and development, procurement, human resources, and sub-systems integration.

Research and development (R&D) is a critically important aspect of inter-firm competition. Britain's Department of Trade and Industry compiles an annual survey of the R&D spending of the top 1,250 companies globally, the "Global 1250." These companies are at the heart of the global economic system. In 2005–6 the firms in the Global 1250 list invested around $430 billion in R&D. They employed around 32 million people, generated sales revenues of around $11.8 trillion, earned operating profits of around $1.3 trillion (i.e. $1,300 billion—11 percent of sales revenue), and had a market capitalization of around $14.6 trillion. The Global 1250 constitutes the core of global technological progress. The list is strongly concentrated by company, sector, and country. The top ten countries (all high-income) account for 94 percent of the total. The top 100 companies account for 61.4 percent of the total expenditure of the Global 1250, while the bottom 150 companies account for just 1.3 percent of the total.

Mainstream economists predict that oligopoly results in a reduction in the level of competition. However, in reality the recent period has seen a drastic increase in the intensity of competition. Investment in technological progress is a key source of competitive advantage. Large companies are pouring money into research and development at an unprecedented rate, in response to intensified competition. Between 2001–2 and 2005–6 total R&D expenditure by the Global 1250 rose by 23 percent. In many sectors profits are growing strongly and companies can afford to spend more on R&D. Where profits are weak, as in the automobile industry, the competition is so fierce that companies dare not cut their investment.

The increased focus on core business among the world's leading firms has enhanced the effectiveness of R&D expenditure, allowing them to benefit from economies of scale and scope. Technological progress in the instruments of R&D, especially IT hardware and software, has enhanced enormously the effectiveness of R&D spending. In addition, the world's leading firms have rapidly increased their R&D bases in low and middle-income countries, which has enabled them to obtain even greater amounts of knowledge per dollar spent on R&D. In 2003, the share of foreign affiliates in total R&D was estimated to be 24 percent in China, 48 percent in Brazil, 47 percent in the Czech Republic, and 63 percent in Hungary.

The past three decades have arguably witnessed greater technological progress than any previous period. This progress has been led by oligopolistic firms which stand at the apex of their respective value chains, and which have powerfully stimulated technological progress at lower levels in the supply chain. I shall examine briefly technological progress in four sectors in the past two decades.

The IT revolution has been at the heart of technological progress in all sectors. The IT hardware and software sector is by far the most important in terms of global technological progress. In 2005–6, the total R&D expenditure of the companies in this sector within the Global 1250 amounted to $111 billion. Within the Global 1250 companies, the IT hardware, software, and computer services sectors contain a total of 326 companies, accounting for 25.8 percent of the total R&D spending. The massive spending of the world's leading IT companies over the past two decades has stimulated a revolution in information generation and transmission. The revolution in IT has transformed the nature both of capital goods and of a large fraction of final consumption. Goods and services in almost every sector have been comprehensively changed by this technological revolution, from complex engineering products, including aircraft, automobiles, farm equipment, and all types of manufacturing machinery, to almost every imaginable service, including mass media, retail, banking, insurance, tourism, transport, and marketing. The IT revolution has universally lowered costs and prices of IT goods and services. It has allowed a dramatic fall in the cost of global communications, transformed the cost and nature of R&D, and facilitated a profound change in the nature of the global firm and its relationship to the surrounding value chain.

In the era of the global business revolution, both passenger and commercial vehicles have altered radically, with large reductions in weight, due mainly to advances in technologies embodied in steel, aluminum, and plastics; large increases in fuel economy, due to weight reduction and advances in engine and tire technologies; large increases in vehicle safety, comfort, ease of use, reliability, and longevity; large reductions in polluting emissions; and radical advances in entertainment and in-car navigation systems ("informatics"). The application of information technology has penetrated every aspect of vehicle operation.

In the aerospace industry, enormous changes have taken place in the nature of passenger aircraft. Large weight reductions per passenger carried have taken place due to advances in aircraft design, through improvements in existing construction materials, and through increased use of composite materials; large advances have taken place due to continuous progress in engine technologies, including weight reduction, increased fuel efficiency, reduced engine noise, increased engine reliability, and advances in ease of engine maintenance; and large advances have taken place in aircraft safety, due to progress in avionics and flight control systems, and improvements in the design and reliability of aircraft components, including seats, engines, landing gear, avionics, and tires.

In the beverage industry, including both soft drinks and beer, quite limited changes have taken place in the nature of the product, but enormous technological progress has occurred in the processes involved in producing and distributing beverages. Filling machinery has greatly increased in speed, reliability, and fuel efficiency, alongside reductions in variability of filling height and in bottle damage. Packaging technologies have altered radically. Metal cans and plastic PET bottles have joined glass bottles to constitute the three main forms of primary packaging. The introduction of metal cans and PET bottles allowed enormous changes in the appearance of primary packaging, increasing customer satisfaction through greater ease of use and attractiveness of design. Improved packaging technologies have increased longevity of beverages at peak condition. All three types of primary packaging have achieved large reductions in package weight, which economizes on the use of raw materials, reduces weight in transport, and improves ease of use by the final customer. These advances have occurred through intense interaction between leading beverage companies and the suppliers of packaging materials (including steel, aluminum, PET, and glass), as well as with the firms that make machinery to produce primary packaging. Large advances have taken place in the machine-building industry to produce PET pre-forms, PET blowing equipment, can-making machinery and glass bottle machinery. They have increased speed and reliability, reduced raw material and fuel consumption per unit, and improved packaging design capabilities. Distribution of beverages is enormously intensive in the use of road transport. Improvements in commercial vehicle technologies have greatly increased fuel efficiency in the distribution of beverages.

As these examples from four different sectors indicate, the focus on core business and expanded firm size among both systems integrators and suppliers has increased economies of scale and scope at every level in the value chain. This applies to almost every sector. Alongside dramatic advances in product and process technologies, there has been a near-universal decline in unit costs and prices, at the same time as great advances in product quality. The era of the global business revolution has seen a large increase in levels of industrial concentration. Ferocious oligopolistic competition has penetrated almost every level of the supply chain, from the systems integrators downwards. Oligopolistic competition at lower levels in the supply chain has been stimulated by intense pressure from above, which "cascades" down through the whole system. Instead of the technological stagnation and real price increases that were predicted by most economists, both "radical" and mainstream, the era has witnessed intense oligopolistic competition, which has been responsible for its extraordinary technological dynamism. This reality has hardly begun to be absorbed and analyzed by mainstream economists.

EXPANDING HUMAN FREEDOM

Of the features which characterise this progressive economical movement of civilised nations, that which first excites attention, through its intimate connection with the phenomena of Production, is the perpetual, and so far as human foresight can extend, the unlimited, growth of man's power over nature. Our knowledge of the properties and laws of physical objects shows no sign of approaching its ultimate boundaries: it is advancing more rapidly, and in a greater number of directions at once than in any previous age or generation, and affording such frequent glimpses of unexplored fields beyond, as to justify the belief that our acquaintance with nature is still almost in its infancy. This increasing physical knowledge is now, too, more rapidly than at any former period, converted, by practical ingenuity, into physical power.

J. S. Mill, *Principles of Political Economy*

Through the ages, the pursuit of profit by business people has stimulated them to respond to the expansion of markets by saving and investing, and achieving technological progress. This has led the way to a progressive expansion of the realm of individual freedom from the numerous forces that constrain the lives of ordinary people. In the past three decades, this process has intensified, producing powerful stimuli for the advance of human freedom.

Freedom from the tyranny of nature

Great technological advances were achieved under the impetus of capitalist markets prior to the eighteenth century. However, the pace of advance accelerated during and after the Industrial Revolution. Economists as different as Karl Marx and J. S. Mill, writing in the midst of this revolutionary process, regarded the profit motive and the extension of markets as fundamental to the liberation of human creative capabilities, which underpinned the technological progress that in turn transformed people's dependence on nature. Writing in 1848 Marx and Engels wrote in the *Communist Manifesto*:

The bourgeoisie, during its rule of scarce one hundred years, has created more massive and more colossal productive forces than have all the preceding generations together. Subjection of Nature's forces to man, machinery, application to industry and agriculture, steam-navigation, railways, electric telegraphs, clearing whole continents for cultivation, canalization of rivers, whole populations conjured out of the ground—what earlier century had even a presentiment that such productive forces slumbered in the lap of social labor?

These forces, which appeared magical in the nineteenth century, have accelerated in the era of the global business revolution, driven by the same forces of capitalist competition, enabling human beings to reach new heights of inventiveness. Technological progress has combined with intense competitive pressure among large capitalist firms and their supply chains to lower real prices, increase consumer choice, and advance human welfare. So great has been the pace and ubiquity of technological progress during the era of the global business revolution that it has become impossible to measure in a meaningful fashion the pace of advance in real incomes and consumption. How can one compare meaningfully the utility derived from an iPod or from a 4G cellphone handset, which offers "high quality service for real time audio, high speed data, HDTV video content and cellphone TV," with the utility that was derived from a 1950s valve radio or typewriter?

Energy supply is central to the world economy. Human ingenuity has increased the availability of primary energy, continually allaying fears that the global economy would run out of primary energy. In 1865, Stanley Jevons, the distinguished British economist, believed that the progressive exhaustion of Britain's coal reserves would spell disaster for the British economy: "It will appear that there is no reasonable prospect of any release from future want of the main agent of industry." Jevons underestimated the capacity of human ingenuity to find new sources of energy and to use old ones in more inventive ways. Fears that the world will run out of energy are based on linear thinking. This view underestimates human beings' capability to innovate in the face of adversity, in response to the stimulus of demand and price signals.

Around four-fifths of global primary energy supply today comes from fossil fuels. Most transport, building, heating, and electricity generation technologies are built around the use of fossil fuels. It is widely thought that the prospects for fossil fuel supply are strictly limited. It is predicted by many experts that at today's level of consumption there are only 40 more years of oil reserves, and 70 years of gas reserves, while coal reserves may last for 200 years. In addition, the rate of increase in demand for primary energy in the low and middle-income countries is accelerating, so that the prospects for global energy supply and demand look even bleaker. However, the reserves of fossil fuel are not absolutely fixed. At prices greater than $70 per barrel, oil reserves are to all intents and purposes infinite. At higher prices, recovery becomes worthwhile using technologies that enable the extraction of a higher proportion of oil, gas, and coal from existing fields. Some estimates of the world's coal reserves consider that there is more than 1,500 years' worth of supply at present levels of consumption. Higher prices also mean that sources of fossil fuels that were formerly uneconomic become economically viable. For example, oil can be recovered from tar sands and shale oil. At a price of above $70 per barrel, there are at least 200 years of oil reserves contained in tar sands. Shale oil contains an estimated eight times more energy than all other forms of fossil fuel combined. This stunning amount of energy is the equivalent of our present total energy consumption for more than 5,000 years. The coastlines of most countries have huge amounts of gas contained within crystals. The *total* reserves of gas in crystals are larger than all known reserves of fossil fuels added together, and the techniques for gaining access to these gases could be commercially viable within a decade or so.

The recent increase in the price of oil has combined with fears over national energy security and global warming to produce a widespread reconsideration of the place of nuclear energy within the energy portfolio in all countries. Nuclear power technologies have made great strides. Technological progress has greatly reduced the construction and operational costs of nuclear power stations, and increased their safety. Modern nuclear fission reactors are designed to shut down in the absence of constant intervention. Fast breeder reactors greatly reduce the demand for uranium, so that there will be almost unlimited availability of the basic raw material for energy generation. In addition, nuclear fusion, which uses ordinary sea water as its fuel, and hence has virtually limitless fuel availability, may become commercially viable within a few decades. After a period when nuclear power was believed to be hopelessly uneconomic, it is now close to competing in real economic terms with gas powered generation. Even after making allowance for decommissioning costs, nuclear power is significantly cheaper than wind or wave power. Such notable figures in the Green movement as James Lovelock have shifted to support for nuclear energy.

By far the most abundant source of primary energy is that which comes from the sun. Science fiction writers, looking far into the future, have long thought that human beings' technological ingenuity would eventually enable them to harness solar energy as their main source of primary energy. They viewed reliance on fossil fuels as a short-term phenomenon associated with an early, primitive phase in human development. It is estimated that the influx of solar energy is equivalent to about 7,000 times today's global energy consumption. Solar energy can be exploited both directly and indirectly. The indirect route is via plant life, which in the very long term provides the basis for fossil fuels. In the short term, solar energy can be harnessed through growing plants. A major advantage of biomass as a source of energy is that it is carbon-neutral, since the emission of carbon dioxide when biomass materials are burned, either as primary fuels or as secondary fuels (such as ethanol), is counterbalanced by their absorption of carbon dioxide during their growth. There has been a great deal of recent technological progress that enables more intensive use of the energy stored within plants, for example in new types of power stations and domestic heating equipment.

The most effective way to make use of solar energy is through the generation of electricity through the use of solar cells or photovoltaic cells. Even with today's technologies, it is estimated that an area of around 250,000 square kilometers (0.15 percent of the earth's land mass) in the tropics could provide all current global energy requirements. Also, solar cells and photovoltaic cell technologies have been advancing rapidly, allowing rapid advances in the effectiveness of capture of solar energy and cuts in the price of harnessing solar energy. Leading international energy companies are now at the forefront of solar energy technologies.

Technological progress in automobile engines, power generation equipment, building design, and packaging, has contributed to large advances in energy efficiency. GDP per unit of energy use rose globally from $4.1 (at constant purchasing power parity, or PPP prices) per kilogram of oil equivalent in 1990 to $5.0 per kilogram in 2005. Progress has been especially striking in developing countries, where the impact of global production technologies in energy generation, transport, and packaging have helped to raise GDP per unit of energy use from $2.9 in 1990 to $4.0 in 2005.

There is, as we have seen above, an almost limitless availability of fossil fuel. The world is now going through a second energy shock, linked to the rise of China and India, with enormous and fast-growing energy needs, political instability in the Middle East, and fears over global warming. These factors have affected both government regulation of the energy sector, notably through the Kyoto Agreement, and energy prices, though the long-term prospect for the likely course of energy prices is still highly uncertain. The main factor in global warming is the production of carbon dioxide by fossil fuels, creating the "greenhouse effect," which traps reflected radiation from the sun in the earth's atmosphere. The level of carbon dioxide production arising from human energy use rose from 17 billion tonnes (metric tons) in 1980 to 27 billion tonnes in 2007, and on present trends will climb to 45 billion tonnes in 2030. However, using technological knowledge that either already exists, or which could soon be brought into existence based on current knowledge, there are numerous ways in which the projected rise in global output could be achieved without any increase in global carbon dioxide output. As well as liberating people from the tyrannies of nature, technology has produced many problems. However, technology also has the capability to solve these problems.

Seven billion-tonne "wedges" have been identified that could help to stabilize carbon dioxide output without any major technological breakthrough. Each one gigaton wedge is the equivalent of taking 250,000 vehicles off the road. These wedges could include 700 1GW nuclear power stations; improving building techniques so that the amount of energy used to heat buildings remains constant (40 percent of primary energy is used to heat buildings); a fiftyfold increase in global wind turbine capacity; doubling the rate of reforestation; 2,500 fossil-fuelled hydrogen power stations, which sequester carbon dioxide in oilfields; a 700-fold increase in photovoltaic cells; and re-powering 1,400 GW of coal-fired power stations with gas.

There are many opportunities for more general use of carbon sequestration technologies so that extensive use can continue to be made of the world's massive coal reserves without contributing to global warming. A variety of possibilities exist through which technological progress might allow large increases in vehicle use to take place without a substantial growth in carbon dioxide emissions. These include improvements in internal combustion engine technologies; the use of hybrid vehicles, which combine the internal combustion engine with the addition of an electric motor; pure electric vehicles, which may ultimately be powered with electricity generated from renewable sources, eventually from solar power, or from fossil fuels accompanied by carbon dioxide sequestration; and expanded use of biofuels, which are carbon dioxide neutral.

For a prolonged period, as average incomes increased, today's developed countries saw large increases in levels of air pollution. As late as the early 1950s, airborne particulates in cities such as London caused severe smogs that caused large-scale loss of life. Government regulation stimulated technological progress through such measures as the introduction of smoke-scrubbing equipment at power stations, the increased use of low-sulfur coal, and improved fuels for vehicles. Particulates in the atmosphere fell dramatically thereafter, reaching levels that today are only a tiny fraction of those in the early 1950s. Many of the technological advances that helped reduce airborne particulates in high-income countries are now embodied routinely in global products that are sold to developing countries, including power stations, vehicle and aircraft engines, and fuels for transport equipment. This tends to reduce the level of particulate emissions in developing countries compared with those experienced in high-income countries at similar levels of real output per person. This ecological "advantage of the latecomer" is demonstrated by the fact that the level of particulates for the urban population in developing countries fell from 98 mcg per cu. meter in 1990 to 61 mcg in 2005.

Technological progress in transport has comprehensively transformed the choices facing people in terms of personal movement. Since the 1970s the real price of air travel and automobiles has fallen tremendously, thereby allowing people with ever-lower income levels to make long journeys on aircraft and acquire cars. The number of outbound tourists from developing countries increased from 212 million individual journeys in 1995 to 419 million in 2006. The number of passenger cars per thousand people in developing countries rose from 24 in 1990 to 39 in 1999–2001. The development of small passenger cars for sale at less than $5,000 will increase still further the penetration of passenger vehicle ownership through the social structure of developing countries. This will enable an ever-wider group of the world's population to experience the independence and convenience of car ownership, and enjoy the pleasures of the open road.

From this hour, freedom!
From this hour I ordain myself loos'd of limits and imaginary lines,
Going where I list, my own master, total and absolute …

I inhale great draughts of space;
The east and west are mine, and the north and south are mine.

Walt Whitman, *Song of the Open Road*

Revolutionary technological advances, especially in semiconductors and software, have contributed to enormous progress in the nature and falls in the price of electronic consumer durables. The transformation of the telecommunications industry has been especially significant for advances in the standard of living of people in developing countries. Increases in average incomes in developing countries have helped to stimulate a growth in expenditure on telecommunications goods and services. In developing countries, the number of telephone lines per thousand people rose from 29 in 1990 to 130 in 2006, and the number of cellphone subscribers rose from zero per thousand people in 1990 to 310 in 2006. By 2002, for every thousand people in developing countries, there were 257 radios, 190 TV sets and 28 personal computers. The technological and business transformation of the global media industry, and the liberalization of national controls, has widened the range of broadcast information to which people from almost all income brackets have access. These developments have helped to provide people with enormously enhanced freedom of choice both for entertainment and for the acquisition of knowledge.

Freedom from control by others

In the past three decades capitalist globalization has stimulated rapid urbanization in developing countries, the urban population rising from 24 percent in 1965 to 44 percent in 2006. The transformation in the living and working environment from a rural, isolated setting, with limited connection to markets, negligible opportunities for changes in work and housing, and a restricted, unchanging set of interpersonal relationships, to an urban capitalist environment characterized by engagement with the market for the employment of one's labor power, wide opportunities for changes in work and housing, and access to a broad and changing set of interpersonal relationships, has comprehensively transformed the outlook of the new generation of urban dwellers. Their children's outlook contrasts even more with that of their parents and grandparents. The pace of change in people's consciousness has been accelerated by the transformations in the mass media facilitated by institutional change and by technological progress in telecommunications and electronic consumer goods. The new generation of urban dwellers operating in a capitalist environment are vastly more independent than their forebears, with far greater opportunities to resist pressures from parents and kin groups, and (in the case of wives and daughters) from husbands, fathers, and brothers. Capitalist urbanization has stimulated demands for political liberties. Whereas in 1985 38 percent of the world's population lived in the world's most democratic countries, by 2000, the share had risen to 57 percent. The share living in authoritarian regimes had fallen from 45 percent to 30 percent.

Growth rates of national output per person have been somewhat faster in developing countries than in high-income countries. Between 1975 and 2002, the growth of per capita GDP in the OECD countries was 2.0 percent per annum, compared with 2.3 percent per annum in developing countries as a whole. Studies which measure global inequality using country averages weighted by population totals have found there has been a small decline in income inequalities during the last quarter of a century. They estimate that the global Gini coefficient, the generally accepted measure of inequalities in income distribution, fell from around 0.58–0.62 in 1980 to around 0.52–0.56 in 1998.

Freedom from poverty

The rapid increase in output per person in developing countries during the period of the global business revolution have contributed to a large reduction in global poverty. In developing countries between 1981 and 2002 the share of people living on less than $1 per day fell from 40 percent to 19 percent, and the share of those living on less than $2 per day fell from 67 percent to 50 percent.

All the changes that took places in these years, such as technological advances in medicines and medical equipment, increasing real consumption levels, improvements in national and international government agencies' delivery systems, improved food security, as well as advances in infrastructure provision, better access to reliable drinking water, and improved sanitation; all these have contributed to enormous improvements in health, helping to free people from the threat of illness, pain, and premature death. This has been crucially important for the standard of living in developing countries. In these countries, between 1970 and 2002, infant mortality rates fell from 108 per thousand live births to 61 per thousand, and under-five mortality rates fell from 166 to 89 per thousand, while fertility rates fell from 5.4 births per woman in 1970–75 to 2.9 per woman in 2002–5. Life expectancy at birth in developing countries rose from 56 years in 1970–75 to 65 years in 2000–5. Even in the least developed group of countries, life expectancy rose from 44 in 1970–75 to 51 in 2000–5. It is impossible to quantify the impact of these hugely important advances in human well-being.

In low-income countries, which are particularly dependent on agriculture, population grew by 2.2 percent per annum between 1980 and 2002 (from 1.6 billion to 2.5 billion), while the amount of arable land per person shrank from 0.23 hectares to just 0.17 hectares in the same period. Without large improvements in agricultural productivity in this period, food output per person would have declined and developing countries' susceptibility to famine would have increased greatly. In fact, this period saw unprecedented advances in agricultural technology and rapid farm modernization, including improvements in seeds, farm equipment, transport infrastructure, and information technology. In low-income countries, between 1979–81 and 2000–2 the amount of fertilizer applied per hectare of arable land rose from 289 grams to 717 grams, the number of tractors per square kilometer of arable land rose from 20 to 66, and irrigated land increased its share of total cropland from 19.8 percent to 26.4 percent. As a consequence of this immense investment and technological progress, per capita food output in low-income countries grew by 0.8 percent per annum in the same period. The improvement in agricultural performance in developing countries played a central role in confining famines to sub-Saharan Africa, whereas formerly they affected large parts of the developing world. Moreover, even in sub-Saharan Africa, due to agricultural modernization, output per worker rose by one-fifth between 1990–92 and 2003–5, which helped to reduce the dimensions of famine significantly.

Freedom from war

It is widely assumed that national identification is "so natural, primary, and permanent as to precede history." In fact, in its modern and basically political sense the concept of the nation is a recent one. It is closely associated with industrialization and the growth of the state, emerging in Europe with the mercantilist era in the sixteenth to eighteenth centuries, and reaching its full development with state-led industrialization in the nineteenth century.

During the early phase of capitalist industrialization from the late eighteenth to the mid-nineteenth century, most economists considered that the emerging market economy was essentially international, not national. It was thought that the global market economy would erode national cultural differences. Much of the economics of the period was focused on individual units, whether people or firms, rationally maximizing their gains and minimizing their losses in a market which had no specific spatial dimension. Adam Smith's *The Wealth of Nations* is directed against the concept of a protected national economy based on mercantilist principles. It argued for a cosmopolitan, international economy in which the extent of the market and the division of labor would become ever wider, not halting at national boundaries. It was widely held that the trend of world history was toward the unification of small states into larger ones and, eventually, into a world state alongside a global market.

In 1784, Immanuel Kant wrote an essay entitled "An Idea for a Universal History with a Cosmopolitan Purpose," in which he suggested that history embodied a hidden plan of nature: "[S]uch a plan opens up the comforting prospect of a future in which all the germs implanted by nature can be developed fully, and in which man's destiny can be fulfilled here on earth." He considered that the highest purpose of nature was a "universal cosmopolitan existence," and that this would eventually be realized as the "matrix within which all the original capacities of the human race may develop." In the *Communist Manifesto* Marx and Engels gave voice to this widely held view:

> The bourgeoisie has through its exploitation of the world market given a cosmopolitan character to production and consumption in every country … In place of their old local and national seclusion and self-sufficiency, we have

intercourse in every direction, universal inter-dependence of nations. As in material so also in intellectual production. The intellectual creations of individual nations become common property. National one-sidedness and narrow-mindedness become more and more impossible ... National differences and antagonisms between peoples, are daily more and more vanishing, owing to the development of the bourgeoisie, to freedom of commerce, to the world market, to uniformity in the mode of production and in the conditions of life corresponding thereto.

During the whole of the first century of modern industrial capitalism, from 1815 to 1914, there was no major international conflict among the world's leading economic powers. Despite intense national economic rivalry, rules were established that provided a mutually agreed structure for the peaceful conduct of international trade, investment flows, and migration. However, the widely anticipated move toward peaceful global capitalism did not take place. The late industrializing countries caught up with the first industrial nation, Britain, with the help of powerful state action, especially protection, to support the growth of their national bourgeoisie and to construct strongly felt national identities. The emergence of distinct national identities was stimulated by the spread of universal education, needed to produce capable workers for a modern economy, and the closely associated construction of a unified national language. The strains stimulated by intensifying nationalistic rivalries between the leading capitalist countries finally erupted in the World Wars of 1914–18 and 1939–45.

The establishment after 1945 of a set of international institutions, although not principally aimed at preventing conflict, helped to do so by greatly increasing the sense of shared global responsibility felt by individual countries. The most important of these institutions were established under the auspices of the United Nations. They provided mechanisms for the mutually accepted conduct of international relations, principally, but not exclusively, in the economic sphere. These institutions included the World Bank, the International Monetary Fund (IMF), the General Agreement on Tariffs and Trade (GATT), the UN Conference on Trade and Development (UNCTAD), the Food and Agriculture Organization (FAO), the International Telecommunications Union (ITU), the International Labor Organization (ILO), and the World Health Organization (WHO). Regional political and economic entities such as the EU, NAFTA, ASEAN, and APEC may also be viewed as part of the march toward global political unity.

Membership of each of these organizations involved the sacrifice of a degree of autonomy by participating states. Under the GATT, successive rounds of reform resulted in large reductions in trade restrictions. At least as significant was the decision taken in 1994 to establish the World Trade Organization (WTO) as a successor to the GATT. The GATT had confined itself essentially to cross-border transactions. The WTO was concerned not only with trade in the strict sense, but also with the rights of international firms to establish service activities within other countries, and to invest in other countries without the requirements to transfer technology or join partnerships with local firms, with their right to have equal access with indigenous firms to local markets, and to protect the use of their intellectual property in other countries. The World Bank and the IMF originally had relatively limited objectives, essentially to support long-term investments and relieve short-term balance of payments difficulties respectively. Over time, however, America has made use of its dominant position in these institutions to extend their original, limited objectives into goals characteristic of the Washington Consensus, such as conditionality requirements under which loan recipients undertook to implement comprehensive system reform, involving privatization, price deregulation, public sector reform, and improvements in corporate governance, labor standards, and environmental regulation. The trend in all these cases was toward international harmonization and "deep integration" among economies. Through these steadily advancing arrangements, individual countries sacrificed aspects of their autonomy in the interests of establishing their own markets as part of a unified global capitalist market, with America at its core.

Up until the 1970s, most countries still implemented interventionist policies in important aspects of international economic relations. Most governments supported their national bourgeoisie in various ways, including protection (albeit declining), state ownership of key industries supporting the indigenous private sector, support from the local banking industry, and resistance to foreign acquisition of local firms. However, in due course the web of mutually agreed international economic and political arrangements expanded, thereby reducing the possibility of conflict. In the last resort, this growing network of global regulations has helped to prevent military conflict among capitalist countries by building a common interest in international arrangements that were mutually beneficial economically. After the 1970s, there were massive changes in the way that national and international economic policies were conducted, as national governments across the world abandoned protectionist, state-led strategies. Support for the national bourgeoisie greatly weakened as barriers to international capital flows were extensively dismantled and, for the first time, production systems were established by firms on a global basis, with closely integrated international division of labor within their supply chain.

The importance of international trade has increased sharply during the period of capitalist globalization, and as a consequence global prosperity is more reliant than ever before on the maintenance of friendly relations between trading partners. Exports of goods and services rose from just 11 percent of world GDP in 1965 to 24 percent in 2004, while the total trade in goods and services rose from 40 percent of GDP in 1990 to 55 percent in 2004. The standard of living of consumers in high-income countries has become intimately linked to international trade. Imports of manufactured goods by high-income countries from low and middle-income countries rose from $414 billion in 1994 to $1.4 trillion in 2004. A large fraction of these imports are consumer goods, the real price of which has fallen heavily during this period, contributing significantly to advances in living standards in the high-income countries.

The liberalization of international capital flows means that a large shift has taken place in ownership structures. It is increasingly likely that foreigners will own a substantial share of the equity of a firm headquartered in a given country. These developments mean that firms from capitalist countries are more deeply embedded than ever before in each other's business systems. The degree of internationalization of the world's leading firms has risen steadily in the era of globalization. Capitalist firms have, in the words of Marx and Engels, "nestled everywhere, settled everywhere, and established connections everywhere." By 2003, the 100 largest transnational corporations had an average of 50 percent of their assets and employment, and 54 percent of their sales, in foreign countries. Owners are less and less "national." For example, only 44 percent of the shares of BP, formerly British Petroleum, are owned by British entities, and foreigners own almost one-half of the French stock market.

Between 1995 and 2004 there were more than 800 large cross-border mergers and acquisitions valued at over $1 billion each. In other words, over 800 large "national" firms lost their national identity, surrendered their national "passports" and became "foreign" firms. As a result a large swathe of firms were absorbed into new corporate entities, with their headquarters in another country. Many famous symbols of national economic success were absorbed in this way into international firms with their headquarters in other countries. For example, in Britain "national champion" firms such as Jaguar, Rover, British Steel, Marconi, Pilkington Glass, British Oxygen, Abbey National, Jewsons, Smiths Industries, British Airports Authority, Morgan Grenfell, and Warburgs, were all acquired by international firms.

The corporate culture of successful global firms is increasingly similar. Most leading global firms conduct their internal communications in English, while most international firms are advised by the same group of international investment banks, accountants, consultants, and human resource advisors. Their brands are shaped by the same group of international marketing firms. Corporate identity is decreasingly associated with any particular nation, and corporate names increasingly are acronyms devoid of national identification: AIG, AXA, BAE, BASF, BAT, BBVA, BP, BT, EADS, EDF, ENI, E.on, GE, GKN, HSBC, KPMG, PwC, and WPP. Business leaders are increasingly recruited from a common pool of educational institutions, with the result that a large fraction of the world's top business leaders have studied at a small group of leading international business schools, which teach courses that are indistinguishable from each other. The heads of leading international firms are increasingly from countries other than those in which their firm is headquartered.

Ordinary citizens have been pulled together by the forces of capitalist globalization. English has increasingly become the common global language. Citizens across the world share a common culture through the global mass media. Together they watch the Olympic Games, the World Cup, English football, or *Friends*. They participate in programs with a common international format, like *Who Wants to Be a Millionaire?* and *Big Brother*.

Knowledge about other countries and cultures has accelerated. The period of capitalist globalization has seen a large increase in mass literacy and educational levels. By 2005 the adult literacy rate in developing countries had reached 85 percent for males and 73 percent for females, and at the same time, the instruments of mass communication have become ubiquitously available. By 2004 54 percent of households in developing countries had a television set. International tourism has grown into a mass phenomenon, facilitated by increases in per capita income, by economies of scale in tourism and hotel companies, which has lowered the real price of tourist lodgings, and by technological progress in aircraft design, which has allowed a drastic fall in the real price of air travel. At the same time international tourism has been stimulated by the global mass media. In 2006 there were 419 million individual outbound tourist journeys from developing countries and 533 million from high-income countries. The number of inbound tourists going to developing countries was 332 million compared with 510 million to high-income countries.

International economic and cultural relations have become so closely intertwined that for most people it is unimaginable that there could be a global military conflict. The world can now look back upon more than half a century of peaceful relations among the leading capitalist countries. Increasingly, the period from 1914 to 1945 appears as an aberration in the long march toward global unification achieved by the modern capitalist market economy. The stresses in the international political system in this period can be viewed as the outcome of strains arising from the nation-based pattern of industrialization that was specific to a particular era in capitalist development. Looking back over the development of the modern world economy, the historian Eric Hobsbawm believes that the phase during which economic development was integrally linked to the national economies of a number of developed territorial states can now be seen as situated between two essentially transnational eras. As the capitalist world economy begins finally to take shape after a delay of 100 years, we may be witnessing today the beginnings of the global government structure that was envisioned by nineteenth century liberal economists as the natural consequence of the global economy. In such an environment, the possibility of major international military conflict would cease to exist, thanks ultimately to the cultural "cement" produced by the integration of the international capitalist economy.

1.2 THE CONTRADICTIONS OF CAPITALISM IN THE ERA OF THE GLOBAL BUSINESS REVOLUTION

Unconstrained, "wild" capitalism threatens fundamentally the very existence of the human species. The global ecology is profoundly threatened by the locked-in pattern of consumption, distribution, and energy consumption that is at the heart of capitalist globalization. The world faces an intensifying international struggle for energy security. The large corporation has burst the boundaries of the nation. Giant global firms threaten the indigenous firms that are headquartered in developing countries. At the same time, they are reducing their allegiance to their original home countries. The distribution of income and wealth within both rich and poor countries has become much more unequal as a consequence of capitalist globalization. The revolution in the financial system has produced comprehensively integrated markets, with money creation and speculation on an unimaginable scale. The global financial system is "flying blind," in the throes of a crisis on a scale that is unprecedented since the 1930s. If human beings are to resolve these contradictions and avoid the looming disaster, it is urgently necessary to establish global mechanisms to contain the self-created monster of unconstrained global capitalism and guide its immense energy in a direction that serves the common interest of all.

MANKIND'S embrace of the forces of capitalist competition can be compared with the pact between Faust and Mephistopheles. The drive to make profits has stimulated human ingenuity over millennia. In the era of the global business revolution this fundamental force, the "electricity" of the economic system, has been liberated to operate even more powerfully than in previous eras. It is a force that human beings themselves have created unconsciously. However, this force also enslaves them. Through the pursuit of profit, mankind is allowed to win ever-greater mastery over nature, and achieve ever-greater levels of consumption, but at a high price. As with Faust, the pact may be of fixed duration. In return for the transitory pleasures that he was granted, Faust agreed that eventually he would give up his life:

> *Faust:* Then take my soul for I desire to die;
> And that's a wager!
>
> *Mephistopheles:* Done!
>
> *Faust:* And done again!
> If to the fleeting hour I say
> "Remain, so fair thou art, remain!"
> Then bind me with your fatal chain,
> For I will perish in that day.
> 'Tis I for whom the bell shall toll,
> Then you are free, your service done.

For me the clock shall fail, to ruin run,
And timeless night shall descend upon my soul.

Goethe, *Faust*, Part 1

Mankind stands at a crossroads in which the very existence of the human species is threatened through the "magical" forces that we have ourselves conjured up. We live in "the best of times," but also "the worst of times."

ECOLOGY, ENERGY, AND THE ENVIRONMENT

[Can] any civilization wage relentless war on life without destroying itself, and without losing the right to be called civilized ... We now stand where two roads diverge ... The road we have long been traveling is deceptively easy, a smooth superhighway on which we progress with great speed, but at its end lies disaster. The other fork of the road—the one "less traveled by"—offers our last, our only chance, to reach a destination that assures the preservation of our earth. The choice, after all, is ours to make.

Rachel Carson, *Silent Spring*

Ecology

The world's population began its accelerated modern growth in the eighteenth century, increasing by around one-fifth, from 610 million in 1700 to 720 million in 1800. In the nineteenth century the rate of growth increased, with the total world population more than doubling, to reach 1.6 billion in 1900. However, in the twentieth century the world's total population increased almost fourfold, exceeding 6 billion by the year 2000. By the late twenty-first century it is likely that the world's population will reach a peak of around 9–10 billion, and the world will have passed through the critical bottleneck of population growth. Technological progress in medicine, transport, building technologies and advances in educational levels have all contributed to the dramatic growth in the numbers of human beings since the eighteenth century.

In order to feed the huge and growing global population and meet the demands for a more varied diet as incomes rise, technological progress has brought unprecedented advances in the application of science to the food industry. It will need to continue to do so in order to meet the increase in population and incomes in the decades ahead. Technological progress, spurred on by the pursuit of profit in all branches of the food industry, has enabled larger quantities of food to be provided more reliably than at any point in human history. The risk of famine has been confined to the margins of the human population. For the world's middle-class consumers, the safety, quality, and variety of food have never been greater. However, progress has come at a high price in terms of the natural environment which human beings share with other living things, both plant and animal.

The World Wildlife Fund (WWF) has constructed a Living Planet Index, which tracks the populations of 1,313 vertebrate species—fish, amphibians, reptiles, birds, and mammals—from all around the world. It concludes that between 1970 and 2003 the index fell by around 30 percent, a global trend which suggests that we are degrading natural ecosystems at a rate unprecedented in human history. However, these aggregate global trends mask important regional differences. The principal declines in wildlife populations in the high-income countries had already been completed by 1970. Between 1970 and 2003, the populations of temperate terrestrial species stabilized, as did those of marine species in the Pacific, Arctic, and Atlantic Oceans. However, between 1970 and 2003 the populations of tropical terrestrial species declined by around 55 percent on average, while those of marine species in the Indian Ocean and Southeast Asian seas saw declines of over 50 percent. In the case of freshwater populations, both temperate and tropical species experienced declines of around 30 percent from 1970 to 2003.

The consequence of uncontrolled pursuit of profit by global capitalism can be seen vividly in the fishing industry, which has witnessed high-speed advances in technology in recent years, including the use of information technology by giant trawlers to identify the location of large concentrations of fish. At low levels of income there is a high income elasticity of demand for fish, and fish consumption is rising fast in developing countries, leading to overfishing. Pollution and global warming have in turn compounded the effects of overfishing. A report in *Science* in 2006 presented a dire warning of the consequences of uncontrolled fishing in the "global commons" of the high seas. It defined a "collapsed species" as one for which the catch has dropped to below ten percent of the recorded maximum catch, and estimated that the proportion of fish species that have collapsed rose from zero in 1950 to 29 percent in 2003. It concluded that, if commercial fishing continued at present levels, there would be a complete collapse of fish species by around 2050, which means that there would be no commercial fishing at all within 40 years. Less than one percent of the world's ocean surface is protected from overfishing. There is no global agreement to prevent overfishing, except for a moratorium on commercial whaling. It is alarming that the European Union, with an income level far above the global average, has a record that is far worse than the global average, with around 80 percent of its fish stocks reported to be overfished, compared with a global average of 25 percent.

The main cause of the decline in terrestrial wildlife populations has been the destruction of forests in order to support agriculture. According to the Harvard ecologist Edward Wilson, the loss of forest during the past half century is "one of the most profound and rapid environmental changes in the history of the planet … Its impact on biodiversity is immediate and severe." As recently as 1950 the earth's old-growth woodland occupied 50 million square kilometers, or nearly 40 percent of the ice-free land surface. Today, its cover has shrunk to 34 million square kilometers and is shrinking fast. Half of what survives has already been degraded, much of it severely.

During the era of capitalist globalization, important changes have taken place in the level, distribution, and composition of the world's forested area. During the 1990s the overall forested area contracted by 2.4 percent. However, in the high-income countries between 1990 and 2000, the forested area actually grew by 0.1 percent per annum. The factors causing this reflected the high standard of living achieved in these countries, leading to population stability, deindustrialization, government regulation, secure property rights over forests, and the establishment of large areas as nationally protected wilderness areas. However, the base from which the forested area in high-income countries began its recent small increase is historically extremely low, given that there has been a large decline since the late Middle Ages. Today, the high-income countries account for only around one-fifth of the world's total forested area.

In developing countries, which account for around four-fifths of the world's forested area, between 1990 and 2005 the forested area fell by around 0.2 percent per annum, more than double the rate at which it was expanding in the high-income countries. The pressures that led to this decline in developing countries are rooted in underdevelopment. At best, it will be a long time before developing countries achieve the per capita income levels of today's high-income countries. Therefore, it is likely that the current trends of severe contraction of the forested area in developing countries will continue for many decades. The recent rapid growth in the production of biofuels to provide fuel for automobiles, including the expansion of sugar cane production in Brazil and palm oil in Malaysia, threatens to accelerate the rate of destruction of forest resources.

The global consequences of the decline in the forested area are especially significant because the largest declines in forested area took place in tropical or subtropical regions, which have a far greater density of species diversity than forests in other regions. Within the overall decline in forested area in developing countries between 1990 and 2000, Brazil alone accounted for over one-fifth, and ten developing countries (including Brazil) accounted for almost four-fifths of the total. There are 25 "environmental hotspots," in which the most species are at risk of extinction. Of these, 15 are mainly covered by tropical rainforests. The environmental hotspots account for just 1.4 percent of the world's land surface, but they account for no less than 44 percent of the world's plant species and more than one-third of all species of birds, mammals, reptiles, and amphibians.

The rate of species extinction has risen dramatically during the era of capitalist globalization. The World Conservation Union's Red List estimates that almost one in four of the earth's mammal species are at some degree of risk of extinction. Edward Wilson warns that as the threats intensify, more and more new species are pouring into the threatened categories of the Red Lists and sliding down the ratchet toward oblivion. He predicts that if current policies continue, by 2030 at least a fifth of the species of plants and animals will be gone or destined for early extinction, and that by the end of the twenty-first century, one-half will have become extinct.

It was in 1962 that Rachel Carson's book *Silent Spring* alerted the world to the terrifying consequences of the unregulated use of the natural environment as an economic resource to be exploited unrestrainedly for commercial profit: "Over increasingly large areas of America, spring now comes unheralded by the return of the birds, and the early mornings are strangely silent where once they were filled with the beauty of bird song." She warned that "the control of nature" is a phrase "conceived in arrogance, born of the Neanderthal age of biology and philosophy, when it was supposed that nature exists for the convenience of man." In high-income countries, government regulation has eliminated some of the most obviously destructive aspects of the human impact upon the natural environment which Rachel Carson catalogued in *Silent Spring*, such as the widespread use of DDT. However, because of the large increase in population and rising incomes, facilitated by technological progress, the era of capitalist globalization has witnessed an alarming overall acceleration in the destruction of the world's natural environment. Three decades later Edward Wilson conjured up a nightmare vision of the world if we continue along our present "well-trodden path":

> In 2100 the natural world is suffering terribly. The frontier forests are largely gone ... and with them most of the biodiversity hotspots. Coral reefs, rivers, and other aquatic habitats have deteriorated badly. Gone with the richest ecosystems are half or more of the earth's plant and animal species ... To travel around along any chosen latitude is to encounter mostly the same small set of introduced birds, mammals, insects and microbes ... The Age of Loneliness lies before humanity.

Environmental transition

The ability to provide a clean environment is closely related to levels of per capita income. In the high-income countries environmental standards have steadily improved since the 1970s. However, in fast-growing developing countries, ecological conditions have deteriorated seriously. The most likely prospect is that the low and middle-income countries will endure a long period of output growth in which they become increasingly polluted before they can become rich and clean. The governments of developing countries face massive environmental difficulties. Not only are they struggling to devise policies that protect their own vast populations from the awful environmental consequences of early-stage industrialization, but also the high-income countries expect them to grow in a fashion that does not damage the rest of the world through global warming.

The case of China provides a stark illustration of the difficulties facing developing countries. In terms of conventional measures of economic development, China is the most remarkable success story of capitalist globalization. However, as we will see in more detail later, China's economic success has been achieved at a high price in terms of deterioration of the environment, which has been damaged severely by the rampant growth of the market economy. China faces the world's most daunting environmental problems, with persistent environmental degradation and ever-worsening industrial pollution. China is likely to remain for many years firmly locked into the phase of environmental deterioration unless drastic action is taken by the Chinese state. China has gone from "poor and clean" to "large and dirty." It faces a mighty challenge if it is to become clean before it becomes rich. China's Vice-Minister of the State Environmental Protection Agency (SEPA) considers that "China's economic miracle is a myth," since environmental degradation is costing the country nearly 8 percent of its annual GDP.

Energy and international relations

Oil has been a key factor in international conflicts during the past few decades, and the possibility of conflict over access to finite oil supplies has become an increasingly important issue in international relations. There is little prospect of renewable energy replacing fossil fuels in the next two to three decades, and coal is therefore likely to remain the most important source of primary energy for electricity generation for the foreseeable future. However, oil is critically important for road and air transport, which are both growing at high speed, especially in developing countries.

Global oil demand is increasing rapidly. America consumes a quarter of the world total, compared with 30 percent in the Asia–Pacific region. Total world oil consumption increased by 19 percent from 1995 to 2005, driven largely by increases of 17 percent in America and 33 percent in the Asia–Pacific region. Oil production, on the other hand, is falling in America and stagnant in the Asia–Pacific region. Consequently, oil imports in both regions are rising rapidly. Global oil imports rose by 23 percent from 1998 to 2005. Out of the total increase in world oil imports from 1998 to 2005, America accounted for 33 percent, compared with 25 percent for China and 24 percent for the rest of the Asia–Pacific region, excluding Japan. As developing countries raise their level of per capita income and expand their transport systems, their demand for oil will increase greatly. For most of the Asia–Pacific region, increased oil consumption will need to be satisfied mainly through increased imports. However, America is likely to remain the most important single oil importer for a long period ahead. By 2004 American net oil imports amounted to 58 percent of its total oil consumption, and it is predicted that by 2025 oil imports will account for close to 70 percent of American consumption.

Between them, the Muslim countries of the Middle East account for over two-thirds of the world's oil reserves, and their share of global output is predicted to rise from 27 percent in 2000 to 43 percent in 2030. Five countries in the Persian Gulf region, namely Saudi Arabia, Iran, Iraq, Kuwait, and the United Arab Emirates, between them have 60 percent of total world oil reserves. The share of the Gulf countries in world oil trade is predicted to rise from 41 percent to 70 percent in 2030. The struggle for oil from the Middle East has been a central factor in international conflict in the past, not least in terms of the relationship between the

Muslim world and the West. It has the potential to become an even more important focus of international conflict in the future, until the world enters an era in which solar power becomes the dominant form of primary energy.

Global warming

James Lovelock regards the earth as a self-regulating system made up of an interconnected totality of organisms, including the surface rocks, the ocean, and the atmosphere. Lovelock terms this system "Gaia." He believes that human beings have deeply disturbed this self-regulating system: "With breathtaking insolence humans have taken the stores of carbon that Gaia buried to keep oxygen at its proper level and burnt them. In so doing they have usurped Gaia's authority and thwarted her obligation to keep the planet fit for life; they thought only of their comfort and convenience."

Burning fossil fuel has been at the heart of much of humanity's technological progress. Human beings have long used fire to clear forests and make way for settled agriculture. Burning coal was at the heart of the Industrial Revolution and the Age of Steam. In the twentieth century, burning oil in the internal combustion engine transformed the way in which people and goods were transported, and coal is still of central importance in electricity production. In James Lovelock's view, fire is centrally important in the ecological challenge that faces humanity: "Perhaps our and Gaia's greatest error was the conscious abuse of fire. Cooking meat over a wood fire may have been acceptable, but the deliberate destruction of whole ecosystems by fire merely to drive out the animals within was surely our first great sin against the living earth. It has haunted us ever since and combustion could now be our *auto da fe* and the cause of our extinction" (James Lovelock, *The Revenge of Gaia*). Perhaps Zeus was correct in the punishment he meted out to Prometheus, chaining him to a barren rock for the crime of teaching humanity about fire:

> *My appointed fate I must endure as best I can,*
> *Knowing the power of Necessity is irresistible.*
> *Under such suffering, speech and silence are alike*
> *Beyond me. For bestowing gifts upon mankind*
> *I am harnessed in these torturing clamps. For I am he*
> *Who hunted out the source of fire, and stole it, packed*
> *In pith of a dry fennel-stalk. And the fire has proved*
> *For men a teacher in every art, their grand resource.*
> *That was the sin for which I now pay the full price,*
> *Bared to winds of heaven, bound and crucified.*

Aeschylus, *Prometheus Bound*

Technological progress has greatly reduced the consumption of energy and other inputs per unit of final product. Nevertheless, in the era of unrestrained capitalist globalization, the pace of growth of final consumption, based around the locked-in pattern of production and distribution, has produced high rates of increase in the consumption of primary energy, including oil. Economic activity has developed in a fashion that has been locked into an environmentally damaging structure from which it has been difficult to depart. At the heart of the capitalist free market system is a vast interrelated structure of personal consumption and road transport. Within this system, individual consumer freedom and rights dominate. The right of consumers to consume freely is nurtured by giant capitalist firms whose interests are served by increased personal consumption. Marketing by global firms in financial services, entertainment, retailing, automobiles, airlines, holidays, food and drink, electronic goods, and IT equipment and services, encourages people to borrow more, spend more, and pursue increased consumption rather than greater happiness. This has been fueled by the explosive growth of personal debt, which has in turn been facilitated by the speculative boom in asset prices.

The individual freedom to consume has expressed itself in a system of personal transport that has been dominated by the private automobile. The automobile industry sits at the center of global capitalism, with a vast supply chain surrounding the core manufacturers. Under capitalist globalization, consumers are locked into a pattern of final consumption organized around packaged and processed goods, which in their turn support a global packaging industry that uses vast quantities of plastics, steel, and aluminum. Intermediate and final products are distributed mainly by road-based commercial transport systems. It is likely that the use of battery-powered electric vehicles will increase substantially in the near future, but this merely transfers the problem of carbon dioxide emissions from vehicle exhaust pipes to the power stations that produce the electricity to power the vehicles. Only if there is a radical advance in conventional power generation technologies, in the program to construct nuclear power stations, and/or in carbon sequestration technologies, will battery-powered vehicles help to provide a solution to the global warming crisis. Roads in their turn require a network of supplier industries, including aggregates, cement, and steel. The production of commercial vehicles itself requires a global network of supplier industries, including steel, aluminum, plastics, and glass. Individuals have exercised their freedom of choice by demanding individualized transport systems in the shape of the automobile. Without exception, developing countries have allowed the same pattern of development in their transport systems and the same freedom of individual consumer choice as exists in the high-income countries.

Despite the unprecedented advances in energy efficiency over the past two decades, energy use is rising rapidly. Between 1990 and 2005, global consumption of primary energy increased by 31 percent, and the prospects are for continued rapid growth. Moreover, even the high-income countries are still expanding their consumption of primary energy. Between 1990 and 2005, their total primary energy consumption rose by 21 percent, and accounted for almost one-half of the total global increase, despite large advances in energy efficiency. As developing countries achieve increases in per capita incomes, they will move steadily toward the levels of primary energy use of today's high-income countries. In 2005, levels of per capita energy use in low-income countries still stood at only 486 kg (oil equivalent) per capita compared with 1,486 kg in middle-income countries, 3,961 kg in the eurozone and 7,983 kg in America. In 2005, the number of motor vehicles per thousand people stood at just nine in low-income countries and 66 in middle-income countries, compared with 604 in the eurozone and 814 in America.

The WWF estimates that from 1960 to 2003 the ecological footprint[4] for low-income countries remained unchanged at around 0.8 "global hectares" per person, while it rose slightly for middle-income countries, from 1.2 hectares to 1.8 hectares per person. In the high-income countries, however, it increased from 3.0 hectares in 1960 to 6.5 hectares in 2003.

In February 2007 the UN's Intergovernmental Panel on Climate Change (IPCC), published its landmark report. A decade previously, the IPCC was only able to conclude that "on balance" human actions were the likely cause of climate change. Its 2007 report concluded that there was "unequivocal evidence" that climate change is caused by fossil fuel combustion. An important secondary cause of global warming is increased cement production. The level of carbon dioxide in the earth's atmosphere is estimated to have risen from around 260 parts per million (ppm) before the Industrial Revolution to 397 ppm in 2005. If current trends in the use of fossil fuels continue then levels will rise to 400 ppm by 2015 and 800 ppm in 2100, and global temperatures will rise by around three degrees centigrade by 2100.

If this continues it will threaten global civilization. The threat will take the form of a rise in world sea levels, an increase in extreme weather, and damage to agriculture. It is likely that the Arctic ice cap will disappear completely by 2060 whatever action is taken in the next few years, since it takes many years for carbon dioxide to disperse from the atmosphere. Managing the consequences of global warming will pose a large challenge even for high-income countries, but for poor countries, especially those in Asia, the challenge will be even more serious. It is now widely accepted that a global turning point has been reached and a choice must be made within this decade if a disaster for the earth is to be avoided.

Under the Kyoto Protocol, the main body of high-income countries, apart from America and Australia, committed themselves to restricting their carbon dioxide emissions by the year 2012 to roughly the level of 1990. The principal mechanism through which they hope to achieve this is by trading carbon permits. These permits are allocated to production establishments in the main polluting industries, which can then trade the resulting right to pollute, selling the permits if they produce less than the fixed target, or buying them if they overpollute relative to the target. Financial institutions are extremely enthusiastic about carbon trading, which they anticipate will create great opportunities for them in the various related financial products. However, it is debatable whether the carbon trading approach, in which the giant financial institutions have a strong vested interest, is superior to other forms of regulation, notably taxation of polluting activities. Since the introduction of carbon trading, the price of carbon has fluctuated wildly, failing to provide polluters with a reliable long-term signal. The carbon trading system only came into force in 2005, just five years before the expiration of the Kyoto Protocol. It is uncertain what form of agreement, if any, will operate after 2012.

Developing countries were not required to implement the conditions of the Kyoto Protocol. By the year 2004, their emissions of carbon dioxide had overtaken those of the high-income countries, standing at 51 percent of the world's total emissions, although the carbon emissions per capita in developing countries stood at less than one-fifth of those in the high-income countries. In the absence of the requisite pace of technological progress, the process of catch-up in developing economies will lead to globally unsustainable increases in carbon dioxide emissions. The wide differences in per capita emissions between rich and poor countries make global agreement on a successor to the Kyoto Protocol especially difficult to achieve.

If the development of solar energy technology is successful, then this may eventually lead to a widespread substitution of fossil fuels by solar energy, including in developing countries. However, even the most optimistic predictions do not consider that this is likely to begin to take place before 2030–40. The period between now and the possible widespread use of solar energy will be extremely challenging for global policy makers. This will be the "eye of the needle" that the world needs collectively to pass through, before solar power becomes commercially viable, before global population has peaked, and before irreparable damage is done to the global environment through global warming.

Despite increases in the use of nuclear power, wind power, and hydro power, it is likely that fossil fuels will remain the main source of primary energy for several decades to come. During this phase it will be necessary that technological progress occurs at such a pace as to ensure that increases in carbon dioxide emissions into the atmosphere from fossil fuels are kept within sustainable levels for the planet. In many developing countries, including India and China, coal will continue to be used as the main source of primary energy, due to its low price and local availability. Techniques of carbon sequestration, however, are still in their infancy, with great uncertainty as to the pace of technological progress and the costs of these techniques once they are developed. Perhaps just as importantly, vehicle use for passengers and freight is likely to expand enormously in developing countries in the next few decades, given that vehicle companies are working intensely to develop cheap cars for the mass of emerging middle-class customers in developing countries.

The high-income countries, with only 16 percent of the world's population, account for 49 percent of the world's carbon dioxide production. Despite technological progress to increase the amount of GDP generated per unit of energy use, developing countries are fast increasing their production of carbon dioxide as their per capita income advances. As we have seen, their total carbon dioxide emissions have now surpassed the total emissions of the high-income countries.

However, their levels of carbon dioxide production per capita are still far below those of the high-income countries. In 2004 the carbon emissions per capita in developing countries stood at just 2.6 kg, compared with 8.2 kg in the eurozone and 20.6 kg in America.

During President Clinton's second term in office, the American Senate refused, by a majority of 95–0, to ratify the Kyoto Protocol. Though faced with the growing evidence of global warming and its relationship to fossil fuel burning, America refused to introduce measures that would interfere with Americans' "long love-affair with the car," such as congestion charges, incentives to use car pools, increased public transport, and an increase in excise taxes on fuel. America also refused to raise the fuel economy standard for passenger vehicles; the current standard of 27.5 miles per gallon was fixed in the mid-1970s and has remained unchanged.

Within the EU there is intense political pressure to resist sharp reductions in carbon dioxide emissions. European consumers are reluctant to pay extra for clean cars. In 2007, in the face of fierce lobbying from Germany's Chancellor, Angela Merkel, and the automobile industry, the EU scaled back its plans to reduce car emissions. The EU car companies warned that the stricter targets were "unrealistic," "technologically unfeasible," and would make large parts of the European industry unprofitable. At its key meeting on climate change in December 2008, the EU agreed to set the broad goal of a 20 percent cut in carbon dioxide emissions by 2020 compared with 1990. However, in response to intense lobbying pressure, it was agreed that most of Europe's heavy industry would receive a large percentage of their tradable permits free, and that many other manufacturers would also be exempted from paying for their permits on the grounds that they faced competition from non-EU rivals. The EU's decision to water down its proposals to deal with climate change has reduced its credibility in trying to establish global cooperation to fight climate change.

Governments in developing countries are primarily interested in increasing per capita income. The negative consequences stemming from continued use of polluting fuels and technologies will take place mainly at a global level. Action by any individual developing country, however large, to limit carbon dioxide emissions has little benefit for the country concerned, but may on the other hand involve large sacrifices in terms of extra costs required to provide energy for economic growth. Fast-growing developing countries are strongly committed to using motor vehicles as the core of their transport systems for both people and goods. They also prize the vehicle sector because of its pervasive linkage effects with the rest of the economy. Governments and consumers in these countries feel that they have the right to replicate the pattern of development of today's high-income countries.

Developing countries have the fastest-growing markets for passenger vehicles, trucks, roads, housing, steel, cement, and power stations. In the absence of extraordinarily rapid technological progress or fundamental changes in the nature of economic development, economic catch-up in developing economies will lead to globally unsustainable increases in carbon dioxide emissions. It would require an immense effort of creativity by the governments of developing countries to develop a new approach to transport and consumption that was built around a different pattern of development, avoiding the "lock-in" that characterizes today's high-income countries. This would mean far-thinking efforts to regulate the market and to resist the push upon government policy that arises from the free market. With the rapidly increasing presence in developing countries of global firms in both the vehicle sector and closely related sectors, the possibility of such a creative policy response is fast receding.

The global economic crisis has important implications for global warming. On the one hand, the recession will lead to a substantial decline in oil demand. However, it will also reduce the level of corporate investment, which will tend to slow down the rate of introduction of energy-efficient equipment, including trucks and power stations, as well as other forms of equipment. Global oil prices hit a peak of nearly $150 per barrel in May 2008. By December 2008 the price had fallen below $40, which greatly reduces the incentive to purchase energy-efficient equipment. In the face of the economic crisis, the first priority for all national governments has been economic stability and employment rather than long-term goals relating to climate change. The crisis has led governments around the world to take measures to support their domestic vehicle industry and associated infrastructure, thereby reinforcing the "locked-in" pattern of personal and goods transport.

Conclusion

One of the driving forces of capitalist globalization is the freedom of capitalist businesses to nurture individual wants through the mass media and global marketing machines. The exercise of individual freedom of choice has allowed the evolution of patterns of consumption, production, and distribution that are severely damaging to the natural environment of the whole world. Not only do they damage the global environment for today's inhabitants, but they threaten the future for generations yet to come. Within the existing locked-in structure there is a wide and growing gap between private short-run costs and benefits, and long-run costs and benefits for the world, including its future inhabitants. Human beings' growing mastery over nature has taken place alongside a disintegrating control over the direction in which the whole structure is moving in respect to the natural environment. Many of these processes are already irreversible, though the full impact of some of them may only become apparent at some point in the future.

While there is a strong coalescence of interests among countries in certain respects, especially in relation to the long term, in other respects their interests conflict seriously. There is a potential for profound conflicts between different segments of the world population over issues of fundamental importance to the sustainability of human life on the planet, including access to finite energy resources and responsibility for ecological damage and global warming. Managing these conflicts will be a major challenge for the capacity of human beings to work harmoniously and achieve outcomes that are in their collective interest.

THE GLOBAL BUSINESS REVOLUTION

> *The bourgeoisie, by the rapid development of all instruments of production, by the immensely facilitated means of communication, draws all, even the most barbarian, nations into civilization. The cheap prices of its commodities are the heavy artillery with which it batters down all Chinese walls, with which it forces the barbarians' intensely obstinate hatred of foreigners to capitulate. It compels all nations, on pain of extinction, to adopt the bourgeois mode of production; it compels them to introduce what it calls civilization into their midst, that is, to become bourgeois themselves. In one word it creates a world after its own image.*

Marx and Engels, *The Communist Manifesto*

In the 1990s, many of the constraints on the growth of firms were removed. Vast regions of the world that were formerly isolated from the international economy were opened for competition. Privatization was enacted in most countries. Cross-border restrictions on mergers and acquisitions were removed from all but a few sectors. Developing countries face the challenge of unprecedented concentration among the world's leading systems integrator firms. However, the depth of this challenge is even greater than it appears at first sight. In addition to intense concentration among systems integrators, high-speed industrial concentration has taken place across large swathes of the global value chain.

Systems integrators and the cascade effect

The global business revolution has witnessed massive asset restructuring, with firms extensively selling off non-core businesses in order to develop their core businesses and upgrade their asset portfolios. The goal for most large firms has become the maintenance or establishment of their position as one of the handful of top companies in the global marketplace. An unprecedented degree of industrial concentration has been established among leading firms in sector after sector. By the 1980s, there was already a high degree of industrial concentration in many sectors within individual high-income countries. However, the global business revolution has seen for the first time the emergence of widespread industrial concentration across all high-income countries, as well as extending deeply into large parts of the developing world.

Global markets are highly segmented, divided between the goods and services sold to the relatively small numbers of people in the global middle class and those sold to the vast mass of poor people who make up the bulk of the world's population. Global consumption by households is hugely skewed toward the high-income countries. They have just 16 percent of the world's population but account for 77 percent of global consumption. The developing countries have 84 percent of the world's population, but account for just 22 percent of world consumption. The top ten percent of the world's population account for 59 percent of global consumption, and the top 20 percent account for 77 percent, while the bottom 50 percent account for a mere seven percent of the total. Contrary to the popular view in business schools, there is no "fortune at the bottom of the pyramid," simply poverty.

Within the high value-added, high technology, and/or strongly branded segments of global markets, which serve mainly the middle and upper-income earners who control the bulk of the world's purchasing power, a veritable law has come into play. A handful of giant firms, the systems integrators, occupy upwards of 50 percent of the whole global market. In sector after sector, leading firms, with powerful technologies and marketing capabilities, select the most capable of their suppliers, in a form of industrial planning, adopting aligned suppliers who can work with them across the world. Thus, across a wide range of activities a cascade effect is at work, in which intense pressures develop for suppliers of goods and services to the global giants to themselves merge and acquire, and develop leading global positions.

The cascade effect observed: aerospace and beverages

The impact of consolidation and the cascade effect can be seen in two very different industries, aerospace and beverages. A single large commercial aircraft costs over $200 million, whereas a single serving of a soft drink or a beer costs only around one dollar. However, common processes are at work in both industries through the impact of high-speed industrial consolidation and the cascade effect.

Large commercial aircraft and advanced military aerospace equipment contain bundles of the world's most advanced technologies. The design, assembly, marketing, and upgrading of this equipment embody powerful economies of scale and scope. The design of a new aircraft requires enormous investments, with significant up-front costs during the launch stage. The industry has large economies of scale in assembly, which comes from spreading planning efforts and high tooling costs over large outputs of one type of aircraft. Economies can be achieved through lessons learned in the course of producing large numbers of a given aircraft model. Having a family of aircraft with common platforms enables the manufacturer to spread given R&D outlays over a larger number of aircraft, to obtain economies of scale in procurement of components, and to achieve large operating benefits for customers. Branding is critical in the aerospace industry. A large installed base itself is the best demonstration of product reliability, operating efficiency, and technological leadership.

In the 1950s and 1960s there were over a dozen firms producing large commercial aircraft. During the era of capitalist globalization, the real value of world commercial aircraft sales has increased many times over. If the view of mainstream economists was correct, if the world of industrial competition was flat and resembled the "trees in the forest," then there should be far more commercial aircraft assemblers today than in the 1960s. In fact, the industry has become a duopoly, with just two large commercial aircraft makers, Airbus and Boeing, left.

The systems integrators, Airbus and Boeing, have huge procurement budgets, totaling more than $30 billion annually in Boeing's case. They focus increasingly on coordinating and planning the supply chain, rather than direct manufacture. As much as 60–80 percent of the end-product value of aerospace products is now derived from the external supply network. Both systems integrators have shifted toward the final assembly of large subsystems, choosing risk-sharing partners that develop and design important subsystems of the aircraft. These require massive R&D investments. As aircraft technology becomes more complex and the cost pressure increases, the systems integrators have pushed more development and design activities down the supply chain to their subsystems integrators. The systems integrators have radically pruned their supply chain. The reduction in the number of direct suppliers allows them to form a closer collaboration with their direct suppliers and maintain tight control over aircraft design and assembly as technology and cost requirements continue to increase. The way in which Airbus and Boeing have reorganized the institutional structure of the supply chain in order to reduce the number of suppliers and nurture large-scale subsystems integrators constitutes a form of industrial policy, with the systems integrators picking and nurturing winners.

In order to meet the demands of the systems integrators, the major aerospace subsystems and key component suppliers themselves must invest heavily in R&D, and expand in order to benefit from cost reduction through economies of scale and scope. A powerful merger movement has taken place at all levels of the supply chain, and the level of concentration in the upper reaches of the aircraft industry supply chain has increased rapidly. Through a series of mergers and acquisitions of core businesses that meet their strategic goals, and through selling non-core businesses in order to upgrade their asset portfolios, a group of giant subsystems integrators have established or strengthened their competitive positions in businesses covering one or more aircraft subsystems. All of these suppliers are headquartered in, and have their main production facilities in, developed countries, especially America. Leaders in their respective industries, all of them are global giants themselves, with billions of dollars in revenues and large R&D outlays. They dominate every major subsystem of the aircraft.

Engines are by far the most expensive aircraft subsystem, involving enormous development costs and R&D outlays. There are now only three engine makers, namely GE, Rolls-Royce, and United Technology (Pratt & Whitney), that are able to produce large modern jet aircraft engines. Aircraft structures are dominated by a handful of companies, including Vought, Finnemeccanica, Mitsubishi, Fuji, and Kawasaki Heavy Industries. Honeywell is by far the most powerful firm in the supply of avionics systems, with Smiths Industries, Goodrich, and Rockwell Collins as its major competitors. Snecma and Goodrich dominate the supply of landing gear, wheel, and braking systems. Snecma is the world leader in wiring systems on large commercial aircraft. Jamco is sole supplier to Boeing for aircraft lavatories. Recaro and B/E Aerospace account for most of the market for seats on large commercial aircraft. Michelin, Goodyear, and Bridgestone are the only firms capable of supplying tires for large commercial aircraft. Saint-Gobain is the sole supplier of aircraft glass to Airbus. Alcoa and Alcan account for most of the world's supply of aluminum for aircraft assembly. Each A380 uses two million of Alcoa's titanium lock bolts.

Unlike the aerospace industry, beverages are technologically simple products which change little over time, and there are low entry costs to the industry. In the era of capitalist globalization the value of global beverage sales has increased many times over. In the 1960s most cities across the world contained numerous small beverage firms, each supplying their local market. If the view of mainstream economists was correct, if the world of industrial competition was flat and resembled the trees in the forest, then there should be far more beverage firms today than in the 1960s. In fact the global beverage industry has witnessed high-speed consolidation. In the carbonated soft drinks sector, just two firms now account for around three-quarters of total global sales. In the broader category of non-alcoholic drinks, just five firms account for over one-half of the global market. Following the acquisition of the giant American brewer Anheuser Busch by Inbev in 2008, the world's top four brewers accounted for almost three-fifths of the world's beer market by volume, and even more in terms of revenue.

The massive procurement expenditure on material inputs and services by the world leading beverage producers has increased the pressure for consolidation from the higher reaches of the supply chain. In many areas, the cascade effect pressures on the supply chain from the beverage industry are applied simultaneously by the food industry. This cascade effect has stimulated a wave of consolidation in the beverage industry's supply chain. Moreover, as the higher reaches of the supply chain have struggled to meet the global needs of the world's leading beverage companies, the process of consolidation within their ranks has produced further cascade pressure on the supply chain of these firms, as they struggle to lower costs and achieve the technological progress necessary to meet the fierce demands of the world's leading system integrators who stand at the center of their respective supply chains.

Over 200 billion beverage cans are consumed annually. Since the late 1980s, the world's metal can industry has rapidly consolidated. Three firms now stand out as the global industry leaders, with a combined global market share of 57 percent. The industry leader, Rexam, makes 54 billion metal beverage cans per year, that is to say, around ten cans for every person on the planet. It sells almost one-half of these to its largest customer, Coca-Cola. The metal can industry is a major consumer of both steel and aluminum, and places intense pressure on the steel and aluminum industries to achieve technological progress, improve product quality, and lower costs. The other major users of primary metals have also consolidated at high speed during the global business revolution, including the automobile, aerospace, construction, and household durable goods industries. They also place heavy pressure on the steel and aluminum industries, which have as a consequence experienced rapid consolidation. The top five firms produce 44 percent of total world production of aluminum, and an even higher share of the aluminum sheet for beverage cans. In the steel industry, leading steel firms focus on high value-added, high-technology products for global customers, including steel for beverage cans. Although the top ten firms account for "only" around 27 percent of total global output by weight, following the merger of Arcelor and Mittal Steel, they account for around three-fifths of total global sales revenue from the steel industry.

Glass bottles are still the main form of primary packaging in the beer industry, and, despite its relative decline, the glass bottle remains an important form of packaging for soft drinks, especially in developing countries. Following successive rounds of mergers and acquisitions (M&A), the glass bottle industry has become highly consolidated. The two super-giants of the industry (Owens-Illinois and Saint-Gobain) now account for around seven-tenths of total glass bottle production in Europe and North America. Between them they produce more than 60 billion glass bottles annually.

PET bottles were developed in the late 1960s, and quickly became the most important form of primary packaging in the soft drinks industry. By 2003, excluding the production by beverage companies for self-consumption, the top four firms accounted for almost two-thirds of the total production of PET bottles in North America and Europe respectively. Much of the technological progress in the PET bottle industry has been achieved by the specialist machine builders, who make two different types of machinery, namely "pre-forms" and the equipment that "blows" the pre-forms into their final bottle form. Each of these sectors is dominated by specialist high-technology firms. One firm alone (Husky) accounts for around three-quarters of the total global market for high-volume PET injection machines, while another specialist firm (Tetra Laval) has a near monopoly on the purchase of advanced blowing equipment by the world's leading beverage companies.

In the supply of beverage filling line equipment, the high value-added, high-technology segments of the market supplying the world's leading beverage companies are dominated by just two firms (KHS and Krones), the product of unceasing M&A in recent years, which together account for almost nine-tenths of global sales of high-speed beverage bottling lines. The world's leading beverage companies have bought machines almost exclusively from these two companies because of their high levels of reliability, low operating costs, high speed, consistent filling height, and low rates of damage to bottles and product. Each of them spends heavily on research and development.

The advertising and communication sector, which is crucial for branding global businesses, has witnessed intense M&A activity and global expansion of its main customers. In addition, they face increasingly powerful global media companies, such as Disney, News International, Time Warner, and Viacom, with which they place their products. The advertising and communication industry has become polarized into a small number of immensely powerful firms and a large number of small firms. By 2001, the top four firms in the sector (WPP, Omnicom, Interpublic, and Publicis) accounted for almost three-fifths of total global advertising revenue.

The world's leading beverage companies are among the largest purchasers of trucks, either directly, or through their third party logistics suppliers. Their truck fleets are enormous, amounting to hundreds of thousands of trucks for the industry leaders. The world's leading truck manufacturers are under intense pressure from their global customers to reduce costs and improve technologies. This intensifies the pressure to increase scale in order to achieve greater volumes of procurement and push down costs across their own value chains, including suppliers of truck components (engines, brake systems, tires, exhaust systems, seats, informatics, and ventilation systems) and materials (steel, aluminum, and plastics). Greater scale also enables them to achieve faster technological progress through economies of scope (especially in relation to technological progress that can be used in different divisions of the company), in order to provide the customer with more reliability, lower fuel costs, greater safety, and more effectiveness in meeting pollution control requirements. By the late 1990s, the world's top five truck makers accounted for one-half of total global sales in terms of the number of units sold, but a much higher share of the total market value, as the leading truck companies tend to produce vehicles with far higher levels of technology than do truck makers in developing countries. Moreover, three of the world's leading truck makers, MAN, VW and Scania, are in the middle of a long-drawn-out process of merger, which will greatly increase the already high degree of concentration in this industry.

Planning and coordination: the external firm

Through the increased planning function undertaken by systems integrators, facilitated by recent developments in information technology, the boundaries of the large corporation have not only shifted, so that a wider range of goods and services is procured from outside the firm, but the very boundaries of the firms have become blurred. The core systems integrators across a wide range of sectors have become the coordinators of a vast array of business activity outside the boundaries of the legal entity in terms of ownership. The relationship extends far beyond the purchase price. In order to develop and maintain their competitive advantage, the systems integrators penetrate the value chain deeply both upstream and downstream, becoming closely involved in business activities that range from long-term planning to meticulous control of day-to-day production and delivery schedules. Competitive advantage for the systems integrator requires that it must consider the interests of the whole value chain in order to minimize costs across the whole system. The extent of the "visible hand" has increased greatly.

If we define the firm not by the entity which is the legal owner, but by the sphere over which conscious coordination of resource allocation takes place, then, far from becoming "hollowed out" and much smaller in scope, the large firm can be seen to have enormously increased in size during the global business revolution. As the large firm has "disintegrated," so has the extent of conscious coordination over the surrounding value chain increased. In a wide range of business activities, the organization of the value chain has developed into a comprehensively planned and coordinated activity. At its center is the core systems integrator. This firm typically possesses some combination of a number of key attributes, including the capability to raise finance for large new projects, and the resources necessary to fund a high level of R&D spending to sustain technological leadership, to develop a global brand, to invest in state-of-the-art information technology, and to attract the best human resources. Across a wide range of business types, from aircraft manufacture to fast-moving consumer goods, the systems integrator interacts deeply with the major segments of the value chain.

A large corporation may have a total procurement bill of several billions, or even several tens of billions, of dollars. The procurement could involve purchases from numerous firms that employ a much larger number of full-time equivalent employees "working for" the systems integrator than are employed within the core firm itself. A leading systems integrator with 100,000–200,000 employees could easily have the full-time equivalent of a further 400,000–500,000 employees "working for" the systems integrator, in the sense that their work is coordinated in important ways by the core firm. In this sense, we may speak of an "external firm" of coordinated business activity that surrounds the modern global corporation and is coordinated by it.

Conclusion

It is widely believed that in recent years, the landscape of global industrial competition has become flat, with the prospect of an ever-increasing role for firms from developing countries within the global economy. In fact, the competitive landscape facing firms from developing countries is much more challenging than most analysts appreciate.

This section has examined the value chains in two very different sectors. It has shown that these sectors have striking similarities in the way in which the core systems integrators have stimulated a comprehensive transformation of industrial structure across the whole supply chain. The most easily visible part of the structure of industrial concentration is the well-known firms with powerful, globally recognized technologies and/or brands. These constitute the systems integrators or "organizing brains" at the apex of extended value chains. As they have consolidated their leading positions, they have exerted intense pressure across the whole supply chain in order to minimize costs and stimulate technological progress. At every level, an intense process of industrial concentration has taken place, mainly through merger and acquisition, as firms struggle to meet the strict requirements that are the condition of their participation in the systems integrators' supply chains. This "cascade effect" has profound implications for the nature of competition.

The commanding heights of the global business system are almost entirely occupied by firms from high-income countries. The firms that have their headquarters in the high-income countries stand at the center of the global business system. In the era of the global level playing field, the landscape of industrial competition is extraordinarily uneven. The high-income economies contain just 15 percent of the world's total population. Firms headquartered in these countries account for over nine-tenths of the companies listed in both the *Fortune 500*, which ranks firms by sales revenue, and the *FT 500* list of the world's leading firms, which ranks firms by market capitalization. They account for almost all of the world's top 1,250 firms ranked by expenditure on research and development, which is a critical indicator of the distribution of global business power. There is not a single firm from the low and middle-income countries among the world's top 100 brands.

At the dawn of the twenty-first century, the reality of the intense industrial concentration among both systems integrators and their entire supply chain, brought about through pressure from the cascade effect, presents a comprehensive challenge for both firms and policy-makers in developing countries. The nature of capitalist freedom, with its inherent tendency toward industrial concentration and inequality in business power, means that firms from developing countries are in a massively unequal position to take advantage of that freedom. On the level playing field of the global free market, large firms from developing countries find it almost impossible to catch up with the established industry leaders from the high-income countries. Not only do they face immense difficulties in catching up with the leading systems integrators, the visible part of the iceberg, but they also face immense difficulties in catching up with the powerful firms that now dominate almost every segment of the supply chain, the invisible part of the iceberg that lies hidden from view beneath the water. In the past, the latecomer countries, from Britain in the late eighteenth and early nineteenth centuries, to America, Continental Europe, Japan, and Korea, all used state industrial policy to stimulate their respective national firms. Only through such state industrial policy, adapted for the conditions of the early twenty-first century and the particular circumstances of each country, can large firms from developing countries hope to catch up with the world's leading firms. High-income countries cannot be surprised, nor do they have any basis for objecting, if developing countries employ the same measures as they did to build their own powerful domestic firms.

CLASS STRUCTURE

> *Wherever there is great property, there is great inequality. For one very rich man, there must be at least five hundred poor, and the affluence of the few supposes the indigence of the many ... Servants, labourers, and workmen of different kinds, make up by far the greater part of every great political society. But what improves the circumstances of the greater part can never be regarded as an inconvenience to the whole. No society can surely be great and flourishing of which the far greater part of the members are poor and miserable. It is but equity besides, that they who feed, clothe, and lodge the whole body of the people, should have such a share of the produce of their own labour as to be themselves tolerably well fed, cloathed and lodged.*

Adam Smith, *The Wealth of Nations*

> *[T]he disposition to admire, and almost to worship, the rich and powerful, and to despise, or at least, to neglect persons of poor and mean condition, though necessary to maintain the distinction of ranks and the order of society, is at the same time, the great and most universal cause of the corruption of our moral sentiments.*

Adam Smith, *The Theory of Moral Sentiments*

Gross national income per person in the countries of the Sahel region of Africa averages around $300–400. In January 2008, the *Financial Times* reported that Vivat Bacchus, a restaurant in London's Canary Wharf financial district, which contains offices of most of the world's major banks, was offering a special "Bonus Tasting Menu" (see page 62). Vivat Bacchus was inundated with bookings. The basic price per person for the Bonus Tasting Menu was £1,000 (i.e. almost $2,000). However, for a supplementary fee customers could upgrade their vintages. The restaurant's owners were "amazed" at the quality and expense of the wines being chosen by diners when the restaurant reopened after its two-week break over Christmas and the New Year.

Capitalist globalization is massively unjust. The freedom of the global capitalist market economy has been accompanied by staggering inequality, with a yawning gap between the global elite and the mass of humanity. At the end of three decades of capitalist globalization, the stark contrast is grotesque.

Global inequality

Those employees who work in the upper reaches of the value chain of global firms inhabit an increasingly homogenized environment, with a common culture and incomes far above the global average, let alone those of the lowest segments of the world's population. It is increasingly common for the senior managers of giant global firms to be drawn from countries other than those in which the companies are headquartered. The global elite is a tiny fraction of the world's population, and its members are made conscious of their special position in many ways. They share a common language, English. They move their main place of residence frequently

Menu

January 2008

Glass of Billecart Salmon Rosé

Royal Sevruga caviar with buckwheat blinis, crème fraîche and lemon

Kauffman Frozen Vodka

Fresh Bahama rock lobster linguini flavoured with 40-year-old Armagnac

Forester Meinert Chenin

Hand-sliced Joselito *gran reserva* ham

Vega Sicilia Unico

Grilled Wagyu fillet steak (marbling score 9),
with red onion marmalade,
seared goose fois gras, Pont Neuf
and sauté green beans

Chateau Lafitte Rothschild

Cheese board of 15 varieties, quince jelly, fruit, and biscuits

1963 Taylors Port

Valrona chocolate soufflé with clotted cream

Chateau D'Yquem

Coffee/Tea with petits fours

Martell Cordon Bleu

Price: £1,000 per person (min 2, max 6)

Accompanying wine by the glass

from country to country. They share common values, read the same newspaper (the *Financial Times*), and stay in the same hotels. They communicate across their respective companies continuously, connected by ever-advancing information technologies. They buy the same globally branded luxury goods. Their children attend the same international private schools and finish their education at the same elite universities. They typically own residences in more than one country. Their homes are increasingly physically isolated from those of ordinary people. They have less and less attachment to a particular country, both at the level of the company and as a social group.

The long-term trends in global income inequality are not disputed. If global inequality is measured in terms of the average per capita income of countries (using the PPP exchange rate,[5] unweighted by population) then the Gini coefficient more than doubled from 0.20 in 1820 to around 0.52 in the 1980s. However, changes in global income inequality during the period of capitalist globalization are complex. The Gini coefficient of international income inequality (using the PPP exchange rate, unweighted by national population) rose from around 0.46 in the late 1970s to around 0.55 by the year 2000. The trend in inequality weighted by countries' populations (again using the PPP exchange rate) is ambiguous. If China is included, then the Gini coefficient declined slightly from around 0.55 in the late 1970s to around 0.50 in 2000. However, if China is excluded, the Gini coefficient rose slightly from around 0.52 in the late 1970s to around 0.55 in 2000. In other words, the trend reduction in global income inequality using this measure is entirely due to the rise in China's average income.

The above measures do not take into account the distribution of income within countries, which has become more unequal in most countries in recent years. Calculations which include intra-country income distribution (using the PPP exchange rate) estimate that in 1998 the Gini coefficient of global income distribution was 0.64, far above the figure for measures that do not take account of intra-country inequality. The income share of the top five percent was 33 percent, and that of the top ten percent was 50 percent, while the bottom five percent received just 0.2 percent of global income, and the bottom ten percent receive just 0.7 percent. The ratio of the top five percent to the bottom five percent was 165:1, and the ratio of the top ten percent to the bottom ten percent was 70:1. Using this measure, there has been no trend change in global inequality during the era of modern capitalist globalization.

However, there are question marks around the accuracy of current estimates that use "purchasing power parity" dollars (essentially using American prices) to measure national output (see footnote above) and global inequality. For example, it is extremely difficult to adjust fully for differences in the quality of goods and services consumed by people in rich and poor countries. Using the official exchange rate rather than PPP dollars, and taking into account intra-country inequality, it is estimated that the global Gini coefficient in 1998 was no less than 0.80. By this measure, the top five percent take 45 percent of total global income, and the top ten percent take 68 percent. The ratio of the top five percent to the bottom five percent is 300:1, and the ratio of the top ten percent to the bottom ten percent is 150:1. There was a small trend increase in global income inequality by this measure during the era of capitalist globalization, from 0.77 in 1988 to 0.80 in 1998.

The world is now more than three decades into the era of capitalist globalization. In the year 2000 total global household wealth amounted to $125 trillion, roughly three times the size of global GDP. This estimate uses the official rate of exchange rather than the PPP exchange rate, since a large share of global wealth is owned by people who can readily travel and invest their wealth internationally. In the year 2000, the top ten percent owned 85 percent of total global wealth, while the richest two percent held more than one-half of total global wealth. The richest one percent alone accounted for 40 percent of all household assets. The entire bottom half of the world adult population owned barely one percent of global wealth. The Gini coefficient for the global distribution of wealth is 0.89. The same value of Gini would be obtained if $100 were shared among 100 people in such a way that one person receives $90 and the remaining 99 get ten cents each.

The distribution of global wealth is heavily concentrated in the hands of those who live in high-income countries. Although it has only six percent of the total global population, North America accounts for 34 percent of global household wealth. The high-income countries of North America, Europe, and the Asia–Pacific region account for 88 percent of the global total. China and India together account for two-fifths of the world's population, but they account for only four percent of global wealth. Membership of the pinnacle of the world's wealth distribution is even more highly skewed by region. Among the top one percent of the global wealth distribution, 39 percent live in North America, 27 percent in Japan, and 23 percent in Western Europe.

Inequality within high-income countries

Capitalist globalization has led to fundamental threats to the labor market organization that has gradually developed in the high-income countries. The free movement of capital, combined with the impact of information technology, has made it possible for firms to establish global production systems. Globally integrated markets tend to produce a single global market for both goods and services (the "law of one price"). Global capital can move to where labor is cheapest and markets are growing fastest. Slow-growing markets and high labor costs in high-income countries have encouraged firms to relocate production to fast-growing developing countries in order to sustain profits. Liberalization since the 1970s has not only opened up a vast world of low-priced, low-skilled labor, but has also opened up a sea of highly skilled labor across the "transition" and developing countries. Labor market competition for employees in high-income countries has been affected by cheap imports of both final and intermediate goods (such as components for final assembly of complex products in high-income countries), as well as through the replacement of exports to world markets by exports from production systems established in fast-growing low and middle-income countries by firms from high-income countries.

Initially, the segments of the labor market that were most affected were relatively limited and confined mainly to the manufacturing sector. In America between 1970 and 2000, the number of manufacturing jobs fell by around six million. However, the impact has since spread to most segments of the workforce. Pressure to compete in labor markets that have become effectively global in scope in many sectors has forced major changes in conditions of work, as well as placing downward pressure on real wages across large segments of the workforce. This has meant that the globalization of capitalism has provided an intensifying threat to a large section of the workforce in high-income countries. Across both America and much of Continental Europe this has helped to produce a political crisis, as ordinary people have increasingly come to believe that multinational corporations are becoming divorced from their interests. Far from producing a homogenization of class interests, the progressive unification of global labor markets has produced an intensified conflict of interest between workers in rich countries and workers in poor countries, as the latter are perceived to be undermining conditions of work for a large segment of the former.

The profound impact of the integration of global labor markets upon the conditions of employment in high-income countries has been compounded by the simultaneous impact of unprecedentedly rapid technological change achieved by the ferocious oligopolistic competition of the global business revolution. The revolution in information technology has greatly changed the nature of demand for labor in lower-skilled occupations, with widespread substitution of labor by information systems. A vast swathe of occupations that were formerly undertaken by skilled clerical and manual workers is now undertaken by computer systems, due to the technological achievements of the giant capitalist firms in the information technology sector, resulting in an explosive growth in information processing capabilities and a simultaneous explosive fall in their real price. Those who have the skills to devise and apply the new information technologies have achieved large increases in their relative incomes.

Across a wide range of high-income countries, in the era of capitalist globalization there was a decline in the relative wages of low-skilled workers compared to skilled workers. The World Bank estimates that between the late 1970s and the late 1990s, the gap increased by 29 percent in America, 27 percent in Britain, 15 percent in New Zealand, 14 percent in Italy, and 9 percent in Canada. At the same time the gap in income between the global elite and the local population in high-income countries widened sharply. Between 1994 and 2005, in 16 out of the 19 OECD countries for which data are available, the earnings of the top ten percent grew faster than those of the bottom ten percent. The American Congressional

Budget Office reported that between 1979 and 2001, the after-tax income of the top one percent of American households jumped by 139 percent to more than $700,000 (adjusted for inflation), while that of the middle fifth rose by 17 percent, and that of the poorest fifth by only 9 percent. In 2004 the top 0.1 percent of the American population included around 145,000 taxpayers, each with an income of over $1.6 million, and with an average income of $3 million. Their share of America's income rose from around 3.5 percent in 1980 to over 10 percent in 2000. The widening gaps in income in America are reducing the degree of intergenerational mobility.

Inequality within developing countries

During the early phase of industrialization, the distribution of income typically becomes more unequal for a significant period of time. During this phase, the majority of a given developing country's workers are underemployed in the farm sector on close to subsistence levels of income. As the modern sector expands, the growing army of rural–urban migrants is pulled into permanent wage employment, but mostly on low incomes in unskilled occupations. This is the so-called "Lewis phase" of economic development with unlimited supplies of labor (named after Arthur Lewis). On the one hand, rural–urban migration to permanent wage employment has contributed to the decline in absolute poverty in many developing countries in recent decades. On the other hand, although a growing fraction of the urban workforce has gradually moved into higher-income occupations, a fundamental constraint is set to the growth of real wages for urban unskilled labor by the availability of unlimited supplies of underemployed rural labor.

Around two billion people work in the non-farm sector in developing countries. The majority of these work as unskilled labor in the "informal" non-farm sector, unprotected by trade unions, health and unemployment insurance, effective minimum wage legislation, or government supervision of conditions of work. A large number of them work in arduous, physically dangerous and psychologically stressful conditions. They typically have temporary contracts, no health or old-age insurance, and wages of around $1–3 per day. For example, in China during the period of capitalist globalization, the total numbers employed outside agriculture expanded at a phenomenal rate, from 118 million in 1978 to 413 million in 2002. However, most of the increase was in the informal sector, in which the number of employees rose from just 23 million in 1978 to over 300 million in 2002. Among these were over 130 million rural–urban migrants, almost all of whom worked in the informal sector. The pressure of rural underemployment, however, has severely constrained or even prevented the growth of real wages in the informal non-farm sector during the era of capitalist globalization.

Within the fastest-growing parts of developing countries, leading multinational firms have established production systems that dominate large swathes of the host economy, and that employ a fast-increasing fraction of their workforce in developing countries. However, relative to the total workforce of these countries, the numbers involved are small. Development economists used to believe that multinational firms would adjust their "factor proportions" to the conditions of developing countries, employing relatively large amounts of labor for each unit of capital. In fact, the era of globalization has produced globally standardized products using globally standardized technologies in the high value-added market for both final and intermediate products. Global procurement, global branding, globally integrated product design, and globally integrated production technologies require homogeneity in capital/labor ratios across countries at every level of income. Global firms employ international workers at international income levels. Local employees of multinational firms in developing countries tend to work at income levels considerably above those of comparably skilled local workers who work for local companies. Moreover, a disproportionate fraction of the local employees of multinational companies are people with relatively high skill levels. Conditions of work approximate to those in high-income countries, even for manual work. Multinational firms must adopt global employment standards, or their reputation will be damaged. Also, it is impossible to manage a multinational firm using a wide variety of different employment practices across different subsidiaries of the company in different locations. Insofar as local firms are able to compete with the global firms, they also must adopt global standards in order to attract high-quality local labor.

In recent years, income inequality has increased in fast-growing developing countries. Many of them have seen the Gini coefficient of inequality in income distribution rise from 0.2–0.3 to 0.4–0.5. According to the World Bank, inequality in East Asia has increased significantly in recent decades. For example, in China, the reported Gini coefficient of urban income distribution rose from 0.16 in 1978 to 0.34 in 2002, while the overall Gini coefficient rose from 0.30 to 0.45 in the same period. In Latin America, inequality increased almost uniformly in the 1980s, though the increase was less pronounced in the 1990s. The World Bank estimates that after three decades of capitalist globalization, the "global middle class," with a per capita income between that of Brazil and Italy, still accounted for only eight percent of the global population and 14 percent of global income. The "global rich," with an income level above that of Italy, amounted to 11 percent of the global population, but accounted for 58 percent of global income. The "global poor," with incomes below the average of Brazil, still accounted for 82 percent of total global population, but for only 29 percent of global income.

The era of capitalist globalization has seen the emergence of two worlds within fast-growing developing countries. One is the world of the twenty-first century, with modern apartment blocks and villas for the globalized elite, with modern sanitation and water supplies. This elite live and work in physically segregated environments; they are protected by private and public police forces; they buy globally branded consumer goods produced to global standards; they invest their wealth in global assets; they send their children to "global" private schools and universities; they receive healthcare from global-standard private hospitals using global medical equipment and pharmaceuticals; they stay in global hotel chains; and they holiday in foreign countries.

The other, and vastly larger, world is that of the mass of underemployed farmers and the permanent members of the urban informal sector. For the two billion or so farmers in developing countries, the period of capitalist globalization has witnessed important advances, including significant advances in health, education, and life expectancy, as well as a significant rise in labor productivity. However, across most of the developing world annual output per farm worker is still painfully low, even after three decades of capitalist globalization. Value-added per farm worker in the eurozone is $23,000, and in America $42,000. Value-added per farm worker is $335 in sub-Saharan Africa, $406 in South Asia, and $445 in East Asia and the Pacific. Value-added per farm worker in both China and India is $400, i.e. around $1 per day, which is one-sixtieth of that in the eurozone and less than one-hundredth of that in America.

The large numbers of people who work in the non-farm informal sector across the developing world are employed mainly in millions of small-scale establishments, in the informal mining, manufacturing, construction, transport, and service sectors. They work in arduous, often dangerous conditions, with a high degree of insecurity. They live in low-quality, overcrowded housing, and often inhabit *favelas*, slums, and shanty towns, without running water or modern sanitation. The official police force often fears to tread in such places, and law and order is often in the hands of the local mafia. The only available schools are those run by the hard-pressed local government, staffed with overworked, underpaid teachers. Only a small fraction of the children in these schools are able to escape to study in the public sector's hard-pressed universities. "Wealth management" typically means borrowing from the informal banking sector at high interest rates to meet pressing living expenses. Illness has to be dealt with by using overworked, understaffed public health facilities, or entering crippling indebtedness by resorting to private-sector medicine. Such people travel on overcrowded buses and trains, never on planes. They do not possess a passport. Buying a single tall skinny latte at Starbucks would require more than a day's income. This is the world of the eighteenth century, but with access to the information technology of the twenty-first century.

Conclusion

The period of the global capitalist business revolution has seen a large increase in inequality in the fast-growing developing countries. The freedom of people in these countries to migrate out of their underemployed rural environment has stimulated the growth of a vast sea of urban informal sector workers, earning low and stagnant incomes, living in low-quality physical environments, with great personal insecurity, with low-quality healthcare and educational services. Their conditions of work and life are fundamentally constrained by the existence of a deep pool of underemployed rural workers at low levels of income who are ready to migrate to the cities. This situation is unlikely to change for several decades, until the industrialization process has run its course and the rural reserve army of labor has dried up, allowing urban real wages for unskilled labor to be bid up by the market. Alongside them, the freedom of global capital to move to low and middle-income countries has stimulated the growth of enclaves of global modernity of working and living. In these enclaves, people live "global" lives, isolated from the realities of daily life for their fellow citizens. This immense inequality has been produced by the freedoms of the global capitalist system.

The current phase of global capitalist development closely resembles that of Britain in the early nineteenth century, in the sense that the world is still in the phase in which there is a huge global rural reserve army of underemployed people. This sets the parameters within which the global capitalist accumulation process operates. The class interests of those at the apex of the capitalist system dictate that they should support undemocratic systems of government which restrict the voice of poor people in global institutions. However, the contradictions involved in this stage of the capitalist accumulation process are profound, with a yawning gulf between the emerging global elite, which has less and less commitment to any particular country, and the mass of poor people, whose lives are still bound by their nation state. In addition, a large part of the workforce in the high-income countries feels that its interests are threatened in fundamental ways by the economic progress of developing countries.

Today's high-income countries all experienced severe class struggle during the early stages of modern capitalist industrialization, but ultimately the capitalist system survived. After three decades global capitalism has arrived today at the equivalent of 1848. It remains to be seen whether the surging contradictions within countries and across countries are sustainable within the current institutional structures. Britain's Industrial Revolution began in the late eighteenth century, and by the 1840s Britain had become the "workshop of the world." However, it was not until 1918 that Britain achieved universal adult male suffrage. Late eighteenth and early nineteenth-century liberals in Europe regarded a narrowly restricted franchise as essential to social and political stability. In his book *The Great Transformation*, published in 1957, Karl Polanyi observed: "In England it became the unwritten law of the constitution that the working class must be denied the vote ... The Chartists [in 1848] had fought for the right to stop the mill of the market which ground the lives of the people. But the people were only granted rights when the awful adjustment had been made."

How committed to "world democracy" are the people and their leaders in the high-income countries? That there should be such extreme inequality of income, wealth, and life opportunities after three decades of capitalist globalization is a cause for profound reflection on the nature of capitalist freedoms and their ability to produce a just outcome. A democratic system of global governance would be one in which the whole world's adult population voted for a global parliament. One can imagine that many of the policies that were supported by the bottom 90 percent of the world's wealth distribution, who possess a combined total of only 15 percent of the world's wealth, and mostly live in deeply polluted environments, might be radically at odds with those of the top 10 percent of the world's wealth distribution, who live in pristine environments in the high-income countries or in isolated enclaves in developing countries, and possess 85 percent of the world's wealth. If the world were governed by a single representative political body elected by the whole global electorate consisting of the 4.5 billion people in the world over the age of 18, it is hard to imagine that large-scale global redistribution of income and wealth would not command wide support.

FINANCE

We shut the cellar door behind us, and when they found the bag they spilt it out on the floor, and it was a lovely sight, all them yaller-boys. My, the way the king's eyes did shine ... They pawed the yaller-boys, and sifted them through their fingers and let them jingle down on the floor ... When we got upstairs, everybody gathered around the table, and the king he counted it and stacked it up, three hundred dollars in a pile—twenty elegant little piles. Everybody looked hungry at it, and licked their lips.

Mark Twain, *Huckleberry Finn*

May this Ring be accursed. Its Gold gave me unmeasured power;
Now its magic shall breed death for him who wears it.
Care shall consume whoever possesses it;
Whoever possesses it not, envy shall gnaw.
All shall lust after its possession but none shall delight in its use.

Wagner, *Das Rheingold*

Monkey:
Just throw the dice
That shall suffice
To make me wealthy.
Life isn't healthy,
But, given gold,
I'd be consoled,
Sober and nice.

Mephistopheles:
How happy would the greedy monkeys be
To live on gambling or on lottery!

Goethe, *Faust*, Part 1

The financial crisis: the bubble inflates

In 2005, floods from Hurricane Katrina submerged New Orleans. The chaotic scenes of poor, mainly black, people left unaided to endure the impact while better-off, mainly white people, fled the scene, shocked America and the world. Global sea levels are rising inexorably as a result of global warming, threatening to submerge large areas of the world's low-lying regions, such as New Orleans. This process will take many years. However, today the global economic system is at risk of being submerged by the "money tsunami" that built up during the era of globalization. Since ancient times, philosophers and religious thinkers have worried about the potential of the real world to be driven by the greed that attracts people to money. During the era of capitalist globalization, the dykes, levees, and national sea defense systems that protected economies from the potential devastation of financial floods were torn down. Walls of money were instead permitted to wash across the world as never before. The height of the waves rose unceasingly as the money tsunami careered uncontrollably across the oceans of the global economic system, swollen by the forces surging underneath the water, invisible to most people. It is the poorest people who will suffer most from the rising sea levels caused by global warming. They will be the ones who also suffer the most from the consequences of the global money tsunami.

Mainstream economists mostly believe that stock markets and currency markets are fundamentally efficient, and based on rational expectations. John Maynard Keynes strongly attacked such views, likening unregulated financial markets to a casino: "Speculators may do no harm as bubbles on a steady stream of enterprise. But the position is serious when enterprise becomes the bubble on a whirlpool of speculation. When the capital development of a country becomes a by-product of the activities of a casino, the job is likely to be ill-done." He believed that speculation is an unavoidable outcome of liquid investment markets. Indeed, he believed that as the organization of investment markets improves, the risk of speculation increases. His critique of unregulated financial markets has been echoed in the writings of C. P. Kindleberger, J. K. Galbraith and Hyman Minsky.

Despite fundamental critiques from non-mainstream economists, most modern finance textbooks have continued to promote the view that markets work rationally and efficiently, but they have failed to provide arguments for why feedback loops supporting speculative bubbles cannot occur. Typically, they do not even mention bubbles or Ponzi schemes, conveying instead a sense of orderly progression and mathematical precision in financial markets. As C. P. Kindleberger's study *Manias, Panics, and Crashes* and J. K. Galbraith's *The Great Crash* pointed out, asset bubbles have occurred repeatedly. The initiating factor in a financial bubble is often the optimism generated by a feeling that the economy has entered a "new era." Once the speculation process gets under way, powerful positive feedback loops drive markets ever higher. Credit is extended on the basis of increased collateral asset prices, which supports still further increase in asset prices, and still further credit expansion. The more one can borrow, the greater the leverage, the more profit one can make in the upswing of the financial cycle. Unregulated financial markets are subject to frequent crises, due to periodic and alternating bouts of irrational exuberance and pessimism among investors, which are largely unrelated to economic fundamentals. The counterpart of the tendency of financial markets to produce self-reinforcing bubble effects is the tendency to produce self-reinforcing market collapse: bubbles tend to burst, rather than slowly deflating.

Numerous factors interacted to permit the unprecedented asset bubble of the era of wild capitalist globalization. A profound sense developed that the world economy had entered a new golden age, with a new paradigm of economic expansion and prosperity that differed from all previous eras. This feeling was reinforced by the opening up of large tracts of both the communist and the non-communist world that had formerly been closed behind protectionist barriers and inward-looking policies. This allowed a vast new terrain for capitalist expansion. The defeat of communism and the triumph of free market ideas reinforced the sense that a new common ground had opened up across the world, in which all people were united in a world that had finally moved beyond ideology. The sense of entering a fundamentally new era in world history was reinforced by the unprecedented technological progress, especially the dazzling advances in information technology. The longer the "golden age" lasted, the more embedded the feeling became that a new world of unlimited capitalist growth had arrived. The charts on the investment analysts' PowerPoint presentations pointed endlessly upward. Few concepts expressed this new age so powerfully as the idea that the BRIC countries (Brazil, Russia, India, and China), with their population of 2.8 billion, would spearhead global growth and profits increase for decades ahead. The self-congratulation of the annual Davos Economic Forum crystallized the unbounded optimism among the world's leading capitalist firms in the age of wild capitalist globalization.

At the core of the economic policies of this era was the determination to keep strict control of consumer price inflation, which had been widespread in the high-income countries up until the 1980s. This determination was reflected in the decision in the high-income countries to establish independent central banks with responsibility for controlling the rate of consumer price inflation through their interest rate decisions. In America the Federal Reserve had for almost 100 years had a broad mandate that included trying to maximize employment, stabilize prices, and moderate long-term interest rates. From the mid-1990s on, in the face of "irrational exuberance" in the stock market, the decision was taken to give priority to the stability of consumer prices, and to allow the asset bubble to increase in size. In the view of Alan Greenspan, an asset bubble could only be identified ex post. In the late 1990s, the independent European Central Bank (ECB) was established and the Bank of England was given independent status. In fact, the so-called "independence" of the central banks in Europe was an illusion, since their mandate was tightly constrained by the government, which required them to concentrate on consumer price inflation rather than asset price inflation in their deliberations on interest rate changes. From this point onward the central banks in most OECD countries used a low interest rate as an "anchor" for consumer price inflation by limiting inflationary expectations. In essence, the independent central banks raised the rate of interest if they considered the economy was overheating, and reduced the rate of interest if they felt the economy could safely be stimulated without causing inflation. Endless debate surrounded the periodic minute changes in the rate of interest by the independent central banks.

The decision to target consumer price inflation was a critically important policy choice. It liberated financial institutions to make money from asset price inflation in the secure knowledge that asset price increases were a "one-way bet," with the central banks prevented by law in Europe and by policy choice in America from intervening to prevent this vast expansion of money-making. The rate of interest in the high-income economies fell to unprecedentedly low levels in the early years of this century, and provided a powerful incentive for businesses and individuals to borrow. Unsurprisingly, giant financial firms were strong advocates of such central bank "independence."

Other factors helped to keep interest rates down. The low rate of interest in the high-income countries was also stimulated by the increase in foreign exchange reserves in East Asia and the oil-exporting countries, which flowed into the high-income countries. The large and fast-growing foreign exchange reserves from East Asia and the oil exporters greatly increased financial flows onto global markets, especially into America. Between 1995 and 2006 the total reserves[6] of East and Southeast Asia as well as the main oil-exporting countries rose from $714 billion to $3,704 billion. Within this total, Japan's share fell from 27 percent in 1995 to 24 percent in 2006, while China's share rose from 11 percent to 29 percent (less than three-tenths of the total) over the same period. A significant proportion of the foreign exchange reserves of these countries was invested in American government Treasury Bills, notes, and bonds. The availability of such vast and fast-rising foreign exchange reserves meant that the American government found it relatively easy to borrow from international markets, and helped to keep the rate of interest low. The inflow of funds also helped to prop up the American dollar. Throughout most of this period, Japan was by far the largest purchaser of American government paper, not being overtaken by China until November 2008, after the asset bubble had already burst. This was arguably the biggest "vendor-financed purchasing program in history," in which the savings of poor people in export-surplus countries helped to finance the consumption of rich people in high-income countries.

America's own policies were centrally important in producing this outcome. The IMF and the World Bank are the core institutions of the Washington Consensus. As Zbigniew Brzezinski noted, "The International Monetary Fund and the World Bank can be said to represent 'global' interests, and their constituency may be construed as the world. In reality, however, they are heavily American-dominated and their origins are traceable to American initiative, particularly the Bretton Woods Conference of 1944." Brzezinski regards them as a key part of America's "global web of specialized institutions." The Asian financial crisis illustrates this very clearly. The crisis had a devastating impact on East and Southeast Asia. Among its central causes was the liberalization of East Asian financial markets, following constant urgings from the IMF. This resulted in a flood of capital into the region, to be followed by a massive, destabilizing outflow during the crisis. The photograph of Michel Camdessus, Managing Director of the IMF, standing over the humiliated figure of President Suharto as he signed his agreement to the IMF's terms for Indonesia's rescue package, burned deep into the consciousness of Asian people. The crisis was followed by countless analyses from Western academics and the Washington Consensus institutions of the alleged failures of East Asian "crony capitalism." The crisis prompted intense efforts by East Asian governments to follow mercantilist policies, increasing export surpluses in order to expand their foreign exchange reserves, in the hope that this would insulate them from the impact of such a crisis in the future. In 1995, East Asia and the Pacific (excluding Japan) had a combined current account deficit of $17 billion. By 2006 they had a combined surplus of $260 billion. It was hoped that the large accumulations of reserves would provide an insurance against any future financial crisis and allow them to avoid having to rely on the IMF to bail them out, with all the conditions and humiliations involved.

In addition, the rise in oil and gas prices after the turn of the millennium stimulated increased export surpluses and foreign exchange reserve growth in the oil-producing economies, which increased sixfold between 1995 and 2006. The price increase was stimulated by the Middle Eastern crisis provoked by the American invasion of Iraq and the uncertainty caused by the intensification of American hostility toward Iran. In their turn, these stemmed from the locked-in pattern of consumption based around intensive energy use and an automobile-based transport system in the high-income countries. The large profits that the oil-rich countries' national oil companies earned at the new, higher prices, reduced their incentive to invite international oil companies to help them to expand production. The liberalized financial markets entered increasingly into speculation in commodity markets, of which oil is much the most important, with the price reaching $150 per barrel at the peak of the commodity price boom.

Money is an elusive phenomenon, and difficult to fix in some desired quantity for any given economy. Variations in the velocity of circulation and the invention of new forms of money make it difficult to control the quantity of money. A minority of economists, such as J. M. Keynes, J. K. Galbraith, C. P. Kindleberger and Hyman Minsky, have argued that fluctuations in the supply and use of money are "endogenous" to the economic system. During an economic boom, despite the efforts of monetary authorities, both money supply and the efficiency of its use expand to meet the needs of asset speculation. In 1930, in his *Treatise on Money*,

Keynes observed that "for many purposes the acknowledgements of debt are themselves a serviceable substitute for money proper in the settlement of transactions." In 1959, the Radcliffe Commission produced a path-breaking report on the British monetary system. It observed that in a developed economy there is an "indefinitely wide range of financial institutions" and "many hold highly liquid assets which are close substitutes for money, as good to hold and only inferior when the actual moment of payment arrives."

During the era of capitalist globalization government regulators in the high-income countries permitted the explosive proliferation of new financial institutions and new forms of debt, which are close substitutes for money. Moreover, the explosion of integrated international money markets made it increasingly difficult for any national or regional monetary authority to control the supply of money within its borders. The relevant framework for monetary policy became the whole world. The international subsidiaries of the giant global financial institutions that emerged in this era could now "make money" anywhere in the world, not only in the place that their headquarters happened to be located.

In the era of capitalist globalization government regulators permitted the range of financial institutions to expand beyond imagination. Traditional commercial banks now competed routinely with investment banks, credit card companies, insurance companies, and the financial branches of supermarkets, automobile companies, aircraft manufacturers, oil companies, and diversified conglomerates such as GE. So-called "hedge funds" hardly existed before the 1990s. Between 1995 and early 2008, however, the total assets of hedge funds rose from $170 million to $2,650 billion. In fact, the term "hedge funds" is a misnomer. In their pursuit of high returns, hedge funds made aggressive use of leverage, pursued short-term momentum trading, and became heavily involved in esoteric and illiquid markets. By 2006 it was estimated that, although hedge funds accounted for only around two percent of total financial assets, due to their high leverage, their use of derivatives, and their active trading policy, they accounted for around two-fifths of daily trading in equity markets in Britain and America, and on some days their share was as much as 70 percent. America is by far the most important home to hedge funds. In 2007 American-based hedge funds (mainly based in New York) accounted for around three-fifths of total hedge fund assets.

Government regulators permitted the sources of debt to expand into forms that were unimaginable before the global business revolution. Investors now had a dizzying array of debt instruments, such as "derivatives," to choose from. At the beginning of this era, derivatives didn't exist. Derivatives are so called because they derive from the price of another product. No matter how sophisticated the calculations and hedging devices may be, derivatives all constitute a form of betting. A wide variety of derivative products emerged, based on predictions of price changes in currencies, property, interest rates, bonds, equities and equity indices, and commodities. These "assets" could now be traded instantaneously on a global basis. National restrictions on the flow of capital across borders were lifted, and markets were made more "perfect" by "real time" global electronic trading technologies. Currency and interest-rate derivatives together accounted for around two-thirds of the total derivatives market. The foreign exchange market is by far the world's biggest financial market in terms of trading volume. By April 2004, the daily turnover on the world's foreign exchange markets had reached $1,900 billion, compared with the average global daily output of goods and services of around $113 billion. The market for credit derivatives and the associated new types of debt grew exponentially. These include such structured credit instruments as residential mortgage-backed securities (RMBS), commercial mortgage-backed securities (CMBS), and numerous other asset-backed securities (ABS) including collateralized loan obligations (CLOs), and collateralized debt obligations (CDOs). CDOs consist of repackaged pools of credit derivatives based on dozens of corporate credits.

An "alphabet soup" of derivatives emerged, and derivatives became a centrally important part of the global financial system. These developments had enormous implications for the real world. The volume of new "money" that was created through speculation in newly developed financial instruments now dwarfed the real economy in which tradable goods and services are produced. The ratio of global financial assets to world output soared from 109 percent in 1980 to 316 percent in 2005. At the end of 2006, central bank "power money" amounted to around 10 percent of global GDP, but amounted to just one percent of total global liquidity. So-called "broad money" amounted to around 122 percent of global GDP, but still accounted for only around 11 percent of total global liquidity. Securitized debt amounted to around 142 percent of global GDP, but still accounted for just 13 percent of total global liquidity. Derivatives amounted to no less than 802 percent of total global GDP, and fully 75 percent of total global liquidity. In other words, "cyber money" now amounted to more than eight times the total global output of goods and services and three-quarters of global liquidity. The "casino economy" had grown to monstrous proportions. It is estimated that the volume of outstanding derivatives reached a peak of $516 trillion (i.e. $516,000 billion) in 2007, amounting to around ten times total global output.

Government regulators permitted much of the credit expansion to take place outside the formal system of bank regulation. Under this system of "vehicular" finance, banks devised myriad vehicles through which to repackage debt and distribute it widely throughout the economic system. These unregulated money market funds themselves accumulated large amounts of debt, with escalating levels of leverage, which allowed credit creation beyond the wildest dreams of high-street bankers. The packages of debt created off the balance sheets of the formal, regulated bank system were bought by individual retail investors, attracted by the high returns on offer, as well as by pension funds, local authorities, schools, and hospitals. Banks routinely encouraged their customers to "maximize their wealth" by investing in these funds. Some analysts called this the "shadow banking system," because it had "lain hidden for years, untouched by regulation, yet free to magically and mystically create and then package loans in ways that only Wall Street wizards could explain." It was estimated that in America, by 2006–7 around one-half of all net new credit creation was taking place in this unregulated shadow financial system.

The complexity of the new financial instruments made it difficult for both investors and regulatory authorities to understand systemic global financial risk. The problem for regulators was exacerbated by the fact that the global financial system developed instruments of such great complexity and at such a high speed, that no one understood how to regulate the whole system, even assuming that the political mechanisms existed to do so. The spread of financial innovation was so dramatic that regulators, lawyers, and rating agency officials struggled to keep up. Even the heads of leading global financial institutions acknowledged that they didn't understand many of the more complex products that their own firms were selling. Moreover, the massive extent of repacking and sale of debt meant that debt was far more widely distributed throughout the economy than was the case before the global business revolution. This provided a source of stability and enhanced the ability of the financial system to ride out relatively small-scale crises, but meant that the whole global financial system was far more susceptible to a giant financial crisis should it erupt.

The ease with which lenders could repackage loans and move them off their balance sheets meant that they were able to lend even more, as regulatory rules permitted banks to reduce their reserves of cash against their loans if these were securitized. The ease of securitizing loans had a powerful "moral hazard" effect for banks, since it meant that they felt that they were insured against default. These processes further encouraged lending and the inflation of asset bubbles in a self-reinforcing cycle. National regulators now had little idea of the origin of the funds that supported the derivatives market. This greatly reduced the effectiveness of national monetary policy.

The period of capitalist globalization and financial liberalization witnessed an increase in the number of financial crises in developing countries. These include the Mexican "Tequila Crisis" of 1994–95, the Asian financial crisis of 1997–98, the Russian crisis of 1998, and the Argentine crisis of 2001–2. In addition there have been numerous smaller financial crises. However, the high-income economies survived the impact of the crises in developing countries. They also survived the collapse of Long-Term Capital Management, of the IT bubble, and the collapse of Enron, as well as the impact of 9/11. A deep and growing confidence developed that the high-income countries had entered a new era of sustained economic growth with low inflation, from which the risk of a financial crisis had been banished forever, brought about through the application of modern, sophisticated, scientifically guided economic management techniques.

A small group of non-mainstream critics, however, drew attention to the dangers that were building. The writings of Kindleberger and Galbraith on financial crises were consistently on the bestseller lists, especially in the midst of a passing mini-crisis, but they were regarded as of historical interest only. They served only to emphasize the progress that had been made in the management of the global economy since the far-off days of financial crisis and bank failures in the high-income countries. The deep warnings they contained went unheeded. Financial sector profits swelled to undreamed-of levels. Between its low in the first quarter of 1982 and its peak in the second quarter of 2007, the share of the American financial sector's profits in America's GDP rose more than sixfold. The mass of the population were willing accomplices in the deregulated asset bubble. People in high-income countries felt secure in their ballooning personal wealth. The asset price bubble, especially the bubble in property, formed the foundation for an explosive growth of credit, to fund both speculation and current consumption. A sea change in attitudes toward personal debt and consumption occurred in the high-income countries, driven by the asset price bubble. The main body of the population was warmly wrapped in the cocoon of the IT-based communication revolution, with music from their iPods accompanying them on their travels to exotic destinations. A brave new world had arrived, courtesy of the asset bubble.

Increases in personal consumption were further propelled by the trend decline in the real prices of final goods and services, caused partly by the entry into the market of a vast number of new workers at low wages from the former communist planned economies and from the formerly inward-looking developing countries. The enormous increase in low-cost, low-price exports underpinned the decline in the price of a wide range of goods and services, though this decline was also due in part to intense oligopolistic competition among giant firms, which compete by forcing down prices along their respective supply chains and investing large amounts in technological progress.

In the first half of 2007, however, there was a palpable sense of unease among financial regulators as their concerns deepened about the extent of the asset and credit bubble, and the absence of control over the global financial system resulting from the new forms of debt creation. Malcolm King, managing director of the Bank for International Settlements, said: "Financial innovation has produced vehicles for leverage which are very hard to measure ... liquidity is increasing very rapidly and this is affecting asset prices ... Central banks are scrambling to address the problem ... but international cooperation and data gathering efforts need to be deepened." Jean-Claude Trichet, President of the European Central Bank, warned: "[T]here is now such creativity of new and very sophisticated financial instruments ... that we don't know fully where the risks are located. We are trying to understand what is going on, but it is a big, big challenge." Kenneth Rogoff, former chief economist at the IMF, launched a devastating attack on the absence of a global plan to ensure the safe operation of the financial system: "Whatever happened to all the grandiose plans for improving the global financial architecture? Over the past couple of years, all introspection seems to have vanished. Instead, the policy community has developed a smug belief that enhanced macroeconomic stability at the national level, combined with financial innovation at the international level, have obviated the need to tinker with the system." He argued that, despite improvement in central bank cooperation in recent years, "contrary to market perceptions, global central banks have only very limited instruments for dealing with a genuinely sharp rise in global volatility, particularly one that is geopolitically induced."

The financial crisis: the bubble bursts

In spring 2007 the global financial crisis that many had feared began to unfold. The first phase of the crisis lasted for around one year. During this time it was hoped that the crisis would remain confined mainly to America, and would be resolved relatively quickly by appropriate government policies. There was a deep reluctance to acknowledge that the crisis might be any more serious than other crises during the period of capitalist globalization. The starting point was the losses incurred by financial institutions that had invested in the American "sub-prime" housing market. It was increasingly realized that the repricing of assets might cascade across other markets and asset types, including commercial property, equities, commodities, and, even, works of art. It was gradually realized that what had previously been regarded as a great strength of financial innovation, namely the wide distribution of debt throughout the global economy, might be a fatal weakness. Fear entered the financial system in the high-income countries as the asset bubble began to move into reverse, spreading out from the sub-prime market. There began a flight from debt that was as potent as the rush toward it had been in the upswing. Liquidity started to dry up as banks became afraid to lend even to each other, since they were uncertain of where the final credit risks lay. A credit squeeze developed across the high-income countries.

By the early years of the new century, the global financial system had become comprehensively integrated across national boundaries, far more even than was the case with the integration of production systems. However, the transition from primarily national to global markets was not accompanied by a strengthening of international regulatory governance. This was resisted fiercely by America, especially through its influence upon the IMF. The IMF was established by the United Nations at the end of World War II with the memory of the Great Depression of the 1930s at the center of its thinking. It is the institution above all others that is capable of exerting collective global control over the world's financial system. However, during the dramatic changes after the 1980s it failed to perform this function, leading it to be described aptly as a "rudderless ship in a sea of liquidity." It was the very absence of regulation that permitted giant financial institutions to earn such enormous profits during the era of capitalist globalization. The largest and most influential banks were American, and they had a powerful voice in shaping the American government's attitude toward the IMF. The financial sector is able to pay enormous sums of money to those who can defend it effectively against the threat of regulatory interference.

In America there is an especially close interweaving between leading personnel in the financial sector and government policy-makers. For example, Robert Rubin worked for Goldman Sachs for 29 years, becoming co-chair in 1990–92. He became assistant to the President for Economic Policy (1993–95), before becoming Treasury Secretary (1995–99). He then returned to the private sector to work at Citigroup, becoming chair in 2007. Hank Paulson was staff assistant to the Secretary of Defense (1970–72) and to the President (1972–73). He then worked at Goldman Sachs for 32 years (1974–2006), becoming successively president and chief operating officer (1990–95), and chair and chief executive officer (1996–2006). In 2006 he was appointed as Treasury Secretary.

The IMF (along with the World Bank) is the core institution of the Washington Consensus. If it is to function as an institution that controls the global financial system in the common interest of the global community, it is essential that its governance be organized justly and equitably. In fact, since their inception in the 1940s, the IMF and the World Bank have been dominated by America, and, to a lesser extent, by western Europe. The high-income countries account for only 16 percent of the global population, but they have 61 percent of the votes in the IMF. America has less than five percent of the world's population, but it has 17 percent of the IMF voting rights, which gives America an effective veto, since important decisions require an 85 percent majority. India and China have a combined population of 2.4 billion (37 percent of the world total), but they have a combined total of 5.6 percent of the voting rights in the IMF. Switzerland, Belgium, and the Netherlands have a combined population of 33 million (0.5 percent of the world total), but they have 6.0 percent of the voting rights in the IMF. The head of the IMF is always a European, and the head of the World Bank is always an American. In recent years, however, there has been increasing pressure from developing countries to reform the IMF to make it truly representative of the global community, and thereby facilitate global collective action to regulate the world's financial system.

As the global financial crisis entered its early phase in the autumn of 2007, it was anticipated that the annual meeting of the IMF in late October 2007 would make progress in the regulation of global financial markets and in the task of institutional reform to better reflect the voice of developing countries. On both fronts the meeting was a complete failure. The participants failed to reach agreement on concrete steps to change the institutional structure of the IMF to reflect more accurately the voice of developing countries. Moreover, prior to the meeting, the Europeans had insisted on their right to choose the next head of the IMF, with Rodrigo Rato replaced by Dominique Strauss-Kahn. The Americans had insisted on their right to choose the head of the World Bank, Robert Zoellick replacing Paul Wolfowitz. These developments greatly undermined the legitimacy of the Washington Consensus institutions in the eyes of developing countries at a point when the world needed their leadership most urgently. It appears to developing countries as though Europe and America feel that only "their" people can be trusted to guide the world through the crisis. David Dodge, the outgoing Governor of the Bank of Canada, warned: "This is precisely the time we need the fund's skills to deal with global imbalances ... We didn't make any progress this weekend. It is a pretty big disappointment. The IMF stakeholders have not even settled the principles, let alone the details of institutional reform. The continued stand-off over reform will undermine the IMF's ability to play an orderly role bringing about an orderly realignment of international currency imbalances. The question is whether we end with some huge bloody crisis or whether we can do it a reasonably smooth manner."

On September 12, 2007, Mervyn King, Governor of the Bank of England, argued that bailing out financial institutions that had made unwise lending decisions and accepting an increased range of assets as collateral for central bank lending would create moral hazard, and "sow the seeds of a future financial crisis." Within a week the Bank of England was forced into a humiliating reversal of its position. For the first time since the 1860s, a British financial institution experienced a mass run on a bank. Amid intense controversy the Treasury stepped in to guarantee deposits in Northern Rock. In March 2008, after a long delay, the British government finally took the failed bank into public ownership. The episode was especially significant as Britain had pioneered the "Big Bang" in financial services, and was widely regarded as a model for regulation of financial markets. It was deeply damaging to the model of bank privatization and reliance mainly on self-regulation that had been advocated around the world by the British government.

In the autumn of 2007 the central banks in the high-income countries introduced piecemeal measures to attempt to deal with the unfolding crisis, but these failed to reassure the financial markets. By mid-December 2007 the credit squeeze had lasted for four months, and on December 12 the central bankers in the high-income countries agreed on a coordinated effort to restore liquidity to financial markets. The American Federal Reserve, the European Central Bank, the Bank of England, the Bank of Canada, and the Swiss Central Bank announced simultaneously that they were taking steps to make cash more readily available to the banks and that they would accept a much wider array of assets as collateral. However, the coordinated intervention by the central banks did not address the fundamental problem of the asset bubble that had accumulated over the preceding three decades.

The decline in asset prices gathered momentum in early 2008, as the Federal Reserve undertook ever more drastic interventions to try to prop up collapsing financial markets. However, it became increasingly clear that conventional monetary policy measures were powerless to "catch the falling knife" of declining asset prices and prevent the toxic interaction of the financial crisis with the real economy.

In March 2008 it emerged that a leading American investment bank, Bear Stearns, was virtually bankrupt. The value of its assets had crumbled during the financial crisis. Its clients rushed to withdraw their funds. Credit lines seized up. Its share price plunged from $169 in January 2007 to just $3.67 on March 17, 2008. Bear Stearns was deeply embedded in the American (and global) financial system. In a hugely significant move, the Federal Reserve decided that in the interests of financial system stability it would provide $30 billion to clean up Bear Stearns' holdings of devalued mortgage securities. Simultaneously, J. P. Morgan agreed to buy the stricken bank at a fire sale price. The bailout prompted intense debate about its implications for the world's deregulated financial markets. Following the Federal Reserve's rescue of Bear Stearns, Martin Wolf, associate editor of the *Financial Times*, commented: "Remember Friday 14, March 2008: It was the day the dream of global free market capitalism died." In the same week, Joseph Ackerman, chief executive of Deutsche Bank, made the historic admission: "I no longer believe in the market's self-healing power."

The gravity of the financial crisis was increasingly acknowledged. In its Annual Report in spring 2008 the Bank for International Settlements warned: "The current market turmoil in the world's main financial centers is without precedent in the postwar period. With a significant risk of recession in the US, compounded by sharply rising inflation in many countries, fears are building that the global economy might be at some kind of tipping point. These fears are not groundless." In April 2008 the IMF estimated that the losses from the write-down of assets in America would total $945 billion, equivalent to around seven percent of American GDP. Goldman Sachs estimated that the overall losses to the American economy from the write-down of asset values would total around $1.2 trillion. The American economist, Professor Nouriel Roubini, predicted that losses from the decline in American house prices (which he predicted would eventually be 30–40 percent) would total $6 trillion, or 42 percent of American GDP. Furthermore, he estimated that there were likely to be trillions of dollars of losses due to falling commercial property prices and a $5–6 trillion loss due to the decline in stock prices. In total this might equal the entire American GDP.

Like a writhing monster, the global asset bubble refused to die quietly. Instead of the simultaneous collapse of all asset classes, the process of credit creation and speculation shifted to the commodity sector. Between 2000 and 2007, world commodity prices had already doubled. The belief gained ground that commodity markets had entered a new Malthusian world of severe natural resource depletion, driven by industrialization in the developing world, which would drive up the long-term price of natural resources. As prices of natural resources rose, speculative flows into the sector surged. On June 6, 2008, the world oil price experienced its largest ever one-day rise, reaching a record level of $139 per barrel, recording a $16 per barrel increase in just two days, rising eventually to nearly $150 per barrel. Only a decade previously, oil had been a mere $8 per barrel. To impartial observers the drastic increase in 2007/8 was driven by speculation chasing the gains from the price increases themselves. In the second half of 2008, the commodity bubble burst. The global commodities index plunged from its peak of 480 (1967=100) in July 2008 to around 360 in early October 2008. In the same period the oil price fell from its peak of almost $150 per barrel to $72 per barrel, and by the year end it stood at less than $50 per barrel.

In autumn 2008, the crisis entered a new and even more dangerous phase. Between early September and mid-October the global financial system was shaken to the core. The events of these weeks brought the era of wild capitalist globalization to a dramatic end. In America a series of shattering blows hit the country's leading financial institutions, including Fannie Mae and Freddie Mac, Lehman Brothers, Merrill Lynch, AIG, Washington Mutual, and Wachovia.

Between them the giant "government sponsored entities" (GSEs) Fannie Mae and Freddie Mac either owned directly or guaranteed almost one-half of total American mortgages, which total around $12 trillion. Their level of leverage was extremely high. As the financial crisis deepened, American home prices fell and foreclosures rose across the country. Fannie and Freddie both incurred huge losses, their borrowing costs increased and their relatively slim capital base was severely eroded. In the first week of September, their share prices plummeted. Over the weekend of September 6–7, the American government placed Fannie and Freddie under the direct control of the government's regulator, amounting to *de facto* nationalization of a vast segment of the American economy. The scene was set for a further dramatic turn in the financial crisis.

Prior to the financial crisis, Lehman Brothers was the world's fourth largest investment bank. As a non-deposit-taking bank it relied on borrowing from money markets and high levels of leverage to undertake a wide variety of investment banking operations. It had a key role in the derivatives market, with hundreds of billions of dollars worth of derivatives contracts, covering everything from oil-price hedging to insurance on corporate debt to bets on the rise of stock indices. It also had a large body of real estate assets, a substantial portion of which were deemed to be "toxic" due to the collapse of the American property market. By September 12 Lehman's share price stood at just $3.83, compared with a peak of $80 in June 2007. The American government took the momentous decision not to save the bank, and allowed Lehman Brothers to file for bankruptcy. This decision was widely hailed as correct, since it meant that the risk of moral hazard, which would have stemmed from government support, was avoided.

The collapse of Bear Stearns and the unfolding crisis at Lehman Brothers produced a wave of fear about the prospects for stand-alone investment banks, including even the three giants, Goldman Sachs, Merrill Lynch, and Morgan Stanley. On Monday, September 15, Merrill Lynch announced that it had agreed to be acquired by Bank of America. Over the weekend of September 20–21, the American government announced that it would allow the remaining giant investment banks, Morgan Stanley and Goldman Sachs, to become "bank holding companies," which would enable them to take deposits from the general public and gain permanent access to Federal Reserve funds, and which would also mean that they would be subject to the same regulatory regime as the commercial banks.

Prior to the financial crisis, American International Group (AIG) ranked among the world's top 20 companies in terms of both revenue and market capitalization.

Its operations were global. AIG's main business traditionally was insurance. As financial markets around the world liberalized it expanded into a sprawling global empire of diversified financial activities, including aircraft leasing (it became the largest in the world, with $55 billion worth of aircraft assets), consumer finance, and asset management. In September 2008 its financial products division had a total derivatives exposure of $441 billion. On Monday, September 15, 2008, AIG's share price fell by 60 percent, and its market capitalization ended the day at $7.5 billion, compared with $175 billion in March 2007. Its collapse into bankruptcy would have had profound consequences for the financial system both in America and around the world. Consequently, on September 16 the American government announced that the Federal Reserve would lend AIG up to $85 billion in emergency funds in return for a government stake of 79.9 percent. In other words, AIG was nationalized by the American government.

On September 12, 2008, the American government announced an emergency package of proposals to try to stem the crisis. The most dramatic of these was Hank Paulson's proposal to establish a "bad bank" to take on the toxic mortgage-related assets in the financial system, allowing banks to stem their losses, recapitalize, and return to normal business. The plan became know by its acronym, TARP, or "troubled assets relief program." The newly established government bad bank would involve the American government spending around $700 billion of taxpayers' money up front to absorb the toxic assets. The plans met with intense opposition in Congress, however, throwing the Republican Party into ideological disarray. Leading Republicans denounced the plan as "un-American," "financial socialism," and even as "trickle-down communism." There was a massive public outcry against the perceived bailout by the American taxpayer of wealthy Wall Street bankers who were regarded as having created the financial crisis in the first place.

The *Financial Times*, more than any other publication, has become identified with the era of capitalist globalization. It has grown from being an oddly colored (pink) British newspaper into the newspaper of choice for the global capitalist class. The dramatic and grave state that world financial markets had reached was illustrated by the paper's historic full-page, large print editorial of Saturday, September 27. The editorial was entitled "In praise of free markets." It read:

> The financial system has reached the point of maximum peril ... If the unravelling of the banking system continues, the economic consequences will be dire ... Capital markets clearly need better regulation, but policy-makers should guard against unintended consequences ... This is a difficult time to defend free markets. Nevertheless, they must be defended, not only on their matchless record when it comes to raising living standards, but on the maxim that it is wise to let adults exercise their own judgement. Market freedom is not a "fundamentalist religion." It is a mechanism, not an ideology, and one that has proved its value again and again over the past 200 years. The *Financial Times* is proud to defend it—even today.

On Monday, September 29, the House of Representatives voted to veto the proposed rescue package. Republicans voted against the bill by two to one. The response of the world's financial markets was dramatic. On the same day, following Congress's rejection of the Paulson rescue plan, the S&P (Standard & Poor) 500 stock market index experienced its largest one-day decline for over 20 years. Stress in world credit markets reached a new intensity. Banks almost ceased to lend to each other. The shocking impact on financial markets of Congress's rejection of the rescue plan caused intense public debate in America. On Wednesday, October 1, the Senate passed the rescue plan, and by Friday, October 3, the House of Representatives had finally agreed to pass a much-amended plan.

Even as Congress was debating the rescue plan, news came of the largest-ever American bank collapse. Washington Mutual (WaMu) had become the country's largest mortgage originator when it acquired Fleet Mortgage in 2001. As of June 30, 2008, it was the sixth largest American bank. As the financial crisis intensified confidence in WaMu drained steadily. Depositors began to fear for its solvency, and in September 2008 there was a run on the bank. On September 25 American regulators closed the bank and seized direct control of its operations. Simultaneously, J. P. Morgan agreed to acquire WaMu for just $1.9 billion, a tiny fraction of its market capitalization in 2007. Immediately after the collapse of WaMu came the news that Wachovia was in severe difficulties. In 2007 Wachovia was the fourth largest American bank by revenues. In 2006 it had acquired the California-based mortgage company, Golden West Financial, which had greatly increased its exposure to the American property market. Wachovia's share price and market capitalization fell heavily in 2007, collapsing disastrously in September. Faced with Wachovia's possible bankruptcy, on September 29 the government stepped in to broker the bank's sale to Citigroup. However, no sooner had the deal been agreed in principle than a counter-offer was made by Wells Fargo, America's fifth largest bank by revenue. Wells Fargo agreed to buy Wachovia outright for around $15.1 billion in an all-share deal, without any support from the government.

Alongside the dramatic developments in America, in late September deep new cracks opened up within the European financial system. The British bank HBOS was formed in 2001 through the merger of the Halifax building society and the Bank of Scotland. It had grown at high speed, taking advantage of Britain's property boom and turning to the wholesale markets for almost one-half of its funding. By 2005, it had risen to become the world's tenth largest bank by revenue. Tightening conditions in money markets and the fall in British property prices placed intense pressure on the bank. By mid-September 2008 its market capitalization had shrunk to less than one-fifth of the level it had been at in March 2007. The British government was terrified lest HBOS should become bankrupt, and on September 17 it waived the normal requirements of the country's competition rules in order to allow Lloyds TSB to acquire HBOS. The new bank would hold a commanding position in the British banking market, with 35 percent of the current account market and 28 percent of the mortgage market.

Confidence in the British banks that were heavily involved in the mortgage market reached a new low point. The next crisis involved Bradford and Bingley, which had been created in 1964 from a merger of two building societies. In 2000 Bradford and Bingley was floated on the stock market as a normal commercial bank, and by 2008 almost nine-tenths of its loan book was made up of buy-to-let mortgages and self-certified mortgages. As the crisis intensified, the money market tightened, and property prices fell, speculation about the bank's solvency increased, and in late September 2008 its share price plummeted, leading to large withdrawals of deposits. On September 28 the British government stepped in and nationalized the bank, taking over its £42 billion loan book. The banks' deposits and branch network were taken over by Banco Santander, which now became one of the largest banks in Britain, following its earlier acquisition of Abbey National, and Alliance and Leicester.

The period of capitalist globalization had witnessed the emergence of a group of immensely powerful European banks headquartered in relatively small economies. As the financial crisis developed, the question was asked: have some European banks not only become "too big to fail," but might they also have become "too big to save"? Prior to the financial crisis, Fortis was a giant bancassurance company, the world's 14th largest company by revenue. The bank is headquartered in Belgium, and its assets amount to around three times the size of Belgium's entire GDP. In late September 2008 shares in Fortis plummeted, and on September 28 the governments of Belgium, Luxembourg, and the Netherlands partially nationalized the bank, buying 49 percent of its national arm in each of the three countries. Only a few days later, the Dutch government decided to wholly nationalize the Dutch segment of Fortis. This was followed by the Belgian government's controversial decision to allow France's BNP Paribas to acquire Fortis's Belgian and Luxembourg operations. If this is finally approved, BNP Paribas will become the largest eurozone bank in terms of the size of deposits.

In the 1990s Iceland privatized and deregulated its banking system, winning high praise from international financial experts. Its banks borrowed heavily abroad to finance their expansion. The property market and stock market boomed, and by the second quarter of 2008, the international debts of Icelandic banks had reached six times the total value of Iceland's GDP. In late September and early October 2008 the country's top three banks collapsed, and on November 20 Iceland borrowed $10 billion from the IMF and a consortium of European governments, an amount roughly the size of its entire GDP. The Icelandic population of 320,000 faced the prospect of a brutal recession, with an enormous debt burden that would hang over the country for years.

Along with Iceland, Ireland was a model of the benefits to be derived from the financial free market. The "Celtic Tiger" achieved high-speed growth on the basis of financial market liberalization and buoyant property prices. As the global financial crisis deepened, fears about the robustness of Irish banks grew. On Monday September 29, Ireland's leading banks experienced a large-scale withdrawal of deposits and a massive decline in their share price. The Irish government intervened to issue a blanket guarantee for two years on all deposits. The government was accused of taking unilateral action that was out of line with the rest of the eurozone, but its finance minister answered: "I accept it is a tendency toward economic nationalism, but we're here on our own in Ireland and the government had to act in the best interests of the Irish people."

The German bank Hypo Real Estate (HRE) is one of Europe's biggest lenders for commercial property. In early October 2008 the central government stepped in to underwrite a 28 billion euro bailout of HRE. The attempted bailout collapsed, however, leading to panic in the German financial markets. On October 5 the German government shocked financial markets by announcing, without any consultation with other EU members, that it was guaranteeing all private bank deposits. The German Chancellor, Angela Merkel, said: "We want to tell people that their savings are safe." Only a week later, the government put into place a 50 billion euro bailout for HRE. The examples of Ireland and Germany raised the specter of each national government in Europe following its own rescue path and competing to attract international capital to its own system.

In the week of October 6–10 the financial crisis entered its most critical phase so far. The global financial system "looked into the abyss." *The Economist*, which had been one of the principal cheerleaders for deregulated capitalist globalization, featured a front cover with a lone figure staring into a black abyss.

The turmoil in financial markets had gathered force ever since the American government's shocking decision to allow Lehman Brothers to go bankrupt. It was now widely acknowledged that the era of American-led free market financial capitalism was over. Even the most ardent advocates of the financial free market were forced by the gravity of the crisis to acknowledge that the model was broken and that a new era had begun, in which governments would play a far deeper role in regulating financial markets. It became increasingly obvious that the financial crisis would lead to a deep global recession.

In the course of the week of October 6–10 the dam burst. The stock market fell by 23 percent in New York, 21 percent in London, 25 percent in Tokyo and 22 percent in Frankfurt. The emerging markets stock market index fell by 26 percent, with a decline of 57 percent from the peak of one year previously. The share price of leading banks fell precipitately. The world's financial markets faced Armageddon. The *Financial Times* editorial of Monday, October 13, was entitled: "A minute before midnight for banks." It said: "The banking system of the Western world is suffering the equivalent of cardiac arrest. It is virtually impossible for any institution to finance itself in the markets any longer than overnight. This is a measure of the panic-stricken collapse of confidence that has seized the system … The heart of the world's financial system has stopped beating. It must be restarted."

Of all the large high-income countries Britain was most at risk, due to the size of the property bubble, the extent of household debt and the degree of importance of the financial sector in the economy. During the week of October 6–10 the share price of Barclays fell by 44 percent, Lloyds TSB by 35 percent, and RBS by 62 percent. Faced with the prospect of a complete meltdown of the British financial system, on Wednesday October 8 the British government introduced a rescue plan of extraordinary dimensions. It included a massive £400 billion rescue package for British-based financial institutions, including £250 billion in guarantees for new short and medium-term debt. However, most revolutionary of all was the decision to make available up to £50 billion in permanent capital in order to raise the banks' Tier One capital ratios. This involved the state taking large shares in the leading British-based banks that wished to take advantage of the offer. The *Financial Times*'s editorial of October 14 was entitled: "Nationalize to save the free market."

Worst hit of the British banks were RBS and HBOS, which had only just announced its merger with Lloyds TSB. RBS had, since 2000, completed more than 25 mergers and acquisitions, and it relied on dangerously high levels of leverage through borrowing on the inter-bank market. Between October 2007 and early October 2008 RBS's share price plunged from 469p to 66p. It had little option but to accept the bailout offer, after which the British government would own around 57 percent of its equity. HBOS also agreed to accept a capital injection of around £12 billion, after which the British government would own around 58 percent of the bank. Lloyds TSB agreed to accept a capital injection of around £5 billion. Following the merger between Lloyds TSB and HBOS to form the Lloyds Banking Group, the British government would own around 44 percent of the combined entity. Britain had led the world in financial liberalization with the "Big Bang" of the 1980s. Under both Conservative and Labour governments it had stood shoulder to shoulder with America in arguing around the world for the benefits of lightly regulated banks owned by private shareholders. The gleaming buildings of the new City of London at Canary Wharf stood at the center of global financial market innovation. By mid-October 2008, a large part of the British banking system, including RBS, Lloyds Banking Group, Northern Rock, and Bradford and Bingley, had been brought under full or partial public ownership. Britain stood humiliated before the world.

During the dramatic events of the week of October 6–10 it seemed that each of the European countries would try to find their own national solution to the crisis. In the face of the devastating events of that week, over the weekend of October 11–12 the main Continental European governments, faced with the threat of meltdown of their financial systems, finally agreed to a coordinated response to the crisis. The German government provided around 100 billion euros in fresh capital for both existing state-owned banks and for privately owned banks, in exchange for government shares. In addition, it agreed to provide up to 400 billion euros in guarantees for bank debt. The French government announced a 360 billion euro rescue package, including 320 billion euros in guarantees for new debt and 40 billion euros to establish a state-owned bank to acquire shares in troubled banks. The other major European economies took similar steps to deal with the crisis.

On Tuesday, October 14, the American government announced that it was introducing emergency measures along the same lines as the Europeans. The government announced that the remit of the Federal Deposit Insurance Corporation would be greatly extended. Even more dramatically, it announced that $250 billion of the $700 billion TARP package would be used to purchase government stakes directly in banks. The immediate objective was to "circle the wagons around a core group of banks"—Bank of America, J. P. Morgan, Wells Fargo, Citigroup, Goldman Sachs, Morgan Stanley, Bank of New York, and State Street. The government was to purchase preferred stock in this core group of banks, including $25 billion in Citigroup, Wells Fargo, and J. P. Morgan, $20 billion in Bank of America, and $10 billion in Goldman Sachs and Morgan Stanley, further extending the government's direct ownership role in the American financial system.

When he introduced the measures, a grim-faced Treasury Secretary, Hank Paulson, said: "America is a strong nation. We are a confident and optimistic people. Our confidence is born out of our long history of meeting every challenge we face. There is a lack of confidence in our financial system ... It poses an enormous threat to our economy. Investors are unwilling to lend to each other, and healthy banks are unwilling to lend to each other ... Government owning a stake in any private US company is objectionable to most Americans, me included. Yet the alternative of leaving businesses and consumers without access to financing is totally unacceptable." The *Financial Times* spoke of Hank Paulson "performing the last rites on US capitalism." Within a month, however, Paulson announced formally that the government had abandoned the idea of using the TARP (troubled asset relief program) funds to purchase toxic assets from banks, deciding that it had no way of knowing the correct price at which to buy the assets. The government's comprehensive *volte face* on such a critical issue dismayed most analysts. It suggested that the core of the American financial policy-making establishment had little idea of how to deal with the crisis.

From financial crisis to economic crisis

By November 2008, the first act of the global crisis had drawn to a close. Through dramatic government intervention in both America and Europe, including a massive extension of state ownership and control over the banking industry, the world had pulled back from the abyss of comprehensive financial meltdown.

In the second act of the crisis, the real economy was increasingly severely affected. The extent of "financialization" of the economy during the era of capitalist globalization had greatly exceeded anything known previously, and as a result the collapse of asset prices consequent on deleveraging had its own momentum. As the real economy became ever more deeply affected, the damaging impact on banks' balance sheets continued to grow in a vicious circle, including continuing write-downs on property-related debt, credit card debt and personal loans, which reduced consumer demand, in turn further eroding banks' balance sheets. By late November 2008 it was reported that the total losses through write-downs and credit losses in global financial institutions were approaching $1 trillion. The IMF had raised its estimate of the total eventual losses to $1.4 trillion, nearly 50 percent greater than its estimate in April 2008. The value of global assets in 2008 fell by around $50 trillion, roughly equivalent to the total global GDP in the same year. It was impossible to predict how far asset prices would ultimately fall.

In late 2008 the situation in the global real economy deteriorated at an alarming pace. OECD governments attempted to stimulate the economy by the usual method of cutting the official rate of interest. By late December 2008 the official policy rate of interest had fallen to 2.5 percent in the eurozone, and 2 percent in Britain. In early January, the Bank of England lowered the rate to 1.5 percent, the lowest since the bank was founded in 1694, and this was followed almost immediately by the ECB's (Euro Central Bank) decision to lower its interest rate to 2 percent. In America, on December 17, 2008, the Federal Funds target rate of interest (the official "policy rate") was reduced to a band between zero and 0.25 percent, representing a remarkable milestone in modern economic history. This decision was closely followed by the Bank of Japan's decision to cut the official rate of interest to 0.1 percent. By early November 2008, the main weapons available to OECD governments to avert a recession had already been used. However, conventional tools of monetary policy proved powerless in the face of the continuing unwinding of the biggest asset price bubble in history and the consequent "great deleveraging."

The continuing decline in asset prices, including both property and stock markets, had a profound effect on the wealth of OECD citizens, leading to a widespread effort to rebuild household finances by saving more and spending less on inessentials. Property prices continued to fall across the high-income countries, and it was now widely expected that the eventual fall in America and Britain would reach as much as 50 percent compared with the peak of the market. The fall in stock markets also continued, with only temporary corrections along the way. By late November 2008 the S&P 500 had fallen by 50 percent from its peak in October 2007. This was now without question the worst bear market since the 1930s. The wealth effect upon consumption was reinforced by greatly increased insecurity, including the prospect of reduced pensions, and by tightening bank lending. The severe economic downturn was leading to a massive second wave of credit losses on consumer and corporate loans, which caused further deep damage to the already eroded capital bases of banks and other financial institutions, in turn causing further restrictions to bank credit. The market for a wide array of assets had dried up as the leverage machine went into reverse and everyone tried to get to zero leverage.

From fears about inflation during the final phase of the asset bubble, global markets suddenly realized that the OECD countries faced a high possibility of a long period of "malign" deflation, with a high risk that a negative spiral would be set in motion in which people postponed spending in the hope of further price falls. Moreover, during this process the real value of debt would increase, further damaging households' wealth, and so, in a further vicious twist to the downward spiral, reducing their incentive to spend. The shocking realization loomed that the world faced the prospect of enduring on a global scale the ills that had afflicted Japan on a national scale in the 1990s following its asset bubble in the 1980s.

Despite having pulled back from the abyss of financial collapse, there were still deep problems in the financial sector. In late November 2008, it was revealed that Citigroup had an estimated $306 billion worth of "troubled assets," including home loans, commercial loans, and commercial mortgages. In the course of the week of November 17–21, Citigroup's share price fell by 60 percent. The American government decided that it could not afford the collapse of another major financial institution and invested $20 billion in Citigroup preferred shares, bringing to $45 billion the government's total recapitalization of Citigroup. Further, it agreed that it would bear any losses exceeding $29 billion that Citigroup incurred due to its troubled assets. On January 16, Bank of America announced a loss of $2.4 billion in the final quarter of 2008. The American government agreed to a $20 billion capital injection and a $118 billion loss guarantee. By mid-January the market capitalization of the world's financial firms had shrunk to $3.6 trillion, compared with $8.5 trillion in August 2007, a fall of almost three-fifths. Once again, the world waited with bated breath for further disastrous news from the leading financial institutions as the real world economic collapse fed back into the banks' balance sheets.

As the full extent and probable duration of the global recession became clear at the end of 2008, investors "flocked to safety," purchasing American government Treasury bills in record amounts. For the first time ever, the Treasury sold a four-week bill at a discount rate of zero. So frantic was the search for safety that the yields on three-month Treasury bills sank to negative levels for the first time since 1940. At negative yields, the investor is essentially paying someone to own the security. The yield on 10-year American Treasury debt fell below 3 percent for the first time in 50 years. The American 30-year bond yield generally reflects views on the long-term prospects for inflation and economic growth, and in late November the yield fell below 4 percent for the first time. The dramatic decline in bond yields reflected the incredibly high prices investors were prepared to pay for a guaranteed fixed yield. The only historical precedent for such low bond yields is the 1930s.

By the end of 2008 it was universally accepted that the global economy faced the prospect of a deep recession. In early November the IMF forecast that in 2009 there would be negative growth across the whole of the OECD, with a decline of 0.2 percent in Japan, 0.5 percent in the eurozone, 0.7 percent in America, and 1.3 percent in Britain. In the ensuing weeks the IMF's assessment of global economic prospects deteriorated steadily.

One of the central hopes of the era of capitalist globalization was that developing countries had entered into an independent growth process that decoupled them from the high-income economies. By late 2008 it was clear that decoupling was a mirage, inconsistent with the basic philosophy of the Washington Consensus, namely deep integration with global capitalism. In December 2008 the World Bank predicted that world trade would contract by over two percent in 2009, with devastating consequences for the developing countries that followed the export-led manufacturing sector growth strategies advocated by the Washington Consensus. Those developing countries that relied heavily on primary product exports faced the prospect of drastically reduced export earnings due to the collapsed primary product prices. Between October 2007 and October 2008 the emerging markets stock market index fell by 57 percent. The World Bank predicted that total private sector capital flows to developing countries would fall from $1 trillion in 2007 to $530 billion in 2009. In December, the UN Conference on Trade and Development predicted that global FDI would fall by around 12–15 percent in 2009.

The combination of bank bailouts and stimulus packages across the high-income countries has enormous implications for global financial markets, because of the unprecedented volume of government borrowing. By late 2008 it was forecast that in 2009 government borrowing in America would reach 1,011 billion euros (equivalent), amounting to 10.3 percent of GDP; in Germany government borrowing was forecast to reach 238 billion euros, amounting to 9.4 percent of GDP; in Italy government borrowing was forecast to reach 220 billion euros, amounting to 13.6 percent of GDP; in France, government borrowing was forecast to be 175 billion euros, amounting to 8.6 percent of GDP; while in Britain government borrowing was forecast to be 182 billion euros, amounting to 9.9 percent of GDP. The world has never seen simultaneous government borrowing across the high-income countries on this scale. It raises the question of whether there will be enough investors willing to buy the vast quantity of bonds that will come to the market, and the terms on which the government will be able to sell its debt. It also raised the possibility of the operation of the so-called "Ricardo effect," under which consumers fear that an increase in government spending will lead to higher taxes in the future, causing them to reduce spending and increase saving. The implications for developing countries too are extremely serious; there is a risk that these countries will simply be crowded out of the global market for government debt.

In the space of two months in autumn 2008, the *Financial Times*'s articles on the crisis had moved from "global financial crisis," to "global economic slowdown," to "world in recession." The *Financial Times*'s headline on November 21 read: "Fear stalks the world economies." Its headline on November 22 read: "Dark days see warnings of far worse yet to come." The article below warned: "Any lingering hopes that some parts of the world economy, particularly the fast-growing emerging markets such as China, would remain immune from the crisis were snuffed out. With remarkable speed in the past two months, a worrying but apparently manageable credit crunch has turned into a global financial crisis and a recession across much of the world's economy."

Towards global financial regulation?

The events of September–November 2008 marked the decisive end of three decades of wild capitalist globalization. America, within which the financial sector has tremendous lobbying power, had used its influence over the Washington Consensus institutions, especially the IMF, to prevent them from acting in a way that would bring the global financial system under collective control. For three decades the Washington Consensus institutions, closely supported by international firms, relentlessly hectored the governments of developing countries to privatize and liberalize their financial systems in order to obtain the benefits from free markets in finance. In 2007, the world's top 20 banks (ranked by net income) had total profits (net income) of $209 billion, an average of over $10 billion each. Of these, eight were American, four were British-headquartered, and the rest were all from other OECD countries. None was from a developing country. The key to the vast profits earned by the giant financial firms based in the high-income countries was their freedom to act almost without restraint in order to achieve huge increases in leverage. The American-led global free market in money was at the core of capitalist globalization. It provided undreamed-of opportunities for the world's leading financial firms to, in effect, make money from money.

After years of lectures from the high-income countries to the developing world about the unfairness of state support for their national firms and the inappropriateness of state ownership, there was a tremendous irony in the high-income countries being forced to provide vast sums of money to support their respective national banks and take large ownership shares in them. After long years of lecturing developing countries on the importance of a hard budget constraint in all sectors of the economy, and the dangers of moral hazard if the state propped up failing firms, the governments of high-income countries were now perpetrating a "soft budget constraint" and engaging in moral hazard on a gigantic scale.

At the core of the Washington Consensus was the confidence that unregulated financial markets based on privately owned banks were self-correcting. The financial crisis demolished this market fundamentalist view. In April 2008, following the collapse of Bear Stearns, George Soros observed: "All the innovations—risk management, trading techniques, the alphabet soup of derivatives and synthetic financial instruments—were based on that belief. The innovations remained unregulated because authorities believe markets are self-regulating." At the same time Paul Volcker, former chairman of the Federal Reserve, concluded: "The bright new financial system—for all its talented participants, for all its rich rewards—has failed the test of the marketplace."

As the financial crisis has unfolded, the voices calling for greatly increased regulation of financial markets have gathered strength. The late J. K. Galbraith insisted that speculation and its aftermath are "recurrent and inherent, unfortunate characteristics of markets, extending over many centuries." He argued that while each episode superficially has new characteristics, the essence is the same and is intrinsic to the market mechanism itself: "[T]he speculative episode, with increases [in asset prices] provoking increases [in asset prices], is within the market itself. And so is the culminating crash." By the end of 2008 it was undeniable that the basic cause of the crisis was within the market itself. In May 2008 the former head of the IMF, Horst Köhler, delivered a devastating verdict on liberalized global financial markets, likening them to Mary Shelley's Frankenstein monster: "The complexity of financial products and the possibility to carry out huge leveraged trades with little capital have allowed the monster to grow … The only good thing about this crisis is that it has made clear to any thinking, responsible person in the sector that international financial markets have developed into a monster that must be put back in its place." In the story, the mass of citizens in the end destroyed Dr. Frankenstein's monster.

It is now widely acknowledged that banks are a public utility and that money should be closely regulated in the public interest. Even the most staunch free market economists and commentators have been forced to acknowledge that a new era of financial market regulation is upon us. It is now widely recognized that the core agencies needed to regulate financial markets must be global in scope. The precise shape of the regulatory structures can only be perceived in embryo, but there is universal acceptance that a new era of financial market regulation has begun. In its own way, these developments are as significant as the fall of the Berlin Wall and the collapse of communism in Eastern Europe.

Increasingly, the protestations of bankers that they are best placed to regulate the financial industry have fallen on deaf ears. On his visit to America in mid-April 2008 the British Prime Minister, Gordon Brown, stated that the world stood in "a new dawn in collaborative action" to tackle the "terrifying risk" of the next century. He argued that the IMF ought to be reshaped radically in order to create a system providing early warnings of financial crises. In September Nicolas Sarkozy, the French President, called for a "regulated capitalism" to replace a world financial system that had "become unhinged." The President of the European Central Bank, Jean-Claude Trichet, called for a review of the full body of the global financial system: "Things have to change in absolutely all parts and parcels of this global financial system without any privilege to anybody, any institution or any instrument." Gordon Brown called for a "Bretton Woods II," with a new regulatory mandate for the IMF that extends far beyond its original purpose. His call was endorsed by several European heads of government, including both Nicolas Sarkozy and Angela Merkel. Without American support, however, such a dramatic institutional change will not happen. In Gordon Brown's view, "American leadership is and will be indispensable." Given that it led the charge toward global financial market deregulation, this is a severe challenge for America. At the height of the crisis on October 10, President Bush himself acknowledged: "The world is sending an unmistakable signal: we're in this together and we'll come through this together."

Turning such broad statements into a concrete reality is a huge challenge for world politics. There is still deep resistance from bankers to substantially increased regulation. There remain deep differences of interest among the high-income countries. Among developing countries there is a deep legacy of distrust of the IMF, which has come to be widely perceived as an instrument of American foreign policy. Moreover, many powerful interests within the OECD countries remain skeptical of extending control over the global financial system to a wide group of developing countries. Although the global financial crisis offers the opportunity to advance global collective action, powerful forces push in the opposite direction. It is an open question whether the centripetal (i.e. center-seeking) forces win out over the centrifugal (i.e. center-fleeing) forces in the resolution of the financial crisis and its ensuing impact on the real economy.

Conclusion

Financial speculation, and the corresponding creation of money to meet the needs of speculation, are a fundamental part of the freedom of capitalism. The natural working of free markets, allied to the motives of fear and greed, have repeatedly produced financial cycles. Money was widely used in ancient Greece several centuries before the birth of Christ, and the beneficial stimulus it provided for specialization and exchange was widely appreciated. Its magical and universal ability to reduce anything that could be exchanged in the marketplace to a common denominator stimulated great discussion among philosophers. Equally, the unique character of "money to make more money," and the open-ended incentive this provided for human greed, aroused great nervousness. In his *Politics*, Aristotle argued: "Very much disliked is the practice of charging interest; and the dislike is fully justified, for the gain arises out of the currency itself, not as a product of that for which the currency was provided." Currency was intended as a means of exchange, whereas interest represents an increase in the currency itself. Hence its name (*tokos*, i.e. offspring), for each animal produces its like, and interest is currency born of currency. And so of all types of business this is the most contrary to nature.

The crisis facing the world today originates in the freedom of the financial system to pursue profits blindly through speculation, "money to make more money." The risk for the global community has been greatly increased by the application of sophisticated new technologies to create money. These technologies are the product of many of the most creative minds in the world today. Giant global financial firms have vied with each other to attract brilliant young mathematicians and physicists to enroll as sorcerers' apprentices, as it were, in the creation of new forms of money. The free, unregulated exercise of their intelligence in the pursuit of profit has taken the world to the edge of a financial and economic abyss.

Effective regulation of the global financial system is desperately needed, but the power and short-term self-interest of giant financial firms has combined with the ineffectiveness of international political institutions to prevent such mechanisms being put into place. The Asian financial crisis demonstrated vividly that the fire of a financial crisis moves at high speed, fanned by self-created winds, and swiftly spreads into the economic, social, and political sphere. The current financial and economic crisis is already global in scope. A phrase that was much-repeated during the Asian financial crisis was "when the tide goes out, the rocks appear" (*shui luo shi chu*). When this tide goes out the rocks that appear may dwarf even those of the Great Depression. Of all the regulatory tasks facing global institutions, this is by far the most urgent. Even the threat of global warming is some way off. We are in the midst of a truly global financial crisis, which is rapidly transforming itself into a global economic crisis. It may well be transformed further into a social, political and international relations crisis. The first tentative signs of a drive for coordinated global regulation of financial markets are emerging, but the prospect is uncertain and the obstacles are great.

CONCLUSION

Capitalist freedom is a two-edged sword. The same force that has propelled forward human ingenuity for over two millennia has reached a new peak in its stimulus to human creativity. However, it threatens fundamentally the very existence of the human species.

The global ecology is profoundly threatened by the consequences of the uncontrolled, locked-in pattern of consumption, distribution, and energy consumption that is at the heart of capitalist globalization. Responsibility for the lion's share of past global warming lies with the high-income countries. Developing countries are rapidly increasing their contribution to global warming, and there is the prospect of an increasing confrontation between rich and poor counties over their respective responsibility for resolving the issue. The world faces an intensifying struggle for energy security among the main importers of oil and gas, which will remain the core of the primary energy supply for the world's transport systems for decades to come.

The large corporation has burst the boundaries of the nation in the pursuit of profit on the global stage, creating profound contradictions in the nation states in which they grew. The fact that global firms are fast diminishing their allegiance to their original home countries is creating fissures within the political systems of the high-income countries. At the same time, giant global firms, winning the battle for survival in the global marketplace, threaten the indigenous firms in developing countries.

The distribution of income and wealth within both rich and poor countries has become much more unequal as a consequence of capitalist globalization. A large mass of citizens in both sets of countries believes the other set of countries is largely responsible for this situation. A global capitalist class has developed rapidly, with shared interests that are at odds with those of the nations within which the global firms had their origins.

The revolution in the financial system has produced comprehensively integrated markets, with money creation and associated speculation on an unimaginable scale, powerfully supported by the creativity of financial technicians, and facilitated by the revolution in information technology. There is no global entity with the power and authority to regulate the global financial system. The system is "flying blind," and is in the throes of a global financial crisis of a scale that is unprecedented since the 1930s. The crisis threatens to interact with the contradictions in the realms of ecology, income and wealth inequality, and the changed nature of the large firm and its relationship to the nation state. It threatens to have severe social, economic, and political consequences. It is quite possible that the crisis will be of such severity as to cause a prolonged period of social instability within both rich and poor countries, which would pose severe challenges for political institutions, and in addition there are likely to be important consequences for international relations.

Behind all of these issues lies the fact that politics is mainly conducted at a national level, while the capitalist system has become global in scale. The mechanisms for the world's citizens to control the global capitalist system are weak. The interests of individual nations are strong, and military force remains a central part of the reality of international relations. America possesses a vast and immensely effective nuclear arsenal. Russia also still possesses a vast nuclear arsenal, and in early 2007 it announced a large increase in military spending in order to fund a new generation of intercontinental ballistic missiles, nuclear submarines, and aircraft carriers. France, Britain, China, India, Pakistan, and Israel all have nuclear weapons. The human species could be catastrophically damaged in the twinkling of an eye. In the 1930s Keynesian policies, insofar as they were applied, did not prevent a deep recession of many years' duration. The crisis was only resolved conclusively with the rise of fascism in Germany and Japan, and the onset of war.

If human beings are to resolve these contradictions and avoid the looming disaster it is urgently necessary to establish global mechanisms to contain the self-created monster of unconstrained global capitalism. It will require comprehensive regulation of global markets. The name that one gives to such a system (whether "regulated capitalism," "socialism," or even "communism") is irrelevant. However, to establish the regulation for sustainable global development will require cooperation between countries whose national interests and cultures often diverge. It will also require cooperation between groups of nations at different levels of economic development. The richer group of countries have many interests in common that diverge from those of the developing countries.

Although America's power and influence are already on the wane, it is still the central driving force of global economic and political activity. America is the Dr. Frankenstein who has produced the monster that now threatens the human species. The global free market policies that lie beneath the crisis are the child of the Washington Consensus, which was dominated by America, and therefore America bears a heavy burden of historical responsibility and future duty. Given that it leads the global system of political economy, it has the opportunity to grasp the nettle of leadership and build on its own traditions to lead the world toward cooperation and harmony; or it can pursue its own self-interest, wrapped in the cloak of ideology, and lead the world toward disaster.

Two of the most urgent issues that require resolution in the years ahead concern America, namely its relationship with China and its relationship with the Muslim world. Both can use their own rich traditions to contribute to a sustainable future for humanity in the twenty-first century, but the likelihood of their doing so will be greatly increased if America is able to develop an evolving pattern of constructive engagement with both. Destructive engagement, on the other hand, will lead to disaster. The second part of this book examines the contradictory character of capitalist globalization in relation to these centrally important issues, and the challenge they pose for the government and people of America in the years ahead.

Hands of God and Adam, detail from "The Creation of Adam," 1511 by Michelangelo di Lodovico Buonarroti Simoni (1475-1564) Sistine Ceiling, (fresco) (pre restoration) Vatican Museums and Galleries, Vatican City, Italy / The Bridgeman Art Library

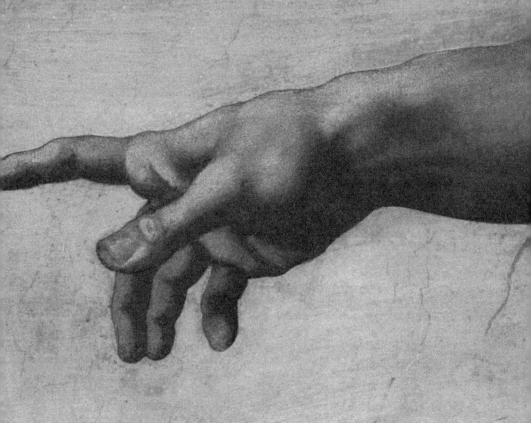

Part 2

Groping for a way forward: Conflict or cooperation?

Gradually, but unmistakably America is showing signs of that arrogance of power which has afflicted, weakened, and in some cases destroyed great nations in the past. In so doing, we are not living up to our capacity and promise as a civilized example to the world ... [The] great challenge in [America's] foreign relations is to make certain that ... the strand of humanism, tolerance and accommodation, remains the dominant one ... [The] stakes are high indeed: they include ... nothing less than the survival of the human race in an era when, for the first time in human history, a living generation has the power of veto over the survival of the next. It is [therefore] not merely desirable, but essential that the competitive instinct of nations be brought under control.

J. William Fulbright, *The Arrogance of Power*, 1965

Only an open and inclusive nation can become strong and prosperous, while a nation that shuts its door to the world is bound to fall behind ... Only by being inclusive, which calls for respect for different cultures and mutual learning, can we enrich and strengthen ourselves. We should boldly absorb and draw upon the achievements of the human society, including those of the capitalist countries, build on them and make innovations ... Only on the basis of mutual benefit and win-win progress can opening up endure and be conducive to the fundamental interests of all peoples and peace and prosperity of the world.

Premier Wen Jiabao, speech at the National University of Singapore,
November 2007

The Chinese emphasis on "harmony" can serve as a useful point of departure for the US–Chinese summits. In an era in which the risks of a massively destructive "clash of civilizations" are rising, the deliberate promotion of a genuine conciliation of civilizations is urgently needed. It is a mission worthy of the two countries with the most extraordinary potential for shaping our collective future.

Zbigniew Brzezinski, January 2009

"Islam" and "the West" are simply inadequate as banners to follow blindly ... [F]or future generations to condemn themselves to prolonged war and suffering ... without looking at interdependent histories of injustice and oppression, and without trying for common emancipation and mutual enlightenment seems far more wilful than necessary. Demonisation of the Other is not a sufficient basis for any kind of decent politics ... It takes patience and education, but it is more worth the investment than still greater levels of large-scale violence and suffering ... Those of us with a possibility for reaching people who are willing to listen—and there are many such people in the United States, Europe, and the Middle East, at least—must try to do so as rationally and patiently as possible.

Edward Said, "Collective Passion," in *The Observer*, September 16, 2001

Introduction

While the capitalist system has become global in scale, politics is mainly conducted at a national level. The mechanisms for the world's citizens to control the global capitalist system are weak, while the interests of individual nations are strong. Military force remains a central part of international relations. If human beings are to resolve the surging contradictions of capitalist globalization and avoid the looming disaster, it is urgently necessary to establish global mechanisms to contain the self-created monster of unconstrained global capitalism. However, to establish the regulation for sustainable global development requires cooperation between countries whose national interests often diverge. It also requires cooperation between groups of nations at different levels of economic development. The richer group of countries have many interests in common that diverge from those of the developing countries. America sits at the center of this drama. The central challenge in establishing global regulation of wild capitalism will be America's relationship with China and with the Muslim world.

BETWEEN them China and the Muslim world contain over two-fifths of the world's population. China's rise is a central fact of political economy in the twenty-first century. Its population is around 1.3 billion, and most Chinese live in a single country. At the start of the twenty-first century there were also 1.3 billion Muslims, but unlike the Chinese the Muslims are spread much more evenly across the world. There are around 900 million in 57 independent Muslim states, and 400 million in over 100 communities in the rest of the world. Although they are dispersed across many countries, they have common beliefs that give them a united perspective on some key issues. The way in which America interacts with these two giant civilizations will be central to the possibility of a sustainable path of global development in the early twenty-first century. American foreign policy has been wracked by intense debate about whether to engage in a peaceful or a confrontational fashion with both China and the Muslim world. The way in which America's international engagement is resolved will determine the nature of capitalist globalization in the twenty-first century and the possibility for a sustainable future for mankind.

In recent years the triangular relationship between America, China, and the Muslim world has been through complicated twists and turns. When George W. Bush's administration came to power it seemed likely that it would engage with China in a hostile fashion. Instead, America's confrontational engagement with the Muslim world over a long period stimulated anti-American Islamic terrorism, which culminated in the "blowback" of the attacks of September 11, 2001. This led America to adjust radically its policies toward China and seek a more constructive engagement in the pursuit of what came to be viewed as America's "'war" with "Islamic terrorism." However, the path that America pursues in its relationship with

China as that country's rise continues, and its long-term relationship with the Muslim world, is still unresolved.

2.1 AMERICA

Despite the fact that the zenith of American power has already passed, America sits at the center of the global political economy. The global free market policies that lie beneath the comprehensive global system crisis are the child of the Washington Consensus, which was driven by America. The Social Darwinist policies that America has promoted globally have produced profound contradictions within America itself as well as in the relationship between America and the rest of the world. America bears a heavy burden of historical responsibility. It has the opportunity to grasp the nettle of leadership and build on its own traditions to lead the world toward cooperation and harmony, or it can pursue its own self-interest, wrapped in the cloak of ideology, and lead the world toward disaster. Two of the most urgent issues that require resolution both concern America, namely its relationship with China and its relationship with the Muslim world. Both can use their own rich traditions to contribute to a sustainable future for humanity in the twenty-first century, but the likelihood of their doing so will be much greater if America is able to develop an evolving pattern of constructive engagement with both of them, and if they, in their turn, are able to engage in an evolving pattern of constructive engagement with America. Destructive engagement, on the other hand, will lead to disaster.

AMERICA'S DOMINANCE OF GLOBALIZATION

The high point of America's global dominance has passed. However, America still sits at the center of the global economy as humanity enters the most critical phase in its history. It has benefited enormously from capitalist globalization. America has less than five percent of the world's population, but it accounts for 27 percent of global manufacturing output. In 2006 North American firms accounted for 170 of the *Fortune 500* companies (ranked by sales revenue). America's share of the total value of global stock markets rose from 33 percent in 1990 to 42 percent in 2005. In 2007 there were 184 American firms in the *FT 500* (ranked by market capitalization), accounting for over two-fifths of the total market capitalization of *FT 500* firms. America accounts for 31 percent of global household consumption, and 34 percent of global personal wealth. It accounts for over two-fifths of the world's top 1,250 firms ranked by R&D expenditure (the 'Global 1250'), which constitute the core of global technological progress. Within the Global 1250 there are 336 firms in the IT hardware, software, and computer services sector. Information technology is by far the most important industrial sector; its products are at the core of the global business revolution in every sector, from soft drinks and beer to commercial aircraft and advanced weaponry. Of the 336 IT firms in the Global 1250, no less than 219 (65 percent) are headquartered in America. In other words, America is home to the "brain" of capitalist globalization.

AMERICA'S SOCIAL DARWINIST IDEOLOGY

During the period of capitalist globalization, Social Darwinist ideology has underpinned American support for the free market both within America and in the international economy. A large fraction of Chinese and Muslims view America's international relations as having been ideologically driven, and Social Darwinist ideas do indeed run deep in America. The idea that the pursuit of individual self-interest serves the interests of the whole of human society appeared to receive strong support from Darwin's theory of human evolution, as expressed in his *Descent of Man*, first published in 1871. The idea of the survival of the fittest provides the intellectual foundation for Social Darwinism, which argues that aggression is the key instinct of all animals, including human beings. It views competition between members of the same species as a fundamental driver of evolution. In the late nineteenth century Darwin's ideas were seized upon by American social thinkers such as Herbert Spencer, and for half a century Social Darwinism became the dominant American political philosophy. Social Darwinists advocated deregulation and unconstrained individual competition. For them, freedom properly understood meant the "abnegation of state power and a frank acceptance of inequality." Social Darwinists regarded the true realm of freedom as "the liberty to buy and sell where and how we please, without interference from the state."

Under the impact of the Great Depression in the 1930s and post-war construction in the 1940s and 1950s, Social Darwinism gradually lost its place as the mainstream political philosophy in America. From the 1960s onward, however, the growing influence of social thinkers such as Friedrich von Hayek and Milton Friedman helped to propel the philosophy into the mainstream once again. The dominant attitude to freedom in America once again equated freedom with individual choice in the marketplace and minimal interference from the state.

Hayek's ideas, especially those contained in his book *The Road to Serfdom* (1944), were a clarion call for conservatives to reclaim the word "freedom," which, in his view, had been usurped and distorted by socialists. For Hayek, the foundation of a good society was individual economic freedom. He believed that this was a unique product of Western civilization and the growth of the market economy over hundreds of years. It is this individualism which "from elements provided by Christianity and the philosophy of classical antiquity, was first fully developed during the Renaissance and has since grown and spread into what we know as Western European civilization—the respect for the individual man *qua* man, that is the recognition of his own views and tastes as supreme in his own sphere."

Milton Friedman did more than any other thinker to take Social Darwinist ideas into the mainstream of modern American political economy, especially through his book *Capitalism and Freedom* (1962). He considered that "narrowly materialistic interests dominate the bulk of mankind," that "one of the strongest and most creative instincts known to man" is the "attempt by millions of individuals to promote their own interests," and that the exercise of these instincts through the market has been the central force in human progress. Friedman viewed the freedom of the individual as the ultimate goal in judging social arrangements, and considered that individual economic freedom was the foundation of political freedom. He believed that the foundation of a good society was private property, and argued that the scope of government should be limited, confined to preserving law and order, enforcing private contracts, and fostering competitive markets. Friedman regarded the central feature of the market system of economic activity as the fact that it "prevents one person from interfering with another in respect of most of his activities."

Friedman acknowledged that the free market with minimal government intervention produces "considerable inequality of income and wealth." The ethical principle by which he justified the unequal distributional outcomes in a free market society is "to each according to what he and the instruments he owns produces." In Friedman's view, the inequality in a free market economy mainly "reflects differences in endowments, both of human capacities and property." Friedman considered that a fundamental tenet of a free society is the right of inheritance of property. He acknowledged that some people are fortunate to be born into better circumstances than others, and asks the reader to consider the imaginary case of four Robinson Crusoes marooned on desert islands. Three of them are on small and barren islands, while one of them is on a large and fruitful island. He writes: "Of course, it would be generous of the Crusoe on the large island if he invited the others to join him and share its wealth. But suppose he does not. Would the other three be justified in joining forces and compelling him to share his wealth with them?" Friedman answers emphatically that this would be an infringement of the freedom of the Crusoe on the large island: "The unwillingness of the rich Crusoe to share his wealth does not justify the use of coercion by the others." Friedman broadens the argument to a global scale: "Are we prepared to urge on ourselves or our fellows that any person whose wealth exceeds the average of all persons in the world should immediately dispose of the excess by distributing it equally to all the rest of the world's inhabitants? We may admire and praise such action when undertaken by a few. But a universal 'potlatch' would make a civilized world impossible."

The collapse of the Soviet Union reinforced Americans' confidence in the free market, and in the country's duty to lead the world toward this as a universal form of socio-economic organization. By the 1990s in America there was no serious intellectual challenge to the philosophy of the free market as the moral basis of the good society. Social Darwinist ideas reached a new apogee under President George

W. Bush. In the wake of September 11 the American government affirmed its duty to spread the moral principle of the free market across the whole world:

> The great struggles of the twentieth century between liberty and totalitarianism ended with a decisive victory for the forces of freedom—and a single sustainable model for national success: freedom, democracy, and free enterprise. Today, the US enjoys a position of unparalleled military strength, and great economic and political influence ... We seek to create a balance of power that favors human freedom ... The US will use this opportunity to spread the benefits of freedom across the globe ... We will make freedom and the development of democratic institutions key themes in our bilateral relations. (*National Security Strategy*, September 2002.)

The American government committed itself to "use this moment of opportunity to extend the benefits of freedom across the globe." In other words, September 11 was viewed as an opportunity to push forward, under the guise of a "War on Terrorism," American ideas of a new world order based on the American model. At the start of the twenty-first century the idea that the free market is a moral concept stood at the center of political discourse in America: "The concept of 'free trade' arose as a moral principle even before it became a pillar of economics. If you can make something that others value, you should be able to sell it to them. If others make something that you value you should be able to buy it. This is real freedom, the freedom for a person—or nation—to make a living." (*National Security Strategy*, September 2002.) In his speech to the West Point Military Academy in 2002, President Bush said: "Moral truth is the same in every culture, in every time, in every place." In his State of the Union Address in 2003, President Bush said: "The liberty we prize is not America's gift to the world, it is God's gift to humanity."

AMERICA'S GLOBALIZATION CHALLENGE

The central drive of American foreign policy in the era of globalization has been to open the global economy to free trade and the free movement of capital. America's wish for a global free market has been substantially granted. However, the contradictions of capitalist globalization are far greater than American policy-makers imagined. Many countries have a version of the same saying—"Beware lest your wish be granted."

Social contradictions

As consumers, Americans have benefited enormously from capitalist globalization, with an unprecedented fall in the real price of most goods and services. An important part of this fall was due to the decline in the real price of consumer goods attributable to greatly increased low-priced imports from developing countries.

However, as producers Americans faced greatly increased pressures. Ordinary Americans are increasingly skeptical of the benefits of globalization. They believe that the interests of American-based multinational corporations and their shareholders are divorced from the interests of ordinary citizens.

The unprecedented pace of technological change in this era, in particular the widespread application of information technology, has dramatically changed the nature of work across the whole spectrum of occupations. A vast array of traditional skills has disappeared in both manufacturing and services. For millions of Americans work has become increasingly homogenized as it has become based on the use of information technology: both bank employees and steel workers sit in front of the same computer screens, tapping the same keyboards. Technological change has replaced a wide swathe of occupations, both blue-collar and white-collar jobs that demanded modest skills, while demand for unskilled or low-skilled jobs in the service sector, such as restaurants, retail, and domestic help, surged.

In addition to the profound impact of technological change, the integration of global markets has had deeply contradictory results for American workers. The liberalization of capital markets has opened up a vast world of low-priced labor across the transition and developing countries, including skilled and unskilled manual labor, as well as scientists, engineers, and managers. In the BRIC countries alone, economic liberalization has added around 1.7 billion people of working age to the international labor market. Global labor markets have been integrated to some degree directly through increased international migration, but this has only been a small part of the integrative mechanism, since high-income countries have retained tight controls over immigration. Rather, the process of integration has mainly taken place indirectly, through the migration of capital to poor countries and through the export of goods and services from poor to rich countries. This has caused intense pressure for international equalization of wages and conditions of work; it is now increasingly being recognized in America that the "law of one price" operates in integrated global labor markets.

A wide range of occupations is susceptible to being outsourced from America to developing countries. Initially the most vulnerable occupations were those in manufacturing. However, the information technology revolution means that a much wider range of occupations is capable of being outsourced than most people initially imagined, including a wide range of service-sector activities. The threat to American occupational security exists at every level of skill and education. The only occupations that will be untouched by this revolution in the global labor market will be personal services, as opposed to impersonal services that can be delivered by wire. The number of Americans who feel that their jobs are threatened by foreign competition has grown greatly in recent years.

During the era of globalization, American workers have been forced to work longer hours, and to accept reduced rates of overtime pay and reduced company contributions to health insurance and pensions. There are 45 million Americans without health coverage, many of whom are full-time workers. American income disparity has greatly increased. The income share of the top ten percent of the American population was stable at around 33 percent from the 1960s to early 1980s, but thereafter it rose to around 44 percent in 2000–02, the same income share that they received in the 1920s and 1930s. The share of the top one percent of the distribution doubled from less than eight percent in the late 1960s and 1970s to around 16 percent at the end of the 1990s. Between 2000 and 2006, median American household income fell by three percent, while the share of corporate profits in GDP rose from seven percent to over 12 percent.

There is a growing discussion in America about the relationship between income, consumption, and happiness. It is now widely accepted that beyond an average per capita income of around $10,000 per annum, increased consumption produces no increase in happiness. In the 1940s Abraham Maslow's pioneering research concluded that there was a pyramid of human needs, at the base of which were basic needs such as food, water, and basic material comforts. Next were safety and security needs. Then came love and belonging, including the desire to feel accepted by the family, the community, and colleagues at work. After that came the need for esteem, both self-esteem and other people's respect and admiration. Finally, at the apex, came "self-actualization," at which point "people achieved the happiness that came from becoming all they were capable of becoming." At this level people might seek knowledge and aesthetic experiences for themselves and help others achieve self-fulfillment. These propositions have been confirmed by recent academic studies of happiness.

Increasing incomes in a free market economy may even contribute to absolute declines in happiness. If the free market determines the nature of transport, living, and working, then increased income may require long hours spent sitting alone inside a metal box on a strip of asphalt. This may in turn accentuate personal isolation and reduce well-being. The dramatic increase in the oil price in 2007–8 temporarily provoked extensive discussion about America's car-dominated pattern of urban living. The whole structure of American urban life, including residential and work patterns and the underdevelopment of public transport, as well as the mentality of Americans, is geared to the automobile. It will be extremely difficult to radically change the dominance of the motor vehicle in the American transport system.

The exercise of individual choice in the food industry may cause a reduction in personal well-being as incomes rise. During the era of globalization America experienced an alarming rise in obesity, which provided a salutary warning to other countries. The country's surgeon-general estimates that 61 percent of Americans are overweight and warns that there are now 300,000 obesity-related deaths per year. Around nine million Americans are morbidly overweight and ten million more are almost there, teetering on the edge. The associated public-health costs are estimated at $117 billion a year, with around $33 billion a year spent on weight-loss products and schemes. The American food industry spends around $4.5 billion each year to advertise its products, with children the prime target for advertising. The average American child watches over 20,000 TV advertisements for food products each year, and "the more television children watch, the more they eat." Children increasingly dictate family food choices in America: "Entire households are immersed in a miasma of one-dimensional sweet taste that reinforces juvenile preferences." However, the food industry has a powerful incentive to persuade children to eat more: "Fat is money. By creating heavier individuals who need more calories to feel satisfied and maintain their weight, the food industry is literally growing a bigger market for itself."

Violence

The resolution of the intensifying social contradictions facing America may not be peaceful. The country has, ever since its foundation, had a long history of social and political violence, beginning with violent conflict with America's indigenous people. Millions of Africans were violently enslaved and brought to North America. In the mid-nineteenth century America experienced the horrors of the Civil War, and between the Civil War and World War I there was intense local violence, closely related to the stresses of industrialization and urbanization. There was serious labor conflict during the Great Depression, often ending in violent confrontation.

After a period of relative calm after World War II, social and political violence escalated in the 1960s. There was massive rioting in Los Angeles (Watts), Detroit, and Newark, which resulted in around 100 people killed and thousands injured. Much of the center of Washington DC was burned down in 1968. One American President (John F. Kennedy) and one presidential candidate (Bobby Kennedy) were assassinated. The nation's civil rights leader, Martin Luther King, was also assassinated. A study of American violence published in 1970 concluded that in terms of total magnitude of strife, America ranked first among 17 Western democracies. It concluded that "violence may be our national nemesis."

On April 19, 1993, federal forces from the FBI and the American army mounted a full-scale attack, including the use of tanks, on the headquarters of the Branch Davidian sect in Waco, Texas. The attack, codenamed "Show Time," took place after a 51-day siege following a raid by the Federal Bureau of Alcohol, Tobacco, and Firearms. Eighty-two Branch Davidians died in the attack, including 30 women and 25 children. None of the federal force died. The precise details of the attack, however, remain mired in controversy. Then on April 19, 1995, the anniversary of the Waco attack, the Alfred P. Murrah Federal Building in Oklahoma City was bombed, killing 168 people, including 19 children, and injuring over 800 people. Until 9/11 this was the deadliest act of terrorism on American soil, but it is an event which is still surrounded by intense controversy. Timothy McVeigh admitted to carrying out the attack; he was sentenced to death and executed in June 2001. McVeigh explained that his principal motive was "a counter-attack for the cumulative raids ... that federal agents had participated in over the preceding years (including, but not limited to Waco)." He regarded his attack as a form of warfare against the American state: "Bombing the Murrah Federal Building," he is quoted as saying, "was morally and strategically equivalent to America hitting a government building in Serbia, Iraq or other nations ... From this perspective what occurred in Oklahoma City was no different than what America rains down on the heads of others all the time ... The bombing of the Murrah Building was not personal, no more than when the Air Force, Army, Navy or Marine personnel bomb or launch cruise missiles against [foreign] government installations and their personnel."

America's gun culture and the associated violence have been endlessly debated. Recently a long legal battle took place in the Supreme Court about the interpretation of the right to possess firearms granted to American citizens in the Bill of Rights (1791), which states: "A well-regulated militia, being necessary to the security of a free State, the right of the people to keep and bear Arms, shall not be infringed." The case revolved around the issue of whether this right applies to individuals, or only to the collective right to bear arms in the National Guard or other state militia. In June 2008, the Supreme Court voted to strike down the District of Columbia's 32-year-old ban on handguns. It affirmed that American citizens have a constitutional right as individuals to keep and bear arms. There are estimated to be around 220 million handguns in America, and over two-fifths of the adult population own at least one gun. In the third quarter of the twentieth century around 800,000 Americans died from gunshots; almost one-half of the deaths were homicides, and the rest mainly suicides. In 1996 two people in New Zealand were murdered using handguns, 13 in Australia, 15 in Japan, 30 in Britain, and 106 in Canada, compared with 9,390 in America.

America's violent culture extends to the treatment of criminals. America is the only Western democracy that permits capital punishment, and 37 of its states currently permit the death penalty. Between 1976 and April 2008, 1,099 Americans were executed, including 405 in Texas alone, and in April 2008 there were 2,263 people on death row. America is also far more inclined than other OECD countries to imprison criminals. In 1998 there were 1.87 million people in American prisons. The American incarceration rate is around 1 in 170 people, eight to ten times greater that in western Europe. A further 3.95 million Americans are on parole, which yields a total population of around 5.8 million Americans under correctional supervision.

The impact of Hurricane Katrina in August 2005 shocked Americans. Civil order in New Orleans collapsed, with widespread looting and violence. It prompted much public debate about the fragility of American society and the possibility of social disorder in the face of an economic crisis or an ecological disaster. The social fabric of America will be sorely tested by the unfolding recession. In 2008 alone, 2.6 million Americans lost their jobs. A comprehensive social contract that rebuilds the welfare state and guarantees social security for all Americans is essential in order to ensure that the country survives the deep crisis with its social fabric intact.

Ecology

When the first European colonists arrived in North America, the vast territory may have had around 15–16 million native human inhabitants. The physical beauty and abundance of wildlife deeply impressed the colonists as they spread across the territory. Nineteenth-century writers such as Emerson, Thoreau, Whitman, and Catlin left lyrical accounts of America's natural environment.

In the 1830s, George Catlin wrote a series of letters from the Far West, where he spent many years among the native people, painting their portraits and the landscapes in which they lived. He wrote in wonder about the herds of bison, which "graze in countless numbers on these beautiful prairies." He marveled at the "endless variety of wild flowers," and "the abundance of delicious fruits": "Whilst wandering through the high grass, the wild sun-flowers and voluptuous lilies were taunting us by striking our faces; whilst here and there in every direction, were little copses and clusters of plum trees and gooseberries, and wild currants, loaded down with their fruit; and amongst them, to sweeten the atmosphere and add a charm to the effect, the wild rose bushes seemed planted in beds and in hedges, and everywhere were decked out in all the glory of their delicate tints, and shedding sweet aromas to every breath of the air that passed over them" (George Catlin, *North American Indians*).

American capitalism has waged a relentless war upon the natural environment, both inside and outside the country. Herman Melville's *Moby-Dick* is arguably the most powerful of all American literary works. It bursts out of the confines of domestic American life. The world's oceans form its vast canvas, and the world's largest living creature its central subject matter. The story of a mighty industrial, profit-seeking machine (the whaling ship) obsessively driven by its captain to pursue and destroy the most famous of all creatures in the natural world stands as a poignant warning to human beings in the age of globalization. The object pursued destroys its pursuer. Few works of art have better captured the self-destructive potential of human nature. The whaling industry was in the forefront of American capitalism's assault on the natural environment:

> [T]hese Nantucketers ... first caught crabs and quohogs in the sand; grown bolder, they waded out with nets for mackerel; more experienced, they pushed off in boats and captured cod; and at last, launching a navy of great ships on the sea, explored this watery world ... and in all seasons and all oceans declared an everlasting war with the mightiest animal mass that has survived the flood ... And thus have these naked Nantucketers ... overrun and conquered the watery world ... two-thirds of this terraqueous world are the Nantucketer's. For the sea is his; he views it, as Emperors own empires.
>
> Herman Melville, *Moby-Dick*

Alongside its destruction of the natural environment, America has long had a powerful ecological movement. In the person of Rachel Carson it had arguably the most powerful of all twentieth-century advocates for the importance of the natural environment for human beings' spiritual well-being:

To stand at the edge of the sea, to sense the ebb and flow of the tides, to feel the breath of a mist moving over a great salt marsh, to watch the flight of shore birds that have swept up and down the surf lines for untold thousands of years, to see the running of old eels and the young shad to the sea, is to have knowledge of things that are as near eternal as any earthly life can be. These things were before ever man stood on the shore of the ocean and looked out upon it with wonder; they continue year in, year out, through the centuries and the ages, while man's kingdoms rise and fall.

Rachel Carson, *Under the Sea-Wind*

Today over four million Americans are members of the country's leading environmental groups, including the World Wildlife Fund, the Nature Conservancy, the National Wildlife Federation, the Sierra Club, the National Parks, the Conservation Association and the National Audubon Society. The American government has passed important legislation to protect the environment, including the US Wilderness Act (1964) and the US Endangered Species Act (1973). However, these have not altered fundamentally the "locked-in" character of America's pattern of economic development.

Despite the increased awareness of ecological issues, the exercise of individual consumer freedom with minimal environmental consideration has led to America having an economy that is extraordinarily profligate in the use of its own and the rest of the world's natural resources. The WWF estimates that between 1975 and 2003 America's annual ecological footprint (see note 4) per person rose by 38 percent, compared with 31 percent in the EU, 14 percent in the middle-income countries, and just eight percent in low-income countries. In 2006 America's annual ecological footprint amounted to 9.6 global hectares per person, twice that for the EU, 4.3 times the global average, and twelve times that for low-income countries. Within its overall ecological footprint, America's footprint for built-up land is six times the global average; for carbon dioxide emissions it is 5.3 times the global average; and for grazing land it is 3.3 times the global average. America has a large "ecological deficit," using 4.8 global hectares per person more than it has available to it within its own territory. A large fraction of its ecological footprint is provided from outside its own territory. In ecological terms this is America's "ghost acreage."

Edward Wilson of Harvard University is one of the world's most influential writers on ecology. In his view, in order for the rest of the world to reach the American level and style of consumption, with existing technologies, would require four planet earths. The present trajectory of capitalist development will take the rest of the world increasingly toward America's pattern. If this trajectory continues, then even the most optimistic projections, with moderate increases in population, food and fiber consumption, and carbon dioxide emissions, suggest that by 2050 humanity will require resources at double the rate at which the earth can generate them. This degree of overshoot would risk not only the loss of biodiversity, but also damage the ability of ecosystems to provide the resources and services upon which humanity depends.

Energy and the environment

During the three decades of capitalist globalization America has remained locked into its pattern of development, dictated by the workings of the free market and the primacy of individual freedom to choose. This has resulted in a reinforcement of its position as by far the world's largest consumer of primary energy. This in turn has had large implications for its international relations.

Although America has less than five percent of the world's population, it accounts for 21 percent of the world's primary energy consumption. Between 1990 and 2005 America's total energy use rose by more than 21 percent. In 2005 America consumed 7,893 kg (oil equivalent) of energy per person, compared with 3,961 kg in the eurozone, 1,486 kg in middle-income countries, and 486 kg in low-income countries. The share of net imports in American energy consumption rose from 14 percent in 1990 to 30 percent in 2005. During the last 30 years America's dependence on oil imports in particular has increased rapidly. Oil accounts for over two-fifths of total American primary energy consumption, and transport accounts for around two-thirds of the country's oil consumption. America's oil production fell from 8.4 million barrels per day in 1990 to 7.2 million in 2004, while its oil consumption rose from 17.7 million barrels per day to 20.5 million barrels in the same period. Net oil imports rose from 45 percent of total consumption in 1994 to 58 percent in 2004, and the prospects are for a further increase in America's dependence on oil imports.

These developments have grave implications for American energy security, which has become a critically important issue in American foreign policy. They have become fundamentally important in America's relationship with the Muslim world and form an increasingly important part of its relationship with China, each of which will be examined in detail later.

The freedom of Americans to own motor vehicles for private use and for commercial transport is at the root of the country's addiction to oil. In 2006 America had 814 motor vehicles per 1000 people, compared with 604 in the EU, 66 in middle-income countries and nine in low-income countries. Since 1985, due to the proliferation of large minivans and SUVs, the fuel economy of American vehicles has fallen from around 30 miles per gallon for new vehicles in 1985 to 29 miles per gallon in 2006. The proportion of American households with more than three cars rose to over one-third, facilitated by the falling real price of vehicles and the easy availability of auto loans. The average distance driven by Americans has risen by 80 percent in the past two decades. In June 2006, petrol cost just 60 cents per liter in America, compared with $1.60–1.70 in the EU. It is more accurate to describe America as addicted to the car than addicted to oil *per se*. The entire American pattern of urban residence and daily life, as well as the country's individualistic psychology, is intimately connected with the fact that Americans believe they have a right freely to own and drive cars.

America's profligate use of oil is important not only for the country's energy security, but also for its interaction with the rest of the world over global warming. It is locked into a growth pattern that uses fossil fuels as the main source of primary energy. America produces 22 percent of global carbon dioxide emissions. Its level of emissions rose by 23 percent between 1990 and 2004, accounting for one-fifth of the total global increase. The rise was largely due to the increase in the number of motor vehicles and the distance traveled per person. Between 1983 and 2007 the total mileage traveled by American vehicles on the country's roads increased from 1.6 trillion miles to 3 trillion miles. America consumes over 1,600 liters of petrol per capita annually compared with 250 liters in Europe. America's per capita emissions of carbon dioxide (20.6 tonnes) are 23 times those in low-income countries (0.9 tonnes), over five times those in middle-income countries (4.0 tonnes), and 2.5 times those in the eurozone (8.2 tonnes).

Over the first six years of his administration President George W. Bush denounced fuel economy standards as "a drain on the US economy and a threat to the safety of American drivers." America was not prepared to sign up to the Kyoto Protocol unless matching action was taken by the world's poorest countries. The Bush administration increased the resources allocated to alternative fuels and more efficient fuel use technologies, but failed to introduce any measures that might significantly reduce energy consumption in the short term.

After 2006 attitudes shifted rapidly among the American public and American business leaders. Several individual states announced their own plans to limit carbon dioxide production, and in May 2007 President Bush astonished the world by announcing that he had been persuaded by new scientific evidence on global warming. He pledged to help establish a new framework on greenhouse gases when the Kyoto Protocol expires in 2012, and he accepted the need for a long-term global goal for reducing greenhouse gases. America participated fully in the UN meeting on climate change in Bali in December 2007. Although it was heavily criticized for blocking agreement over precise targets for emissions, America accepted that the scientific evidence for global warming was unequivocal, and signaled its willingness to work within the UN framework to establish a successor to the Kyoto Agreement. At the G8 summit in July 2008 President Bush signed a communiqué in which the G8 leaders agreed to "consider and adopt ... the goal of achieving at least a 50 percent reduction in global emissions by 2050, recognizing that this global challenge can only be met by a global response." The American position on global warming, however, was still far more cautious than that of Europe. Moreover, America placed great emphasis on the importance of developing countries contributing to measures to contain global warming. Nevertheless, in the final years of the Bush administration tremendous changes took place in the American government's position on global warming, suggesting that America recognized the necessity for cooperating with the global community to resolve one of the critical problems facing humanity.

Finance

The achievement by America of its goal of establishing a global level playing field in trade and investment, and the removal of the constraints on financial markets, has resulted in a massive financial crisis, which has quickly moved into the real economy. The consequences for personal and national finances in America are immense.

During the 30 years of wild globalization, ordinary Americans watched in wonder as they became steadily wealthier. The process, however, went into a shocking reversal in late 2007. In the following year their household wealth shrank drastically, and was poised to shrink much further as the decline in asset prices continued. National self-confidence, which had grown steadily during the era of globalization, was punctured. The national mood had altered dramatically. The global financial crisis will have a deep impact on the daily lives and outlook of Americans. The decline in banks' ability to extend personal credit, and the attempt by Americans to rebuild their household wealth through increased saving, will produce a profound change in American households' behavior after three decades of ever-increasing debt. It is highly likely that America will enter a deep recession, perhaps even matching that of the 1930s; as we have seen, by the end of 2008 the American government had exhausted the conventional tools of economic policy. The official "policy" rate of interest was almost at zero, and the government had introduced a vast package to recapitalize the country's banks. However, the economy was in free fall.

America entered the recession with unprecedentedly large public and private debt. Between 1990 and the middle of 2008, total public and private debt rose from around 155 percent of GDP to almost 356 percent. American households, in other words, entered the recession in a perilous position. The average level of household debt had risen from around 75 percent of annual disposable income to almost 130 percent on the eve of the crisis. The increase in household debt was closely connected with the bubble in the American housing market, which greatly increased household wealth and the value of the collateral against which households could borrow. This is a tremendous burden to carry into the recession. The destructive unwinding of the global asset price bubble has already had damaging effects on the welfare of American citizens, and the effects were intensifying explosively in late 2008. By the end of the year it was estimated that the economy was contracting at an annualized rate of five percent. The total losses on risky assets were estimated to be in the range of $2.8–6.0 trillion. The S&P 500 index had fallen by 43 percent from its level in late 2007, while prices of both residential and commercial property were in free fall.

Americans and their political leaders may increasingly cast around for scapegoats for the reduced household wealth, increased economic insecurity, and deteriorating conditions of employment that face a substantial segment of the population.

In early December 2008 it was reported that America had lost 1.2 million jobs since the start of September, the largest three-month loss since the months immediately following the end of World War II. The job losses were widespread, as labor-shedding moved from the earlier focus on manufacturing and construction into the service sector. Moreover, for those in employment, the average length of the working week was shrinking. The number of people in part-time employment rose by 2.7 million in 2008, reaching 7.3 million in November. The median price of existing homes fell by 11.3 percent in October year-on-year, the biggest drop on record, and was widely expected to fall much further before hitting the bottom. The "roll rate" on mortgage repayments records the degree to which borrowers fall behind on their second and third payments and ultimately enter foreclosure. The national roll rate increased from an average of 12–15 percent in recent years to 30 percent in November 2008, reaching no less than 65–75 percent in Florida and California. The collapse of asset prices, including the stock market, has sharply reduced pensions for American retirees. Retail sales in October fell by 2.8 percent, the biggest drop on record.

During the period of capitalist globalization America has stood at the center of the world's financial system, and the US dollar has been at the center of America's dominance. That position is now under threat. The collapse of large segments of the "commanding heights" of the American financial system and its rescue by the government has deeply shocked all sections of the population. The prospect for the dollar is highly uncertain. In the early phase of the global financial crisis, international capital flowed into America in large quantities, in a mass "flight to safety," which helped to support the dollar. However, it is highly uncertain whether such inflows will continue at anything like their current level. If substantial flows of capital start to move out of the economy, there is a danger of a "rout of the dollar" that gathers speed in a vicious circle as international confidence in the American economy declines.

The wide variety of government interventions in response to the crisis is set to greatly expand the American budget deficit. By the end of 2008, taken together, the loans, investments and guarantees made by the Federal Reserve and the Treasury since the financial crisis began totaled $7.8 trillion, in addition to a pre-crisis debt of around $10 trillion. With assets approaching around $2.3 trillion and capital of less than $40 billion, the Federal Reserve increasingly resembled a public hedge fund, with leverage of more than 50:1. The American government's budget deficit increased from 1.2 percent of GDP in 2007 to a projected level of 2.9 percent in 2008. By the end of 2008 it was predicted that the budget deficit in 2009 could rise as high as 12.5 percent of GDP. The American government stands poised on a knife-edge. On the one hand, the measures taken may be unable to prevent a slide into recession and deflation. On the other hand there is a danger that in their efforts to kick-start the economy, the American government embarks on a path of monetary expansion that leads to high levels of inflation.

The euro is only ten years old. The population of the eurozone is 317 million, compared with 299 million in America. While America's GDP is 23 percent larger than the eurozone's, its exports are just 30 percent of those of the eurozone. After a difficult early life the euro has begun to establish itself as a credible reserve currency. In 2006 the value of euro notes in circulation exceeded that of dollar bills, and the euro also overtook the dollar as the main denomination for international debt issuance. The share of foreign exchange reserves held in euros has risen from around 19 percent in 1999 to almost 30 percent in 2007. The share of global foreign exchange reserves held in American dollars, meanwhile, declined from around 80 percent in the late 1970s to around 70 percent at the time of the euro's launch, falling to just over 60 percent at the end of 2007. Economists at the American National Bureau of Economic Research estimate that, if present trends continue, the euro could overtake the dollar as the leading currency for international foreign exchange reserves by 2022. A survey conducted at the end of 2008 reported that around 60 percent of the population of the main eurozone countries believe that the euro will overtake the dollar in importance within just five years. This possibility would be hastened by the admission of other countries to the eurozone. As the global crisis deepens, it is possible that more countries might seek shelter within the relative safety of the euro. The most important such admission would be Britain, which would bring the eurozone's GDP to the same size as America's and increase the gap in exports even further. It is possible also that Poland, Hungary, and Denmark might join at some point. Furthermore, the attractiveness of holding foreign exchange reserves in euros rather than dollars has increased due to the appreciation of the euro, which has risen from $0.83 per euro in October 2000 to $1.40 on December 30, 2008, having reached a high of $1.60 per euro in April 2008.

Although the *renminbi* (China's currency) is not fully convertible at present, it has long been made clear that eventually, when conditions are appropriate, it will become fully convertible and, when that happens, its role as a reserve currency is sure to grow. In the short term, there has been wide speculation that China has been slowly reducing the share of its foreign exchange reserves held in US dollars. Also there has for many years been discussion of the possibility over the long term of an Asian Currency Unit emerging in the same way that the euro emerged, after long years of economic integration. Twelve Asian countries, including India and South Korea, have increasingly traded as a bloc, with a gradually strengthening network of free trade agreements and cross-investments, creating conditions similar to those in Europe which paved the way for the introduction of the euro. Although it is far from being a reality, discussion of this possibility was stimulated by the Asian financial crisis and could re-emerge in the face of the current crisis.

At the end of October 2007, the outgoing head of the IMF, Rodrigo Rato, warned that there was a risk that the American currency could suffer a dramatic fall that would shake confidence in American assets. This would have a major impact on America's position in the world. At the end of the Opec summit in December 2007, Hugo Chavez announced triumphantly that the "empire of the dollar is crashing." Kenneth Rogoff warned in more sober fashion at the end of December 2007:

"Americans will certainly find global hegemony a lot more expensive if the dollar falls off its perch … American voters, who are famously loath to increase taxes, might start to think harder about the real economic costs of their country's superpower status. In the absence of international government coordination, there is a danger that the fall in the value of the dollar will produce a one-way bet against the dollar as an attractive one for international financial institutions to make." America may find itself subjected to the kind of financial pressure that the American government and its financial institutions have exercised in the past toward other countries. The global "money tsunami" stemming from financial liberalization, conjured up in order to serve the interests of Wall Street, may yet flow back upon America itself.

Soft power

The early phase of capitalist globalization may well have increased America's soft power in the world (its ability to influence through non-military means). Its policies toward Israel, however, substantially weakened its soft power in the Muslim world, and its invasion of Iraq further eroded its soft power among Muslims. The Asian financial crisis greatly eroded its soft power in Asia. However, the global financial crisis has dramatically accelerated the decline in America's soft power. At international policy discussions, in universities, and in the popular media, it is no longer credible to argue for the virtues of the American-led unregulated free market. America's soft power can only be restored if its leadership fully recognizes the disastrous outcome of the path it has advocated for the past 30 years, and works in close partnership with the global community toward intelligent regulation of the market in the collective interest of all human beings.

2.2 AMERICA AND CHINA

America and China will be the most important actors in the global political economy in the first decades of this century. The prospects for global sustainable development hinge around the relationship between these two mighty forces. Despite their immense respective strengths, each of them has its own internal contradictions, brought about mainly by the impact of capitalist globalization on the two economies and societies, one aspect of which is their growing mutual economic integration. The combination of political stability under the leadership of the Chinese Communist Party with experimental economic system reform and opening up to the outside world has resulted in the most remarkable era of development the world has ever seen. However, China's deepening engagement with global capitalism has led to an explosive growth of inequality, a drastic deterioration in the physical environment, the harsh challenge of the global business revolution for large Chinese firms, widespread corruption, and deep challenges in reforming the financial sector. The two countries' growing interaction may yet end in terrifying conflict. The prospect, literally, of the end of the world, may however encourage the evolution of a cooperative relationship based on enlightened self-interest, which attempts to resolve the contradictions of capitalist globalization, in respect of their internal development, of their mutual relationship, and of their joint role in the international political economy. China and America can both gain greatly by cooperation to solve the global challenges produced by capitalist globalization, and working together to build the global institutions that are necessary to ensure a sustainable future for the human species.

America and China are of identical size, both occupying a land area of 9.6 million square kilometers. Each has a giant river that flows across the center of the country—the Chang Jiang ("Yangtse") in China, and the Mississippi ("Old Man River") in America—forming a central theme in each country's history and culture. However, China's population stands at over 1,300 million compared with just 300 million in America. The different levels of population in these vast territories is central to the two countries' respective patterns of long-term development. China has only been able to support such a huge population because the patterns of collective and state action that have evolved over millennia have permitted the country to develop intensive agriculture based on sophisticated water control. The filling up of America by immigrants and their descendants over the past two centuries, and their violent conflict with the indigenous inhabitants, is central to American culture.

From the late 1970s onward, under the leadership of the Chinese Communist Party's policy of "reform and opening up," China became ever more deeply integrated with the capitalist global economy. This enabled it to benefit from the "advantages of the latecomer," including access to international markets, capital, and technology, and to the release of its latent productive forces, which are based on a long history of capitalist development. It has produced remarkable economic growth and a transformation of the Chinese people's standard of living. However, the very success of China's engagement with global capitalism has resulted in profound challenges, including sharply rising inequality, declining energy security, worsening ecological damage, and serious difficulties in competing with the world's leading firms. China's leaders recognize these challenges, and resolving them is their central task in the years ahead. This is a "choice of no choice." Sustainable development in China requires that it must achieve balanced development and establish a "harmonious society."

As we have seen, capitalist globalization has also had a contradictory impact on America. It has brought great benefits to American firms, shareholders, and consumers. However, it has also brought profound challenges. These include a sharp increase in inequality, a decline in energy security, and an increased threat to the natural environment, the erosion of national identity among leading American firms, and serious financial instability. China's rise has increasingly become the scapegoat for America's difficulties arising from capitalist globalization.

Despite its universal character in the era of globalization, capitalism retains deep roots within individual nations, with their own national interests and internal contradictions that shape their international relations. The tension between the universal impulse of capitalism and the archaic structure of the nation state remains intense. The contradictory character of capitalist globalization is crystallized in Sino-American relations. There is a possibility of serious conflict between them, which would be a catastrophe for humanity. Faced with such a possibility, Sino-American cooperation is the only rational path for the leaderships of the two countries to pursue. They can benefit from mutual support in resolving the stresses that capitalist globalization brings to both countries and to the whole global community. However, the difference in their histories, culture, and population size, as well as their stages of development, creates severe difficulties in finding cooperative solutions.

If America and China were to come into violent conflict, both would fight under their respective national flags. Compared with most other nations, the national flag plays an exceptionally powerful role in America's public life. It is flown in front of people's homes and businesses, in concert halls and sports stadiums, in clubs, and in classrooms. The cult of the flag is a product of the American Civil War and the subsequent patriotic nation-building era. The American flag became almost a religious symbol, with many states passing laws prohibiting the "desecration of the flag." Johnny Cash's song "Ragged Old Flag" taps into the deep reservoir of American patriotic feeling associated with the flag: "So we raise her up every morning, take her down every night. We don't let her touch the ground, and we fold her up just right."

At dusk each day on Beijing's Tiananmen Square, thousands of people gather around the national flag. When people from other parts of China visit Beijing they love to come to watch the flag raising at sunrise and the flag lowering at sunset. Throughout China, the national flag has deep significance. In June 1990, China's People's Congress passed the National Flag Law, which prohibits the "desecration of the national flag." Here, a Chinese scholar recalls her relationship with the national flag:

We were told that the red color of the national flag symbolized the blood of countless revolutionary pioneers in history who had sacrificed their lives for the "standing-up" of the country. We were told the larger yellow star represents the leadership of the Chinese Communist Party and the four smaller stars surrounding the larger star represent the unity of people.

I was appointed the flag-raiser (*sheng qi shou*) of my school when I was in the second year of high school. It was an honor the school awarded to students who demonstrated high academic achievement as well as integrity.

When my teacher told me the task, I did not feel anything special about myself being a "good student" but an enormous amount of responsibility. It was my responsibility to raise the national flag every morning before class, lower it down every evening after school, look after it and keep it intact.

Every morning before class, the students of the whole middle school gathered together in the school's sports ground to attend the flag-raising ceremony. While my fellow classmates walked toward the sports ground, I would take the flag to the mast and tie it to the rope along the mast, waiting for the headmaster's announcement. When the national anthem began, I started to pull the rope and raise the flag. I needed to make sure that the flag reached the highest point of the mast at the final note of the national anthem. It took me a few times to get this right. Meanwhile, all the students stood solemnly, paying tribute to the flag. The ceremony was followed by the morning broadcast calisthenics.

After school, I would walk to the flag mast and lower the flag. I would fold it neatly and hand it back to the school office. This would be a one-person ceremony and I performed the duty on my own. A couple of times, I went straight back home after school, leaving the flag behind. Then at the dinner table, I suddenly realized I forgot to perform my duty and rushed to school to complete the task. I still remember the terrible feeling I had for my "mistake."

If it suddenly rained and I was in class, I would ask for permission to leave to "rescue" the flag from the rain.

If America and China can find a path toward mutual long-term understanding and benefit, the two flags can stand side by side as a symbol of international cooperation and their collective interests, instead of serving as a rallying point in conflict.

Photo: iStockphoto

EMBRYONIC CAPITALISM IN CHINA

Capitalist development has a long history in China. Prior to the early modern period China's embryonic capitalism was far more developed than that of Europe. China's capitalist development took place within the context of a powerful state that, in periods when the system functioned well, shaped the pattern of capitalist development in numerous ways to meet common social interests. China's policy-makers today can gain inspiration from this experience ("using the past to serve the present") as they struggle to find their own path through which to relate to capitalism's surging power and contradictory character. In its search for a way forward amid the immense difficulties that it confronts, China's leaders can turn to the country's own past for a source of inspiration. They can use this rich history to provide intellectual nourishment for the attempt to maintain the non-ideological approach of trying to "grope for a way forward," an approach that "seeks truth from facts," devising policies in a pragmatic, experimental fashion to solve concrete problems as they emerge.

The monumental work of the Cambridge historian of science, Joseph Needham, has shown that in many important fields China made great technological advances before the West. Recent research by many Chinese economic historians has shown that the traditional Chinese economy was far more dynamic over the long term than had formerly been thought. From the tenth to the thirteenth century China set out along the path of the "Second Industrial Revolution" well before Europe. A steady stream of significant technological advances was made thereafter up until the nineteenth century without China making the leap to a full-fledged modern Industrial Revolution.

China's technological developments were stimulated by powerful long-term growth in both domestic and international trade. The country was distinguished from the rest of the world by the fact that its central authorities established peaceful conditions over its vast territory. This provided merchants with the confidence to undertake trade that far exceeded that in other parts of the world until modern times. The normally peaceful environment over wide areas provided a powerful incentive to those with capital to undertake long-term investments. It also enabled the entire territory of China to form a single unified free trade area. In the nineteenth century there are estimated to have been a total of 35,000 "standard" and "intermediate" market towns. Above this dense local trading structure were a further 2,300 "central market towns," 932 cities and 26 "metropolitan trading systems," which in turn formed eight great economic systems. Among these were cities of a size and level of sophistication that far exceeded those of contemporary Europe until late in the latter's development. The degree of state interference in trade was small, in normal times confined mainly to taxation of a small number of key items. Therefore, long before any other comparable region of the world, China was able to enjoy for a long period the powerful stimulus of specialization, the division of labor, the rapid spread of best practice techniques, and powerful incentives to accumulate capital. The same processes that Adam Smith identified as being responsible for the wealth of the British nation were responsible also for the wealth of the Chinese nation.

The textile industry was much the most important industry in traditional China, as it was in early modern Europe. Towards the end of the Ming dynasty (1368–1644) cotton replaced hemp and silk as the principal fabric for daily wear. The spinning and weaving of cloth became the largest handicraft industry, and by the early nineteenth century there were around 60–70 million rural households engaged in these occupations as a subsidiary activity to farming. Around one-half of the cloth was for home consumption, and the other half for sale on the market. Of the marketed cloth, it is estimated that around 15 percent entered long-distance trade. By the early Qing dynasty (1644–1911), in the late seventeenth and early eighteenth centuries, there were many examples of large-scale businesses, many of them in the metallurgical industries, in both iron manufacture and mining, though there were also many examples of large-scale businesses in industries such as salt-making and trading, in porcelain, and in the manufacture of iron products.

It is estimated that in 1750, China's share of global manufacturing output stood at 33 percent, compared with 25 percent in the Indian subcontinent and just 18 percent in the West. In 1800, China's per capita GNP was $230 (at 1960 prices) compared with $150–200 for England and France. As late as 1798, Malthus declared China was the richest country in the world. In his description of Lord Macartney's mission to China in 1793, Sir George Staunton said that "in respect to its natural and artificial productions, the policy and uniformity of its government, the language, manners, and opinions of the people, the moral maxims, and civil institutions, and the general economy and tranquillity of the state, it is the grandest collective object that can be presented for human contemplation or research."

The traditional Chinese state combined a hereditary emperor with a large professional civil service, selected mostly by competitive examination. In addition there was a much larger number of members of the local "gentry" (*shenshi*), who dealt with many affairs in their local communities for which the official government had no time. The dominant ideology of bureaucratic rule was taught continuously through the examination system. Confucian ideology, the foundation of the examination system, was the key to the system's long-term stability and cohesion. Its overriding values were the primacy of order and stability, of cooperative human harmony, of accepting one's place in the social hierarchy, and of social integration. China's long tradition of political philosophy emphasized that the sole test of a good ruler was whether he succeeds in promoting the welfare of the common people. This, the most basic principle in Confucianism, has remained unchanged throughout the ages.

During the long periods in which it functioned effectively, the Chinese state provided a framework of law and order and protection for property rights, within which considerable long-term economic development took place, matched by corresponding technological progress. Chinese merchants were never able to develop the independence from the state that began to develop in increasingly autonomous towns in late medieval Europe. However, the control exercised by the state ensured that in the long periods when the central government functioned well, the cities provided a secure setting in which to conduct business, not only as a result of the peaceful environment, but also as a result of the state's protection of property rights. The vast quantities of merchandise could only be safely stored and traded because the corresponding contracts were legally enforceable, and because robbery of merchants' property was illegal. There were all manner of written commercial agreements, including shipping orders, bills of lading, promissory notes and contracts of sale, all of which were routinely circulated and legally enforceable.

In the traditional Chinese economy, exchange was almost always a monetary transaction. Marco Polo was fascinated by the control exercised by the central authorities over the supply of money. During the Yuan dynasty, the Mongol rulers presided over the first economy in the world to have paper money. The Chinese government has been aware for over two thousand years of the importance of money to a sound economy. One of its ongoing struggles was to ensure that the money supply was not debased, and that the quantity of money corresponded to current economic needs. The central government tried persistently to maintain central control over the amount and nature of currency in circulation. Detailed accounts from the early Qing dynasty show the way in which the central government closely monitored the money supply, frequently changing the specified weight and composition of coins in response to changing economic conditions, and attempting to maintain a constant exchange rate between copper cash and silver coinage.

The most important function of the traditional Chinese state was water control, for both drainage and irrigation, as well as for transport. Large water-control projects were almost exclusively public, organized either directly by the central government, or by lower levels of the bureaucracy. Water-control activities carried a grave moral imperative for government officials, with a similar responsibility as national defense. The central administration had important functions in inter-district water projects or projects with large expenses, such as Yellow River flood control, as well as building and maintaining the Grand Canal. The Grand Canal played a significant part in providing a transport system linking the productive south with the political north, engaging the attention of the best minds of China for more than ten centuries. Local government officials had an important role in water control. For almost any local water works beyond the capacity of the peasants of a single village, the magistrate intervened to mobilize forced labor, supervise the construction of local works, and regulate the use of water by rival villages. There was a heavy moral burden upon local officials to ensure that the innumerable local water-control activities were provided at an adequate level. The ideal magistrate was "an official close to the people, and flood and drought should be of as much concern to him as pain or sickness of his person."

Famine relief was a critically important state function in traditional China. Official famine prevention measures had been formulated as early as the Song dynasty (AD 960–1279). They included famine investigation, providing relief funds, supplying relief grain, controlling prices, and strengthening and rebuilding production. The detailed and formalized procedures for combating famine were only possible thanks to the sophistication, centralization, and stability of the Chinese bureaucratic system. Many of the measures adopted anticipate the analysis of famine made by modern economists, including use of the market wherever possible. From very early on, China's bureaucrats were aware of the dangers that speculation posed for the livelihoods of ordinary people. As early as in the Warring States Period (475–221 BC) the government held that fluctuations in the price of grain should be kept within a certain range for the benefit of both production and distribution. Marco Polo described the way in which the emperor purchased grain during times of plenty, accumulating "vast quantities of corn and every kind of grain and stores them in huge granaries," and when crops failed "releases enough for all … throughout all parts of his empire."

The Qing government established a vast network of "evernormal granaries" across the country in order to stabilize grain prices. In addition to maintaining emergency reserves, the purpose of the evernormal granaries was to cushion the impact of seasonal price fluctuations by buying up grain immediately after the harvest, when prices were low, and reselling it at a low price during the lean period before the new harvest came in. The spring sales and autumn purchases by the evernormal granaries were supposed to even out prices by compensating for the weakness of the private sector or by competing with it when it tended to take advantage of and speculate on seasonal and/or regional price differentials. The sale of public grain became one of several strategies available to the state to combat a subsistence crisis.

The Chinese state strongly encouraged the development of the traditional market economy. The state stepped in when markets failed, not only in respect of immediate growth issues, but also in relation to the wider issues of social stability and cohesion. It nurtured and stimulated commerce but refused to allow commerce, financial interests, and speculation to dominate society. Behind the edifice of authoritarian imperial rule was a pervasive morality based on the necessity of all strata of society observing their duties in order to sustain social cohesion, to achieve social and political stability, and to ensure social sustainability. When these functions were operating effectively there was "great harmony" (*da tong*), a prosperous economy, and a stable society. When they were operating poorly there was "great turmoil" (*da luan*), economic retrogression, and social disorder.

If by the "Third Way" we mean a creative symbiotic interrelationship between state and market, then we can say that China practiced its own "Third Way" for two thousand years. This was the foundation for its hugely impressive long-term economic and social development. The Chinese "Third Way" was not simply an abstract set of rules about intervening with the market, but was a complete philosophy that combined comprehensive analysis of concrete ways of both stimulating and controlling the market, with a carefully thought-out system of morality for rulers, bureaucrats, and ordinary people. When the system worked well, the philosophical foundation was supplemented by non-ideological state actions to try to solve practical problems that the market could not solve. Confucianism nurtured a deeply developed concept of duty, which was considered to be the foundation of collective action and social prosperity. The fact that the system went through regular cycles when these principles were poorly observed, rulers and bureaucrats were corrupt, and the economy and society foundered, should not blind us to the underlying coherence and lasting benefit from this integrated system of philosophy and public action.

China under Chairman Mao

From the mid-nineteenth century to the late 1940s, China endured almost 100 years of political turmoil. A substantial degree of capitalist modernization took place within and around the Treaty Ports, where extraterritoriality provided relative security for capitalists. However, the overall pace of economic growth was painfully slow, and for long periods the country was in the throes of either civil war or war against an invading foreign army. In the 1940s China was still a poor, backward country. In 1949 the Chinese Communist Party (CCP) seized power, and Chairman Mao Tse-tung led the party until his death in 1976. In the early years after the revolution, the party allowed a mixed economy in the cities, and in the countryside it allowed private agriculture alongside the development of mutual aid institutions to meet people's needs in health, education, and finance. However, in 1953, amid intense inner-party struggle, Chairman Mao led an ideological push toward "socialist transformation" and away from the subtle balance between state and market that had characterized China's political economy for two millennia. By 1956 most farmers had entered collective farms, most of the industrial means of production had been nationalized, most prices were under direct state control, foreign assets had been expropriated, and international trade was strictly regulated. For the next two decades the market economy was driven underground. Indeed, during the Cultural Revolution capitalism was likened to a "dog in the water," to be "beaten with a stick and drowned."

Chairman Mao believed that under the leadership of the communist party it would be possible to build a non-capitalist, humane society which provided an opportunity for the whole population to fulfill their human potential. It was a philosophy that was powerfully driven by the intention to restrict drastically the population's "negative" freedoms to act in accordance with their individual wishes free of external restriction, while providing the maximum equality of opportunity for citizens to achieve their "positive freedoms." Under Chairman Mao's leadership the explicit goal of the party was to lead society toward the goal of communism, beyond even the socialist stage.

From the mid-1950s through to the mid-1970s, China made great progress in many key aspects of social and economic development. The growth rate of national product was faster than in most developing countries, and in normal times the mass of the people enjoyed a high degree of livelihood security. Most impressive of all, the country achieved enormous advances in health and education. By the mid-1970s, China's levels of infant mortality and child death rates had fallen to exceptionally low levels compared with other developing countries. The system also provided a high degree of security, drastically reducing the age-old fear of an unforeseen personal, natural or economic disaster that was the reality for every farm family and for a large fraction of the urban workforce in pre-revolutionary China. These achievements were widely applauded by Western scholars as evidence that redistributive policies could enable low-income countries to achieve high levels of basic needs long before average per capita incomes had risen to high levels.

The Maoist period also resulted in deeply problematic outcomes. Diversity of thought was crushed, as large numbers of people were imprisoned for their political views. Freedom of cultural expression was dramatically narrowed, causing large-scale damage to people's welfare. The intense political struggles to limit social inequality caused immense suffering to innumerable people. Although growth rates were high, they were achieved in a highly inefficient way, with slow technological progress, a long-run fall in capital productivity, and stagnation in average per capita incomes after the mid-1950s. Apart from improvements in consumption of a narrow range of consumer durables (the "four big goods"—watches, bicycles, radios, and sewing machines), per capita consumption of most other items either stagnated or declined. Although basic needs indicators improved greatly, the proportion of the population in absolute poverty remained at around 30 percent in the mid-1970s, totaling around 270 million people, compared with around 190 million in 1957. The utopian attempt to leap into a communist society during the Great Leap Forward resulted in a colossal man-made disaster: work incentives eroded, production schedules were wrecked by the focus on political struggle, and ill-conceived schemes of capital construction (notably the massive movement to extend the amount of irrigation, and the ill-fated "backyard iron and steel campaign") caused immense waste. The result was an estimated collapse in national output of around 35 percent from 1958 to 1962. The collapse in farm output caused the biggest famine of the twentieth century, with as many as 30 million "excess deaths."

Under Chairman Mao the Chinese people paid a high price for the attempt to suppress market forces completely, to cut the country off from the global economy and society, to drastically constrain the dimensions of inequality, to eliminate material incentives, to radically limit cultural freedom, and to lead society in wild, nationwide mass movements. From the late 1970s on, China put into place policies of experimental economic reform and opening-up ("groping for stones to cross the river"), under tight political control by the Chinese Communist Party. However, few people in the West believed that a dynamic market economy could exist under the Chinese Communist Party. Most considered that capitalism was fundamentally incompatible with rule by the party. China's cautious, experimental approach, which involved a large role for the state in regulating the market, ran counter to the philosophy of the Washington Consensus. By the late 1980s, the mainstream of Western commentators considered that China's reforms had failed. Anti-communist pro-reform Chinese intellectuals who left their country were welcomed in leading American universities as the brave harbingers of a better world that was about to come into being. The Tiananmen events of 1989 appeared to confirm that "socialism with Chinese characteristics" could not achieve successful modernization.

In the wake of the Tiananmen events of 1989, and in the face of the collapse of Soviet communism, the near-universal judgment in the West was that the Chinese Communist Party could not survive much longer. Indeed, in the immediate aftermath of Tiananmen, mainstream Western opinion considered that communist rule in China would be ended within a few months. The mainstream of Western opinion believed that the Soviet Union under President Gorbachev was pursuing the correct path to reform of a communist system of political economy, with a "Big Bang" of openness in the political system (*glasnost*) providing the necessary precondition for a "Big Bang" to restructure the economic system (*perestroika*). When President Gorbachev visited his Chinese counterpart Deng Xiaoping in May 1989, the two men were unable to leave the Great Hall of the People by the front exit due to the teeming protests on the square in front of the building. Thousands of student protesters dropped little glass bottles (*xiao ping*) as a silent protest against Deng Xiaoping. Gorbachev basked in Western media adulation for initiating the self-destruction of the "evil empire," and was feted by President Reagan and Margaret Thatcher, the British Prime Minister. China's leaders, by contrast, were vilified in the West.

In fact Gorbachev's reform policies in the Soviet Union, which had been loudly applauded by Western commentators, destroyed a functioning system of political economy, albeit one that was functioning a long way from its full potential. Far from it being necessary that the Soviet economy collapse, the Soviet system actually contained immense possibilities for judicious reforms to produce accelerated growth and great advances in living standards. Instead, Gorbachev's reforms and those of his successor, President Boris Yeltsin, which were also loudly applauded by the mainstream of Western social science, ushered in a disastrous decade of "*katastroika*," in which a small group of people looted the economy during the period of "wild privatization," while the living standards of the mass of ordinary citizens collapsed, resulting in deep psychological trauma, accompanied by an unprecedented peacetime rise in mortality and decline in life expectancy. President Gorbachev is now reduced to the humiliating role of appearing in advertisements for Louis Vuitton luxury goods. One can only wonder at his thoughts as he looks at the advertisements.

In China, by contrast, against all expectations from the mainstream of Western social scientists, under the leadership of the Chinese Communist Party (with around 74 million members), the country has become the most dynamic part of the whole global economy. The Chinese Communist Party penetrates the Chinese bureaucracy deeply. The combined structure constitutes the "system" that has been at the heart of China's successful modernization since the 1970s, and which is the heir to the traditional Confucian bureaucratic structure. Once people are accepted into the system, advancement through the strict hierarchy of ranks is based on comprehensively demonstrated ability, including technological skills, personal character, and judgment. Those within the system are expected to observe high professional standards and accept strict discipline. At every level there is a continuous process of education in the acquisition of professional skills, as well as in a broader understanding of China's development challenges, both domestically and internationally. As in traditional times, the model official works formidably hard for only a modest income to serve the public interest, and does so at the expense of family life, and even in the midst of personal adversity. Unlike in the West, where policy-makers often lose their positions after elections, the absence of a multi-party system means that senior Chinese officials all have deep experience developed over a whole lifetime spent working within the system, which typically means that they have greater experience and professional expertise in the area for which they are responsible than their elected or politically appointed Western counterparts possess.

After the death of Chairman Mao, China's public policy returned to a non-ideological, pragmatic state, which had deep roots in Chinese history. It produced remarkable results. The growing impact of market forces, and increasing integration with the global economy, produced one of the most extraordinary periods of growth the world has ever seen, and the contrast with the period of Maoist planning was dramatic. China's policy-makers achieved this remarkable result through cautious, experimental engagement with the market economy, both domestically and internationally. They resisted constant hectoring from the Washington Consensus institutions and their many supporters within China, who urged China's policy-makers to move rapidly toward a "normal" market economy, in which there are no state-owned enterprises, in which there is no state industrial policy, and no restrictions on foreign direct investment, and in which there is a freely floating exchange rate and capital can flow freely into and out of the country. Those who opposed these views were labeled "hardliners" and ridiculed for their lack of understanding of modern economics.

China's "rise" and Russia's "fall" constitutes a comprehensive refutation of the ideas of the mainstream of Western social science, as embodied in the Washington Consensus institutions.[7] The judgment of the herd, the mainstream Western conventional wisdom, was wrong, just as it was to be wrong in its judgment about the consequences of the deregulation of financial markets. This judgment was bound within the narrow, analytical framework of mainstream social science as it had developed since the 1960s, a framework which had largely eviscerated the role of history, psychology, philosophy, culture, literature, and social structure from social analysis. It eschewed fieldwork investigation of the daily reality of the economy within firms and among individual consumers. Instead, it aimed at creating a "science" of society to stand alongside the natural sciences. Its practitioners considered that they were engaged in testing "theories" in the same way as natural scientists.

Social science came to be dominated by mathematical models, obsessed with quantification based on the correlation of measurable variables ("econometrics"). Data were selected to reflect an imaginary world as the social scientists wished it to be, rather than investigating in an open-minded fashion, with diverse analytical tools, of which econometrically based quantification is just one, the messy reality that is the real material of social science. This pseudoscientific approach came to dominate research not only in economics departments, but also in sociology, economic history, political science, business schools ("management science"), and, even, the study of the mind, in the shape of the modern "science" of psychiatry. The mainstream of the new social "science" constructed a stultifying and boring abstraction from reality. The dying breed of university scholars who thought differently were ridiculed as "unscientific." Young students who thought in a different fashion either never entered the social sciences or soon left them.

If we are to judge the value of theories by their power to predict, then we must conclude that the mainstream of Western social science failed abysmally in the era of capitalist globalization.

From 1990 to 2004 China's GDP growth rate averaged 10.3 percent per annum, compared with 4.1 percent among developing countries as a whole and 2.6 percent for high-income countries. China rose from the world's seventh largest producer of manufacturing output in 1990 to the third largest in 2005, accounting for almost one-fifth of the total global increase in manufactured output, and it rose from the world's 28th largest exporter in 1980 to the third largest in 2005. Its export growth was critically important in sucking in as many as 150 million low-skilled rural workers into non-farm employment, which made a large contribution to poverty reduction. Global corporations view China as central to their long-term strategy; in

2002 China overtook America as the country with the largest FDI inflows. Over the past two decades China's indigenous large enterprises have undertaken large-scale evolutionary institutional change; they have grown rapidly, absorbed modern technology, learned how to compete in the marketplace, and a large group of them has floated on international stock markets. The number of mainland Chinese firms in the *Fortune 500* increased from just three in the late 1990s to 22 in 2007.

The explosion of market forces in China since the 1970s, alongside the progressive deepening of China's engagement with global capitalism, has transformed the lives of ordinary Chinese people. The proportion of urban dwellers in China's total population rose from 18 percent (172 million) in 1978 to 43 percent (562 million) in 2005, and the share would be even higher if long-term unofficial residents (as many as 150 million people) were included. The nature of employment has changed decisively away from farming: the number employed in the non-farm sector rose from 119 million (30 percent of the labor force) in 1978 to 412 million (56 percent) in 2005. The World Bank has estimated that the proportion of the Chinese population living on less than $1 per day fell from 64 percent (634 million) in 1981 to 14 percent (180 million) in 2002, representing "a speed and scale of poverty decline that is unprecedented in human history." The infant mortality rate fell from 85 per thousand live births in 1970 to 26 in 2004, while life expectancy at birth rose from 63 years in the 1970s to 73 years in 2005.

The extraordinary success of the 2008 Beijing Olympics appeared to cement firmly China's rise and the fact that it had once again resumed its historical place among the world's leading nations. The success of the Games produced an intense patriotic celebration of the role that China now played in the world. The Games took place in the 30th year after the launching of China's policy of "reform and opening up," and China's population could look back with immense pride on the achievements of this period.

CHINA'S GLOBALIZATION CHALLENGE[8]

Alongside the immensely positive impacts, China's close engagement with capitalist globalization was accompanied by surging contradictions. China's leadership is trying hard to identify and implement policies that tackle these problems.

Ecological implosion

China's high-speed economic growth has been accompanied by an ecological implosion caused by the impact of rampant market forces. China's population inhabits an environmental nightmare. The country's grasslands are receding by around one million hectares per annum. China's intense and growing population pressure means that the amount of arable land per person is among the lowest in the world, standing at only around 0.10 hectares, compared with a world average of 0.24 hectares. The average quality of farmland is falling due to the conversion of high-quality land, especially in eastern China, to industrial and residential use. The area affected by serious soil erosion has increased to include around 38 percent of the entire country, and the area of desert is increasing at the rate of around 2,500 square kilometers per year. Acid rain affects about one-quarter of the country's land area. China's area of natural forests is falling at an alarming rate, and its large reforestation programs have produced poor results.

There is rampant water pollution, and a serious and worsening shortage of fresh water. Nearly a quarter of China's rivers fail to meet its own irrigation standards, and significant levels of pesticide residues are found in more than half of the foods grown in the suburbs of major cities. China's emissions of organic water pollutants are as large as those of America, India, Russia, and Japan combined. Overall, China is not short of water, but distribution is highly uneven, and nearly half of the population lives in critically water-short areas in northern China. Groundwater levels over large parts of the North China Plain have fallen due to overextraction for irrigation and urban water supply. Among the 600 major cities, 300 face severe water shortages. State standards for drinking water quality are met in only six of China's 27 largest cities, and groundwater standards are met in only four of them. Access to piped water is critical for human health, but only around 33 percent of rural households and 54 percent of urban households have access to piped water. However, even access to piped water is no guarantee of water quality in the home. Even in large cities, only around 15 percent of residents have access to comprehensively treated piped water.

Most industrial wastewater is untreated or has passed only rudimentary pretreatment processes, and wastewater and hazardous waste discharge at most township and village enterprises is unmonitored. Less than one-tenth of municipal wastewater receives any form of treatment. In all, roughly 200 million people live in 20,000 small towns without any sanitation other than, at best, pipes that lead wastewater to the nearest ditch. Only 18 percent of households have flush toilets in their home, and 28 percent have no access to a lavatory of any type. China's estuaries and coastal areas are threatened by increasing occurrences of red tides, oil spills and pollution from inland sources. A combination of pollution and overfishing has caused a serious drop in fish catches from coastal waters.

Generation of solid waste in large Chinese cities is growing by around 10 percent annually. Although waste treatment has made progress, less than one-half of municipal waste is treated. Chinese industry generates five times as much solid waste as the municipalities. Of this less than 10 percent is reported to be "discharged." Much of the remaining 90 percent is dumped in an uncontrolled manner, leading to pollution of adjacent land, water sources, and air. Less than one-half of hazardous waste is treated to a reasonable degree or re-used, while the rest joins the uncertain fate of other industrial solid waste streams.

Air quality in many Chinese cities falls well below international standards. Sixteen of the world's 20 most polluted cities are in China. Air pollution in Chinese cities associated with direct burning of coal and lead from car exhausts has declined due to strict government regulation. However, the volume of motor traffic is rising rapidly. Four-fifths of the country's air pollution is accounted for by vehicle emissions, and by 2010 it is predicted that vehicles will account for over three-quarters of emissions of nitrous oxide, carbon monoxide, and hydrocarbons in China's largest cities. Nearly 200 Chinese cities fall short of the WHO's standards for airborne particulates. The area affected by acid rain has grown steadily, and now affects around one-third of the whole country, while the steady march of desertification has led to increasingly frequent sandstorms in northern cities, including Beijing. The vast number of rural township and village enterprises are frequently in the heavy industrial sectors, such as cement, chemicals, and metallurgy, and they account for a growing fraction of China's carbon dioxide and sulfur dioxide emissions.

The country's rapid industrial growth since the late 1980s, which has been deeply integrated into capitalist globalization, has been highly "commodity-intensive" and energy-intensive. China's output of heavy industrial products has risen at a fantastic rate. In 1978 it ranked third in the world in coal production, fourth in cement production, and fifth in steel production. By 2004 it was by far the largest in the world in each of these products. In 2005 China accounted for around four percent of global GDP, but it consumed nine percent of global crude oil, 20 percent of aluminum, 30–35 percent of steel, iron ore, and coal, and 45 percent of cement. This pattern of industrial growth has had profound implications for the Chinese environment, as well as for China's energy security.

Energy security

Between 1994 and 2004 China's primary energy consumption increased by 71 percent, and its share of global primary energy consumption increased from ten percent to 14 percent. The rapid growth of passenger vehicles and trucks has contributed significantly to China's accelerating demand for oil, and the stock of vehicles is predicted to rise from 24 million in 2005 to 100 million in 2020. Between 1994 and 2004 China's oil consumption increased by 113 percent. However, China's oil reserves amount to only around 1.4 percent of the world total, and from 1994 to 2004 China's oil production grew by only 19 percent. By 2004 China was importing 2.5 million barrels of oil per day, and the price of these imports has risen greatly since the mid-1990s. It is forecast that by 2020 China will be importing as much as three-quarters of its total oil consumption.

National energy security is of central importance for China, and the pressure will intensify as the economy expands. This will increase the incentive to rely on coal as the main form of primary energy supply. China has large coal reserves, estimated to be around 13 percent of the world total. The relatively low cost of coal provides a strong incentive to continue to use it as the main source of primary energy. In 1994 coal accounted for 69 percent of China's total primary energy consumption. By 2012 China plans to install nearly 600 new coal-fired power stations, around one-half of the world total, and to greatly increase the supply of oil from coal (coal liquefaction). By the mid-1990s China had already overtaken America as the world's biggest coal producer, and today it accounts for almost one-third of total global output. China's high dependence on coal has enormous environmental implications, for both China and the rest of the world.

Global warming

China's per capita consumption of primary energy is only around one-ninth of that in America. In America, consumption of primary energy per person today is around eight tonnes (oil equivalent), compared with around 0.9 tonnes per person in China. By 2001, China was the world's second largest producer of carbon dioxide, standing at 50 percent of the level of America, although its per capita emissions are still a mere 11 percent of those of America. The International Energy Agency estimates that in 2007 China overtook America as the world's largest producer of carbon dioxide.

China's leaders fully appreciate the need to find a new path of economic development that is less energy-intensive and less polluting than that of America today. They need to do so for reasons of national energy security, as well as to protect China's domestic environment and to prevent international conflict over China's impact on the global environment. If China were to climb to the current American level of per capita consumption of primary energy it would consume even more than the total world energy consumption today.

In March 2007, at a meeting with international business leaders in Beijing, the Chinese Premier, Wen Jiabao, said that it would be a disaster for China to follow the American path of vehicle development. China's 11th Five-Year Plan has called for the ambitious goal of improving the country's energy efficiency by 20 percent by 2010. In part this will be achieved by technological progress in the leading firms that produce complex machines such as power stations, vehicles, and aircraft, as well as in the technologies of building construction. Progress in energy efficiency will take place in part through greater use of taxation and the price mechanism, as well as through advancing the country's energy efficiency codes. The Chinese government has responded to the intensifying ecological degradation with numerous laws and regulations on resource protection and pollution control, including strict regulations to control vehicles emissions. From July 1 2006 all new vehicles were required to meet fuel economy standards that are stricter than those in America. New construction codes encourage the use of double-glazed windows to reduce air-conditioning and heating costs. The government restricts the construction of small power plants, encouraging instead the installation of large, modern power plants which use coal-heated steam at high temperatures and generate 20–50 percent more electricity per unit of coal than older Chinese power plants. It is also encouraging the installation of power plants that use integrated gasification combined cycle (IGCC) technologies, which produce more electricity per unit of coal, and allow the possibility of carbon dioxide being separated and pumped underground (carbon sequestration) for storage. Existing coal-fired power plants are required to have sulfur filters on each smokestack by the year 2010.

However, there are still enormous environmental problems facing China. The State Environmental Protection Agency still has a low standing, with just 300 employees, while for local government officials the priority remains economic growth and employment creation. There is a strong incentive for profit-seeking power generation companies to choose cheaper indigenous power plants that have older technologies. The technology for advanced coal-fired power stations is mainly in the hands of the leading international power station producers (GE, Siemens, Alstom, and Mitsubishi) and is costly for operators to install. Sulfur filters in power stations are also costly to install and operate, putting pressure on operators' profit margins. In 2002 the government vowed to reduce sulfur emissions by 10 percent, but instead they rose by 27 percent. Solutions to urban air pollution, which is increasingly caused by automobile traffic, have been sought mainly through technological improvements rather than in alternative transport systems.

China's unbalanced growth path

Prior to 1978, the so-called "planned economy" was locked into a development path that had a high rate of savings and investment alongside unbalanced growth of heavy and light industry. This was widely attributed to the inefficiency of resource use under the planned economy. It was argued that the move toward a market economy would change this growth pattern. In fact the growth pattern intensified as the market economy penetrated more deeply. China's savings rate has risen from 43 percent in 1990, already a very high rate in international comparative terms, to 54 percent in 2006, almost twice the average for developing countries. By contrast, the share of consumption in GDP has fallen from 42 percent in 1990, already a low share in comparative terms, to just 33 percent in 2006, far below the average for all developing countries. The economy has relied on a very high rate of investment to generate growth. In 2006 the share of gross capital formation in GDP stood at 45 percent, compared with 27 percent for all developing countries. This suggests a continuing inefficient, wasteful pattern of resource use, with low technological progress over a large part of the economy, and a high incremental capital/output ratio, with a large amount of additional investment needed to generate an additional unit of output. In 1990 the share of heavy industry in China's overall industrial output was already high, standing at over 50 percent of the total gross value of industrial output. By 2006 the share of heavy industry had risen to 70 percent. This reflects the highly resource-intensive pattern of development over much of the economy, including low-technology manufacturing for the mass of the Chinese population, and a large role for infrastructure investment.

Since the policies of "reform and opening up" began in the late 1970s China has become ever more deeply integrated into the international economy. Since the 1980s, no other economy has achieved such rapid export growth as China. Between 1985 and 1995 its export volume grew by 15 percent per annum, and between 1995 and 2006 the rate of growth accelerated to 20 percent per annum. The share of foreign trade in China's GDP rose from 10 percent in 1978 to 33 percent in 1990, and reached no less than 67 percent in 2006. China's foreign trade ratio today is far above that in other large, continental-sized economies, such as America, Russia, Brazil, and India, or, even, Japan. International firms investing in China have become central to the country's economic growth. Foreign-funded enterprises account for 57 percent of export earnings and 90 percent of China's exports of "new and high technology products." Two-thirds of the patents granted in China are awarded to foreign enterprises and people.

China's deep integration with the international economy has brought large gains from comparative advantage, enabling China to export labor-intensive goods in huge quantities. However, it has also China left deeply vulnerable to fluctuations in the international economy. The global recession is having a deep impact on China. Seventy percent of China's total exports (direct plus net re-exports through Hong Kong) go to the OECD countries, which face a severe downturn in consumer expenditure. In addition, China's exports to the primary commodity-producing countries are also affected by the collapse of world commodity prices. It is likely that China's export growth in 2009 will fall to negligible levels and may even become negative. This is a tremendous macro-economic shock after the sustained explosive growth of exports over the last two decades. It is the first time during the era of reform and opening up that the economy has received a shock of this magnitude; few people in China's policy-making circles had anticipated such a situation.

The impact of the global recession is felt especially severely in the areas that are most deeply integrated into the global economy, notably the Yangtze River Delta, which includes Shanghai, Southern Jiangsu and Northern Zhejiang provinces, and the Pearl River Delta in Guangdong province. These areas have been the engine for China's economic growth under the policies of reform and opening up. Together they account for 28 percent of China's GDP, 58 percent of its FDI (41 percent for the Yangtze River Delta and 17 percent for the Pearl River Delta), and 66 percent of its exports. Because of this, they are now receiving the full force of the global recession. The possibility of socio-political instability is increased because of the spatially concentrated nature of the impact of the downturn in global demand for Chinese exports. The key export-oriented areas contain the workplaces of a huge number of rural-urban migrants in low-skilled or unskilled occupations.

Poverty and inequality

Behind China's development process in the early twenty-first century lies the harsh reality of the "Lewis phase" of economic development with unlimited supplies of labor. China has a population of almost 1.3 billion, almost 70 percent of whom still live in the countryside. The World Bank has estimated that in 2004 over 500 million Chinese people were living on less than $2 per day, and around 100 million were living on less than $1 per day. In 2007, the World Bank dramatically re-estimated China's national product, reducing its estimate in terms of PPP dollars (see note 5) by no less than 40 percent. As a result, it tripled its estimate of the number of people living on less than $1 per day to 300 million. China's own official statistics estimate that the average per capita income of China's 750 million rural dwellers is only $1.1 per day (at the official rate of exchange). China may well become the world's largest economy while it is still locked in the Lewis phase of development. Moreover, China faces the prospect of a rapid rise in the dependency ratio in a few years' time as the population ages, due to the "echo" effect from the one-child policy introduced in 1980, which would put upward pressure on unskilled wage levels before China had reached upper-middle income levels. China would then be in the unique position of having passed through the Lewis phase of development while still a lower-middle income country.

The great extent of rural underemployment and the low level of average rural incomes powerfully stimulate rural–urban migration, and provide severe downward pressure on non-farm wages in unskilled and low-skilled occupations. There are as many as 150 million rural migrants working in the urban areas. They are predominantly unskilled labor, earning the equivalent of around $1–3 per day.

The Grand Hyatt Hotel in Shanghai is a visual metaphor for the city's modernization. It is a triumph of modern architectural technology. The hotel proper only begins on the 50th floor. The bedrooms are arranged in a circle around the outside of a vast central atrium that stretches up a further 40 floors to the sharp, distinctive pinnacle at the top of the building. Lying in a bath situated next to the window, the guest looks down 50 floors or more to the ground below, safe amid the storms that often lash the building and cause it to sway alarmingly. The price of staying a single night is $300 or more. The building was constructed by large teams of migrant workers. The guests are secure in their rooms, their only fears arising from vertigo, from the swaying of the building in a storm, or, perhaps, from the dark, as they fumble, jet-lagged, and irritated, to locate the light switch amid the complex high-tech lighting system. It is hard to imagine the fear and risks involved for the young migrant men from far-off villages who worked in all weathers to construct such a building. They earned not much more in a year than the guest pays for a single night's stay.

Around 300 million Chinese workers, a large fraction of whom are illegal "immigrant" workers from the countryside, are now employed in the non-farm "informal" sector, without the protection of trade unions, mainly in small enterprises with little regulation over conditions of work, and they are often without unemployment or health insurance. Furthermore, after the mid-1990s, around 40–50 million workers lost their jobs as a result of reform in state-owned enterprises.

Alongside these developments, large amounts of FDI by multinational firms helped to produce clusters of modern businesses and residential areas, in which the relatively affluent urban middle class is isolated and protected from the surrounding mass of poor people, often living in gated communities protected by armed guards.

The national Gini coefficient for China's income distribution rose from 0.28 in the early 1980s to 0.50 in 2005. In 2002, the Gini coefficient for the distribution of wealth reached 0.55, while that for the distribution of financial assets was 0.74. In 2002, the top ten percent of the Chinese population accounted for 32 percent of national income, 41 percent of total wealth and 48 percent of financial assets. One of the leading international banks estimates that the top one percent of the Chinese population (i.e. around 13 million people) has 67 percent of the country's household wealth, while the top 0.1 percent (i.e. around 1.3 million people) has no less than 41 percent of the total.

The global business revolution [9]

Since the 1980s China has implemented industrial policies intended to nurture a group of globally competitive large indigenous firms. This period has, at the same time, witnessed a revolution in world business. It has seen a unique intensity of merger and acquisition, which presents a comprehensive challenge for Chinese firms. Not only do they face immense difficulties in catching up with the leading systems integrators, who occupy that part of the "iceberg" that is visible "above the water." They also face immense difficulties in catching up with the powerful firms that now dominate almost every segment of global supply chains, the invisible part of the iceberg that lies hidden from view.

China is far from being the technological "workshop of the world" in the sense that Britain was in the nineteenth century. China's firms are far from the global technology frontier. More than one-half of China's exports, and around 90 percent of its exports of electronic and information technology products, are produced by foreign-owned factories. The key components in a wide range of electronic and information technology products manufactured in China are imported from the world's leading firms in the sector. China's exports are heavily dependent on imports of semiconductors, which rose from $3 billion in 1995 to more than $90 billion in 2005. In the latter year China's imports accounted for two-fifths of total global semiconductor output. The 21 Chinese firms in the *Fortune 500* (2007) are all majority-owned by the Chinese state. They are from a small number of strategic industries (including banking, telecoms services, steel, power transmission, railway construction and engineering, and oil and gas), and obtain most of their revenue from the protected domestic market, in which they face little competition from multinational firms. None of them has yet established a significant presence in international markets. Successful latecomer industrializing countries, from America in the late nineteenth century to South Korea in the late twentieth century, have all produced a group of globally competitive firms. China is the first successful latecomer not to have done so. The fact that the world's sixth largest economy (the second largest in PPP terms) has not produced a substantial group of internationally competitive large firms is highly significant in the history of modern capitalist development.

China's policy-makers recognize that the challenge facing the country's large firms on the "global level playing field" is far greater than had been imagined prior to China joining the WTO. The country's policy-makers are intensely investigating ways in which to build powerful Chinese firms that can compete with the global giant firms in a range of strategic industries, including financial services, telecommunication services and equipment, oil and gas, metals and mining, power generation and equipment, automobiles, and aerospace. This effort is focused on a group of around 150 large state-owned enterprises.

China has eschewed the long-term protectionist approach that America itself adopted. In the nineteenth century, America achieved rapid industrialization behind high protectionist barriers, which it maintained for over 100 years. America began its heavy protection of indigenous industries in the late eighteenth century, immediately after Independence. The policies were the brainchild of Alexander Hamilton, the first American Treasury Secretary. In Hamilton's view, if America was to survive in a dangerous world, its government needed to be strong and, above all, "energetic." In January 2004, Senator Ernest Hollings (South Carolina) drew attention to Hamilton's role in the construction of America's industrial policy in his testimony before the US–China Economic and Security Commission:

In the earliest days, the Brits, right after we had won our freedom, corresponded to the colony and said, "you trade with us what you produce best and we'll trade back with you what we produce best": David Ricardo, *The Doctrine of Comparative Advantage*. And Hamilton wrote a booklet. And it's called *The Report on Manufacturers*. In a line, Hamilton told the Brits to bug off. He said, "we are not going to remain your colony, shipping you our rice, our cotton, our indigo, our lumber, our iron ore, and bringing in the manufactured goods; we are going to build up our own manufacturing capacity." The first bill was for the seal of America. The second bill to pass the Congress of America, on July the 4th, 1789, was protectionism [the first American Tariff Act]. A tariff bill of up to 50 percent on some sixty articles … After a hundred years, in 1900 … America was so rich in goods and services that she was more self-sustaining than any industrial power in history … Now we had the real super power, because that's economic power.

After Senator Hollings had made his speech, Commissioner Reinsch observed: "Your comments about Alexander Hamilton and manufacturing I thought were interesting, and something I learned a long time ago and forgotten. I can't help but think though in a way what you're telling us is that Hamilton had the right approach. It seems to me that one could argue the Chinese are doing exactly the same thing, so they're smart too, right?"

In fact, in contrast to the policy of America in the nineteenth century, China's policy since the 1980s has been consistently based on an open economy, culminating in its decision to join the WTO. China is searching for a new form of industrial policy, in which it builds a group of large, globally competitive firms in key strategic industries in the context of an open economy that is deeply integrated into the capitalist global business system, with high levels of trade, and is open to foreign investment.

The capability and role of the state

China's outstanding economic performance since the 1980s is inseparable from the firm leadership and political stability provided by the Chinese Communist Party. However, the country's engagement with capitalist globalization also raises profound issues for the nature and function of the Chinese state.

The party is intimately intertwined with every aspect of socio-economic life. In the late 1980s and early 1990s, Deng Xiaoping warned repeatedly of the dangers of China collapsing into chaos. Since then China's leaders have repeatedly warned of the importance of "enhancing the art of leadership," and "resisting corruption." There are over 74 million members of the Chinese Communist Party. There has been widespread insider dealing and corruption during China's economic system restructuring. One important aspect of this process of "primitive accumulation" has been the ubiquitous triangular relationship between the local communist party, the banks, and the development of publicly owned land. Administrative decisions to redesignate land can vastly inflate the value of a piece of land. Such key decisions in the hands of local government officials include the redesignation of a piece of suburban land from agricultural use to residential and commercial use, and redesignation of urban land from "suitable for low-rise dwellings" to "suitable for high-rise residential and commercial development."

Corruption has also been deeply embedded in the privatization process. In the initial phase of Chinese enterprise privatization, the main target was the privatization of the large number of small and medium enterprises, which were typically under the control of the local government. In recent years Initial Public Offerings (IPOs) of a minority share of the equity of China's leading state-owned companies have raised many tens of billions of dollars. In 2007 alone the total value of IPOs by mainland companies in Hong Kong and the mainland was $62 billion. In 2006 the average first day price rise for IPOs of Chinese mainland companies was 23 percent in Hong Kong, while in the mainland in 2006–7 the average first day rise was 97 percent. It is estimated that the IPOs of indigenous Chinese companies "left $25 billion on the table" in 2006–7. Unsurprisingly, both in Hong Kong and in the mainland, applications for share allocations have typically vastly exceeded the number of shares available. This has provided large opportunities for "spinning," whereby well-connected entities and individuals obtain privileged access to the shares issued in IPOs. Well-connected insiders have made huge personal fortunes from this near risk-free chance to double their money.

The level of party members being sentenced for corruption has risen to include many in high positions. An official report to the National People's Congress in 2005 declared that 2,960 officials at or above county level were investigated for corruption in 2004, 11 of whom were at the provincial or ministerial level.

Corruption is not unique to China today and it is possible for corrupt regimes to grow successfully. It is political stability and security of property rights that are critically important in the early phase of capitalist development. In most cases the early phase of modern capitalist development, including in America, was mostly accompanied by extensive corruption and class struggle. In almost every case too, including in America, the early phase of capitalist industrialization was accompanied by violent confrontations between workers and government forces. None of today's high-income countries experienced political revolutions during this turbulent process; instead, they all experienced political evolution. Capitalist development led to the gradual unfolding of citizens' opportunities and political consciousness, and to the steady advance in their assertion of their rights, rather than to a violent political revolution. Democracy typically followed, however slowly, rather than preceded, or even accompanied, the early phase of capitalist development. China's moves toward political democracy have been slow, experimental, and cautious. So far, they have mainly been confined to local political institutions. In other words, in its cautious development of democratic structures and practices, China is following a well-trodden path.

China is a vast, poor country with urgent development needs, which can only be met by state action. China's deepening engagement with capitalist globalization is associated with a deep crisis in the country's welfare system. China has experienced a process of "state desertion" comparable to that in the former Soviet Union. As the role of the market economy increased, the state's fiscal capability declined seriously. Government revenue as a share of GDP fell from 31 percent in 1978 to under 14 percent in 2000, and there was at the same time a large rise in the share of welfare expenditure from fees paid by private individuals. In 1980 more than 75 percent of educational funding came from the government, but by 2000 this had fallen to just 54 percent; this had serious implications for social equity because it resulted in the exclusion of many poor children. By 2002–3 China's medical insurance system covered less than half of the urban population, and only one-tenth of the rural population.

Under the planned economy, work units guaranteed all Chinese citizens incomes in their old age, though the level of income guaranteed varied widely depending on the nature and location of the place of work. This system is now undergoing comprehensive transformation. China is still in the early stages of establishing a pension system consistent with the emerging market economy. In 2002, only around 55 percent of the urban workforce and 11 percent of the rural workforce were covered by public pensions. The problems of building an insurance system are complicated by the dramatic changes taking place in China's demography. The one-child policy, introduced in the late 1970s, and the effects of urbanization, have produced a large decline in fertility. China's birth rate in 2004 (12 per thousand) was as low as that in the high-income countries. Also, there has been a steady rise in longevity. It is projected that the share of the population over the age of 60 will rise from 11 percent in 2005 to 28 percent in 2040. Unlike the West, which became "rich" before it became "old," China is set to become the world's first major economy to become old before it becomes rich.

Financial institutions

Engagement with the international financial system is, arguably, the most sensitive and difficult aspect of China's involvement with global capitalism. Since the 1980s the world's leading financial firms have been through a period of unprecedented merger and acquisition. This period has seen the emergence of super-large financial services firms, such as Citigroup, J. P. Morgan Chase, Bank of America, and HSBC, which rapidly acquired dominant positions in Latin America and Eastern Europe. After its acquisition of Banamex, one of Mexico's largest banks, Citigroup proclaimed: "China is top of our radar screen." After China joined the WTO in 2001 there was relentless international pressure for the country to open its financial system fully to competition from international financial firms, as a *quid pro quo* for the fact that the high-income countries had opened their markets to China's surging exports.

The Asian financial crisis provided a shocking insight into the fragility of China's financial institutions. China appeared at first to escape any effects of the crisis, due to the fact that the *renminbi* was not fully convertible. In fact the crisis had a powerful impact through the medium of Hong Kong and the massive debts accumulated there by mainland "trust and investment" and "red chip" companies, and other mainland-based entities operating in Hong Kong. The most visible of these were GITIC (Guangdong International Trust and Investment Corp.) and GDE (Guangdong Enterprises), which included five floated "red chip" companies. During the Asian financial crisis, GITIC went into bankruptcy, while GDE was insolvent and comprehensively restructured. Prior to the crisis both companies had been regarded as model institutions by international lenders, but GITIC's bankruptcy and GDE's restructuring allowed the outside world to look closely for the first time inside large Chinese companies. The investigations revealed a comprehensive failure in corporate governance, including disastrous lending practices: a large fraction of their loans had been made to firms and institutions that were unable or unwilling to repay their debts. A substantial part of their investments were highly speculative, including heavy participation in the property boom in Guangdong province and in Hong Kong.

After the Asian financial crisis the central government undertook a massive clean up of the country's financial institutions. It revealed shocking evidence about the state of corporate governance in China's main banks. Since the late 1990s the

Chinese government has made immense efforts to restructure the country's four largest commercial banks, each of which is a majority state-owned enterprise. Beginning in 1999, specially created asset-management companies (AMCs) relieved the four big banks of an estimated $328 billion in non-performing loans, which as a result fell from over 31 percent of their loan balance at their peak to around ten percent at the end of 2005. The government also made great efforts to improve the quality of corporate governance and to upgrade the technological capabilities of the banks, including their risk evaluation and information technology systems. The banks sold minority shares of their equity to leading international banks, who then helped to improve the technological skills at the head offices of their Chinese partners. Following reconstruction of their internal operations, the leading state-owned Chinese banks established strong balance sheets, and then floated a minority share of their equity on the domestic and international markets. By 2007 China had three of the world's top ten banks in terms of market capitalization.

However, despite progress in restructuring their internal operations, large challenges remain for China's top banks. There is still a long way to go before they can compete with the world's leading banks in international markets. Compared with the world's leading banks they have made only limited progress toward operating on a commercial basis, and they still have high cost structures and limited risk-assessment skills. The top Chinese banks are still firmly controlled by the state, which appoints their top managers. Only a small fraction of their equity is publicly traded; the rest is owned by the Chinese government. Their high stock market capitalization is based on the questionable assumption that if all the shares were publicly traded, they would trade at the same price as the publicly traded shares. They operate in a heavily protected domestic market, and only a small fraction of their business comes from competitive international markets. A large share of their revenue comes from the margin between government-set deposit rates and lending rates. China's financial institutions also suffer seriously from corruption. In the first half of 2005, the party's Central Disciplinary Inspection Commission punished over 1,600 financial-sector employees for fraud and other related crimes. Of these, 570 managers and branch heads were imprisoned or fired. Intense debate surrounds the level of non-performing loans in the Chinese financial system. China's banks still face intense pressure to make loans as directed by central and local party leaders, rather than according to commercial criteria. In the past few years, new non-performing loans may have replaced the old ones on a large scale during the explosive growth of credit which helped to fuel the rapidly inflating bubble in Chinese asset prices in 2006–7, including both property and equities.

The global recession is likely to affect seriously the balance sheet of Chinese financial institutions. It is even possible that a banking crisis might develop. The impact on the banking sector might occur through several channels. First, there are direct losses resulting from the international operation of China's big financial institutions. Hong Kong is a point of particular vulnerability due to the absence of supervision by mainland supervisory bodies and the difficulty that Hong Kong's regulators have in supervising the internal workings of mainland entities operating in the territory. In November 2008 it was reported that CITIC Pacific had lost around $2 billion on its investments in foreign exchange derivative markets. It was reported also that China Steel Construction and China Railway Construction Corporation, which are both listed in Hong Kong, had substantial losses arising from their foreign exchange investments. These large losses may be merely the tip of the iceberg. The operation of Chinese financial institutions in international markets beyond Hong Kong also poses significant risks. As of September 2008, leading Chinese financial institutions had substantial holdings of American assets, the value of which fell heavily in 2008.

Secondly, the possibility of a banking system crisis may be increased through the continued impact of political pressure on lending by financial institutions, especially, but not exclusively, at the local branch level. Such pressure will intensify as China's economy is buffeted by the global recession. The effect of such decisions on bank balance sheets will be compounded by the effect of the domestic economic downturn. "When the tide goes out, the rocks appear" (*shui luo shi chu*), as was the case in the Asian financial crisis. As economic growth slows down, non- performing loans are likely to increase, and the effect will be most pronounced in the areas that are most deeply integrated into the international economy. If economic growth declines substantially, many investment decisions which were justified by high rates of growth and short payback periods will become loss-making. In addition, if growth declines, the likelihood of excess capacity will increase, in both the export-oriented industries and also in the industries that supply them with capital goods and current inputs. This will also tend to increase losses at marginal enterprises in those sectors. Thirdly, the collapse of the domestic stock market and the decline in real estate prices will affect banking sector profits. This will arise due to the fact that at least 25–30 percent of bank loans in recent years have been made to property developers and construction companies. Banks have also made their own direct investments in the booming property and stock markets in recent years. Some of these are reportedly very large. In addition, many large state-owned enterprises have been heavily involved in investment in the stock market and the property sector, the decline in which will damage their profitability and reduce their ability to service their debts to the banking sector.

China as a developing country

Over the past few years there has been a daily outpouring of Western fears that China has surpassed one or other OECD country by some measure or another. It is equally often pointed out that it will overtake the American economy at some point in the not-too-distant future. This trivializes and misunderstands the nature of the national catch-up challenge that faces China's leaders. China's population is 27 percent larger than that of all the high-income countries combined. As China faces the intense challenge of the global financial crisis it is especially important to evaluate carefully the degree to which China has, indeed, caught up.

The table on p148 shows "the world turned upside down." The high-income countries as a whole have a population that is less than four-fifths of China's. Each Chinese person has the same basic rights as a human being as a citizen of the high-income countries. As a human being, a poor migrant worker in China earning two or three dollars a day on a building site, or assembling electronic goods, is intrinsically worth as much as a car worker in Detroit earning $300 per day (excluding fringe benefits), or the head of a Wall Street bank earning tens of millions of dollars in a year.

Despite immense progress since the 1970s in economic terms, China is still far behind the West as a whole. The fact that China has in certain respects overtaken individual high-income countries is misleading in terms of the overall level of catch-up that it has achieved. China's total national product (in PPP dollars) is still only 17 percent of that of the high-income countries (the "West"), and its per capita national product (also in PPP dollars) is only 13 percent of that of the high-income countries. China's total household consumption is less than one-tenth of that of the West. China's "massive" exports are only 11 percent of those of the high-income countries. China has only 16 companies in the *FT 500* and 21 in the *Fortune 500*. The West has 428 and 448 respectively. China has five companies in the Global 1250 of the world's top firms by R&D expenditure, while the West has 1,166 companies in the Global 1250. China has three percent of global household wealth. The West has 88 percent. Despite the fact that its population is so much larger than that of the high-income countries, China has only 3.66 percent of the votes in the IMF, while the West has 60.5 percent. If the West is in "decline" relative to China, the decline still has a long way to go before development parity has been established.

If China's growth continues at the same rate as for the past three decades, it will catch up with the high-income countries at some point. However, that point is much further away than most people realize. Even if China continues to grow rapidly, during the critical "bottleneck" phase of the next twenty to thirty years, before global population reaches a peak or technological progress allows the harnessing of solar power, China will remain far behind the West in many critical development indicators.

However, there is no certainty that China will continue to grow at the same pace as in recent years. In most respects China is still at the early stage of modern economic growth. During this phase today's high-income countries all experienced large cyclical fluctuations, with pronounced booms followed by violent slumps and depressions. In the case of Britain in the first half of the nineteenth century, as it was being turned into the "workshop of the world" it experienced no less than four major cycles of boom and slump. The last of these plunged the working class into utter penury and unleashed a wave of business bankruptcies. Moreover, in 1845–50, under British rule, one million Irish people died of famine out of a total Irish population of around nine million. It will be a tremendous policy achievement if

China manages to avoid major cyclical fluctuations, and food security is a central concern for the leadership. China also faces the special challenge that, before it becomes "rich," it will become "old" and will move out of the "Lewis phase" of development with unlimited supplies of labor, as well as still being locked into the "large and dirty" phase of development.

The global economy is entering a period of intense crisis. This will have enormous repercussions for China, which has locked itself deeply into the international economy. China must face this crisis as a country that is still far from having caught up with the high-income countries.

If the world is to make progress toward collective action to resolve the challenges it faces it is essential for the high-income countries to realize that there is a wide development gap still existing between China and themselves. This means that there are still profound differences both of interest and capability to contribute to collective solutions. These differences will persist throughout the critical period ahead in the next 10–20 years, during which the world must move toward new forms of collective regulation of the global market economy.

China and the West: the world turned upside down

	China	High-income countries	China as percentage of high-income countries
Population (million) (2006)	1,312	1,031	127
Gross National Income (at official rate of exchange) (2006)			
– Total ($ billion)	2,621	37,732	6.9
– $ per person	2,000	36,608	5.5
Gross National Income (PPP $) (2006)			
– Total ($ billion)	6,119	36,005	17.0
– $ per person	4,660	34,933	13.0
Household consumption (billion PPP $, 2006)	2,019	22,323	9.0
Exports ($ billion) (2006)	969	8,451	11.5
Imports ($ billion) (2006)	791	8,984	8.8
FT 500 companies (2007)	16*	428	3.7
Fortune 500 companies (2007)	21	448	4.7
DTI Global 1250 companies (2006)	5	1,166	0.4
of which: top 100	0	100	
Global household wealth (%)	3	88	
IMF voting rights (%)	3.66	60.5	
CO_2 emissions (mmt, 2004)	5,006	13,382	37.4

* including Hong Kong.

RESOLVING THE CONTRADICTIONS: CONFLICT OR COOPERATION?

In 1988 Bob Dylan was in New Orleans recording "Oh Mercy." During a difficult phase in the recordings he took some time off with his wife and rode his Harley-Davidson around the Mississippi Delta: "The air smelled foul. Still water—humid air, rank and rotten." They rode to Morgan City: "Dust was blowing, my mouth was dry and my nose was clogged." They turned south to Houma, and kept riding until they saw the oil rigs and supply boats. They spent the night in a motel at Napoleonville. Setting off the next morning, "a nipping wind hit me in the face, but it was a beautiful day." They circled around Lake Verret, "riding on high trails, cruising by giant oaks, pecan trees—vines and cypress stumps down in the swamps." They stopped at a petrol station off Route 90 near Raceland. Across a vacant field stood "an obscure roadside place, a gaunt shack called King Tut's." It sold trinkets, newspapers, sweets, and handicraft items, and was run by Sun Pie, "one of the most singular characters you'd ever want to meet." Sun Pie was short, old, "wiry like a panther", and "on his bones was the raw skin of the earth." Posters were displayed on the walls of Sun Pie's shack, one of Bruce Lee and one of Chairman Mao. Behind the counter was a photograph of the Great Wall of China taped to a mirror. On the other wall was a jumbo-sized American flag.

> *"You a praying man?" said Sun Pie.*
> *"Uh-huh."*
> *"Good, gonna have to be when the Chinese take over ... You know, the Chinese were here at the beginning. They were the Indians. You know, the red man. The Comanche, the Sioux, the Arapaho, the Cheyenne—all them people—they were all Chinese. Came over here about the time when Christ was healing the sick. All the squaws and chiefs came from China—walked across from Asia, came down through Alaska and discovered this place. They became Indians a lot later."*
> *"Chinese huh?"*
> *"Yeah, that's right. Trouble was they split up into parties and tribes and started wearing feathers and forgot they were Chinese ... They're coming back, these Chinese, millions of them. It's preordained, and they won't have to use force. They'll just walk in, take up where they left off ... People think I'm crazy, but I don't mind. The Chinese are solid—they don't use vulgar language. The Chinese nightingale will sing in the land. They don't have the ten commandments, either, don't need 'em. All the way from here to Peru, Chinese."*
> *A subtle change came over Sun Pie, and he turned his face toward the poster of Chairman Mao: "War is not a bad thing. It thins out the population. You got to let it all float up to the surface."*
> *In my mind's eye I saw blood being splattered and spilled.*

> Bob Dylan, *Chronicles*, Volume One

America and China will be the most important actors in the global political economy in the first decades of this century. The prospect for global sustainable development hinges around the relationship between these two mighty forces. Despite their immense respective strengths, each of them has its own internal contradictions, brought about mainly by the impact of capitalist globalization on the two economies and societies, one aspect of which is their growing mutual economic integration. Their growing interaction may yet end in terrifying conflict. However, that prospect may encourage the evolution of a cooperative relationship based on enlightened self-interest, which attempts to resolve the inherent contradictions of capitalist globalization, in respect both to their internal development, to their mutual relationship, and to their joint role in the international political economy.

Conflict?

In China some people believe that it is quite possible that there will be a military conflict with America. Wang Lixiong's novel *Yellow Peril* is a bestseller among Chinese readers worldwide.[10] It identifies a scenario in which political disintegration in China leads to a global nuclear holocaust: "He did not want there to be a mystery forever as to who had fired the 40 nuclear warheads. The message to be repeated by the beacon informed Russia, America, and the world that China had settled accounts for the 205 missiles it had received ... It was time. The preparations were complete, the arming program faultlessly installed. He pressed the firing key with his finger: the last time he would touch anything."

In America China's rise alarms many people. They consider it to be an inevitable adversary. Several books have been published in America in recent years outlining different scenarios under which a military conflict with China might erupt. They believe that it would be sensible to act soon to restrain China before it becomes too powerful. In America in recent years there has emerged a deeply rooted "politics of anxiety," stemming from the possibility that the interaction of political and ecological issues might produce a catastrophic international conflict. In 2007 Cormac McCarthy was awarded the Pulitzer Prize for Fiction for *The Road*, which presents a terrifying vision of a world following a holocaust in the near future: "They followed a stone wall past the remains of an orchard. The trees in their ordered rows gnarled and black and the fallen limbs thick on the ground. He stopped and looked across the fields. Wind in the east. The soft ash moving in the furrows ... He looked back at the boy. He looked at the dry grass where it moved and at the dark and twisted trees in their rows. A few shreds of clothing blown against the wall, everything gray in the ash."

American hegemony In the early 1990s, following the collapse of communist rule in the Soviet Union and Eastern Europe, and the Tiananmen events of 1989 in China, the American leadership turned its attention toward assessing the country's long-term international relations strategy in the radically changed international situation. The American political establishment unashamedly welcomed the fact that America had established global hegemony and considered that this served the interests of both America and the world. America felt itself to be leading the world toward a period of unprecedented economic and social progress in which all countries would adopt American-style democracy and free markets.

The first important statement of America's strategic readjustment was contained in the draft Defense Planning Guidance (DPG) document for 1994–99. The DPG was prepared secretly in 1992 in the Department of Defense at the instruction of Defense Secretary Dick Cheney. It enunciated a plan for America to maintain permanent global military superiority and world dominance: "Our first objective is to prevent the re-emergence of a new rival, either on the territory of the former Soviet Union or elsewhere, that poses a threat on the order of that posed formerly by the Soviet Union ... [This task requires] that we endeavor to prevent any hostile power from dominating a region whose resources would, under consolidated control, be sufficient to generate global power."

In her *Foreign Affairs* article in 2000 Condoleezza Rice set out the foreign policy position that guided both Bush administrations thereafter: "The process of outlining a new foreign policy must begin by recognizing that America is in a remarkable position. Powerful secular trends are moving the world toward economic openness and—more unevenly—democracy and economic progress. Some hold on to old hatreds as diversions from the modernizing task at hand. But America and its allies are on the right side of history." Rice proclaimed that "American values are universal" and argued that "the global economy demands economic liberalization, greater openness and transparency." She argued that the decisive tools in shaping international politics are "international economic policies that leverage the advantages of the American economy and expand free trade." [11]

When George W. Bush came to power in January 2001, the principle of overarching American global dominance was the cornerstone of American foreign policy. In the wake of the attacks of September 11 he said: "America now faces a choice between the path of fear and the path of confidence ... This administration has chosen the path of confidence ... We fight our enemies abroad instead of waiting for them to arrive in our country. We seek to shape the world, not merely be shaped by it ... The path we have chosen is consistent with the great tradition of American foreign policy ... To follow this path, we must maintain and expand our national strength so we can deal with threats and challenges before they can damage our people and our interests. We must maintain a military without peer ... America must continue to lead." The National Security Strategy of 2002 made it clear that America reserved the right to undertake "pre-emptive attacks on the enemy:" "When the consequences of an attack with WMD are potentially so devastating, we cannot afford to stand idly by as grave dangers materialize. This is the principle and logic of pre-emption." It committed America to establishing a world that conformed with its own values: "Economic freedom is a moral imperative ... Greater economic freedom is ultimately inseparable from political liberty ... History has judged the market economy as the single most effective economic system and the greatest antidote to poverty."

At the time of the original DPG document in 1992 there was an array of possible rivals for America to consider as future superpowers. By the end of the decade the possible superpower rivals had been reduced to one, namely China. As China continued its rapid growth, so it acquired an ever-greater importance in American foreign policy.

In her *Foreign Affairs* article in 2000 Condoleezza Rice warned that China was a "strategic competitor," which constituted a potential threat to stability in the Asia–Pacific region: "China is a great power with unresolved vital interests, particularly concerning Taiwan. China resents the role of America in the Asia–Pacific region. This means that China is not a status quo power but one that would like to alter Asia's balance of power in its own favor. That alone makes it a strategic competitor, not the 'strategic partner' the Clinton administration once called it." Rice argued that America should "promote China's internal transition through economic integration," while "containing Chinese power and security ambitions." On the one hand, China's deepening integration with global capitalism would provide a key mechanism for political change in China: "[T]rade and economic interaction are good, not only for America's economic growth but for its political aims as well ... Trade can open up the Chinese economy and, ultimately, its politics too. This view requires faith in the power of markets and economic freedom to drive political change, but it is a faith confirmed by experiences around the globe." On the other hand, Rice argued that America "should never be afraid to confront Beijing when our interests collide." The American policy of containment of China was explicit: "The United States must deepen its cooperation with Japan and South Korea and maintain its commitment to a robust military presence in the region. It should play closer attention to India's role in the regional balance ... The United States has a deep interest in the security of Taiwan ... If the United States is resolute, peace can be maintained in the Taiwan Strait until a political settlement on democratic terms is reached."

America's need for enemies The fact that America's population is composed of the descendants of immigrants and slaves, that there was a prolonged process of territorial expansion within North America, and that the country has a highly unequal socio-economic structure, has meant that the construction of a common national identity has been of great importance for America. These challenges remain today as the country engages ever more deeply with capitalist globalization. They form the central theme of the late Samuel Huntington's final book, which has the evocative title *Who Are We?*.

Religion and military violence have played a central role in the construction of American national identity. Around three-fifths of Americans today are Protestants.

The core of American culture was established by the Protestant settlers in the seventeenth and eighteenth centuries, and became the foundation of American identity in the nineteenth century into which successive waves of immigrants were absorbed. The core values included liberty, equality before the law, individualism, representative government, and private property. These values formed the ideology that helped to unify a society that was in fact highly unequal from its inception. In the late eighteenth century it was already the case that the top ten percent of the white population in the colonial territories owned around one-half of the total wealth and held around one-seventh of the population as slaves.

From the earliest days of settlement through to the late twentieth century the American military tradition has involved "total warfare," which blurs or even erases the boundaries between combatants and non-combatants. From the late sixteenth century through until the late nineteenth century the American nation was forged through relentless violence within North America itself. At the center of this was the genocide against the indigenous "Indian" population. The early Puritan colonists believed that divine providence had given them the right to occupy North America. As America expanded its territory westwards the idea of "Manifest Destiny" grew even stronger. Central to this was the view that had been expounded by John Locke, that the indigenous inhabitants had failed to make good use of the abundant resources of the continent and, therefore, had forfeited their right to ownership of the resources they occupied. The indigenous population of North America had originally been around 15–16 million, but by the late nineteenth century it had been reduced to less than one million. In part this was due to the impact of European diseases, but to a significant degree it was due to unceasing violence that only concluded in 1890 with the Battle of Wounded Knee.

In a precursor of modern guerrilla warfare, both sides indulged in ferocious attacks on civilians. From the earliest days of frontier warfare up until the late nineteenth century, white Americans made widespread use of violence directed systematically against Indian non-combatants as a means of undermining enemy morale. Such a method of warfare (the "first way of war") was deemed as morally legitimate because the enemy were regarded as "savages" and less than human beings. In the first way of war guerrilla fighters with greatly inferior armaments live among the mass of the population, indistinguishable from the ordinary citizens. Only by attacking civilians and the economic resources that support the guerrillas can the colonizing force defeat the indigenous resistance movement. Guerrilla warfare by poorly armed freedom fighters typically involves great suffering for the civilian population that harbors the guerrillas.

The number of slaves grew from around 500,000 in 1790 to around four million by 1860. By the 1960s, when the civil rights movement erupted, there were around 23 million African Americans. The long-term impact of slavery on the American national psyche has been incalculably large and multidimensional. After emancipation in 1865 freed black slaves were barred from taking advantage of the opening of the West to improve their economic status through land acquisition. During the Reconstruction period after the Civil War black Americans were finally given the vote. From 1890 onward, however, they were progressively disenfranchised in the South. The focus on race in the interpretation of the boundaries of political democracy helped to solidify a sense of national identity among the diverse groups of white people of British and Continental European origin that made up America's free population.

The indignities suffered by black Americans extended deep into the texture of daily life. The Plessy decision of 1896 affirmed the right of the state of Louisiana to segregate black people from white people on the railroads. It was quickly followed by state laws which required racial segregation in every aspect of life, from schools to hospitals, waiting rooms to restrooms, pay windows to cemeteries. As late as the 1960s, 17 states still had laws on their statute books that prohibited mixed-race marriages. The imposition of its own conception of human rights has been central to American foreign policy for decades. Yet within America the struggle by black Americans for human rights went on for more than four centuries. Despite the tremendous progress since the 1960s, extending even to the election of a black president of America, the impact of slavery still looms large in the American psyche.

The Mexican War (1846–48) and the Civil War (1861–65) played critical roles in constructing the American national identity. The Mexican War concluded with the absorption of the vast territories of New Mexico, Utah, Arizona, Nevada, part of Colorado, California, and Texas. The Civil War, which forced the rebellious Confederate states back into the Union, was the first large-scale war fought with modern industrial technology. It was extraordinarily violent, resulting in around 623,000 deaths and 470,000 people wounded, out of a population of 30 million.

There has been only one large-scale attack by foreigners on civilians in America, namely the attack of September 11, 2001, in which around 3,000 people in total died, of whom around 2,000 were American citizens. Since America took up the baton as the dominant global power following the attack at Pearl Harbor, it has systematically employed bombing of civilian targets (so-called "strategic bombing") in order to break the will of the enemy population.

In 1945 under General Curtis LeMay, the US Air Force undertook systematic fire-bombing of Japanese cities. In a single night, in "ideal conditions for creating a firestorm," over 100,000 people died in Tokyo. LeMay's attack on Tokyo set the course for a relentless bombardment of Japanese cities. In total, several hundred thousand people died in these attacks, explicitly aimed at civilians. American submarines sank almost 2,000 Japanese merchant ships, killing over 100,000 civilians. In Europe the last months of World War II witnessed strategic bombing by the American and British air forces on a massive scale. Around 600,000 civilians died in the allied bomb attacks, and a much larger number of people were injured. The nuclear bomb attacks on Hiroshima and Nagasaki killed over 300,000 people in total.

The "first way of war" is unforgiving. During the Korean War, American bombing of the North was so devastating that it was halted because there was nothing of any consequence left to bomb. American bombers targeted North Korean dams, the destruction of which, as anticipated and intended, caused immense loss of civilian life, both directly and indirectly, through its effect on agriculture. More than four million Koreans died in total during the conflict, of which a large fraction were civilians who were killed as a direct or indirect result of American bombing.

During the war in Vietnam large areas of the country were declared "free fire zones," which American planes bombed at will. By the end of the war seven million bombs had been dropped on Vietnam, more than twice the total dropped in Europe and Asia in World War II. Haiphong and Hanoi were fire-bombed more than once by the US Air Force. Large quantities of poisonous sprays were used to destroy trees and any kind of vegetation in the large areas on which they were dropped. Horrific attacks on Vietnamese civilians were carried out by American troops on the ground, including the infamous My Lai massacre, in which 450–500 people, mostly women, children, and old men, were shot. At least two million people died in the Vietnam War, of whom a large number were civilians who died as a result of the direct and indirect effects of American bombing.

In the recent era of globalization the late Samuel Huntington did more than any other scholar to shape the American establishment's view of international relations, notably through his two bestselling books *The Clash of Civilizations* and *Who Are We?*.[12] He believed that America faces serious threats to its national identity and unity arising from the "hispanization" of American culture, from increased domestic social inequality, and from the "globalization" of the American elite. In addition to these factors, America faces large challenges to its national identity in the decades ahead due to the rapid changes in its ethnic composition. The American Bureau of Census predicts that by the year 2050 the total American population will have risen to around 430–440 million, from 300 million today. By 2050, America's non-Hispanic white population is predicted to shrink from 66 percent today to around 46 percent of the total population. The black population, meanwhile, is predicted to rise to almost 70 million (around 15 percent) and the Asian population to over 40 million (almost ten percent of the predicted total). Most significantly, the Bureau predicts that the Hispanic population will increase from around 47 million today to around 130–135 million, doubling its share of the total population from 15 percent to around 30 percent.

Although America sits at the center of the global system of political economy, the immense size and diversity of the country has helped to ensure that its politics and culture are inward-looking. America's national sports of basketball, baseball, and American football are played by a relatively small number of people across the world. Americans tend to go abroad less than the citizens of other high-income countries. In 2007, America had around 66 million outbound tourists, compared with over 70 million for both Britain and Germany, which have far smaller total populations than America.

America's cultural introversion is a challenge to the country's engagement with diverse cultures in the era of globalization. The great works of American literature not only deal mainly with the country's domestic culture, but are strongly regional in their orientation. The writings of John Steinbeck, Jack London, and Raymond Chandler are set mainly in California; those of William Faulkner and Tennessee Williams are set mainly in the Deep South; Mark Twain's main milieu is the Mississippi; most of the writings of Edith Wharton, Scott Fitzgerald, J. D. Salinger, Tom Wolfe, Saul Bellow, and Philip Roth are set in New York and its environs; Ralph Waldo Emerson, Henry Thoreau, Nathaniel Hawthorne, John Updike, and Richard Ford take the northeast as their main subject matter; while Cormac McCarthy's writings are set mainly in the southwest border region. The great "international" works of American literature—such as those of Ernest Hemingway, Henry James, and Joseph Heller—deal mainly with the lives of Americans abroad. In the era of globalization since the 1970s, the most influential works of American literature have dealt almost exclusively with domestic issues.[13]

Huntington pointed out that the existence of an external enemy has played a central role in helping to create national unity out of a people who came to America from all over the world. In his view America's sense of national unity was undermined by the collapse of the "evil empire" of the former Soviet Union. Much of American foreign policy debate since then has involved identifying a new "enemy" that is ideologically hostile, racially and culturally different, and militarily strong enough to pose a credible threat to American security. Huntington considered that there were two possible external enemies who might fulfill this role, namely the Muslim world and China: "[China is] still communist in theory if not in economic practice, clearly a dictatorship with no respect for political liberty, democracy, or human rights, with a dynamic economy, an increasingly nationalistic public, a strong sense of cultural superiority, and among its military and some other elite groups, a clear perception of the United States as their enemy." Many of President George W. Bush's advisers believed that a war with China was likely, perhaps even inevitable, in the next 20 or 30 years. Henry Kissinger warned that the hawks in President Bush's administration saw China as a "morally flawed inevitable adversary." They believe that America should not act as a strategic partner, but instead should treat China as a rival and a challenge, just as it treated the Soviet Union during the Cold War.

William Fulbright was the longest-serving chair of the Senate Foreign Relations Committee (1959–74). In 1965 in the middle of the war in Vietnam, in his book *The Arrogance of Power*, he pointed out that throughout American history two strands, which he terms "democratic humanism" and "intolerant puritanism," had coexisted uneasily. He considered that the growing influence of the "puritan way of thought" had led America to "look at the world through the distorting prism of a harsh and angry moralism." Fulbright believed that the great challenge in America's foreign relations was to "make certain that the strand of humanism, tolerance, and accommodation, remains the dominant one." The foremost need of American foreign policy was a renewed dedication to an "idea that mankind can hold to," and not "a missionary idea full of pretensions about being the world's policeman." Fulbright warned that the stakes were high: "they include ... nothing less than the survival of the human race in an era when, for the first time in human history, a living generation has the power of veto over the survival of the next." It was therefore not merely desirable but essential that the "competitive instinct of nations be brought under control." He urged Americans to remember that "we are not God's chosen savior of mankind," but "only one of mankind's more successful and fortunate branches, endowed by our Creator with about the same capacity for good and evil, no more or less, than the rest of humanity." Fulbright concluded: "Gradually, but unmistakably, America is showing signs of that arrogance of power which has afflicted, weakened, and in some cases destroyed great nations in the past. In so doing, we are not living up to our capacity and promise as a civilized example to the world." Fulbright's solemn warning is as appropriate today as it was when the *The Arrogance of Power* was first published in 1965.

Energy contest with China As America has become increasingly dependent on imported oil, "energy security" has risen to the top of America's political agenda. China's own search for secure sources of international oil has become a key issue in Sino-American relations. America's policy-makers believe that China is increasingly active in striving for energy resources in ways that are in direct competition with America, and that this is producing a potential for conflict between the two nations. China's oil companies have, indeed, increased their efforts to acquire ownership of international oil reserves. However, they have been permitted to acquire only limited ownership and operation rights over the resources controlled by the national oil companies (NOCs) in Latin America, the Middle East, and the former Soviet Union. China's oil supplies from these regions have come mostly through open market purchases rather than through ownership of oilfields.

China's efforts to acquire oil assets have met with the greatest success in Africa. There is a strong symmetry of economic interest between China and Africa. Africa has a low density of population, vast natural resources, and immense potential to benefit from trade with China based on its comparative advantages. China has intensified its efforts to develop supplies of oil from Africa, as well as supplies of other primary produce, including food. Chinese oil companies are fast developing their operations in Africa, including substantial investments in Angola, Nigeria, and Sudan. By 2005 Angola was second only in importance to Saudi Arabia as a source of oil supplies to China, and Africa as a whole supplied almost one-third of China's oil imports.

In 2005, when CNOOC (China National Offshore Oil Corporation) made a bid to acquire Unocal, the American- headquartered oil company, it "sailed into a perfect storm," releasing an avalanche of hostility toward China. When the takeover was blocked by the American Congress, William Reinsch, President of the American National Foreign Trade Council, observed: "We are in a time and place where every single one of these deals is going to go through extra scrutiny, because the deals give fodder to the view that China is the enemy." The intensity of feeling in Congress is remarkable in view of the massive international reserves owned by the leading American and European-based oil companies. These companies typically own 70–80 percent of their oil reserves in foreign countries, whereas for the leading Chinese oil companies, international oil reserves are still only a tiny share of their total reserves. PetroChina has the largest international reserves of any Chinese oil company, but these are only one-tenth of those of Exxon Mobil, the leading American oil company. The widespread feeling among American politicians that China is involved in unacceptable interference in the internal affairs of oil-producing countries is staggeringly hypocritical, given the unceasing, ongoing, and intensifying American involvement in the internal development of oil-producing regions, especially the critically important Gulf region.

Environmental battle In the last few years in the high-income countries, there has developed a gathering concern over the perceived threat to human civilization from burning fossil fuels. China is increasingly perceived by Americans as the major threat to the global environment in the coming century. In his apocalyptic book *Collapse* (2005), Jared Diamond paints a nightmare vision of the environmental implications for America consequent upon China's rise. In a new version of the "Yellow Peril," Diamond warns that if China achieves First World living standards it will "approximately double the entire world's human resource use and environmental impact." He doubts whether even the world's current human resource use and environmental impact can be sustained: "Something has to give way. That is the strongest reason why China's problems automatically become the world's problems."

He forecasts that if current trends continue, with "emissions rising in China, steady in the US [sic], declining elsewhere," by the year 2050 China will account for 40 percent of the world's total emissions of carbon dioxide. He points out that China already leads the world in the production of sulfur dioxide, with an output double that of America. He portrays a terrifying vision of China's export of pollution: "Propelled eastwards by winds, the pollutant-laden dust, sand, and soil originating from China's deserts, degraded pastures, and fallow farmland gets blown to Korea, Japan, the Pacific islands, and across the Pacific within a week to America and Canada. Those aerial particles are the result of China's coal-burning, deforestation, overgrazing, erosion, and destructive agricultural methods."

China will soon overtake Japan as the world's largest importer of tropical timber. Diamond argues that China is, in effect, "conserving its own forests" by "exporting deforestation to other countries, several of which (including Malaysia, Papua New

Guinea, and Australia) have already reached or are on the road to catastrophic deforestation." Diamond argues that several of China's "exports" pose a severe environmental threat to America: "[T]he three best-known pests that have wiped out numerous North American tree populations—the chestnut blight, the misnamed "Dutch" elm disease, and the Asian long-horned beetle—all originated in China or else somewhere nearby in East Asia." He believes that the Chinese grass carp, "now established in rivers and lakes of 45 US states," competes with "native fish species and causes large changes in aquatic plant, plankton, and invertebrate communities."

Diamond is concerned at yet another threat to America from China's rise: "Still another species of which China has an abundant population, which has large ecological and economic impacts, and which China is exporting in increasing numbers is Homo Sapiens. For instance, China has now moved into third place as a source of legal immigration into Australia, and significant numbers of illegal as well as legal immigrants crossing the Pacific reach even the United States."

Trade and finance During the era of capitalist globalization, America and China presented mirror images of each other. China became an important supply engine of the global economy, while America became the world's most important demand engine. Each grew in a seriously unbalanced fashion. In America the share of consumption rose from around 65 percent in the early 1980s to 71 percent in 2004. America accounts for only around six percent of global population, but it accounts for one-third of global consumption. In China, after decades of high levels of welfare security under the planned economy, the transition to the market economy has produced high levels of personal insecurity, helping to stimulate a very high rate of savings. Moreover, China is still a poor country. Despite having over 20 percent of the world's total population, China accounts for only around three percent of global household consumption. By 2004 the American population's savings rate stood at minus one percent, compared with 35 percent in China. During this period America's trade (merchandise plus services) deficit widened alarmingly, growing from 1.6 percent of GDP in 1995 to 6.0 percent in 2006. The almost exact counterpart of this was the rapid expansion of China's trade surplus, from 1.4 percent of GDP in 1995 to 6.3 percent in 2006.

These developments stimulated strong responses within America. There developed a widespread sense among Americans that the Chinese state "cheats" through a variety of channels in order to artificially stimulate its exports. These include holding down the value of the national currency, the *renminbi*; providing subsidized inputs to exporting firms; sacrificing environmental standards and working conditions in China in order to increase export competitiveness; unfairly nurturing "national champion firms" that can compete internationally; and providing abundant credit from state-owned banks on favorable terms to exporters. China's success in increasing its exports was widely perceived to threaten American workers' jobs and conditions of employment. In addition, it has become increasingly widely thought that China bears a heavy responsibility for the American asset bubble due to its large purchases of American government debt consequent upon its large increases in foreign exchange holdings, thought to have been a main cause of the low American interest rates in this period.

The mainstream view on Capitol Hill is fearful of China's rise. The US–China Economic and Security Review Commission (USCESRC) was set up in October 2000 by the American Congress to "monitor and investigate and report to Congress on the national security implications of the bilateral trade and economic relationship between America and the People's Republic of China." The Commissioners are all appointed by Congress. The Commission has produced a succession of reports, each of which expresses deep apprehensions about the implications of China's economic rise for America, including the impact on American employment and conditions of work, and upon America's technological and military superiority. At one of its hearings, Vice-Chairman C. Richard D'Amato commented: "If you can figure out how to integrate a Chinese communist dictatorship with over a billion people who go where they're told to go; who work in the industry they're told to work [in]; who get paid what they're told they're worth; who have no way to answer back; if you can figure out how to integrate that into the world economy, please let me know." Numerous protectionist measures directed against China were ready to be enacted by Congress even before the financial crisis erupted.

In fact the relationship between China's rise and America's economic difficulties is far more complex than is usually suggested. In terms of China's role in keeping down American interest rates, it is a mistake to focus on China. China did not overtake Japan as the largest holder of American Treasury bills, notes, and bonds until late in 2008. Moreover, America's domestic institutions account for around one-half of the total holdings. Despite the rapid increase in China's foreign exchange reserves, they still account for only around one-third of the world total. As a share of GDP the foreign exchange reserves of Singapore, Hong Kong, and Malaysia each greatly exceed those of China. China has built up large foreign exchange reserves by dint of its intense efforts to export. This may be regarded as an umbrella to protect its citizens against unwelcome changes in the economic weather, but there are 1.3 billion Chinese people who need to shelter under the umbrella. In per capita terms, China's foreign exchange reserves are far smaller than elsewhere in East Asia. At the end of 2007, China's foreign exchange reserves per person stood at $1,170, compared with $3,900 in Malaysia, $5,500 in Korea, $6,800 in Taiwan, $7,500 in Japan, $22,000 in Hong Kong, and no less than $41,000 in Singapore.

The American trade deficit increased to a forecast $664 billion in 2008, standing at around two-fifths of the world total. In terms of the role of China's exports in the yawning American trade deficit, the focus on China is misplaced. It was still the case in 2006 that only 11 percent of total American imports were made in China.

Although China's trade surplus rose rapidly during the period of capitalist globalization, so too did those of other countries. It was forecast that in 2008 the total world current account surplus would reach around $2 trillion.[14] China's share of the total is forecast to stand at just 16 percent. The share of the oil-exporting countries is forecast to stand at no less than 40 percent, while that of Japan and Germany together is forecast to stand at 27 percent. Although China has a far larger population, its exports are still only around one-tenth of the total exports of the high-income countries. The main basis of China's exports is labor-intensive, low technology goods. Almost four-fifths of American toys and games are imported from China. The main body of exports to America from Germany and Japan consists of high-technology equipment. Moreover, China's national companies have only negligible production in their international operations, with almost nothing in America, in part due to political restrictions on their inward investment. In addition to their direct exports to America, Germany and Japan have large-scale production facilities there. Moreover, companies from Germany, Japan, and America all have large-scale production and exports from their investments in China. Over 60 percent of China's total exports and over 80 percent of high-technology exports come from foreign-invested firms.

As the global recession bites deeper, a balanced evaluation of the relationship between China's rise and the crisis in America's political economy may be an "inconvenient truth." The chorus of hostile opinion seeking a scapegoat may drown out balanced evaluations. It may be politically more convenient to blame China's rise rather than attribute the crisis in the American political economy to the contradictions of the free market, including America's locked-in addiction to the automobile and to oil, and its consequences for American foreign policy; or to attribute it to the American-led Washington Consensus policies on financial liberalization and their role in the Asian financial crisis and in the response of East Asian countries, and their role too in the global financial crisis.

Military relations The world is in the middle of one of the great historic changes in relative power, and historically such changes have mostly led to conflict. Since the 1980s the world has entered the second era of globalization. The first one began in the second half of the nineteenth century and ended with a series of political and economic disasters in the first half of the twentieth century. If such calamities are to be avoided, much will depend on the relationship between America, which is in relative decline, and a rising China.

There is deep concern in America that China's rise will transform fundamentally the balance of world economic and military power. In the view of the American government, China is the one country that has the potential to challenge American supremacy. The Pentagon's Quadrennial Defense Review of 2006 stated: "Of the major powers, China has the greatest potential to compete militarily with America and field disruptive military technologies that could over time offset traditional

US military advantages absent [sic] counter strategies." In 2002 President Bush warned China:

> In pursuing advanced military capabilities that can threaten its neighbors in the Asia-Pacific region, China is following an outdated path that, in the end, will hamper its own pursuit of greatness. It is time to reaffirm the essential role of American military strength. We must build and maintain our defenses beyond challenge … Our forces will be strong enough to dissuade potential adversaries from pursuing a military build-up in hopes of surpassing, or equaling, the power of the US.

In 1999 America's military budget stood at $253 billion. In the wake of 9/11, the budget rose steeply, and by 2008 America's total military expenditure had reached $696 billion, around $2 billion per day. In the era of the global market economy, which has a central impulse toward universalism that breaks down international economic, social, and cultural differences, it is remarkable that America spends so much on instruments designed to kill human beings from other countries.

America has an ever-expanding military relationship with the countries around China. Japan itself has a large stock of military equipment, mainly purchased from America. America has almost 60,000 military personnel stationed in Japan. Its stock of military equipment in Japan includes around 100 F-16 and F-15 fighters. America also has an aircraft carrier plus support ships headquartered at Yokosuka, which form the core of the American 7th Fleet. Japan and America have established a "joint missile defense shield," the primary motivation for which is their fear of China. Japanese and American officers are engaged in joint efforts to improve their forces' interoperability, and smooth the interface between their respective combat and communication systems. America is also nurturing "trilateral military cooperation" between South Korea, Japan, and America. The Commander-in-Chief of the American Pacific Command (PACOM) has indicated that America's ties with South Korea must adapt to "the changing security environment represented by China's military modernization." South Korea itself has a powerful air force, including almost 500 modern fighter aircraft, all purchased from America. In addition America has around 35,000 military personnel in South Korea, and its military equipment in South Korea includes over 80 combat aircraft. America is also closely involved in Taiwan's military modernization. Taiwan possesses a large modern air force, with more than 500 combat aircraft, including over 230 American F-15s and F-16s.

The world may never face a greater risk of nuclear warfare. America is the only country that has used nuclear weapons to wage war. It dropped the first atomic bomb on Hiroshima on August 6, 1945, and the second one three days later, on August 9, at Nagasaki. When he was informed of the attack on Hiroshima, President Truman declared: "This is the greatest thing that has ever happened." Otto Frisch was working at the Los Alamos laboratory when somebody opened the door and shouted "Hiroshima has been destroyed!" Frisch later recalled: "I still remember the feeling of unease, indeed nausea, when I saw how many of my friends were rushing to the telephone to book tables at the La Fonda hotel in Santa Fe, in order to celebrate." That same evening at Los Alamos Robert Oppenheimer made a speech in the auditorium after walking through a cheering crowd of scientists pumping his fists in the air.

Today America has a stock of 8,000 active or operational nuclear warheads, with an average destructive power that is 20 times that of the Hiroshima bomb, which killed around 200,000 people. Of these nuclear weapons, 2,000 are on hair-trigger alert, ready to be launched with 15 minutes' warning. America has never endorsed the policy of "no first use." Robert McNamara was the American Secretary of Defense (1961–68) during the Vietnam War. In 2005 he wrote:

> We have been and remain prepared to initiate the use of nuclear weapons—by the decision of one person, the president—against either a nuclear or non-nuclear enemy whenever we believe it is in our interest to do so ... On any given day, as we go about our business, the president is prepared to make a decision within twenty minutes that could launch one of the most devastating weapons in the world. To declare war requires an act of Congress, but to launch a nuclear holocaust requires twenty minutes' deliberation by the president and his advisors.

In 2005 America's Annual Report to Congress on "The Military Power of the People's Republic of China" concluded that China will not be ready to fight even a moderate-sized adversary until 2010, and that the People's Liberation Army (PLA) is presently unable to compete directly with other modern military powers. In the view of some American military experts America has succeeded in achieving nuclear primacy. China has a limited nuclear arsenal. It possesses no long-range bombers or modern submarine-based nuclear weapons. China's medium-range bomber force is obsolete and vulnerable to attack. China's entire intercontinental nuclear arsenal consists of 18 stationary single-warhead ICBMs. These are "not ready to launch on warning." Their warheads are "kept in storage" and "the missiles themselves are unfueled." The lack of any advanced early warning system adds to the vulnerability of China's ICBMs. China would have no warning of an American submarine-launched missile attack or a strike using hundreds of stealthy nuclear-armed cruise missiles. Despite much talk about China's military modernization, the odds that China will acquire a survivable nuclear deterrent in the next decade are "slim." Some experts believe that Russia can no longer count on a survivable nuclear deterrent either. The fact that for many years to come America may have the capability to destroy the nuclear weapons systems of both Russia and China without risk of nuclear retaliation can be seen as a force for global stability. It may also be viewed as a dangerous encouragement to America to threaten or even to use nuclear violence in the event of international confrontation.

The American government regards nuclear weapons as central to its military strategy. This provides an intense incentive for other nations to either expand their existing arsenals or develop nuclear weapons if they do not already possess them. Robert McNamara characterized the American nuclear weapons policy as "immoral, illegal, militarily unnecessary, and dreadfully dangerous." The risk of an accidental or inadvertent nuclear launch is unacceptably high. In his view the only rational policy is to "move promptly toward the elimination—or near elimination—of all nuclear weapons."

Fears of China's rise are now embedded deeply in the American intellectual and government elite in relation to China's perceived impact on American inequality, conditions of work, energy security, ecology, and financial security, not to speak of the perceived threat to American global economic, financial, cultural, and military dominance. It requires little imagination to visualize the innumerable different ways in which the contradictory impact of capitalist globalization upon both China and America could erupt into a military conflict.

Cooperation?

China experts often refer to the Chinese word *wei-ji*, meaning "crisis." They point out that the Chinese word *wei-ji* contains two parts. *Wei* can be combined with *xian*, to produce the word *wei-xian*, meaning "danger." *Ji* can be combined with the character *hui* to form the word *ji-hui*, meaning "opportunity." In other words, in the Chinese language, a "crisis" can be viewed as both a "danger" and an "opportunity." The danger of a global catastrophe also contains the opportunity to produce non-ideological Sino-American cooperation in order to solve common problems and contribute to global cooperation to solve the problems that confront all humanity.

While there is deep fear of China's rise among Congressional representatives, the leaders of large American firms are mostly enthusiastic about globalization in general, and about China in particular. American business leaders have become increasingly international in their outlook. Most of them view China's rise as an immense opportunity. Most of them are intensely enthusiastic about China, and often try to understand its history and culture. Many of their children have studied in China.

Apart from the benefit to American firms there are numerous ways in which Sino-American cooperation can work to the advantage of the populations of both countries. Above all, the avoidance of war is in the interests of the mass of citizens of both countries. In the event of nuclear or biological/chemical warfare, no one would escape the impact, whatever their level of income or wealth. China's economy is now so closely integrated with that of America that its political and economic collapse would greatly harm ordinary Americans, not to speak of the mass of Chinese people. The surging inequalities in income, wealth, and life chances in both countries can only be resolved by each of them identifying a new role for their

164

respective governments, coordinating their efforts, and learning from each other's experience, both today and in the past. The two countries need to cooperate closely to resolve the global energy and ecological challenge, and to establish a stable structure for global finance. Some American policy-makers believe that the areas of mutual interest between America and China are greater and more significant than their spheres of potential conflict.

In 2006 the (then) American Deputy Secretary of State, Robert Zoellick, proposed that America try to work with China to become a "responsible stakeholder" in the international system. He argued that there was now a close connection between domestic developments in America and China, and the way in which the two countries interact with each other on regional and global issues. Zoellick believes that China seeks a benign external environment in which to pursue its internal development. He considers that China's philosophy of a "peaceful rise" means that it does not seek to overthrow the international system, but, rather, that it wants to work with America and others to calm anxieties.

Deepening interconnection of American and Chinese political economies In the 1980s the prime goal of American foreign policy was the overthrow of the "evil empire" of the Soviet Union. This goal was pursued through acceleration of the arms race and numerous channels of influence upon Soviet policy-makers. American foreign policy played a significant role in the collapse of Soviet communism and the disintegration of the Soviet Union. Alternative policies pursued by the Communist Party of the Soviet Union could have produced an extraordinary acceleration of Soviet economic growth as the country made use of its abundant natural resources, high scientific achievements, and exceptionally advanced human resources. Gradual reform polices under Communist Party leadership might have allowed the economy to move toward the "production frontier" of what it was capable of achieving with its rich resources. Instead, "regime change" resulted in state disintegration, with disastrous consequences for the economy and for the welfare of most Russians. The Soviet economy had only negligible linkages to the American economy. The Soviet Union accounted for a tiny fraction of American exports, and it received no investment by American multinationals. Soviet exports to America were trivial in scale. The collapse of the Soviet economy had a negligible impact on the American economy other than the short-term fall in American military expenditure.

During the high-speed advance of capitalist globalization since the 1980s the Chinese and American economies and business systems have become closely intertwined. American consumers benefit greatly from the rapid growth of low-priced Chinese exports. American companies and shareholders benefit from China's absorption of booming American investments and from American companies' access to the low-cost manufacturing supply chain in China. American primary product producers (including food, oil, and mining companies) benefit from exports to China, both directly from America and, increasingly, from production bases in other countries. American high-technology firms benefit from the export of products such as aircraft, medical, telecoms and power equipment, semi-conductors, and software. American retailers benefit from low-cost sourcing in China. The American government benefits from Chinese government purchase of its debt. "System disintegration" in China, such as America helped bring about in the Soviet Union, Afghanistan, and Iraq, and may help to bring about in Iran (and, perhaps, more widely in the Muslim world), would have severe economic consequences for America. It is in the interests of American business and the mass of American citizens, not to speak of the rest of the world, to support the efforts of China's Communist Party leadership to achieve the country's "peaceful rise."

China's deep engagement with global capitalism has resulted in an economy that is far more open to the international economy than were most other latecomer countries, including America. By 2003 the ratio of the stock of inward investment to GDP was 35 percent in China, compared with eight percent in South Korea, five percent in India and just two percent in Japan. China's economy is far more open to trade than any other large economy. In 2004 the ratio of China's trade to its GDP reached 70 percent. The foreign trade ratios of America and Japan are both less than 25 percent.

America is critically important for the Chinese economy. America has become one of the largest sources of FDI inflows into China. American investment in China has many benefits. Leading global systems integrator firms from America stimulate other international firms (both from America and elsewhere) within their supply chains to establish production facilities in China. They bring management skills and technologies to China, and exert intense pressure on the whole supply chain within China to advance its business and technological skills. By 2005 America had become the most important market for China's exports, totaling $163 billion, or over 21 percent of China's total exports. In the same year America accounted for just 7.4 percent of China's total imports. However, these consist predominantly of high-technology products, such as semiconductors, aircraft, and power stations, which play an important role in upgrading China's technological base. The recession in America is already having a serious impact on China, an impact which would be greatly exacerbated by American protectionism.

Harmonious society: freedom, state, and market Capitalist globalization has contributed to surging inequality of income and life chances in both China and America. In China there has been intense debate among policy-makers about the rapid growth of inequality, not only in income, but also in education, health, and life chances. The country's leaders have declared their intention to try to establish a "harmonious society" based on a just distribution of income and life chances. In America too, as we have seen, there has been a surge of analysis and discussion of the rapidly growing disparity of income and life chances, with parallels being drawn with the Gilded Age of wealth polarization in the late nineteenth century. Today, as then, many Americans, from widely differing political backgrounds, feel that the American government should play a much larger role in income redistribution and welfare if American society is to remain stable and just, and if freedom is to mean more than simply the freedom to buy and sell.

"Freedom" is a word whose meaning has been the subject of intense debate in America since Independence. At the heart of this debate has been the battle over the role of the state and its function in the achievement of "positive" and "negative" freedoms. This debate has been greatly influenced by Social Darwinism, which was centrally important in American political philosophy from the late nineteenth century until the Great Depression of the 1930s. In fact, however, Darwin's own ideas were far removed from those of Social Darwinism. In *The Descent of Man* Darwin paid close attention to the evolution of moral qualities in human beings, ascribing a central role in human evolution to the development of "social instincts." Darwin ranged widely in exploring the origins of these instincts among human beings; he uses the word "love" more than 90 times in *The Descent of Man*. He argued that primeval men, the ape-like progenitors of man, became social beings through the acquisition of "the same instinctive feelings, which impel other animals to live in a body": "They would have felt uneasy when separated from their comrades, from whom they would have felt some degree of love; they would have warned each other of danger, and have given mutual aid in attack or defence. All this implies some degree of sympathy, fidelity, and courage." Darwin believed that at a very remote period primitive men were influenced by the praise and blame of their fellows, and through this acquired social instincts that helped them to succeed in competition with other groups of their own species. As human society evolved, people's moral sense, or conscience, became more complex, "originating in the social instincts, largely guided by the approbation of [their] fellow-men, ruled by reason, self-interest, and in later times, by deep religious feelings, and confirmed by instruction and habit." He believed that the foundation stone of morality became the motto "do unto others as ye would they should do unto you."

The Gilded Age in America at the end of the nineteenth century witnessed a tremendous concentration of wealth and income. By 1890 the richest one percent of the American population received the same total income as the bottom 50 percent and owned more wealth than the bottom 99 percent. In the 1890s there was violent class struggle. In the face of such extreme inequality and class conflict, American writers such as Walt Whitman in *Democratic Vistas* (1871) and Edward Bellamy in *Looking Backwards* (1888) provided a utopian vision of America in the distant future. Bellamy anticipated that by the end of the twentieth century, buying and selling would be "considered absolutely inconsistent with the mutual benevolence and disinterestedness which should prevail between citizens." He imagined that by the year 2000 "service of the nation, patriotism, and passion for humanity" rather than "self-service" would motivate the American worker. The American Economics

Association was founded in 1885, at the high point of the Gilded Age, with the express purpose of combating Social Darwinism and laissez-faire orthodoxy. The founder of the AEA, Richard T. Ely, wrote: "We regard the state as an educational and ethical agency whose positive assistance is one of the indispensable conditions of human progress." Many younger economists believed that private property had become a means of depriving others of their freedom, and that poverty posed a far graver danger to the republic than an activist state.

During the Progressive Era leading up to World War I, a broad coalition of forces emerged in America to nourish the idea of an activist national state to enable the realization of freedom for the mass of the people. Laissez-faire became "anathema among the lovers of liberty." It was thought that only "energetic government" was able to "create the social conditions for freedom." Progressives such as John Dewey and William Willoughby believed that true freedom required the state to establish the social conditions for the full human development of all citizens. T. H. Green, the British philosopher, made a profound impact with his lectures in America in which he argued that freedom was a positive concept. He explicitly linked the concept of positive freedom with the conditions necessary for people to realize these freedoms, namely education, health, housing, and other cultural and material prerequisites for a fulfilled life.

The Great Depression had a major impact on the struggle over the interpretation of freedom in America. By 1932 over 15 million Americans were out of work. For those able to find jobs real wages fell precipitously. Hungry men and women lined the streets of major cities. Thousands more inhabited the ramshackle shanty towns ("Hoovervilles") that sprang up in parks and on abandoned land. No part of America was untouched by the crisis. When he assumed the presidency in 1933, Franklin D. Roosevelt proclaimed: "For too many Americans, life is no longer free; liberty no longer real; men can no longer follow the pursuit of happiness." Under Roosevelt's guidance, the Democratic Party led the country toward large-scale state intervention to reconstruct the economy and provide citizens with social security. The Depression discredited the idea that social progress rested on the unrestrained pursuit of wealth, and transformed expectations of government. It reinvigorated the Progressive conviction that the national state must protect Americans from the vicissitudes of the marketplace. It placed "social citizenship," with a broad public guarantee of economic security, at the forefront of American discussions of freedom. These ideas remained in the mainstream of American political thought for long into the post-war world, reinforced by the massive task of economic and social reconstruction in war-ravaged Europe.

In recent years there has been intense debate in America about the perception that social cohesion has declined. In *Bowling Alone*, Robert Putnam examined the change in "social capital." He believes that social capital develops because people develop patterns of reciprocal behavior in which mutual support provided by one party to another can enable that provider to benefit at some future point in their own life. Putnam drew a striking conclusion from his research: "For the first two-thirds of the twentieth century a powerful tide bore Americans into ever-deeper engagement in the life of their communities, but a few decades ago—silently and without warning—that tide reversed and we were overtaken by a treacherous rip-current. Without at first noticing, we have been pulled apart from one another and from our communities over the last third of the century." Putnam believes that the drastic increase in the role of TV in daily lives was associated with a pronounced increase in individualistic, materialistic values conveyed through formal advertising, but, also, increasingly, through advertising embedded within programs. The data in Putnam's study pre-dates the revolution in information technology that has taken place since the late 1990s. This revolution, which employs technologically sophisticated marketing techniques, has been the mechanism through which materialist, individualistic values and the instant gratification of consumerist wishes through access to debt have been purveyed ever more powerfully to young people.

Even before the financial crisis the role of state and market were already beginning to be rethought in the light of the surging contradictions of capitalist globalization. It was increasingly realized that the answer to these contradictions was to return to an older tradition that attempts to establish a less ideological approach to the role of state and market. There was an increasing chorus of voices from all parts of the political spectrum that was appalled by the growing inequality of income and life chances that emerged during the era of wild capitalist globalization. By 2006–7 there was widespread public concern across the whole political spectrum about the growth of inequality within America, and its relationship to globalization. A *Financial Times*/Harris poll conducted in spring 2008 found that 78 percent of Americans believe that the income gap between rich and poor citizens has grown too wide. More than two-thirds of Americans believe that the government should raise taxes for rich people and lower them for poor people. It was increasingly recognized that the American government needs to expand greatly its responsibility for supporting and retraining American workers who become displaced by globalization. The impact of the global financial crisis on the American economy and society has intensified the need for the government to increase its intervention in order to ensure that the whole of society pulls through the crisis together. The example of both the New Deal and the wartime economy and spirit were increasingly referred to as relevant to the deepening crisis.

In December 2008 President-elect Obama made it clear that the crisis provided an opportunity to increase government investment in America's crumbling road, water, and public transport infrastructure, and in "green energy," as well as in its education and health system: "As tough as times are right now there is a convergence between circumstances and agenda. The key for us is to make sure that we jump-start the economy in a way that doesn't just deal with the short term, but puts us also on a glide path to sustainable development." The President-elect emphasized that the crisis was not confined to America, and required greatly increased international cooperation: "The reality is that the economic crisis we face is no longer just an American crisis, it is a global crisis—and we will need to reach out to countries around the world to craft a global response." The financial crisis was crucially important in Barack Obama's sweeping electoral victory. It has the potential to legitimize a radical shift in the center of gravity in American politics away from Social Darwinism, which reached its apogee under President Bush, and a return to a tradition in which state action is crucially important to the achievement of a socially cohesive society. It remains to be seen how far this potential is realized.

China also is searching for its own balance of state and market. By the turn of the millennium, China's social welfare system had been substantially dismantled, and most welfare spending came from individuals' personal payments. Under the policies of reform and opening up, the gap between urban and rural incomes has widened, and the huge body of rural migrant workers have found themselves to be second-class citizens in the urban areas. After 2002 the Chinese government acknowledged the shortcomings of a market-dominated approach toward social welfare. It began to reverse the tide and instead try to construct a "harmonious society." Under this philosophy, the goal is to rebalance the development model away from the path followed since the early 1990s. The objective is to redistribute income toward the poorer segments of society, especially those in the rural areas and toward the lower strata of income distribution in the urban areas, including the migrant workers, as well as moving toward a more energy-efficient path of development.

The government is carefully studying the varied experiences of high-income countries, as well as looking back at its own history. China's reforms since the 1970s have been described as "groping for stones to cross the river." It has been widely assumed by American analysts, and indeed by many Chinese commentators, that the other bank of the river for China's reforms is a political-economic system like that of America in the era of capitalist globalization. However, the mainstream of Chinese policy-makers is far removed from this view. The government is trying to devise policies that deal with the surging contradictions of the market economy. It emphasizes the need to use the market to achieve desirable ends, but it recognizes the need to regulate the market in the overall interest of society. It regards the provision of "positive freedom" for all members of society as the bedrock of a "harmonious socialist society":

> We need to ensure that everyone has an opportunity to pursue all-round development in an environment of freedom and equality. Just as promoting economic development and increasing people's welfare is the bound duty of the government, advancing social equity and justice is the conscience of the government ... We should value fraternity rather than self-love, and follow ethical

standards that are higher even than the mountains … Only by appropriately spreading the fruits of economic development among the people can we win their support and maintain social stability. (Premier Wen Jiabao, March 2008)

After 2002, the government took numerous concrete measures to establish a "harmonious society." It rescinded the agricultural tax and introduced substantial subsidies for the main agricultural products, which had a large impact on rural incomes. It stopped collecting tuition fees from the 150 million rural students receiving compulsory education. It instituted free education for students majoring in education in teacher colleges. It promoted a new type of rural cooperative medical insurance, which covered nine-tenths of all counties by 2008. It is building a system of health clinics in every village and creating a rural medicine supply network in order to ensure that rural residents have access to safe, effective, convenient, and reasonably priced medical and health care services. The major communicable diseases, such as AIDS, tuberculosis, and schistosomiasis, are now treated free of charge.

It is working through several channels to improve the social safety net for urban residents, including improvements to the basic old-age pension system, unemployment, and medical insurance. It now provides targeted assistance for the poorer segments of the urban population. It is setting up a nationwide basic minimum cost-of-living allowance system for all residents, and devising policies to address the housing difficulties of poor urban dwellers. It is giving priority in housing development to housing for low and middle-income families and accelerating the construction of low-rent housing for poor families. It is paying close attention to resolving the problems experienced by rural migrant workers and their families in the cities. It has introduced measures to ensure that children from poor families and children of rural migrant workers in cities enjoy the same access to compulsory education as other children of urban dwellers. It is developing an old-age insurance system and is working to upgrade the social safety net for rural migrants working in the cities, including medical insurance for major diseases.

The measures taken by the government since 2002 to improve social welfare for poor people have had a significant effect. However, the challenge to social stability posed by the global financial crisis is deep. In November 2008, in response to the rapidly intensifying impact of the global financial crisis, the government announced a huge $586 billion emergency package to be spent in 2009 and 2010, to include increased expenditure on railways, roads, and airports; on the urban and rural electricity grid; on reconstruction for earthquake-hit areas; on rural residents' livelihood projects and rural infrastructure; on housing projects for low-income urban residents; on ecological and environmental protection projects; on independent innovation and industrial restructuring; and on medical care and education. The global crisis provides an opportunity to accelerate the rebalancing of China's growth model toward one that is more sustainable over the long term, through increased orientation toward social justice and domestic demand, and through increased energy efficiency:

> During the period ahead, it is glaringly obvious that we will face pressure from the global financial crisis, which will become increasingly deep, and from the self-evident slowdown in global economic growth. It is glaringly obvious that we will face pressure from the dramatic decline in external demand and from the gradual weakening of China's traditional competitive advantage. It is glaringly obvious that we will face pressure from increasingly intense international competition and from the rise of trade and investment protectionism. It is glaringly obvious that we will face pressure from the increasingly strong constraints on population, resources, and environment, and from the increasingly urgent need to transform the approach toward economic development. (President Hu Jintao, November 29, 2008)

The accelerated rebalancing of China's development model will reduce the country's vulnerability to economic shocks. Whether it will be sufficient to enable the country to weather the rising storm of the global recession successfully remains to be seen.

China and America have entered the era of capitalist globalization from fundamentally different starting points. China entered it as an isolated, centrally planned, non-market economy. America entered it on the rising tide of free market Social Darwinism. However, they are both groping their way toward a sustainable development path. Despite the enormous discrepancy in their levels of development, they are both experiencing profound system destabilization arising from the surging contradictions of raw capitalist globalization, which have intensified drastically with the onset of the global financial crisis. For both America and China, the global financial crisis and its impact on their economy and society presents an opportunity. In both countries the crisis justifies greatly increased government intervention to protect the interests of all citizens in the face of a serious threat to their economic security.

America and China can both learn from their respective political-economic histories. Both countries are trying to "use the past to serve the present." China is trying to find a new center of gravity after the extremes of the Maoist "instruction economy," and is searching in its own long history for inspiration. In America it is increasingly recognized that the country needs to learn from its own history about the best way in which to control the market in the broad social interest. The financial crisis that erupted in America in 2007–8 could lead to a return to an increased role for the state comparable with the change after the Great Depression and in the post-war period of global reconstruction, when America's leaders tried to build a "Great Society," and it could lead also to America playing a central role in building the global institutions needed to ensure sustainable human development. The deep impact of the global financial crisis upon China has led its government to accelerate the country's move toward a "harmonious society" in order to rebalance the overall development model toward a just and socially sustainable pattern of development. China's deep integration into the global economy means that it also has a strong interest to cooperate with America to build global institutions to regulate international markets in the collective interest.

Science, technology, and the environment America is at the center of global technological progress. Its firms are by far the most powerful in terms of R&D, with particular dominance in information technology, the key to the global business system. In 2002 American companies spent over $21 billion on R&D undertaken in other countries. Of this total, $2.7 billion was in developing countries, of which around $650 million was undertaken by American companies in China. By 2003 foreign companies are estimated to have accounted for around one-quarter of total R&D spending in China. Of this, American companies accounted for around one-third.

The number of students in American tertiary education in technological subjects (science, engineering, and mathematics) is greatly exceeded by the number of such students in China, India, and Russia. In 2000–1 there were 2.6 million students enrolled in tertiary education in technological subjects in China, 2.4 million in Russia, 1.9 million in India, and 1.7 million in America. In 2006 the American National Academies published a report entitled *Rising Above the Gathering Storm*, which argued for a large increase in both the size and the effectiveness of government support for American science and technology if the country is to sustain its technological lead. It recommended that the American government should implement policies to attract an increased share of the world's most able young scientists and engineers to work in America. These would include easing visa requirements, providing priority to doctoral-level scientists and engineers in obtaining American citizenship, and providing international students and researchers in America with access to information and research equipment in American industrial, academic, and national laboratories comparable with the access provided to American citizens and permanent residents of a similar status.

Although Chinese firms still face an intense struggle on the "global level playing field," Chinese people are already making a large and rapidly growing contribution to global technological progress. Chinese engineers and scientists constitute a large and growing fraction of the research force of leading global firms, working both in the high-income countries and, increasingly, in research institutes established by global firms in China. American firms are in the vanguard of global technological progress, and, already, Chinese scientists and engineers are making a large contribution to new knowledge within those firms.

There are many areas in which science needs urgently to produce solutions in order to allow global sustainable development, and nowhere are the challenges more intense than in China. They include improving human physical and mental well-being, overcoming the exhaustion of non-renewable resources, finding new ways to harness renewable energy sources, producing food in sustainable ways, devising new forms of transport and urban living, and shifting the structure of consumption toward a sustainable path. China cannot simply replicate the locked-in growth pattern of today's high-income countries that has resulted from the operation of market forces. Because of its vast size and rapid growth, the difficulties that China confronts are of unique intensity. The very survival of China, and indeed of the whole world, depends on meeting these challenges. By contributing to solutions to these burning problems, Chinese science and technology can make a large contribution to global sustainable development. This contribution can come through Chinese scientists working within global corporations. However, a key part of the contribution may take place through China's core group of around 150 state-owned enterprises. No other country now possesses such a powerful group of state-owned firms. They have the potential to work in a coordinated fashion to meet the long-term needs of China's sustainable development, and, in so doing, to contribute to global sustainable development. This, in its turn, is in the long-term interest of American business and the mass of American citizens.

The energy sector is a critical area of interaction between America and China. Perceptions of the importance of energy security have increased dramatically in America in recent years. In 2006 the Chairman of the Senate Foreign Relations Committee, Richard Lugar, warned: "No one who is honestly assessing the decline of American leverage around the world due to energy dependence can fail to see that energy is the albatross of US national security." He said that America needed to expand international coordination of energy issues, especially with India and China, in order to address the growing global competition for energy resources. He argued that resolving American energy security required "extraordinary international diplomacy."

In some ways China and America face common problems and have common incentives to solve their respective energy problems. They have a common interest in political and social stability in Muslim countries and elsewhere, in order to ensure stability of oil supplies. America and China might benefit from working together to develop and implement utilization of "next-generation fuels" such as hydrogen. They can both benefit greatly by increasing rapidly the share of electricity they generate by nuclear power. They would both benefit from techniques to harness solar, wind, and wave power more effectively. Given that they both have massive coal reserves, there is tremendous potential for them to cooperate in technologies to convert coal to oil, and so ease their respective energy security worries. China's investments in coal liquefaction, using American–South African technology, are already well advanced. They have a common interest in devising ways to use their abundant coal resources so as to be less damaging to the environment, both locally and globally. For example, they have a common interest in the development of carbon sequestration technologies. China can also benefit from American technology in areas that enable it to increase the efficiency of its energy consumption and thereby reduce its reliance on oil. Such areas include reducing energy use through the employment of advanced machinery, clean coal technologies, and combustion efficiency improvements. Each of these areas offers large possibilities for American firms to benefit from policies to control global warming, and to work with Chinese firms to cooperate in advancing such technologies. There are enormous possibilities too, to build on existing relationships between American and Chinese universities to advance these technologies.

The negotiations over the successor to the Kyoto Protocol will involve a good deal of hard bargaining, not least between America and China. However, no one in either America or the Chinese policy-making circles now seriously doubts the weight of scientific evidence concerning global warming. Even under President Bush America radically shifted its stance toward the scientific evidence. America and China are the two most important nations by far in terms of the global environment; between them they account for 38 percent of total world primary energy consumption, 33 percent of global oil consumption, and no less than 59 percent of global coal consumption. Neither of them can escape the consequences of global warming, the ultimate externality. Between them they account for an almost equal amount of carbon emissions, and together they account for 38 percent of global emissions of carbon dioxide. There is a compelling logic to America and China eventually finding a basis for a fair and effective balance between their respective contributions to the resolution of the challenge of global warming. Between them they hold the fate of the world in their hands. An agreement on the contribution that America and China each needs to make would form a solid foundation for the successor agreement to the Kyoto Protocol. The depth of discussion already under way between the relevant policy-makers and business leaders in the two countries provides grounds for optimism that between them the two countries can help to pull the world back from the global warming abyss.

Finance The depth of the global financial crisis, and the severity of the recession that is unfolding, has led to profound reflection on the nature of the global financial system. Increasingly, as the crisis has developed commentators have begun to refer to money as a "public utility" or, even, a "public good." The analogy can be drawn with fire. Fire is essential for human civilization. However, no one would suggest allowing fires to be started uncontrollably. A central task of human intelligence has been to control the application of fire, containing it in vessels that maximize the positive impact of combustion but limit its damaging effects. In the same way, by the end of 2008 it was increasingly recognized that the financial system required regulation at a global level.

America and China are key actors in the attempt to establish a global structure that regulates the financial system in the collective interest of the global community. China has the world's largest foreign exchange reserves. It has overtaken Japan as the country with the largest holdings of American Treasury bills, notes, and bonds. It is the country with the largest current account surplus. China's rise places it at the forefront of the demand to restructure global institutions to reflect the growing importance of developing countries. If they are to be effective, the institutions to govern the world in the twenty-first century must reflect equally the rights of all the world's citizens. They cannot be legitimate if they reflect only the wealth and economic power of certain countries. The change in the relative position of America and China in the key international institutions can serve as an inspiration for the world as it reconstructs global institutions to face the challenges outlined in this book. Among these, the most urgent is that of the global financial system. America and China have a heavy responsibility to ensure that this process succeeds.

The IMF was the key body to emerge from the Bretton Woods Conference of 1944. Right through to the present day it has been dominated by the high-income countries; with only around one-sixth of the world's population, they account for 60.5 percent of IMF voting rights. America alone, with 299 million people, has 17.1 percent of the votes, while China, with 1,312 million people, has just 3.7 percent of the votes. The guiding spirit behind the Bretton Woods Conference of 1944 was John Maynard Keynes. Keynes considered that the financial system instituted by the conference was necessary but dangerous if not properly regulated. He warned that it was highly likely that a deregulated financial system would turn into a "casino" in which speculation dominated the market. Under the influence of the Washington Consensus, with America at its core, the IMF led the drive to deregulate global financial markets from the 1970s onward. The world's financial markets have, as Keynes feared, become ever more like a casino. The "gambling economy" has increasingly gained the upper hand over the real economy where most people live and work.

The driving imperative of the move to deregulate the global financial system was the vested interests of banks in the high-income countries in general and America in particular. During the era of capitalist globalization, the banks headquartered in the high-income countries went through an explosive process of merger and acquisition, and international expansion of their operations. With the notable exception of Britain, each of the high-income countries sought to build national champion banks and were deeply resistant to takeover of national banks by banks from other countries. This did not prevent them, however, from arguing that developing countries should freely allow them to acquire local banks. Their philosophy seemed to be: "Do as I say, not as I do." In 2006, at the end of the era of wild capitalist globalization, out of 133 financial firms in the FT 500 there were just 11 from developing countries, and among the world's top 25 financial firms ranked by total assets there was just one from a developing country.

China was a major exception to the global trend during this period. When China began to reform its major state-owned banks, international banks were skeptical that the reform process would succeed. In a widely distributed analysis published in

2003, Citigroup argued that China should "tear apart the big four banks into relatively small units in order to switch on the process of bank reform ... If the big four are not broken up soon they will face bankruptcy." Citigroup argued that to have a small number of super-large banks posed a serious threat of moral hazard, because the state would go to any lengths to avoid bankruptcy of one of the big four banks. It concluded: "The hope that the big four commercial banks can be transformed into entities possessing competitive strength is manifestly unrealistic, but once the state-owned big banks are split up into several relatively small banks, then the whole picture will be transformed."

In fact, the banking reforms were remarkably successful. China tightly restricted ownership by foreign banks, which are still capped at 25 percent, undertook comprehensive internal reform, and floated minority shares of its leading commercial banks on international stock markets. By 2007 China had three of the world's top ten banks in terms of market capitalization; these three banks are all in the world's top 20 banks ranked by Tier 1 Capital. Chinese banks, however, still face deep challenges. The vast bulk of their business is in the highly protected domestic market. Their international competitiveness is still unproven. The political system still exerts a substantial influence on lending practices, and the impact of the global recession upon China will have a large impact on the domestic banks. However, Chinese banks enter the global recession in a relatively strong position.

The refusal of the Chinese government to allow a "level playing field" for American banks infuriated the leading American banks. Hank Paulson, the American Treasury Secretary, argued ceaselessly that liberalizing the ownership rules in China's financial sector was in the interests of both its people and its economy: "So many of the things they need to do for their own well-being are also the things that benefit the rest of the world ... We have pressed hard on capital markets. I do not understand why there are ownership caps." As the era of capitalist globalization progressed there was an intensifying barrage of argument from Washington Consensus institutions, American policy-makers, global banks, and international economists for China to liberalize its financial structure. Chinese policy-makers, bankers, and economists were criticized for being hardline, ideologically motivated, and technologically illiterate because they didn't understand or wish to acknowledge the benefits of financial liberalization. Not only did China's banks remain under majority state control, but the national currency, the *renminbi*, remained non-convertible, the capital account remained closed, and China's regulators prevented its banks from encouraging the explosion of personal debt that happened across the high-income countries and in those developing countries in which the global giant banks dominated, including large parts of the former Soviet Union and Eastern Europe. The arguments within China were intense. The example of the Asian financial crisis and the immense damage it had caused played a crucial role in enabling China's policy-makers to resist the siren calls from international opinion. China can be thankful that such wise decisions were made. If it had followed the advice of the international community, the impact of the global financial crisis would be far more severe than it is.

The global financial crisis has deeply damaged the banks of the high-income countries. However, the national governments of the high-income countries have not watched passively as their financial firms have collapsed. In only one case, namely Lehman Brothers, did a government allow a leading financial firm to collapse. That searing example of the application of the "hard budget constraint" rapidly disposed of the idea that considerations of moral hazard should govern policy toward insolvent banks. It placed the "soft budget constraint" at the heart of government policy in the high-income countries. The advice that these countries had dispensed around the world for the past three decades was suddenly cast aside, as their governments "circled the wagons" around their banks, which were regarded as too big to fail.

Despite the dramatic difficulties they have faced, it is possible that the banks headquartered in the high-income countries will emerge from the crisis with their competitive position even stronger relative to those headquartered in developing countries. On the one hand, numerous financial institutions have been taken into whole or partial state ownership. On the other hand, an explosive merger and acquisition process was permitted and even encouraged by the national governments of the high-income countries. These included the acquisition of Bear Stearns and Washington Mutual by J. P. Morgan, Merrill Lynch by Bank of America, Wachovia by Wells Fargo, Fortis by BNP Paribas, and HBOS by Lloyds TSB. Moreover, the crisis has dealt at least as much damage to the banks from developing countries, which have seen their local stock markets collapse and their economies enter a recession at least as severe as that in the high-income countries.

At its meeting in April 2006, against the background of increasing nervousness about the global financial system, the IMF announced a plan to give big emerging market economies an increased role in the IMF through an increase in their shareholdings and voting rights. It was hoped that these changes would increase the IMF's legitimacy and bind rising economic powers more tightly into the multilateral financial system. However, in the midst of the emerging global financial crisis in the autumn of 2007, the IMF failed to agree to the details of the major institutional reforms that had been agreed in principle, which would have given an increased voice to developing country governments. Against a chorus of disapproval from developing countries, the high-income countries insisted that, as before, the new head of the IMF be a European and the new head of the World Bank should be an American. It appeared that the high-income countries did not consider that the "natives" in the developing countries were ready yet to participate in the onerous task of governing the world's financial system.

The central arguments that were advanced by the Washington Consensus institutions in favor of global financial liberalization now appear, at best, threadbare. At worst, they appear to have been self-serving in order to meet the interests of the powerful banks headquartered in the high-income countries, with America at their core. The global financial crisis has exposed comprehensively the extreme danger posed by the liberal global financial structure promoted by America and its supporters. Both America and China are being deeply affected by the global recession, the fundamental cause of which lies in the deregulated global financial system put into place under American leadership from the 1970s onward, and which formed the core of wild capitalist globalization. It is in the interest of the citizens of both America and China that the global financial system is brought under the control of a global institution which has legitimacy in the eyes of the entire world, and which is felt to serve their collective public interest. In view of the depth of the crisis, the logic in favor of trying together to lead the world toward root-and-branch reform of the global financial system is compelling. Already the tone of the Sino-American dialogue on economics and finance has changed completely. Having looked into the abyss, the two countries have no choice but to cooperate in leading the world forward to place the financial system under collective control in the common interest of all its inhabitants.

The market and morality, East and West From ancient times to the present day, philosophers have sought to find a pragmatic, non-ideological middle way between competing extremes as the ethical foundation for the good society. If they are to cooperate internationally to solve the challenges created by capitalist globalization, human beings must find a common ethical ground from across the different world civilizations, "using the past to serve the present" to form a common ethic for global survival, which meets people's profound spiritual needs on the basis of a simple rational philosophy that all people can understand. In their search for a good society, China and America can look to the elements in their respective intellectual traditions that constitute a common ethical foundation for social life. The most influential thinkers of all cultures have addressed the fundamental issues of the ethical foundations for human survival, and among the most enduring of these are Confucius and Adam Smith.

Adam Smith provides an intellectual inspiration for free market economists across the world, not least in America. *The Wealth of Nations*, published in 1776, is the most influential book in the history of economics. It was written at a time of rapid socio-economic change in Britain during the early phase of the First Industrial Revolution. It provides an elegant, harmonious integration of individual self-interest and social interests. Smith identified two powerful drivers of economic progress, namely the division of labor and the accumulation of capital. The foundation of Smith's growth model was the division of labor. Smith considered that the fundamental driver of the accumulation process was the pursuit of profit. The possessor of capital directs his stock of capital toward those industries that yield the greatest profit: "[B]y directing that industry in such a manner as its produce may be of the greatest value, he intends only his own gain, and he is in this, as in many other cases, led by the invisible hand to promote an end which was no part of his intention."

Smith believed that these forces were the key to economic development, or, as he put it, the "wealth of nations": "Little else is required to carry a state to the highest level of opulence from the lowest level of barbarism, but peace, easy taxes, and a tolerable administration of justice ... The natural effort of every individual to better his own condition, when suffered to exert itself with freedom and security, is so powerful a principle that it is alone, and without any assistance, not only capable of carrying on the society to wealth and prosperity, but of surmounting a hundred impertinent obstructions with which the folly of human laws encumbers its operation ..."

The Wealth of Nations is a huge work of more than 1,000 pages. Few people read the whole text. Indeed, many professional economists, while freely making use of the idea of the "invisible hand," have never read any part of it. Few of them have read it thoroughly. It is widely assumed that *The Wealth of Nations* proves that the free market, guided by the "invisible hand," is the best arrangement for organizing economic life. Smith's other great work is *The Theory of Moral Sentiments*, published in 1759 and revised by Smith in 1761. Many economists have never heard of this work, and fewer still have read it. Far from being an early work which was superseded by *The Wealth of Nations*, *The Theory of Moral Sentiments* is intellectually inseparable from the former work. While their main topic is different, they share the same fundamental passion about the moral foundations of social life. Smith had grave doubts about the ability of the free market to meet human needs. He believed that the market was a two-edged sword, with unique dynamic qualities but also with deep inbuilt contradictions, though he did not use this word to describe them and gave little clue as to how these might be resolved. Free market economists rarely, if ever, acknowledge his penetrating analysis of the inherent contradictions of the market economy.

Smith viewed the division of labor as a two-edged sword. It promotes productivity growth, the basis for long-term improvements in the wealth of nations, but it also has deeply negative consequences for the mass of the population. Smith believed that people are born with relatively equal potential for self-realization, but their ability to achieve this is largely dependent on their social environment, especially the nature of their work: "The differences of natural talents in different men is, in reality, much less than we are aware of; and the very different genius which appears to distinguish men of different professions, when grown up to maturity, is not upon many occasions so much the cause as the effect of the division of labour. The differences between the most dissimilar characters, between a philosopher and a common street porter, for example, seems to arise not so much from nature, as from habit, custom and education."

Smith was brutally realistic about the consequences of the division of labor for the mass of workers: "In the progress of the division of labour, the employment of the far greater part of those who live by labour, that is the great body of the people, comes to be confined to a few very simple operations, frequently to one or two. But the understanding of the greater part of men are necessarily formed by their ordinary employments. The man whose life is spent in performing a few simple operations, of which the effects too are, perhaps, always the same, or very nearly the same, has no occasion to exert his understanding, or to exercise his invention in finding out expedients for removing difficulties which never occur. He naturally loses, therefore, the habit of such exertion, and generally becomes as stupid and ignorant as it is possible for a human creature to become." Smith warned: "[I]n every improved and civilized society, this is the state into which the labouring poor, that is, the great body of the people, must necessarily fall, unless government takes some pains to prevent it."

Smith thought that great inequality and class conflicts were unavoidable in a society based on private property: "Wherever there is great property, there is great inequality. For one very rich man, there must be at least five hundred poor, and the affluence of the few supposes the indigence of the many." Smith warned that only if the fruits of economic progress trickled down to the mass of the population could a society be judged to be morally satisfactory and secure from social instability: "Servants, labourers, and workmen of different kinds, make up by far the greater part of every great political society. But what improves the circumstances of the greater part can never be regarded as an inconvenience to the whole. No society can surely be great and flourishing of which the far greater part of the members are poor and miserable. It is but equity besides, that they who feed, clothe, and lodge the whole body of the people, should have such a share of the produce of their own labour as to be themselves tolerably well fed, cloathed [sic] and lodged."

Smith believed that class stratification was a necessary condition of economic progress, facilitating the accumulation of capital and the division of labor. However, he believed that this contained the possibility not only of class conflict, but also of the "corruption of moral sentiments," through the construction of social values that justified "neglect of the poor and mean": "[T]he disposition to admire, and almost to worship, the rich and powerful, and to despise, or at least, to neglect persons of poor and mean condition, though necessary to maintain the distinction of ranks and the order of society, is at the same time, the great and most universal cause of the corruption of our moral sentiments."

Smith considered that behind the profit motive for accumulating capital lay a deep psychological drive, namely the desire to acquire "wealth and greatness," which contained its own "deception," or inbuilt contradiction: "The pleasures of wealth and greatness … strike the imagination as something grand and beautiful and noble, of which the attainment is well worth all the toil and anxiety which we are apt to bestow upon it. And it is well that nature imposes upon us in this manner. It is this deception which rouses and keeps in continual motion the industry of mankind." Smith enumerates the dramatic effects of the application of this "industry," impelled by the "deception" of the pursuit of "wealth and greatness": "It is this which first prompted them to cultivate the ground, to build houses, to found cities and commonwealths, and to invent and improve all the sciences and arts, which ennoble human life; which have entirely changed the whole face of the globe, have turned the rude forests of nature into agreeable and fertile plains, and made the trackless and barren ocean a new fund of subsistence, and the great high road of communication to the different nations of the earth. The earth by these labours of mankind has been obliged to redouble her natural fertility, and to maintain a greater number of inhabitants."

Smith believed that the pursuit of "wealth and greatness" was a "deception" because, beyond a certain modest level of consumption, additional consumption brought no increase in happiness, and often brought unhappiness: "In the langour of disease and the weariness of old age, the pleasures of the vain and empty distinctions of greatness disappear … Power and riches then appear to be, what they are, enormous and operose [laborious] machines contrived to produce a few trifling conveniences to the body, consisting of springs the most nice and delicate, which must be kept in order with the most anxious attention, and which, in spite of all our care are ready every moment to burst into pieces, and to crush in their ruins their unfortunate possessor." Smith compared "power and riches" to 'immense fabrics, which "require the labour of life to raise … [They] threaten every moment to overwhelm the person that dwells in them, and which while they stand, though they may save him from some smaller inconveniences, can protect him from none of the inclemencies of the season. They keep off the summer shower, not the wintry storm, but leave him always as much, sometimes more exposed than before, to anxiety, to fear, and to sorrow; and to diseases, to danger and to death."

Smith considered that "frivolous consumption" brought no increase in happiness: "How many people ruin themselves by laying out money on trinkets of frivolous utility … All their pockets are stuffed with little conveniences … They walk about loaded with a multitude of baubles … If we consider the real satisfaction which all these things are capable of affording, by itself and separated from the beauty of the arrangement which is fitted to promote it, it will appear in the highest degree contemptible and trifling … [W]ealth and greatness are mere trinkets of frivolous utility, no more adapted for procuring ease of body or tranquillity of mind than the tweezer-cases of the lovers of toys."

Smith thought that the only worthwhile social goal was the pursuit of happiness, which was to be attained through tranquility, not the acquisition of power and riches: "Happiness is tranquillity and enjoyment. Without tranquillity there can be no enjoyment; and where there is perfect tranquillity there is scarce anything which is not capable of amusing." The attainment of happiness does not require high levels of consumption: "[I]n the ordinary situations of human life, a well-disposed mind may be equally calm, equally cheerful, and equally contented … [I]n the most glittering and exalted situation that our ideal fancy can hold out to us, the pleasures from which we propose to derive our real happiness, are almost always the same with those which in our actual though humble situation, we have at all times at hand and in our power … [T]he pleasures of vanity and superiority are seldom consistent with perfect tranquillity, the principle and foundation of all real and satisfactory enjoyment."

Benevolence, not the pursuit of wealth and greatness, allows the construction of a sense of duty which, in its turn, enables the realization of social cohesion: "The regard to those general rules of conduct, is what is properly called a sense of duty, a principle of the greatest consequence in human life, and the only possible principle by which the bulk of mankind are capable of directing their actions … Without this sacred regard to general rules, there is no man whose conduct can be much depended upon … By acting according to the dictates of our moral faculties, we necessarily pursue the most effectual means for promoting the happiness of mankind." Smith believed unless a society was just, there was a grave danger that it would disintegrate into chaos: "Justice, on the contrary, is the main pillar that upholds the whole edifice. If it is removed, the great, the immense fabric of human society, that fabric which to raise and support seems in this world, if I may say so, to have been the peculiar and darling love of Nature, must in a moment crumble into atoms."

Smith's analysis of the contradictions of the market economy is highly relevant to fundamental issues facing the world today. These fundamental issues include the nature of work for almost one billion people in developing countries employed as "lumpen labor" in the non-farm sector for $1–2 per day; class conflict between capital and labor in developing countries that are still in the early phase of capitalist industrialization; the degradation of work for a large fraction of the service-sector workers in rich countries, who work under intense pressure from relentless monitoring made possible by modern information technology, in order to increase "labor intensity"; the erosion of a sense of social cohesion as "state desertion," in order to provide a good investment environment for global capital, becomes widespread across countries at all levels of development; widespread consumer fetishism promoted by the immense marketing expenditure of global giant firms and commercialized global mass media; and even the very sustainability of life on the planet as fast-growing parts of developing countries move toward the immense per capita consumption levels of the high-income capitalist countries.

Historically, the central preoccupation of Chinese political practice has been the attempt to find a function for the state, and nurture a social ethic, that enables both economy and society to operate in a way that serves the interests of society as a whole. The core of this approach to political theory and practical politics is the desire to establish social cohesion in the interests of all members of society, no matter what position they occupy. These ideas had their foundation in the writings of Confucius. *The Analects* is by far the most influential book in Chinese history, providing the moral foundations for the Chinese state and Chinese society for over two thousand years.

Confucius's ideas, like those of Adam Smith 2,000 years later, were developed during a time of rapid and dramatic social change, in which traditional methods of government and standards of conduct no longer applied. In seeking for a solution to the social and political chaos, Confucius looked back with regret to the stable feudal order of the early Chou dynasty, in which there had been an accepted code of *li*, the rites and manners regulating social relationships. This way of behaving was the "way of the ancient kings." The recovery of the *Dao*, or Way, became the central theme in Chinese philosophy.

Confucius and his followers wished to identify practical solutions for the problems society faced rather than engage in abstract philosophical debate for its own sake. Chinese philosophy has always centered on human needs, on the improvement of government, on morals, and on the value of human life. Chinese philosophers have tended to distrust thinkers who are too logical, seeing them as "triflers with unimportant questions" and "gross simplifiers of important ones." They tend not to waste their time on logic-chopping without practical issue. They possess a genius for devising simple aphorisms which guide thought of the maximum complexity while using the minimum number of words. This method of thinking was influenced by the fact that Chinese words are uninflected, with their functions signified only by particles and by word order, allowing the illusion of looking through language at reality as though through a perfectly transparent medium.

The core of Chinese political philosophy over more than two millennia has been the attempt to build and sustain "great harmony" (*da tong*). Confucianism constituted the moral outlook that bound the population together in pursuit of common interests. Its ultimate goal was to ensure the welfare of the common people. Its ideal was the life lived by the educated "gentleman" (*junzi*): "For the gentleman it is morality that is supreme." The core Confucian value is benevolence, which is "more vital to the common people than even fire and water." The gentleman "instructed in the Way loves his fellow man." The pursuit of benevolence imposes a heavy moral burden: "Is there a man who, for the space of a single day, is able to devote all his strength to benevolence? ... A gentleman must be strong and resolute, for his burden is heavy and the road is long, for his burden is benevolence and the road only comes to an end with death." The gentleman "devotes his mind to attaining the Way and not to securing food." He "worries about the Way, not about poverty." Like Aristotle, Confucius believed that living a moral, good life provides its own reward: "The gentleman is easy of mind, while the small man is full of anxiety."

Confucius and Smith naturally express themselves in different ways. However, from a comparison of the key ideas in Confucius's *Analects* and Adam Smith's key works, *The Theory of Moral Sentiments* and *The Wealth of Nations*, we can see that there are powerful common themes concerning the relationship of the individual to society; the importance of maintaining social cohesion in order to serve the interests of the whole society; the function of morality in maintaining social cohesion; the relationship of material consumption to human happiness; and the function of education in a good society. The same ideas can be found in numerous other parallel sets of thinkers in China and the West, but I have chosen to concentrate on Confucius and Adam Smith, as they are uniquely influential within their respective cultures. Unwittingly, they occupy a broad common ground across the centuries and across cultures.

A Chinese edition of *The Wealth of Nations* has long been available. Chinese scholars have recently produced a meticulously translated edition of *The Theory of Moral Sentiments*, which has made a significant contribution to the discussions about the roles of state and market in building a harmonious society. The Chinese Premier, Wen Jiabao, has frequently used quotations from *The Theory of Moral Sentiments* in his speeches. He has drawn attention to Smith's deep concern for "benevolence" as the basis for social ethics. Smith considered that human psychology required social cohesion as the foundation of a good society in which all citizens could achieve happiness:

All the members of human society stand in need of each others' assistance … Where the necessary assistance is reciprocally afforded from love, from gratitude, from friendship, and esteem, the society flourishes and is happy. All the different members of it are bound together by the agreeable bonds of love and affection, and are, as it were, drawn to one common centre of mutual good offices. The foundation of such cohesion was benevolence: [T]o feel much for others and little for ourselves, to restrain our selfish, and to indulge our benevolent affections, constitutes the perfection of human nature; and can alone among mankind produce that harmony of sentiments and passions in which consists their whole grace and propriety.

Both Smith and Confucius are profoundly spiritual, attempting to address people's fundamental fears and needs. The outlook of both is based on humanistic rationality, which is complementary to, rather than a substitute for, religious belief. Neither of them considers the market is an intrinsically moral entity that should be allowed to dominate society. The restraint of selfishness, or "benevolence," is the moral foundation of both philosophies, not the pursuit of individual self-interest. They share the view that a good society is one in which social harmony is achieved through all the people sharing a common view of social justice. Both emphasize reciprocal social obligations and duties as the foundation of a good society. Both regard the pursuit of wealth and position as damaging to individual fulfillment. Both regard education as the foundation of self-fulfillment and the morality that forms the cement for social cohesion. They share the view that the only rational human goal is happiness, and that this is most completely achieved through the search for tranquility, not the relentless pursuit of material consumption and pleasure.

CONCLUSION

The essence of capitalism is its propensity toward universalism. In the pursuit of profit capitalism pushes beyond local boundaries, whether village, town, region or country. There is a persistent tension between capitalism's universal impulse and the nation. However, in the process of constructing modern capitalism, contrary to the expectations of nineteenth-century analysts, the national state propelled capitalism forward and reinforced the sense of national identity and interests, through the mechanisms of mass education, the mass media, and government ideology. The rise of modern capitalism in the late nineteenth century erupted into the international conflict that dominated much of the twentieth century. Even in the era of capitalist globalization today, there persists a profound tension between the national state and the international impulse of capital. The tension is crystallized today in the relationship between America and China. This relationship is central to the prospect for human survival.

Contrary to most predictions, the combination of political stability under the leadership of the Chinese Communist Party, and a process of experimental economic system reform and opening up, has resulted in the most remarkable period of development the world has ever seen. China has been unique among large latecomer countries in its degree of openness to trade, international capital and business, and international culture. China's ever-expanding incorporation into global capitalism has transformed the country's productive forces and social relationships, producing enormous benefits for the Chinese people. However, it has also led to wide-ranging problems that threaten the entire social, economic, and political system. These include the explosive growth of inequality, a drastic deterioration in the physical environment, the harsh challenge of the global business revolution for large Chinese firms, widespread corruption, and the difficulties of reforming its financial sector.

The Chinese government is working hard to devise polices that can overcome the country's immense internal problems. These include policies to equip the country's leading firms to meet the challenge of the global business revolution, to mitigate the unequal distribution of income, to improve health and educational provision for the mass of the population, to improve energy efficiency, to reduce environmental pollution, and to tackle corruption. No sector is more vital to the government's reform efforts than finance. China is groping for a way to avoid socio-political upheaval in the midst of immense internal difficulties, and to ensure "harmonious development" which establishes a balance between China's inland and coastal regions, urban and rural areas, society and economy, and nature and man. This is a "choice of no choice" for China's sustainable development. The impact of the global recession will exacerbate greatly the challenges facing the Chinese government. It may also offer an opportunity to accelerate the rebalancing of the Chinese growth model toward poor regions and poor people.

Capitalist globalization has also brought enormous benefits to America. China's increasing involvement in the global capitalist economy has contributed greatly to American prosperity. American firms benefit from their investments in China. American high-technology companies benefit by their sales to China and by employing large numbers of Chinese scientists and engineers. American consumers benefit from China's cheap exports. The American government benefits from China's bond purchases. However, global capitalism has also given rise to intense contradictions within American capitalism in respect to social inequality, energy security, the environment, and financial fragility. There is a growing perception that China's rise threatens the dominant position and identity of its firms, as well as its social stability, its energy security, its natural environment, and its financial stability. These perceptions influence decisions taken by the leadership, and they can be exploited by them in a time of socio-economic crisis. America now faces the prospect of a recession that is deeper than any since the 1930s.

The fact that the intense contradictions within both China and America, as well as in their interrelationship, might result in terrifying conflict is attracting increased attention from commentators across a wide spectrum of political persuasions. The degree of interconnectedness in world affairs is now so great that it is no longer possible even for the strongest political economy in the world to establish "national" security within its own borders. It is a delusion to imagine that in a globalized political economy even the most powerful economy can isolate itself securely within its own national boundaries while contradictions rage in the world around it.

Traditional China was the most isolated of the great civilizations of the ancient and medieval world, cut off from them by physical barriers. The concept of "Great Harmony" is not in principle confined to China. Many people in China hope and believe that its ancient civilization can make an important contribution toward building cooperative institutions that can contribute toward ensuring a globally sustainable future for all human beings. China today is deeply integrated into the global capitalist system. Despite its rapid development China is still far behind the development level of the high-income countries, and has many interests in common with other developing countries. It has a highly developed sense of its own national interests and has many urgent domestic development problems that need to be resolved. However, since the 1970s, under the policy of "opening up and inclusiveness," it has set its path firmly toward deep economic and cultural integration with the global community. The Chinese government has repeatedly emphasized its commitment to "reform and opening up," and constructive engagement with the international community of nations in a non-ideological, pragmatic fashion. In his speech in Singapore in November 2007, the Chinese Premier, Wen Jiabao, said:

Only an open and inclusive nation can become strong and prosperous, while a nation that shuts its door to the world is bound to fall behind ... Only by being inclusive, which calls for respect for different cultures and mutual learning, can we enrich and strengthen ourselves. We should boldly absorb and draw upon the achievements of the human society, including those of the capitalist countries, build on them, and make innovations ... Only on the basis of mutual benefit and win-win progress can opening up endure and be conducive to the fundamental interests of all peoples and peace and prosperity of the world. (Chinese Premier, Wen Jiabao, "Only an open and inclusive nation can be strong," speech at the National University of Singapore, November 2007)

If America seeks long-term security, it faces a "choice of no choice." It must cooperate with Communist China to support the construction of a harmonious society internally within China. The areas of necessary cooperation include resolving China's energy needs, its ecological difficulties, its financial system reform, and reform of its health and education system, and supporting China's efforts to establish a just distribution of income. In other words, it must accept and contribute to China's "peaceful rise," even if that means accepting that the resulting system of political economy will look very different from that of America today. China and America have no choice but to cooperate to solve the global challenges produced by capitalist globalization, and to work together to build the global institutions that are necessary to ensure a sustainable future for the human species.

2.3 AMERICA AND ISLAM

There is a widely held view in America that there is a "clash of civilizations" between Western capitalism and the Muslim world. In fact the widespread anger in the Muslim world against America has little to do with "Islamic fundamentalism." From its earliest days through to the present day, most of the Muslim world has enjoyed vibrant capitalist development, with long-standing efforts to mitigate the undesirable consequences of unrestrained free markets. In the pursuit of oil security America has relentlessly intervened politically and militarily in the region that is the core of the Islamic religion, which has resulted in widespread hostility among Muslims. At least as important a factor in Muslim hostility has been America's political, financial, and military support for the state of Israel. The widespread misperceptions among the American public of the history of the foundation and growth of the state of Israel constitute a fundamental barrier to American relations with the Muslim world. In fact there are great opportunities for America to engage positively with the Muslim world, based on a common belief in God and a common search for values that can provide a moral anchor for ordinary people in the turbulent world of capitalist globalization.

Broadly speaking, levels of religious belief decline in line with countries' levels of economic development. In Western Europe, less than 40 percent of the population affirm that they are "strongly religious." The long-term decline in attendance at church services is a recurring theme in the European popular press. There is no agreement on the causes of the decline of religious belief and practice in Europe. Among the hypotheses suggested is the advance of the European welfare state in recent decades, which has helped to reduce people's feelings of vulnerability and isolation. Another factor is increasing levels of education, which raises people's propensity to adopt a "rational" view of religious issues rather than follow a belief based on faith. One of the most popular books in recent years has been *The God Delusion*, in which the Oxford professor Richard Dawkins uses the power of "science" to "prove" that God does not exist. The attempt of the tiny human brain, even one as large as that of Professor Dawkins, to prove or disprove the existence of the unfathomable—God—has always struck me as futile.

America is a striking outlier to the general pattern. The intense religiosity of America baffles most Europeans. Christianity has been central to American identity since the earliest days of colonial settlement. Over two-thirds of the population affirm that they are "strongly religious." Over four-fifths of Americans declare that they are Christians. Over nine-tenths of Americans affirm that they believe in God. Three-fifths of Americans say that they pray one or more times each day and a further 20–23 percent declare that they pray once or more per week. Not only has America remained an intensely religious nation ever since the earliest days of its existence, but in the face of capitalist globalization the religious feelings of Americans seem to have intensified. Samuel Huntington believed that this can be explained by wide concern about the "decline in values, standards, and morality in American society." He believed that "large numbers of Americans came to feel personal needs for believing and belonging that secular ideologies did not satisfy."

Religious belief has assumed a central place in American political life. When he was asked who his favorite political philosopher was, George W. Bush answered: "Christ, because he changed my heart … When you turn your life over to Christ, when you accept Christ as the savior, it changes your life. That's what happened to me." Al Gore has described how he spent a year in divinity school in order to explore "the most important question about what's the purpose of life, what's our relationship to the Creator, what's our spiritual obligation to one another." He concluded that the "purpose of life is to glorify God. I turn to my faith as the bedrock of my approach to any important question in my life … Faced with a difficult decision I ask myself: 'What would Jesus do?'" It is unimaginable that a self-proclaimed atheist could win an American presidential election.

In the Muslim world also, religious belief has maintained deep roots as economic modernization has proceeded, alongside fast-growing urbanization, increased income levels and improvements in mass education. The beliefs have been maintained also in the face of secular ideologies pursued by the governments of many Muslim countries. As in America, religious belief has intensified in the era of capitalist globalization. Both Muslims and Americans have turned increasingly to religion in order to provide a moral compass in the confused world of capitalist globalization.

In the view of scholars such as Bernard Lewis and Samuel Huntington there is a fundamental contradiction between Western capitalism and the Muslim world, which amounts to nothing less than a *Clash of Civilizations*. This view was reinforced by Huntington's book of the same title, published in the 1990s. In the wake of 9/11 Huntington published *Who Are We?*, in which he provided a terrifying analysis of the emerging relationship between the Muslim world and America. He argued that this relationship is comparable to that between America and the Soviet Union during the Cold War. He considered that Muslims are hostile to America because of their "fear of American power, envy of American wealth, resentment of what is perceived as American domination and exploitation, and hostility to American culture, secular and religious, as the antithesis of Muslim culture." He believed that "Muslims increasingly see America as their enemy," and drew an ominous conclusion: "If that is a fate Americans cannot avoid, their only alternative is to accept it and to take the measures necessary to cope with it." In the wake of 9/11 and in the face of numerous violent attacks by Muslim groups in both rich and poor countries, this view struck a deep chord among a large body of the population in high-income countries.

The way in which the Muslim world interacts with capitalist globalization is determined primarily by its relationship with the world's most powerful nation, America. In fact, as we shall see, the reality of Muslim history, beliefs, and economic performance is at odds with Huntington's perception of an inherent *Clash of Civilizations*. Huntington was concerned that significant elements of the American elite are favorably disposed to America becoming a cosmopolitan society. However, he believed that "the overwhelming bulk of the American people are committed to a national alternative and to preserving and strengthening the American national identity that has existed for centuries." In fact, rather than looking inwards, there are great opportunities for Americans to engage positively with the Muslim world, on the basis on a common belief in God and a common search for values that can provide a moral anchor for ordinary people of both the Christian and Muslim religions in the turbulent world of capitalist globalization.

CAPITALISM, DEVELOPMENT, AND ISLAM

There are more than 70 countries each with populations of more than one million Muslims. Although Muslims constitute only 12 percent of the population in India and less than three percent in China, these countries contain around 125 million and 40 million Muslims respectively. America itself contains around six million Muslims. There are 44 countries where Muslims constitute more than one-half of the population. In Africa alone at the end of the twentieth century, there were around 350 million Muslims, including 62 million in Nigeria, 60 million in Egypt, 32 million in Ethiopia, 30 million each in Algeria and Morocco, and 25 million in the Sudan. There are four countries that each have more than 100 million Muslims (Bangladesh, India, Indonesia, and Pakistan), and there are another four countries that each have 50–100 million Muslims (Egypt, Iran, Nigeria, and Turkey).

There has been considerable argument about why people converted to Islam in such enormous numbers. It used to be thought that conversion to Islam was made at the point of the sword, and that conquered people were given the choice of conversion or death. It is now widely accepted among scholars of Islam that conversion to Islam was mostly voluntary; only rarely was it forcible. Muslims of all types emphasize the Koran's principle: "There is no compulsion in religion." From the Sahel (the northern belt of the Sudan region) of Africa and the Indian Ocean, to the Malayan Peninsula and Indonesia, it was spread by peaceful contacts among merchants, preachers, and missionaries. In the cases of North Africa, Anatolia, the Balkans, and India, Islam was brought by nomadic Arab or Turkish conquerors. However, even in these cases, invasion by Islamic forces did not result in forcible conversions; rather, invasion provided the opportunity for Islam to spread peacefully through the same channels as elsewhere.

At least as remarkable as the spread of Islam is its persistence as the dominant religion in such large parts of the world. It sustained its deep roots in society in the face of colonial domination by the British, Dutch, and French, in the face of the secular ideology of the Soviet and Chinese communist parties in Central Asia, and, in recent decades, in the face of capitalist modernization in large parts of the Muslim world and desperate poverty in Africa's Sahel region.

Many non-Muslims have difficulty in making sense of the Koran; they find it hard to understand why the Koran has had such a profound influence in the Islamic world. There are number of reasons for this influence. There is, to begin with, a long and rich tradition of sophisticated Islamic scholarship and research. However, the key to the Koran's deep roots in Islamic society lies in the way in which it is memorized verse by verse, and applied to the concrete issues that people face in their daily lives: "Although Islam is a belief, its main program is the practical sphere of life; it does not remain circumscribed in theoretical discussions and the speculations of theology ... the Koran always appeals to human nature and draws our attention to the signs of God which are within man's soul itself and are all around him ... [Islam] abhors being reduced to pure thought ... and loves to appear personified in human beings, in a living organization and in practical movement" (Sayyid Qutb, *Milestones*).

One reason for Islam's strength is the profound sense which it gives of belonging to a community that transcends race, color, and language: "In this great Islamic society, Arabs, Persians, Syrians, Egyptians, Moroccans, Turks, Chinese, Indians, Romans, Greeks, Indonesians, Africans, were gathered together. Their various characteristics were united, and with mutual cooperation, harmony and unity they took part in the construction of the Islamic community and Islamic culture. This wonderful civilization was not an 'Arabic civilization,' even for a single day; it was purely an 'Islamic civilization.' It was never a 'nationality,' but always a 'community' of belief" (Sayyid Qutb, *Milestones*). The sense of an Islamic community bound together by mutual help is deeply embedded in the Koran: "I swear by this city (and you are a resident of this city), by the begetter and all whom he begot: We created man to try him with afflictions. 'I have squandered vast riches,' he boasts. Does he think that none have power over him? Have we not given him two eyes, a tongue, and two lips, and shown him the two paths? Yet he would not scale the Height. Would that you knew what the Height is. It is the freeing of a bondsman, the feeding, in the day of famine, of an orphaned relation or a needy man in distress, to have faith and to enjoin fortitude and mercy" (Koran, 90).

There is also a long tradition of secular Islam, in which the ethical values that are embedded in the Koran are applied to daily life without participation in religious ceremonies, or, even, without necessarily believing in God. Equally, there is a deeply spiritual quality to Islam, which finds a powerful expression in Sufism, which for long periods was dominant in parts of the Muslim world and is still deeply influential. The Sufi tradition, represented by writers such as Farid Ud-Din Attar and Rumi, has much in common both with the mystical medieval European Christian tradition found in the teachings of Meister Eckhart and *The Cloud of Unknowing*, and the Chinese Daoist tradition, found in writings such as Lao Zi's *Dao De Jing* or Zhuang Zi's writings. In each of these traditions, there is a common element of ecstatic loving union with the immensity of being, which can be called God. Each of the mystic traditions has a central place for removing the sense of self and achieving emptiness in order to accomplish ecstatic union with unbounded existence. Christianity, Daoism, and Islam, all explore the fundamental existential issues of being and non-being. They contain a similar spectrum of perspectives, which include a passive, contemplative withdrawal from reality and a calm involvement with reality, as well as humor:

> One lot cogitates on the way of religion,
> Another ponders on the path of mystical certainty;
> But I fear one day the cry will go up,
> "Oh you fools, neither this nor that is the way"
>
> The Ruba'iyat of Omar Khayyam

The mystical strand of Islam, Christianity, and Daoism is the one that is most easily able to communicate across national, linguistic, and cultural boundaries. It is the most intuitive and the most closely connected with people's deepest hopes and fears. America also has its own mystical tradition:

> Standing on the bare ground—my head bathed by the blithe air and uplifted into infinite space—all mean egotism vanishes. I become a transparent eyeball; I am

nothing; I see all; the currents of the Universal Being circulate through me; I am part and parcel of God.

Ralph Waldo Emerson, *Nature*

In World War I, educated English and American soldiers were reported to have recited Edward FitzGerald's translation of the *Ruba'iyat of Omar Khayyam* as they marched to their deaths on the Western Front. In the 1960s, large numbers of American and European students read Alan Watts's book, *The Way of Zen*, which was closely based on Chinese Daoist philosophy. As the citizens of high-income countries search for meaning in the confusion of capitalist globalization, the "New Age" philosophy they imbibe includes elements from each of these mystical traditions. There is no "clash of civilizations" in New Age culture. Rumi, Meister Eckhart and Lao Zi rub shoulders comfortably together.

Islam and capitalism in the pre-modern world

America is the central force in capitalist globalization. The Twin Towers of the World Trade Center constituted the essential icon of American capitalism and of its dominant position within the globalized world economy. For a large body of the general public in the high-income countries, the attack on the World Trade Center on September 11, 2001, represented an attack on capitalism by Islamic fundamentalists. Many left-wing analysts, however, frustrated at the absence of violent anti-capitalist revolutionary movements in much of the developing world, view "Islamic terrorists" as the vanguard of a global class struggle against the injustices of capitalist globalization. Both groups consider the fundamentals of Islam to be anti-capitalist. Such a view was nurtured in the popular mind by powerful writings such as those of Samuel Huntington. The attack appeared to many to vindicate Huntington's thesis, expounded in the mid-1990s, that there was, indeed, a fundamental "clash of civilizations" between Islam and the West. This view was nurtured by the Zionist lobby in the high-income countries. They used the attack on the World Trade Center as an opportunity to assert their own civilizing role in the midst of what they perceived as the hostile anti-capitalist, anti-democratic, and economically stagnant Islamic world that surrounds Israel.

The idea that there is a fundamental "clash of civilizations" between Islam and the West was not invented by Samuel Huntington. During the Cold War many anti-communist scholars argued that Islam and capitalism were fundamentally incompatible, and feared that communism and Islam would develop a dangerous anti-capitalist alliance. Some scholars, motivated by hostility to Islam, endeavored to show that, by forbidding them from engaging in any progressive economic initiative, Islam doomed its adherents to stagnation. They concluded that Muslims must be vigorously combated if civilization was to progress.

In reality, the Islamic religion is no more anti-capitalist than is Christianity. The Koran has nothing against private property. It even provides clear instructions about the practice of property inheritance and gives strict injunctions against the theft of private property. Wage labor is referred to many times in the Koran as a normal and acceptable practice. The Koran looks favorably upon commercial activity, confining itself to condemning fraudulent practices and urging abstention from trade during certain religious festivals. In the broader Muslim tradition, the search for profit, trade, and production for the market are typically looked upon favorably. Indeed, according to holy tradition, trade is a superior way of earning one's living. The Prophet is alleged to have said: "If God let the dwellers in Paradise engage in trade, they would trade in fabric and the spices." Wealth is not a dirty word for Muslims; on the contrary, wealth creation is a desirable goal, subject only to Islamic moral values and imperatives. Individual freedom, the right to property and enterprise, the market mechanism, and distributive justice are inalienable parts of the Muslim economic framework. It was a moral framework which allowed the medieval Islamic world to develop a sophisticated capitalist economy, with thriving trade and urban commercial centers, widespread production for the market, and a powerful capitalist class.

Mecca was already a vibrant commercial city when the Islamic religion emerged, with large-scale trading networks and extensive money-lending at interest. Muhammad lived and worked in the urban world of Mecca. The city's prosperity at that time was still recent, born of its caravan links with distant cities, which benefited large-scale trade and the emerging capitalism of the Meccan merchants. In a relatively brief period after the death of Muhammad in AD 632, Islam spread across a vast region. The earliest substantial Muslim architectural monument was the Dome of the Rock in Jerusalem, constructed at the end of the seventh century, only 70 years or so after the death of Muhammad, on the spot where it is said that Muhammad had ascended into heaven. By 750 the Islamic empire stretched from the Indus in the east through into North Africa, Spain, and even into southern France. For much of the period from the seventh to the seventeenth century, a large part of the Old World was united under Muslim rule. Arabic provided linguistic unity for the Arab world which was at the core of Islam, and created an essential tool for intellectual exchanges, for business, and for government and administration. Classical Arabic was not only a language, it was also a literature, a philosophy, a fervent universal faith, and a civilization, evolving in Baghdad and from there spreading far and wide.

The Abbasid revolution of AD 750 ushered in the classical period of the economic development of the Muslim Empire, especially its commercial development. For four or five centuries after the death of Muhammad, Islam was the most brilliant civilization in the Old World, but this period was ended by the reconquest of the eastern Mediterranean by Christian Europe in the twelfth century and the intrusion of the Mongols in the thirteenth century. The Abbasid Caliphate was based in a newly established capital city, Baghdad, or the "City of Peace." The ninth-century historian al-Ya'qubi records how the Abbasid ruler al-Mansur halted by the village that was to become Baghdad and said:

This island between the Tigris in the east and the Euphrates in the west is a marketplace for the world. All the ships that come up the Tigris from Wasit, Basra, Ubulla, Ahwaz, Fars, 'Uman, Yamama, Bahrayn, and beyond will go up and anchor here; wares brought on ships down the Tigris from Mosul, Diyar Rabi'a, Adhurbayan, and Armenia, and along the Euphrates from Diyar-Mudar, Raqqa, Syria, and the border marshes, Egypt and North Africa, will be brought and unloaded here. It will be the highway for the people of the Jabal, Isfahan and the districts of Khurasan. Praise be to those who preserved it for me and caused all those who came before me to neglect it. By God, I shall build it. Then shall I dwell in it as long as I live and my descendents shall dwell in it after me. It will surely be the most flourishing city in the world.

A great commercial metropolis developed around the central core of Baghdad, which grew into the largest and richest capital city in the Old World.

The medieval Islamic Empire constituted a massive virtual free trade area, across which goods and peoples could move relatively easily. The density of commercial relations within the Muslim world constituted a kind of world market of unprecedented dimensions. Islam dominated the Old World, and was at the center of a huge entrepôt trade between the Far East, Europe, and Black Africa. Arab sailing dhows used the monsoon cycle to carry on large-scale trade, reaching Canton by the ninth century. Caravans might consist of 5–6,000 camels, with the capacity of a very large merchant sailing ship. Basra imported vast quantities of kermes and indigo to dye textiles red and blue, while coral was transported from North Africa to India, and slaves were bought in Ethiopia. Iron, together with pepper and spices, were brought back from India.

Although there was a huge entrepôt trade with the non-Muslim world, a large part of the trade consisted of exchange within the Muslim world itself and exports from that world to other markets. Many different towns and districts specialized in textile production, including silk weaving, wool, cotton, and linen products; Bokhara, Armenia, and Persia were already famous for carpet manufacture. Other areas specialized in hides, skins, and leather articles. Various districts specialized in the commercial production of weapons, ceramics, copper pans and pails, scales, and articles of furniture. Other districts specialized in the manufacture of soap, ointments, rose water and palm-shoots, scent, honey, saffron, or indigo. There were many agricultural crops produced largely for the market, including cotton, dried fruits, and various fresh fruits, especially dates, sugar cane, and spices. Every year the date trade alone mobilized more than 100,000 pack-camels. Sugar cane cultivation became an industry, and flour milling spread. Water mills and windmills were widely used for various industrial process. Horses and camels were bred for the market, while the dried fish of the Caspian, the Aral Sea and the Persian Gulf were exported widely.

Vast fortunes were made under a capitalist trading system that extended as far as China and India, the Persian Gulf, Ethiopia, the Red Sea, Africa, and Andalusia.

Enormous cities grew up, with trade as their central function; they included not only Baghdad, but also the large city of Samarra, and the great ports of Basra, Cairo, Damascus, Tunis (a reincarnation of Carthage), and Cordoba. In 1326, the Arab traveler Ibn Battuta said of Mecca: "Altogether, every kind of merchandise from every country can be found gathered in this town." For over one hundred years, in the ninth and tenth centuries, Islam dominated the eastern Mediterranean, which breathed life and prosperity into seaports like Palermo, Alexandria, and Tunis.

In the late tenth century the Fatimids broke away from the Abbasid Caliphate, which ruled the empire from its base in Baghdad, and established their own base in Egypt. The Fatimids built the new city of Cairo, with its magnificent al-Azhar mosque, as their capital. They soon extended their sway across the whole of North Africa, and into Sicily, Palestine, Syria, and Arabia, and for a while they greatly surpassed the power of the Abbasid Caliphs in Baghdad. The peak of the Fatamid Caliphate came during the reign of the Caliph al-Mustansir (1036–94). It was a period of great commercial and industrial efflorescence and prosperity.

The Fatimids fully understood the importance of trade for the prosperity of their empire, developing plantations and industries in Egypt, nurturing a powerful export trade, and developing a wide network of commercial relationships, especially with Europe and India. They established close relations with the Italian city-republics, and their ships and merchants sailed as far as Spain. The two main harbors of the Fatimids were Alexandria and Tripoli, both of which were linked to worldwide markets. Their fleets controlled the eastern Mediterranean. In the east, they developed close contacts with India, and gradually extended their sovereignty over both shores of the Red Sea. They shifted the Indian trade route from the Persian Gulf to the Red Sea, and especially to the great Fatimid port of 'Aydhab on the Sudanese coast. After decades of gradual decline, however, the Fatimid Caliphate was finally defeated in 1171 by Saladin, who reunited the main parts of the Islamic world.

The term "Renaissance" has been used to describe the Golden Age of Islam, from the ninth to the twelfth century. In science the Muslims made significant contributions to mathematics, especially in the fields of trigonometry and algebra; in trigonometry the Muslims invented the sine and the tangent. During this period Muslim scholars made great progress in astronomy, optics, chemistry (including the distillation of alcohol and the manufacture of sulfuric acid), and in medicine. In philosophy, the Islamic world rediscovered Aristotle, who was known as the "first master." Muslim humanism, based on Aristotle, was widespread and long-lived throughout Islam. Thanks in considerable degree to the edition of Aristotle's works edited by the Islamic scholar Ibn Rushd (Averroës), Aristotle's ideas re-entered Europe, where they sparked off the great philosophical revolution of the thirteenth century.

The years 1261–1300 saw the establishment of the Ottoman Empire. From the thirteenth century through to the early fifteenth century, however, the Ottomans suffered attacks from the Mongols. Baghdad was conquered in 1258, and destroyed in 1401. It was not until 1453, with the conquest of Constantinople by the Ottoman Turks, that a new era of relatively stable Islamic unity began. By 1687 the Ottoman Empire stretched from Armenia in the east through to Hungary in the northwest, the Crimea in the northeast, Mecca in the south, and Algeria in the west. During this period, the commercial forces that had grown up during the Golden Age of Islam revived and achieved further expansion.

Asia Minor became an industrialized region of the Ottoman Empire long before Western and Russian manufactures began to compete with Turkish and Indian textiles in the late eighteenth century. The Anatolian city of Bursa emerged as a world market in the second half of the fourteenth century; soon, along with Constantinople and Pera, it became one of the main economic foundations of Ottoman power. In the period 1400–1630 Bursa was one of the great world centers for silk commerce and industry. Most transactions there were made on credit, with accounts settled at the end of a defined period. In the fifteenth and sixteenth centuries an important north-south trade developed across the Black Sea; large quantities of silk, cotton, and hemp products were exported from Anatolia to northern Black Sea ports, through which animal and agricultural stuffs were in turn exported to Istanbul. In the Ottoman Empire there developed a large market for Anatolian manufactures, with textiles at its center. From Tokat, Corum, Merdizifon, Katamonu, Borlu, and Konya came cotton cloth; from Bursa came silk; from Tosya and Ankara came mohair; and from Trabzon came hemp.

Jerusalem provides a significant example of a relatively small commercial and industrial center under the Ottomans. The population was four-fifths Muslim, with small Christian and Jewish minorities. The Ottoman rulers provided an environment in which commercial and industrial activity could flourish, but in which the needs of the different segments of the local population could be met through extensive state regulation of economic life. One of the Ottomans' first tasks was to renovate the ancient city walls, and they also rebuilt and improved the city's water supply. The Ottoman authorities undertook to supply the local population with water "night and day, forever and ever." These public works were crucial to the commercial prosperity that Jerusalem experienced in the sixteenth century. In the early years of Ottoman rule charitable Muslim endowments proliferated in Jerusalem.

Under Ottoman rule there were two critically important offices of local government: the *kadi* and the *muhtasib*. The *kadi* was the Muslim judge, who heard legal cases, recorded and notarized decrees emanating from Istanbul, and issued licenses and permits. The *muhtasib* was responsible for inspecting market activities in the widest sense, including patrons, clients, merchandise, and their multi-faceted interrelations. Most economic activities were conducted in self-organized guilds. However, the structures within which they operated were tightly regulated by the Ottoman Empire's local representatives. The *kadi* and *muhtasib* exercised meticulous control over all significant aspects of economic life in Jerusalem, including prices, division of labor, market locations, product storage and quality, weights and measures, and health and safety regulations. Although the central Ottoman authorities set the parameters governing economic and social life in sixteenth-century Jerusalem, the Sultan's local representative enjoyed wide discretion in the administration of these principles, adjusting their application to local conditions.

Under this system, economic activity in sixteenth-century Jerusalem flourished. The city soon became the center of a thriving soap industry. Soap made in Jerusalem was sold throughout Palestine and Greater Syria, and regularly exported to Egypt. The soap industry's growth in turn stimulated commercial olive production around Jerusalem, since olive oil was the main raw material for soap. The merchant class grew in strength during this period. Merchants were closely involved in production as well as in trade; they acquired soap factories and invested heavily in them, as well as buying olive oil and selling the finished soap. In terms of the city's economic and social activity, Jerusalem's merchants set the pace and were at the helm, as entrepreneurs and developers, and even as local leaders.

Through extensive trade networks Islam put down deep roots in the Sahel region of Africa. Timbuktu, in today's Mali, was one of the wealthiest cities in the world in the Middle Ages. Goods from the western Sudan, including gold, ivory, and tortoiseshell, were exchanged with manufactured goods from the leading Mediterranean cities. It evolved into one of the most important medieval centers of Arabic and Islamic studies. For centuries the *ulama* (Muslim scholars) of Timbuktu maintained a rich and vital tradition of Koranic, Hadith, and legal studies, supplemented by classes in theology, linguistics, history, mathematics, and astronomy. In 1526 the Muslim traveler Leo Africanus visited Timbuktu, and wrote: "Here are great stores of doctors, judges, priests and other learned men, that are bountifully maintained at the king's cost and charges. And thither are brought divers manuscripts or written books out of Barbarie, which are sold for more money than any other merchandise."

In the view of Fernand Braudel, a substantial segment of the medieval Muslim economy can be described as capitalist; as a whole it was, until the sixteenth century, more extensive than that in Western Europe. Throughout the Ottoman Empire, a vast economic system based on the market economy took root, with a money economy and commercialization of both industry and agriculture. From one end of Islam's world connections to the other, speculators "unstintingly gambled on trade." Merchants' private wealth was critically important to the medieval Islamic world's role as the organizer of world markets. The Islamic conquest of other territories permitted a vast accumulation of wealth in the hands of merchants. In addition to the development of commercial capital in the medieval Islamic Empire, financial capital grew substantially after the empire's establishment. Money-lending was practiced extensively, despite the Koran's prohibitions of *riba* (interest). Credit was in fact widespread under the Ottoman Empire, with concealed interest added to the payment on credit as if it were a loan, anticipating the methods of modern "Islamic finance." Letters of credit were known from the earliest days of Islam, and became widespread among merchants in the Ottoman Empire.

Modern Islamic capitalism

In January 2008, President Bush visited the Middle East. The set-piece speech of his trip was made in a $3 billion super-luxury hotel in Abu Dhabi. In it, he praised the United Arab Emirates for having "shown the world a model of a Muslim state." Few Muslims, however, would agree with this statement. The UAE is wholly unrepresentative of the Muslim world, with its population of just four million people, and with 3.4 percent of the world's natural gas reserves and 8.1 percent of its oil reserves. The development tasks facing the rulers of Abu Dhabi do not begin to compare with those that have faced most of the Muslim world in recent decades.

There has been much debate about why Islam has remained so deeply rooted in so many countries, with such diverse cultures and historical experiences, and about the reasons for the widespread Islamic revival across Muslim countries in recent years. There is a popular perception in the West that the Islamic revival can be explained by the fact that Muslim countries are development failures. It is thought that "failed Muslim states" provide the opportunity for "Islamic terrorists" to emerge, grow, and prosper among the marginalized sections of stagnant economies. There is a widespread perception that the "Islamic revival" can be equated with the violent anti-Western, anti-capitalist Islamic movements.

There is a widespread perception in the West that the Muslim economies as a whole have performed poorly. In reality, however, the Muslim world has a rich and diverse development experience. It is a world which consists of at least three major groups of countries.

The oil-rich Muslim countries constitute a special form of political economy. They have enormous advantages stemming from their rich natural resource endowment. They also, however, face common problems, which can be summarized crudely as the "curse of oil," and which have nothing to do with the fact that they are Muslim countries. The same problems have affected most oil-rich developing countries, including Angola, Mexico, and Venezuela, regardless of the country's religion. The problems are the result of factors such as fluctuations in export earnings, the difficulty of absorbing large quantities of foreign exchange, and the socio-political consequences of the ruling elite's monopoly over access to the economic rents from oil revenues. In addition, the world's leading powers, especially America, have been deeply involved with their political and military affairs, as their oil production is critical for the high-income capitalist economies. This intervention has helped greatly to reinforce highly unequal systems of political economy, which have been unable to achieve widely based development. As a result of these factors, the oil-producing developing countries have tended to have large fluctuations in their economic growth.

The small group of countries on either side of the Persian Gulf account for less than one-tenth of the world's Muslim population, but they account for almost two-thirds of the world's oil reserves. They have followed a special form of capitalist development. Between them the countries of the Gulf Cooperation Council (Bahrain, Kuwait, Oman, Saudi Arabia, and the United Arab Emirates) have a total population of just 36 million, a tiny fraction of the world's Muslim population. Typically, the vast oil wealth is controlled by a small number of families. Because of the limited channels through which rents are generated in oil-dependent economies, it is relatively easy for a dominant group to seize control of the rents, and use them to further bolster their rule. The family-run states have been heavily dependent for their survival on support from America (and to a lesser extent, from Britain and other European countries) to maintain their authoritarian rule, which has helped to generate intense anger against America. The immense inequalities in the distribution of wealth and income in the Gulf countries, vastly in excess of, and quite different from, those in non-oil Muslim countries, have inspired intense anger from different socio-political groups within the region. Naturally, this has typically taken an Islamic form.

At the core is Saudi Arabia, with around one-quarter of the entire world's oil reserves. The ruling Al Sa'ud family makes no attempt to conceal its ownership of the country's principal natural resources behind the mask of state institutions. Since Saudi Arabia's foundation in the 1920s the Al Sa'ud family have effectively been the country's owners as well as its rulers. Oil is not merely the kingdom's primary national resource; it is first and foremost private, family property. The bulk of the oil revenue is paid directly to the king before it is registered as national income. The royal family decides on its needs, and officials are instructed to act accordingly. In the late 1990s the 6,000-odd members of the Saudi royal family were estimated to receive an average of around $1 million each, in addition to their regular "working salaries" and commissions on business deals. Similar arrangements apply in the other Arab oil-producing countries where rule is vested in a single family. The fact that this political settlement has been maintained with the help of substantial military and political support from America, and its close ally Britain, has exacerbated anti-American feelings among Muslims across the world. In January 2008, as well as making his keynote speech in Abu Dhabi, President Bush visited Saudi Arabia. To honor his achievements the Saudi ruler presented him with a gold chain and a ceremonial sword, and the pictures of him receiving these honors were beamed around the world.

Large numbers of Muslims across the world consider that Saudi Arabia's rulers live in a way that contradicts the basic principles of Islam. The fact that Saudi Arabia is also the site of the Islamic holy places contributes greatly to the deep anger among Muslims, both inside and outside the country.

The population of the Sahel region faces uniquely difficult development challenges, a world removed from the $3 billion hotel in which President Bush made his keynote speech. Almost 200 million people live in the mainly Muslim countries of this region, which stretches in a wide band across the center of northern Africa, from the coastal populations in Senegal, Guinea, Guinea Bissau, The Gambia, and Sierra Leone, through the vast landlocked territories in Mauritania, Mali, Niger, Burkina Faso, Chad, Sudan, and Ethiopia, to Eritrea and Somalia. The core of this region is the semi-arid Sahel zone, which borders the Sahara desert to the north.

Most of the people live a long distance from the coast. Population densities are low, and per capita incomes are falling across most of the region. Agriculture is the main economic activity in the region, typically accounting for 40–50 percent of GDP. The region suffers from deteriorating rainfall, severe droughts, and desertification. The Niger River was formerly the lifeblood of the ancient city of Timbuktu, in Mali. After the disastrous droughts in the 1970s and 1980s, the section of the Niger that flowed through the city dried up altogether. The region has several of the world's poorest countries. Average life expectancy across the region is only around 45–50 years. The population growth rates are high, averaging around 2.5–3.0 percent per annum, and the region's population has doubled in only 20–25 years, putting intense pressure on the already fragile environment. Annual death rates are high, averaging around 20 per thousand, and the probability of not surviving to the age of 40 is around 30–40 percent in most of the Sahel group of countries. Only a small number have the opportunity to migrate to other parts of the world, and many people die on the high seas while they attempt the perilous journey to enter Europe illegally from ports on the West African coast.

To argue that the Sahel's region's shocking development record is caused by the Islamic religion is a travesty of reality. Rather, Islam's survival in the region may be attributable to the fact that it provides spiritual support for the huge population, living as it does in such difficult and worsening conditions. "With every hardship there is ease. When your prayers are ended, resume your toil, and seek your Lord with all fervor" (Koran, 94).

Among the wider group of countries in which Islamic beliefs are dominant, there is a normal distribution of more and less successful development experiences, in which the differing performances are attributable to factors other than religion.

Since the late nineteenth century, whenever there has been political stability and some degree of security to pursue production for profit, the economies of the Muslim countries have experienced significant economic growth. Even under Western colonialism, which governed most of the Muslim world until the middle of the twentieth century, there was a great deal of capitalist development in Muslim countries. Much of this was stimulated by the "demonstration effect" of international trade and foreign investment, and partly it was attributable to the infrastructure constructed under the colonial governments. But to a considerable degree it was due to indigenous capitalist business endeavor. By the 1950s, there were around 1.5 million workers in industry in the Middle East, amounting to around two percent of the workforce in Iran and Egypt, and five or six percent in

Turkey. In addition, there were many people employed in capitalist businesses in the financial, commercial, and infrastructure sectors. The capitalist sector as a whole accounted for 20 percent of annual investment in Iran and Iraq, 50 percent in Turkey, and 80 percent in Syria and Lebanon.

In the 1950s and 1960s, in common with most developing countries, a large part of the Muslim world turned toward state-led industrialization. There was widespread nationalization of banks, public services, and large-scale industry, and even some attempts to set up agricultural collectives. However, even at the height of state-led industrialization, the economies throughout the Muslim world maintained a combination of public and private ownership, far removed from the central planning of the communist countries. This was true for Egypt under Nasser, Iraq under Saddam Hussein, Libya under Gaddafi, Syria under Assad, Tunisia under Habib Bourguiba, and Iran after the 1979 revolution. Each of these countries had a substantial private sector economy, and none of them ever approached the degree of hostility to private enterprise that was the case in the Soviet Union or during the Cultural Revolution in China. Even in Afghanistan under the Taliban, there was an active local exchange economy, albeit with limited international trade and hostility to international investment.

After Nasser died in 1970 there was a widespread move away from Arab socialism toward the policy of an "open door" (*infitah*) for international trade and foreign investment. The collapse of the Soviet Union accelerated this trend. The movement toward opening up after the 1970s was widespread across the Muslim world, producing great opportunities for capitalist development, which built on the ancient foundations of trade and market-oriented production. By the early twenty-first century the Muslim countries as a whole were deeply integrated into the capitalist world economic system.

Trade liberalization stimulated rapid export growth and large increases in the foreign trade ratio in the non-oil producing Muslim countries. By 2004 the share of merchandise trade in GDP stood at 25 percent in Egypt, 33 percent in Pakistan, 36 percent in Bangladesh, 49 percent in Indonesia, 53 percent in Turkey, 55 percent in Morocco, 80 percent in Tunisia, 105 percent in Jordan, and 196 percent in Malaysia. Under the *infitah* policy the Muslim countries experienced widespread increases in foreign direct investment. By 2004, stocks of FDI relative to GDP stood at 27 percent in Egypt, 36 percent in Morocco, 39 percent in Malaysia, 53 percent in Syria, and 62 percent in Tunisia. In the same year stocks of FDI in the Muslim countries as a whole totaled around $220 billion, roughly the same figure as that reported for China ($245 billion in the same year), and greater than that for the whole former Soviet Union and southeast Europe ($200 billion).

Although local financial institutions have traditionally been restricted by formal Islamic prohibitions on the provision of interest (*riba*) and financial speculation (*ghara*), the interpretation of these concepts has always been fraught with controversy, and they did not historically prevent the existence of a large financial sector in the Muslim world. However, in recent years there has been a major change in the nature of financial institutions in the Muslim world, stimulated by the revolution in the nature of financial instruments and the flood of financial assets accumulating in the hands of oil-producing countries, consequent upon the increased price of oil. In Muslim countries banks have begun a comprehensive transformation, with widespread privatization and extensive acquisition by international banks. The floodgates have opened for the provision of "Islamic finance," both by multinational banks and by indigenous financial institutions. "Islamic finance" is now formally legitimated through the use of a variety of techniques that enable Islamic banks to avoid the constraints imposed by the formal prohibitions on interest and speculation.

"Islamic" financial institutions typically avoid investments in areas prohibited by Islam, such as alcohol, pork, gambling, and weapons manufacture. They emphasize their Islamic credentials by paying a portion of their profits in *zakat* (alms) to support social welfare in Muslim countries. There are innumerable ways of paying interest on loans, by redefining de facto interest payments as legitimate profit earned through a business partnership. Islamic financial institutions may circumvent the payment of conventional interest by issuing *sukuks*, bonds that give investors profits from an underlying business that backs a bond. The countries in the Gulf region are vying with each other to become global financial centers, by encouraging international financial firms to operate there, and by nurturing local financial institutions in the hope that they will become globally competitive—which can only be achieved by adopting the same practices as international financial firms. Financial institutions in the Muslim world have also built up substantial ownership stakes in conventional international banks.

Since the 1970s, the non-oil producing Muslim countries excluding the Sahel region have achieved widespread structural change, with large declines in the share of agriculture in national output and employment and large increases in the share of urban population. Under some form or other of capitalist modernization, the non-oil producing Muslim countries overall have grown quite rapidly. From 1975 to 2002 the per capita GDP of the five largest Muslim countries (Indonesia, Pakistan, Bangladesh, Turkey, and Egypt), with a combined population of around 650 million, grew at an (unweighted) average rate of 2.7 percent per annum, almost twice the average rate of growth of the middle-income countries, and considerably faster than the rate of growth of the low-income countries. Over the course of these 27 years, despite rapid population growth, per capita GDP more than doubled in these five large Muslim countries at the core of the Muslim world.

In this period, the growth rate of per capita GDP in the most populous Muslim country, Indonesia, was not far behind that in the Asian Newly Industrializing Countries (NICs). Indonesia's total population is over 200 million, far larger than the rest of the non-communist Asian Newly Industrializing Countries put together. It also lacks the peculiar development advantages enjoyed by Hong Kong and

Singapore. These include their location, the absence of a rural sector, and their rich inheritance from British colonialism, with a developed port infrastructure, and relatively high levels of education and administrative skills. From 1975 to 2002 Indonesia's GDP per capita grew at 4.2 percent per annum, compared with 4.4 percent in Hong Kong, 5.0 percent in Singapore, 5.2 percent in Thailand, and 6.1 percent in Korea. The Muslim world also has its own "Little Asian Tiger" economy, in the shape of Malaysia, whose national output per person rose by around four percent per annum between 1975 and 2002.

Since the 1970s, across a wide spectrum of Muslim countries, capitalist economic growth has resulted in substantial advances in human development. In the Middle East and North Africa the proportion of the population living on less than $2 per day fell from 29 percent in 1981 to 20 percent in 2002. Infant mortality fell dramatically and life expectancy advanced enormously in the Muslim countries. For example, between 1960 and 2004 in Egypt, Iran, and Turkey, infant mortality rates fell from around 160 per thousand live births to 20–30 per thousand, and life expectancy increased from around 48 years to around 70 years. Enrollment rates in education also advanced dramatically. By 2004, in most Muslim countries most females in the relevant age group were enrolled in secondary education. Whereas in 1965 in Egypt, Iran, and Turkey, less than one quarter of the relevant age group were enrolled in secondary education, by 2004 the proportion had risen to 80–90 percent. By 2004 enrollment rates in tertiary education in key Muslim countries were far above those in low-income countries, and substantially above those even in middle-income countries.

Tertiary education in the Muslim world has expanded in part to meet the growing demands of the modern economy for highly educated workers in both scientific and non-scientific subjects. During the period of capitalist globalization, the Muslim world has also produced numerous outstanding scientists. The former Indian President Abdul Kalam is a Muslim. He is one of India's leading scientists, and played a central role in the development of India's nuclear weapons. Abdus Salam, a Muslim from Pakistan, won the Nobel Prize for physics. He once wrote: "The Holy Quran enjoins us to reflect on the verities of Allah's created laws of nature; however, that our generation has been privileged to glimpse a part of His design is a bounty and a grace for which I render thanks with a humble heart." Among many other outstanding modern scientists from the Muslim world are Ahmed Zewali, an Egyptian, who won the Nobel Prize for chemistry; Ayse Erzan from Turkey, who won the UNESCO "Women in Science" award in 2003; Rashid Sunyaev, from Uzbekistan, who is one of the world's leading astronomers; and Mustansir Barma, one of the world's leading theoretical physicists. International scientific journals contain large numbers of articles by scientists from Muslim countries.

In the non-oil producing Muslim developing countries, as is normal in developing countries, enlargement of the modern sector has taken place in the context of a relatively large rural sector containing widespread underemployment of labor. During this "Lewis Phase" of development, capitalist growth has been accompanied by quite high levels of inequality, although these levels are generally lower than in Latin America and sub-Saharan Africa.

Muslim responses to capitalism

The growth of modern capitalism in the Muslim world since the late nineteenth century has brought an outpouring of writing and political movements that has tried to come to terms with the new phenomenon. The responses have been diverse, but they have almost all taken place within the context of Islam. Much of the discussion has harked back to earlier Muslim thinkers who have wrestled over the centuries with the roles of the market, private property, and the state. In response to the challenging realities of modern capitalist development, there has been a ferment of debate, expressed in literature, music, film, and political argument. The debate among Islamic intellectuals and political thinkers has fused together arguments about national liberation from colonial rule and the intrusion of international capital, with analysis of indigenous capitalism, and the associated phenomena of urbanization, changing class structure, and the impact of the modern market economy on people's consciousness.

Anti-Western violence

The 1990s saw a spate of terrorist attacks by Islamic groups against symbols of the West, and especially of America, including an abortive attack on the World Trade Center in New York, large explosions at the American embassies in Beirut and Sudan, and an attack on an American warship, the USS *Cole*. However, the awareness of Islamic terrorism increased massively as a consequence of the astonishing spectacle broadcast live on global television of the destruction of the twin towers of the World Trade Center. The meticulously planned and executed attack was a superlative propaganda coup for its perpetrators.

After 9/11 a succession of violent operations was carried out by Islamic fundamentalist movements, including the bombing of commuters in Mumbai, Madrid, and London. These actions sparked a media frenzy and widespread panic in high-income countries, and the eruption of a veritable industry of apocalyptic fears and predictions about global terrorism and "global *jihad*." A large body of people in the high-income countries believe that the future of civilization is under threat from anti-Western and anti-capitalist Islamic fundamentalists. The images of extreme violence make for shocking and riveting television. It is possible that the numbers killed as a result of Islamic terrorism may increase, perhaps even through the use of a "dirty" nuclear bomb. However, in total the number of fatalities so far is relatively small. Any deaths through terrorist violence are shocking, of course, but it is important to put these attacks in perspective. Over the course of World War II nearly 30,000 people were killed as a result of German bombing in London, while British and American bombers killed around 600,000 people in German cities. Of course, the horrors of World War II in western Europe pale beside those in the Soviet Union, where as many as 28 million people, mainly innocent civilians, perished as a result of the Nazi invasion. Since the late 1940s armed conflicts have resulted in over 20 million deaths, and around one million people have died in total as a result of Hindu–Muslim violence in India. It is estimated that around 20 million people will die between 2000 and 2015 in road accidents, and a further 200 million will be injured.

To people in Muslim countries, the numbers of people killed in high-income countries as a result of attacks by Islamic terrorists since the 1990s pale before the immense numbers of deaths in violent conflicts in their own societies in recent history. These deaths were often the result of military action by outside forces, such as the French in Morocco, Tunisia, and Algeria, the British in Iraq, Egypt, and Sudan, the Soviet Union in Afghanistan, the Dutch in Indonesia, the Israelis in Egypt, Lebanon, and Palestine, and the Americans in Afghanistan and Iraq. In the perception of local people the invading and occupying armies appear as terrorists just as much as the Islamic terrorists appear to citizens of America or Europe when they carry out attack against their citizens. The fact that the invading soldiers wear uniforms does not stop them from being terrorists. Even among the large sections of the population who disagree with violence as the solution to conflict, the local fighters may still appear as freedom fighters rather than terrorists. While the mainstream of Muslims may deplore violence, they may still feel sympathy and admiration for the bravery of the young people who sacrifice their lives.

In the minds of many people in the West "Islamic fundamentalism" is equated with the intensely anti-Western regime of the Taliban in Afghanistan. In fact, the Taliban regime in Afghanistan (1992–2002) was unusual in the history of Islam, with few parallels elsewhere in the Muslim world. It arose in specific circumstances, at a time when Afghanistan was a battleground for the Soviet Union and America. Their activities in Afghanistan had important consequences for its neighbor, Pakistan, helping greatly to destabilize that country's politics. One reason for the eventual success of this particular extreme form of Islam was the strong support it received from both the CIA and the Pakistan Interservices Intelligence organization (ISI). It was in this environment that Al Qaeda was able to grow. The Taliban regime was antagonistic to the West, and especially to America. However, it was anathema for the vast majority of Muslims across the world. The Taliban were poorly tutored in Islamic and Afghan history, in knowledge of Sharia law and the Koran. The rich diversity of Islam and the essential message of the Koran—to build a civilized society that is just and equitable, and in which the rulers are responsible for their citizens—was forgotten.

Anti-capitalist revolution

The inequality and injustice that is inseparable from raw capitalism has regularly produced social movements protesting against the established order in Muslim countries. In the medieval Muslim world, capitalist development produced severe stresses and strains in the social fabric. Alongside flourishing economic and commercial development there was growing class inequality and class conflict in both urban and rural areas, which fostered a revolutionary climate and a long series of urban and agrarian disturbances. The revolts of the medieval Muslim world came in many forms, but they all had in common hostility to the rich, and the use of language and ideals from the Koran. Some of these revolts took the form of ascetic and religious criticism, but many of them were truly revolutionary in purpose, although it is difficult to disentangle the degree to which different rebellions were protests against oppression rather than attempts to establish a millennial, egalitarian society.

One of the most influential thinkers in the radical "communist" tradition of Islam was Abu Dharr al-Ghifari, who was one of the Companions of the Prophet. He shocked people by saying that the Koran's teaching required everyone to spend the whole of their wealth beyond the minimum needed for subsistence in the service of God or on charity. Around ten years after the Prophet's death he declared that the threatening verses in the Koran about rich men unwilling to give alms were applicable to members of the Muslim community no less than to the Jewish and Christians clerics attacked in the preceding verse:

> Believers, many are the clerics and monks who defraud men of their possessions and debar them from the path of God. To those that hoard gold and silver and do not spend it on God's cause, proclaim a woeful punishment. The day will surely come when their treasures shall be heated in the fire of Hell, and their foreheads, sides, and backs branded with them. They will be told: "These are the riches which you hoarded. Taste then what you were hoarding."

Koran, 9:34–35

Abu Dharr is said to have been banished to a remote locality as a danger to society. In the twentieth century, Abu Dharr enjoyed considerable popularity in the Muslim world, being viewed by the socialist and communist Left as a distant precursor of modern communism, or, at least, as a demonstration that socialism is not alien to the Muslim tradition.

In Iran and southern Iraq in the eighth and ninth centuries there was a succession of major uprisings, including the rebellion of the Iranian heretic al-Muqanna ("the Veiled One"), which lasted from 776 to 789. Al-Muqanna allegedly preached and practiced "communism of both property and women." The most serious Iranian rebellion was that of Babak, which lasted from 816 until 837. Babak led large-scale attacks on the landowners and plundered their possessions. Between 869 and 883 there was a large-scale slave revolt in southern Iraq and southwestern Iran, which began among the slaves who worked for large merchants and entrepreneurs on the salt flats east of Basra. Even though many of the slaves were African and not

Muslims, the revolt used Islamic language to express its rebellion against intolerable conditions.

The only major long-term competitor to the Abbasid Caliphate in the medieval Muslim world was the Egyptian-based Fatimid Caliphate, which was founded by the Isma'ilis. The Isma'ili was the most important of a number of sects that flourished in this period, attracting widespread popular support among ordinary people. Its members were highly egalitarian; their orthodox opponents frequently alleged that they practiced "communism of property and women." At the beginning, the Isma'ilis sharply attacked those who acquired wealth, but once they came to power, first in Tunisia and then in Egypt, they adopted thoroughly capitalist principles, allowing a market economy, and doing nothing to encroach upon the right to individual property and wealth.

All of the revolts in the medieval Islamic world were eventually crushed or else disintegrated of their own accord. They had only a limited influence, sometimes abandoning the revolutionary features of their program on their road to power. They left no permanent mark on the course of Islamic history, and wrought no radical changes in the structure of Islamic society. None of these uprisings was able to seize the seat of power at the heart of the Islamic Empire. They have much in common with the violent millennial movements in early modern Europe, which used Christian teaching as the ideology for their attack on the injustice of emerging capitalist society, but which never seized political power.

As modern capitalism evolved in Muslim societies, so there arose a strand within Islam that argued for a revolutionary interpretation of the Koran, harking back to medieval Islamic thinkers such as Abu Dharr and revolutionary leaders such as Babak. The Iranian scholar Ali Shari'ati stands at the forefront of such thinkers. Shari'ati's outlook went through different stages. He was strongly influenced by Sufism, and at one point was sympathetic to Islamic Marxism. However, by the mid-1970s he had concluded that the time was ripe for an Islamic revolution against the Shah. The revolution was to be "a bloody and virulent struggle" until it achieved the "annihilation of the triad of private property, autocratic monarchy and the clerical institution." Shari'ati's standpoint was that of Islamic social justice. He came to view Marxist guerrillas as the allies of Islamic fighters in the battle against the common enemy. In his view, when the Koran talks of property as belonging to God, it means that capital belongs to the whole people. He considered that there was a binary opposition running through the whole of human history, represented metaphorically by Cain and Abel: "[T]he system of Cain [stands for] economic monopoly and private ownership … slavery, serfdom, feudalism, bourgeoisie, industrial capitalism and imperialism (the culmination of capitalism)." By contrast, the system of Abel stands for "economic socialism (collective ownership), pastoral and hunting modes of production and the industrial mode of production (in the classless and post-capitalist society)."

Shari'ati believed that the establishment of an egalitarian, non-capitalist society required leadership by an enlightened vanguard—the *mujahideen*. Members of the vanguard would be people who, through their understanding of Islam and their direct apprehension of the true nature of society (and thus its ills), would be unaffected by the seductions and intimidations represented, respectively, by capitalism and tyrannical power. Shari'ati believed that the *mujahideen* should be armed not only with the Koran, but that it must also engage in violent struggle to overthrow the false gods of capitalism and state power. In a famous speech to his students in April 1972 he urged them: "Die! So that others may live." He believed that the spectacle of violent struggle between small groups of *mujahideen* and the state would awaken public consciousness. He recognized that the *mujahideen* would probably be defeated, but believed that the martyrs would expose the hollowness of the rulers and lead to their eventual downfall. He was contemptuous of debating "scientifically" with his opponents in the face of "people's hunger and the pillage of the capitalists." Shari'ati was imprisoned by the Shah in 1973. On his release from prison, he escaped from Iran and died of a heart attack in England, in June 1977, aged 44.

Only a small segment of the Islamic movement has adopted such a revolutionary anti-capitalist position. Although Shari'ati himself only came to such a position relatively late in his short life, his later writings are deeply influential among those who have adopted a revolutionary outlook. However, only a small part of the violence in Muslim countries in recent decades has been directed against the ruling class. Recent armed struggle within Muslim countries has often taken the form of attacks against Israel, and against the American presence, and the lesser presence of America's allies, in the Middle East, including attacks both in the region itself and in other parts of the world. It has sometimes involved civil war between different Islamic factions, neither of which is anti-capitalist, at other times separatist struggles by armed Islamic groups, or armed struggle against Islamic regimes with a view to replacing them with a regime that is more just, but still recognizably capitalist.

An Islamic 'Third Way'

From the late nineteenth century onward, there was a ferment of discussion among Islamic scholars about the significance of capitalist modernization and the ways in which it might be made compatible with Islamic values. There began a prolonged engagement with the methods through which it might be possible to build a morally acceptable society under capitalism. The goal for which the scholars searched was a society that avoided extremes of wealth and poverty and sustained a harmonious relationship between different members of society. The aim was to restore a moral economy which had been disrupted by modern capitalism and by the attitudes it encourages toward property and wealth creation. The debates that swirled around this central issue harked back to discussions within Islam over the course of more than 1,000 years. These debates, which have formed the focus of intellectual thought within the Muslim world over the last century, have much in common with the debates in the West and in China, which have wrestled with ways in which to tame capitalist forces in the interests of the wider society, albeit that the language is distinctively Islamic and the frame of reference for analyzing the moral economy is the Koran.

In the two centuries prior to Muhammad, a group of thinkers emerged in Iran who advocated a form of communism, involving the collectivization of private property. Muhammad, of course, also preached against riches and the rich, especially at the start of his preaching in Mecca, condemning wealth for turning people away from God. Passages early in the Koran express hostility to the pursuit of wealth because it turns people away from God and away from a harmonious relationship with the rest of society. In some places the Koran exhorts the rich to give away all their possessions to the poor if they wish to be rewarded in the afterlife: "The righteous man is he who ... though he loves it dearly, gives away his wealth to kinsfolk, to orphans, to the destitute, to the traveler in need and to beggars, and for the redemption of captives ..." (the Koran, 2:177). In similar vein, in the New Testament Jesus says: "It is easier for a camel to pass through the eye of a needle than it is for a rich man to enter the Kingdom of Heaven."

However, later passages in the Koran do not attack private property as such. Muhammad's solution to the evils of inequality of possessions was to urge the rich to give alms to the poor, and to tax them. These were "reformist" solutions, even for those times. The main body of medieval thinkers and political activists who used Islam to criticize the existing state of society in the Muslim world operated within the reformist framework. They tried to ensure that the state operated according to the ideals of the Koran. For them this meant treating all believers as equal before the Divine Law. It meant practicing within the Muslim community an advanced form of mutual aid, at the expense of the better-off and to the benefit of the poorer people. This is the ideal that the many Islamic reformist and revolutionary movements strove for repeatedly. However, these movements almost all accepted it as inevitable that there should exist distinctions between free men and slaves, landowners and tenants, rich and poor.

Throughout its history Islam has emphasized that justice is the core of the Islamic economic system. In the eleventh century al-Mawardi argued that comprehensive and multidimensional justice promotes solidarity, law and order, national economic development, expansion of wealth, population growth, and national security: "There is nothing that destroys the world and the consciousness of the people faster than injustice." Ibn Khaldun, the great Islamic scholar who died in 1406, wrote that economic development is only sustainable if there is justice: "Oppression brings development to an end," and "decline in property is the inevitable result of injustice and transgression."

However, in the mainstream of Islamic thinking, a just society has been pursued within realistic constraints about the nature and importance of the market economy. Three centuries before Adam Smith, Ibn Khaldun emphasized the rationality of the division of labor and the market mechanism: "It is well known and well established that human beings are not themselves capable of satisfying all their economic needs. They must cooperate for this purpose. The needs that can be satisfied by a group of them through mutual cooperation are many times greater than what individuals are capable of satisfying themselves." Ibn Khaldun emphasized the positive function that could be played by extension of the market: "[Tools require savings which is the] surplus left after satisfying the needs of the people. Increase in the size of the market boosts the demand for goods and services, which promotes industry, raises income, furthers science and education, and accelerates development." The great Islamic university al-Azhar in Cairo was founded in 970. In 1948, in a famous judgment, it strongly affirmed the reformist view of the Koran. Radical Egyptian Islamists had argued that Islam was inherently communist, making use especially of the writings of Abu Dharr to support their view. The doctors at al-Azhar issued a *fatwah*, proclaiming: "No communism in Islam."

The 1950s and 1960s saw the appearance, across much of the Arab world, of so-called "Arab socialism," at the core of which was state planning and extensive nationalization of the means of production. Egypt under Nasser was the leading force in this movement, which was typically justified in terms of the Islamic tradition, with the state allegedly taking the lead in ensuring that the whole of society's interests were met. However, even at the height of Arab socialism, there was still a large role for the private sector. In the 1960s Nasser's own Minister of the Economy, Ibrahim Qaissouni, said: "Our socialism ... does not aim at allowing the state full ownership of the means of production, but protects private property and stipulates the freedom of private initiative and its equality of opportunity with the private sector." During Nasser's lifetime, an intense debate took place among the reformist mainstream about capitalism in the Muslim world. After Nasser's death in 1970, the discussion centered more firmly around the mechanisms that could guide an essentially private-enterprise capitalist economy toward Islamic ideals. Policy liberalization after the death of Nasser took the Arab socialist countries much more firmly toward mainstream capitalism. It became commonplace among Islamic intellectuals to refer to an Islamic "Third Way" between raw capitalism and state-controlled, materialistic communism. There was heated discussion among Islamic intellectuals about how best to establish harmony in a society disrupted by class antagonisms and driven by the acquisitiveness, competition, and commodification unleashed by capitalism.

Together with Ali Shari'ati, the Egyptian scholar Sayyid Qutb (1906–66) was the most influential internal critic of Muslim governments in the twentieth century. Initially, Qutb was supportive of President Nasser's "Egyptian socialism." However, Qutb came to believe that Nasser had betrayed the fundamental principles of Islam, that he had nurtured a cult of personality, and that he had constructed an authoritarian dictatorship under the flag of socialism. Sayyid Qutb's trenchant criticism led to his being jailed for ten years (1954–64), and he was eventually tried and executed by Nasser in 1966. Qutb was a sophisticated, highly educated scholar, who had obtained a master's degree in America, taught in higher education in his native Egypt, and served as a senior official in the Ministry of Education. There is a widely held view in the West that Muslim scholars and Muslim schools (*madrasas*) are "fundamentalist," anti-Western and anti-capitalist. Given the fact that Qutb is immensely influential in the Islamic world among scholars and students, it is useful to look at his views in some detail.

Qutb's most influential book is *Social Justice in Islam*, originally published in 1949, and still widely read today. For Qutb "justice is the greatest foundation of Islam." People are social beings, who only prosper as a species through mutual support: "The Islamic belief is that humanity is an essential unity ... Life is like a ship at sea whose crew are all concerned for her safety; none of them may make a hole in his own part of the ship in the name of his individual freedom." Islam attempts to find a middle way in balancing the interests of the individual and society: "Justice demands that the social system shall conform to the desire of the individual and satisfy his inclinations—at least so far as will not injure society—as a return for his contribution to it in the way of ability and labor ... [J]ustice is not always concerned to serve the interests of the individual. Justice is for the individual, but is for society also, if we are willing to tread the middle way."

Qutb recognized the need to motivate people through material incentives to work hard, which will be for the benefit of the whole society. He affirmed that private property is an integral part of the Muslim economy. However, the individual must realize that he is "no more than the steward of property": "Property is a trust in the hands of its possessor, who is obliged to use it for the general good of society." Under Islam, "everything belongs to the community, and, therefore, all permission for personal ownership must come from the law, virtually or actually": "Allah is the only true owner of anything." Qutb argued that wealth should be taxed for the benefit of society. Islam prescribes the levying of *zakat* on the usufruct from property. *Zakat* and other state levies are to be used for social welfare to provide all members of society with their basic needs: "Islam disapproves of people being in poverty or need, because it wishes to preserve them from the material cares of life and give them leisure for better things, for things which are more suitable for human nature and to that special nobility with which Allah has endowed the sons of man." Islam should ensure that medical care and education are "provided free to every individual in the country: the rich must not be able, by money, to get more than the poor in schools or hospitals." Islam aims to "create a balance of wealth, to oppose destitution, to establish the responsibilities that exist between rich and poor, and thus to shape a society that has a sense of mutual relationship and mutual help and that is therefore a healthy society."

Qutb emphasizes Islam's hostility to the accumulation of capital through usury, reflecting the deep fears about the socially corrosive impact of "making money from money" that has been widely felt in different cultures since ancient times: "Mutual help is one of the fundamental principles of the Islamic society, but usury destroys mutual help and it vitiates it at its very root." Islam views usury as the means of "amassing a vast amount of capital wealth that does not depend on labor and effort ... Although Allah has allowed bargaining, he has forbidden usury." Usury is viewed as a key mechanism for producing socio-economic inequality, and exploitation of those in a vulnerable position; instead, money should be "loaned to those in need freely and without interest; this is the way to increase affection, cultivate generosity, and create a sense of mutual responsibility between rich and poor, between powerful and weak."

In Qutb's view, the human race is at a critical juncture in its long evolution, due to the contradictory character of capitalism: "[T]he world today is in that state of insecurity and instability where it must look for new foundations and search for some spiritual means of restoring to man his faith in the principles of humanity." He considers that Islam can contribute fundamentally to solving the problems arising from capitalist materialism: "We are indeed at a crossroads ... [Islam] can offer mankind this theory [of social justice] whose aims are a complete mutual help among all men and a true mutual responsibility in society." Islam seeks to provide answers to human beings' most profound spiritual needs. Islam can make a fundamental contribution to the global problems arising from the contradictory character of capitalist materialism: "[T]he philosophy of Western materialist civilization is a danger to the continued existence of man. It breeds in human nature a ceaseless anxiety, a perpetual rivalry, a continuous strife, a degeneration of all human qualities. And this is in spite of all the triumphs of science that could have tended to human happiness and peace and content had it not been that the bases of the Western philosophy of life were purely materialistic and hence unable to guide men along the path to perfection." Such fears are now widely held in the non-Muslim world in the face of the realities of the profound contradictions that have emerged during the era of capitalist globalization.

Today there is hysteria in the West about the perceived threat from Islamic fundamentalism. There is a widespread view that there is indeed a "clash of civilizations" between Islam and the Judaeo-Christian West. However, the mainstream of Muslim thinking today, among both scholars and ordinary people, occupies the reformist ground, just as it did in the medieval world. The mainstream is found neither in the Taliban and Al Qaeda, nor in the American-backed oil-rich authoritarian states on the western side of the Persian Gulf.

In recent decades, across a wide range of Muslim countries, capitalist modernization has been pursued with some form of secular development strategy. Examples of this include Turkey under Kemal and his successors, Iran under the Pahlavi regime, Iraq under the Ba'athist regime, Pakistan under Ayub Khan and Yahya Khan, Egypt under Nasser, Sadat, and Mubarak, Malaysia under Mahatir and Badhawi, and Indonesia under Suharto. These countries have all, albeit to different degrees, achieved successful capitalist modernization. In each of them, despite numerous measures to achieve some form of secular modernization, Islam has remained deeply entrenched. During the era of capitalist globalization there has been a pronounced Islamic revival in all of these countries.

The mainstream of the Islamic revival is far from being a response to state failure and poor economic performance. It has taken place in all parts of the modernizing capitalist Muslim world, including some countries that have grown at much faster rates than average in the developing world, such as Malaysia, Turkey, and Indonesia under Suharto. The revival appeals to all segments of the population, including students, intellectuals, women, businessmen, and both farmers and urban workers.

Among the most striking examples of the Islamic revival has been the electoral victories of the Justice and Development Party (AKP) in Turkey since 2000, including its sweeping success in the 2007 parliamentary elections, in which it won 47 percent of the popular vote. The AKP is a conservative, non-violent Islamic party, which seeks to maintain an open economy and a Western legal system, and which seeks membership of the European Union. Pakistan too has had a powerful Islamic revival, and Islam is central to the daily lives of most people in Pakistan. However, mainstream Muslims in Pakistan are far removed from Islamic fundamentalism. In the 2008 general election less than ten percent of the population chose to vote for the fundamentalist Islamic political parties.

Much more controversial has been the progress made by the Muslim Brotherhood in Egypt. The Muslim Brotherhood is much less well understood by, and inspires apprehension in, the Western media. The policies of President Nasser and his successors, Presidents Sadat and Mubarak, have followed a long tradition of secular modernization under an authoritarian state which stretches back to Muhammad Ali and Ishma'il Pasha in the nineteenth century. Capitalist modernization under the authoritarian Egyptian state has produced tremendous social tensions, such as are typically the case in the early phase of economic development. These are associated with rapid urbanization, social dislocation, and increasing inequality. These tensions have escalated in the era of *infitah*, the open economy, and capitalist globalization. Since the start of the new millennium, foreign direct investment has poured into Egypt, reaching a record of $11 billion in 2006–07, and national output growth has accelerated to over seven percent annually. However, the World Bank estimates that between 2000 and 2005, the number of people below the poverty line rose from 16.7 percent to 19.6 percent. Egypt is described a "one percent society," in which one percent of the population controls almost all the wealth of the country.

The Muslim Brotherhood is the most important element in a broad-based Islamic revival in Egypt. The Brotherhood was founded in 1928, and the late Sayyid Qutb remains its most important figure. The Brotherhood is banned from participating in elections as a political party, but its members are allowed to compete as individuals. In the 2005 elections it won over 20 percent of the seats in the Egyptian parliament. It is widely thought that if it wished, it could obtain a parliamentary majority. The Brotherhood is explicitly committed to parliamentary democracy, non-violence, and private property. It has established deep roots among intellectuals and business people, taking control of the largest professional and student associations. It has established a network of social services in neighborhoods and villages, offering full health insurance as well as other welfare benefits. These organizations provide a sense of community to neighborhoods by helping citizens obtain food, jobs, and healthcare.

The mainstream of the Islamic revival in Muslim countries has not been Islamic fundamentalism, which seeks to return to a mythical Islamic utopia. Rather, the mainstream has been the search for values based on the Koran, which can provide meaning and a moral framework to guide society through the chaotic process of capitalist modernization, including rapid urbanization, in the context of an open economy. The core values of the Islamic revival constitute a form of "Third Way," which is opposed to political violence and which accepts the legitimacy of the electoral process. It accepts the institutions of private property and the market, but wishes to constrain the conditions under which these institutions function, with an ethic that is derived from the Koran. Thinkers and political activists in the reformist approach believe that the Koran provides a moral framework within which private property and entrepreneurial activity can work toward the collective interest.

ISLAM AND THE WEST

Muslim unity

The 1.3 billion Muslims in the world live in several tens of countries, in some of which they constitute a majority of the population. Even the smallest of these countries, such as Kuwait, Bahrain, and the United Arab Emirates, have attempted to build a sense of national identity in the modern era, a form of identity which is often based on a mythical history of national unity. Muslims are divided by the fact that they speak a diversity of languages. There are profound differences of culture, language, and ethnic and national identity between the Muslims in African countries such as Nigeria, Sudan, or Sierra Leone, those of the oil-producing countries of the Arab Middle East, those of Central Asia in Iran, Afghanistan, and Uzbekistan, and those of South and Southeast Asia, in Pakistan, India, Malaysia, and Indonesia. There are also violent conflicts within the Islamic community. The Islamic Kurds have fought a ferocious, long-lasting battle for independence with their fellow Muslims in Turkey, Iraq, and Iran. Islamic Iran and Islamic Iraq fought one of the longest-lasting and most horrific wars of modern times. Much of the Muslim world is riven by the schism between the Sunni and Shi'ite Muslims, just as Europe was for a long period riven by the divide between Protestants and Catholics, and still is in Northern Ireland. The attempts to build Muslim institutions that cross national boundaries have, for the most part, not advanced far. For example, the Arab League, which was founded in 1945 as an "Arab United Nations," has never progressed much beyond a talking-shop.

Despite their internal divisions, the 1.3 billion Muslims are united by a religion, which, for a large fraction of them, remains fundamentally important as a guide to the conduct of their lives. It permeates their daily lives in a way that Christianity has ceased to do for many of those who are nominally Christian. There is a profound sense of Muslim identity that transcends the boundaries of nationality, culture, language, and religious interpretation.

In modern times there has been widespread anti-Western feeling across the Muslim world. This hostility has many causes, including the relatively recent and violent end to colonialism, the intertwining of oil and international relations, and the role of Israel. The language in which this hostility has been expressed by Muslims has been largely couched in terms of the Islamic religion. This also is unsurprising, as Islam is naturally the ethical framework for all Muslims; it provides a language and tradition with powerful emotional appeal.

Europe and Islam

America is central to the relationship between Islam and the West today. However, in the late nineteenth and the first half of the twentieth century, it was Britain and France which formed the front line of Western interactions with the Muslim world. The legacy of this period still affects the way in which Islam interacts with global capitalism, and these two countries remain important actors in the Muslim world today.

Before 1914 a large part of the Middle East was under Ottoman (Turkish) rule. By the late Ottoman period, "Greater Syria" (today's Syria, Jordan, Israel, and Lebanon) and the provinces of Basra, Mosul, and Baghdad (today's Iraq) were developing into an integrated economic unit within the Ottoman Empire, linked by modern infrastructure, and with increasingly closely linked markets. At the end of World War I, with the collapse of Ottoman rule, powerful movements for Arab national self-determination emerged. Arab nationalists began to think in terms of a new political entity that would transcend the boundaries inherited from the Ottoman Empire. Even though the eventual boundaries for the Arab people were imprecise, they might in principle have embraced much of the Middle East, including possibly even Iraq. This entity would have constituted a formidable state, with a common language and culture, linked by both natural waterways (the Tigris and Euphrates) and man-made road and rail links, stretching from the Mediterranean possibly even to the Persian Gulf, and bounded by mountain ranges to the north (separating it from Turkey) and the east (separating it from Iran), and desert to the south (separating it from Egypt). There was considerable sympathy for Arab nationalist views both in America and in some parts of the political establishment in the victorious European states, Britain and France. Moreover, during the war, the British government had encouraged the hope that in return for their support against Turkey, the Arab people might be granted political independence. For the first time, the claim that those who spoke Arabic constituted a nation and should have a state had been to some extent accepted by a great power. Had these aspirations been respected and an Arab state of the Middle East established, relations between the West and the Muslim world would have been fundamentally different.

Instead, after World War I Arab nationalist hopes were dashed. The division of the region into smaller states under separate British and French rule prevented the development of the territory into a single geopolitical unit. At the end of the war, Britain and France together seized control of the Middle Eastern possessions of the Ottoman Empire. They did so under the authority of a "mandate" granted by the newly established League of Nations. Britain was given the mandate for the territory that is now Iraq, Jordan, Israel, and the occupied Palestinian territories, while France was given the mandate for Lebanon and Syria. These areas had been part of the Ottoman Empire, without separate national identities, but now the British and French created the modern Arab states, giving them territorial boundaries and central regimes, and bequeathing to the future the problem of a cultural region partitioned into a number of small states. In the modern world, this outcome finds its analogy in the views of Western strategists who hope for the break-up of China into smaller "warring kingdoms." In the period 1919–39 the British and French intensified their control over trade and production within the region. The granting of the mandates to Britain and France was deeply resented by most Arab people, especially those who had wished for a united independent state after the downfall of the Ottoman Empire.

British troops occupied Egypt in 1882. In 1883 the British Prime Minister, W. E. Gladstone, told the House of Commons: "I must remind the House that the onerous duty which we have undertaken in Egypt is to put down disorder, and thus establish some beginnings of tolerable government. That is a duty we have undertaken, not on our behalf only, but for civilization. We undertook it with the approval of the powers of Europe—the highest and most authentic organ of modern civilization." Britain extended its rule southwards into the Sudan, defeating the forces of the ruling Islamic government at the Battle of Omdurman in 1898. Winston Churchill considered the Battle of Omdurman to be "the most signal triumph ever gained by the arms of science over barbarians": "Within the space of five hours the strongest and best-armed savage army yet arrayed against a modern European Power had been destroyed and dispersed, with hardly any difficulty, comparatively small risk, and insignificant loss to the victors." The Sudanese army, approximately 52,000 strong, suffered losses estimated to be 20,000 dead and 22,000 wounded. By contrast, the Anglo-Egyptian army, some 23,000 strong, suffered losses of 48 dead and 382 wounded.

Egypt remained a virtual colony until the Anglo-Egyptian Treaty of 1936, with repeated violent suppression of nationalist demonstrations, while the Sudan remained under British occupation until 1956. Even after Egyptian independence Britain maintained control of the Suez Canal, which was owned mainly by

Anglo-French shareholders. It was nationalized by the Egyptian government in 1956. In a secret tripartite agreement Britain, France, and Israel agreed to use the decision as a pretext for overthrowing the socialist government of President Nasser. The short-lived Franco-British invasion intensified anti-British (and anti-French) sentiment in the Middle East.

By the end of World War I Britain had established a dominant position in the Persian Gulf. Kuwait remained a British protectorate until 1961, and it was not until 1971 that the British withdrew finally from the states of the lower Gulf, including Bahrain, Qatar, the United Arab Emirates, and Oman. Further south, in the Gulf of Aden, the port of Aden had been a British colony since 1839, and the surrounding territory had been a British protectorate from 1896. This area did not gain independence from Britain until 1967.

In the interwar period Britain maintained a network of military facilities in the Middle East, including ports, airfields, and army bases. In this period, British forces carried out bloody suppressions of revolts in both Iraq and Palestine, which in one incident involved the use of the Royal Air Force to drop chemical weapons in Iraq. As we shall see, the British government's Balfour Declaration was critical to the Jewish colonization of Palestine. Under British aegis, large-scale Jewish immigration into Palestine was permitted up until World War II. Britain played, and continues to play, a significant role in buttressing the authoritarian governments in the Arab oil-producing countries, through the sale of weapons and the provision of military advice and training. Moreover, British policy in the Muslim world was overshadowed by the catastrophe of the handover of power in South Asia in 1947. The appalling violence, with Muslims at its center, was widely perceived to have been a consequence of bungled policy by the British colonial rulers. The legacy of the disastrous handover persists to this day in the form of hostility between India and Pakistan and deep antagonism between Muslims and Hindus within India.

France's role in the Middle East in the interwar period was deeply resented because of its establishment of de facto colonies in the mandated territories of Syria and Lebanon. In Lebanon, France's "divide and rule" policy exacerbated an already complex situation, by encouraging the different religious and linguistic groups to maintain separate educational systems. The French mandate over Lebanon was warmly welcomed by the minority Catholic Maronite population, which had centuries-old religious, cultural, and business links with France. As well as its mandate over the former Ottoman territories in the Middle East, France had for a long period controlled colonies in North Africa, including Tunisia (occupied by the French army in 1881), Morocco, and Algeria. In Morocco the French defeated an armed movement of national resistance in 1926, and by the late 1920s they had conquered most of the country. The French army and navy had a network of bases spread across the Maghrib, protecting France's extensive economic interests in the region.

Unlike other French colonies, the vast territory of Algeria was fully integrated into France's political structure. By the early 1950s there were around 1.3 million French immigrants (*colons*) in Algeria, compared with around nine million Arab people. The French colonists dominated the economy, controlling the most fertile land and the most productive agriculture. The national liberation movement, the FLN (Front de Libération Nationale), fought a prolonged and violent war with the French armed forces. Algeria did not achieve independence until 1962. It did so at great cost. A large part of the Muslim population was displaced in the struggle, and around 300,000 or more (out of a population of around nine million Muslims) were killed.

France played a significant role in relations with the Muslim world in other respects too. As we shall see, in 1956 France began to supply Israel with advanced conventional weapons and provided the technological capabilities that enabled Israel to build nuclear weapons. There was strong support for the Zionist movement at high levels of the French government, and Israeli scientists in turn helped the French solve technological problems as they moved toward the final stages of building their own nuclear bomb. A key element in the relationship was the Algerian independence struggle. The Algerian national liberation movement attracted widespread support in the Muslim world, especially in the Arab countries, and the French government believed that Egypt was playing an important role in the struggle against the French. They agreed to help Israel to acquire nuclear technology in return for Israeli agreement to provide intelligence information to the French about Egyptian activities in Algeria. Moreover, in the wake of the French humiliation by President Nasser over the Suez debacle, the French government promised to work with Israel to topple President Nasser.

Energy security, American foreign policy, and the Middle East

America's free market pattern of development became locked into a structure that was addicted to the automobile and to oil. As America's own oil production declined and its dependence on imported oil became ever larger, so the importance of secure access to oil rose ever higher on the American foreign policy agenda. By far the largest oil reserves in the world are located within the national boundaries of the country that was the birthplace of the Prophet Muhammad and in which the Islamic religion arose. A large fraction of the remaining reserves of oil are located in the surrounding territories in the Arab world that formed the early core of Islam. Together, the Muslim countries of the Middle East account for over two-thirds of the world's oil reserves, and their share of global output is predicted to rise from 27 percent in 2000 to 43 percent in 2030. The share of imports in the American oil supply is predicted to rise from 54 percent in 2001 to 68 percent in 2025. Five countries in the Persian Gulf region, namely Saudi Arabia, Iran, Iraq, Kuwait, and the United Arab Emirates, between them have 60 percent of total world oil reserves, and the share of the Gulf countries in world oil trade is predicted to rise from

41 percent to 70 percent in 2030. The American government's National Energy Policy document of 2001 concluded: "Middle East oil production will remain central to world oil security ... [and] the Gulf will be a primary focus of US international energy policy." The central role of the Middle East in global energy supply has led America to be intimately involved in the political economy of the Middle East, especially that of the key oil-producing states, Saudi Arabia, Iran, and Iraq. It is said repeatedly that the Gulf is a "vital strategic area" for America: "strategic" is shorthand for saying that the region is home to two-thirds of the world's oil reserves.

We have seen that the lobbying power of Wall Street financial firms has greatly influenced America's international relations in the era of capitalist globalization. We will see later that the American Zionist lobby has also deeply influenced American foreign policy in this era. As will see in this section, the giant American oil companies have also greatly influenced American foreign policy. In each case the long-run interests of ordinary Americans have been sacrificed to the interests of a particular segment of the American political economy, each of which possesses enormous lobbying power.

Saudi Arabia The modern state of Saudi Arabia came into existence in the 1920s, when the Saudi royal family seized control of the holy places of Mecca and Medina and assumed their custodianship. The Saudi state has since then been governed as the personal property of the ruling family. Its legal code is based on the Wahhabi branch of Islam, which is conservative and austere in its application of Islamic principles, based on the supposed application of the "fundamental principles" embodied in Muslim scriptures. Saudi Arabia makes extensive use of the death penalty (including the execution of child offenders) and application of the lash by its courts. There has been pervasive discrimination against women, with more complete sex segregation outside the home than in any other Muslim country.

Oil exploration in Saudi Arabia began in the 1930s. Toward the end of World War II the Saudi Arabian monarch, King Ibn Saud, made it clear that if Washington agreed to supply the country with foreign aid he would offer the American government special access to Saudi oil. In February 1943 the American President authorized Lend Lease assistance to Saudi Arabia, and America began its long and deep involvement in Saudi Arabian politics and oil. A year later, in February 1944, a famous discussion took place between Lord Halifax, the British Ambassador in Washington, and President Roosevelt, in which Roosevelt showed the ambassador a map of the Middle East and said: "Persian oil is yours. We share the oil of Iraq and Kuwait. As for Saudi Arabian oil, it's ours." In October 1950, American President Harry Truman wrote to King Ibn Saud: "I wish to renew to your majesty the assurances which have been made to you several times in the past, that the United States is interested in the preservation of independence and the territorial integrity of Saudi Arabia. No threat to your Kingdom could occur which would not be a matter of immediate concern to the United States." Ever since 1943, America has provided the basic guarantee of Saudi Arabian territorial integrity and independence and has closely supported Saudi Arabia's autocratic ruling family, both politically and militarily. Many prominent members of the House of Saud are friends of senior American politicians, including both Bush presidents, and are investors in firms managed by prominent Republicans, including former Secretary of State James Baker and former Secretary of Defense Frank Carlucci.

Iraq At the end of World War I, as we have seen, Britain took control of Iraq from the Ottoman Empire, and ruled it as a colony on the Indian model. In 1930 Iraq became formally independent, but Britain still retained control over Iraq's foreign and military affairs. It was not until the overthrow of the Hashemite monarchy in 1958 that British influence was finally thrown off. In 1963 the Ba'ath party seized power and set Iraq on its modern course. It declared Iraq to be a socialist society and nationalized the main banks and industries. Nationalization of the country's oil resources was completed in 1972. Iraq declared itself an Islamic state, but it was far removed from the "fundamentalist" Islamic government that was to come to power later in Iran, let alone that of the Taliban in Afghanistan.

In 1979 Saddam Hussein came to power. Despite the harshness of his rule, the Ba'ath state created a wide base of public acceptance, providing extensive subsidies for urban middle-class education and health policies. Iraq attempted to build itself into the dominant power in the Arab world. First it attempted to capture the oil resources of western Iran, which led to a prolonged and brutal war between the two countries. Then it invaded Kuwait, in order to add Kuwait's huge oil resources to its own. The central importance of the region in American foreign policy was demonstrated by the First Gulf War, in which America drove Iraq out of Kuwait and restored the country's vast oil reserves to its autocratic rulers. At the end of that war the giant oil producers, Iraq and Iran, on the northern and eastern sides of the Gulf respectively, were both ruled by regimes hostile to America. The oil-producing countries along the western side of the Gulf, which were all characterized by an absence of political democracy and extreme inequality in the distribution of income and wealth, were heavily reliant on American support, both diplomatically and militarily. This fact was made abundantly clear by the First Gulf War.

American policy throughout the 1990s aimed at encouraging internal dissatisfaction and the overthrow of Saddam Hussein. After his defeat and eviction from Kuwait, America stationed large numbers of troops in Kuwait and Saudi Arabia, maintained no-fly zones over northern and southern Iraq, and, along with Britain, undertook intermittent bombing inside Iraq. America enforced a blockade of Iraq's ports, which drastically restricted its international trade and severely damaged its economy. The oil industry was crippled under the combined impact of prohibitions of international investment and bans on imported equipment, and as a result, Iraq's oil production fell to less than one-half its capacity. The American-enforced blockade contributed to the deaths of hundreds of thousands of Iraqi children due to lack of adequate food and healthcare. The suffering caused by American policies generated popular sympathy for the Iraq government both within Iraq and among the international Muslim community.

Three of the world's top five oil companies (ExxonMobil, Chevron and Conoco Phillips) are American, and the other two giants, BP and Shell, have a large share of their business in America. In the 1990s they had hoped to gain increasing access to the 70 percent of the world's oil reserves that are controlled by the national oil companies (NOCs). They were broadly unsuccessful, however, and they were instead forced increasingly to develop expensive and inaccessible fields independently of the NOCs. The oilfields (and gas fields) of Iraq and Iran are huge and low cost, and the prospect of increased access to them was immensely attractive to the giant international oil companies.

Prior even to his assumption of the American presidency in 2001, George W. Bush's top advisers believed that America should invade Iraq, oust Saddam Hussein, and replace him with a new regime friendly to American interests. In 1998 a group of eighteen leading American political figures signed a highly publicized letter to President Clinton, urging him to act decisively to pre-empt Iraq's possible acquisition of weapons of mass destruction before it was too late. The signatories included Donald Rumsfeld, Paul Wolfowitz, Richard Perle, Robert Zoellick (now president of the World Bank), and Francis Fukuyama. Most of them became officials in George W. Bush's administration, and they continued to push strongly for military action in Iraq.

Following the attacks of September 11, 2001, America invaded Afghanistan in order to overthrow the Taliban regime. In early 2002 the Bush government prepared its plans to invade Iraq. In August 2002 Vice President Cheney warned:

Should all [of Saddam Hussein's WMD] ambitions be realized, the implications would be enormous for the Middle East and the United States. Armed with an arsenal of these weapons and seated atop ten percent of the world's oil reserves, Saddam Hussein could then be expected to seek domination of the entire Middle East, take control of a great portion of the world's energy supplies, directly threaten America's friends throughout the region, and subject the United States or any other nation to nuclear blackmail.

A *New York Times*/CBS poll prior to the American invasion of Iraq after 9/11 reported that only six percent of Americans opposed military action, "even if many thousands of innocent civilians are killed." A substantial majority favored the American invasion. In the teeth of widespread international opposition, including mass protests across the length and breadth of Europe, the Americans invaded Iraq (in "Operation Iraqi Freedom") in a military campaign designed to "shock and awe" the Iraqi population. Despite constant references by the military to a new type of weaponry with precision targeting, tens of thousands of Iraqi civilians died during the American invasion, certainly a vastly greater number than had lost their lives in the destruction of the Twin Towers. In addition, large numbers of people were wounded, lost their homes, were displaced due to the American invasion, and/or suffered psychological traumas from the violent military operation.

Senior American officials went to great lengths to avoid mentioning oil as a *causus belli.* The principal official justifications given for the invasion were that Iraq had played a role in the 9/11 attacks on the Twin Towers and that Saddam Hussein had developed weapons of mass destruction. Both of these claims were later shown to be false. Most people in the Muslim world, and indeed in the world at large, believe the inconvenient truth that both the First Gulf War and the invasion of Iraq in 2003 were closely connected with America's search for energy security, with its desire to gain access to Iraqi oil for Western oil companies, and especially for American ones. In his memoirs published in 2007, Alan Greenspan said: "I am saddened that it is politically inconvenient to acknowledge what everyone knows: the Iraq war is largely about oil."

At its meetings in 2002–3 the American State Department called for the opening up of Iraq's state-owned oil sector to outside investment after a period of rehabilitation of the oilfields. The Department of Defense developed plans to seize control of Iraq's oilfields immediately after the invasion and prevent their destruction. American oil companies did not disguise their hopes that they would be at the center of the Iraqi oil industry under the post-Saddam government. The Bush government hoped that the invasion would replace Saddam Hussein with a stable pro-Western government that would boost oil output with the large-scale involvement of Western oil companies.

In the event, the invasion of Iraq produced results that were seriously damaging to America's own foreign policy objectives. As most Middle Eastern experts had predicted, the country descended into anarchy and civil war. Saddam Hussein's authoritarian but stable and long-lasting regime was replaced by violent chaos. Representatives from the majority Shi'ite population dominated the new Iraqi government which was elected in 2005. The overthrow of Saddam Hussein by America's violent intervention inflamed Arab public opinion on all sides against America. It also provided an opportunity for Iran to extend greatly its influence in the region, through the closeness of its relationship with the Shi'ite majority that now ruled Iraq. The previously dominant Sunni minority entered a bitter civil war with the now dominant Shi'ite majority. The war resulted in a drastic deterioration in the welfare of the Iraqi population; a report in the British medical journal *The Lancet* in 2007 estimated that there had been 655,000 "excess deaths" in Iraq since the American invasion, equivalent to 2.5 percent of the total Iraqi population. The collapse of order in Iraq, and the threat of wider political ramifications, was a major factor in the rapid increase in the world oil price. This in turn strongly assisted the oil-producing economies by greatly increasing their foreign exchange earnings. It contributed to greatly increased confidence among the governments of oil-exporting countries, including that of President Putin in Russia. It provided greatly increased resources for the budgets of populist anti-American governments, such as those of Mahmood Ahmadinejad in Iran and Hugo Chavez in Venezuela, with which to support anti-poverty polices and win political influence both domestically and in the surrounding region.

The increased oil price greatly reduced the incentive for NOCs to involve the leading international oil companies in the development of their oilfields. By late 2006 it was widely accepted that Iraq had descended into civil war, that America had lost the war in Iraq and now faced the prospect of a humiliating withdrawal, analogous to its withdrawal from Vietnam. The disaster in Iraq threatened to produce a domino effect in terms of the comprehensive destabilization of the Middle East. The war in Iraq had produced a growing interdependence between the formal mortal enemies, Iran and Iraq, bringing together their mainly Shi'ite populations in a way that threatened fundamentally to reshape the region.

The bipartisan American Iraq Study Group published a report in December 2006, which repudiated virtually all of the policies that President Bush had been pursuing toward Iraq since 2002. It underlined the "staggering cost of a war that is failing," both in terms of the almost 3,000 American troops killed and the $400 billion spent on the war to date. The report disputed the American government's assertion that the violence in Iraq was mainly due to Al Qaeda, arguing that Al Qaeda was responsible for "only small portions of the violence." In December 2006, Zbigniew Brzezinski, the former American national security adviser, concluded that the war had been a disaster. He warned of the potentially disastrous impact of American Middle Eastern policies upon American foreign policy interests:

[T]he US role in the world is being gravely undermined by the policies launched more than three years ago. The destructive war in Iraq, the hypocritical indifference to the human dimension of the stalemate in Israeli–Palestinian relations, the lack of diplomatic initiatives in dealing with Iran and the frequent use of Islamophobic rhetoric, are setting in motion forces that threaten to push America out of the Middle East, with dire consequences for itself and its friends in Egypt, Jordan, and Saudi Arabia.

By mid-2008 the intensity of internal conflict in Iraq had abated somewhat, as a result of the "troop surge" and of the ceding of a large degree of control to forces that had previously been opponents of the American army of occupation. On July 1, 2008, the Iraqi government invited foreign companies to bid for contracts to develop eight of its oil and gas fields, including six fields that constitute the backbone of the Iraqi oil industry. Iraq's national oil companies were to have no more than a 25 percent stake in these projects. This historic announcement allowed international oil companies back into Iraq for the first time in 30 years. It was expected that the deep involvement of the international giants would help to lift Iraq's oil output to 4.5 million barrels per day by 2013, compared with 2.5 million barrels per day in 2007. It appeared that President Bush would leave office having accomplished the first phase of the reopening of Iraq to the international oil companies.

Iran Oil was first discovered in Iran in 1908. Production was dominated by the Anglo-Persian Oil Company, in which the British government established a controlling interest in 1914. In 1919 the ancient state of Iran was made a virtual protectorate under the Anglo-Persian Treaty. In 1921, however, the treaty was denounced by the Iranians, and in 1925 the modern Iranian state came into being when Reza Khan seized power as head of the army, declaring himself the Shah of Iran. Under his rule Iran developed into an authoritarian, secular, and modernizing state. It built a powerful army and established a secular education system. The 1920s and 1930s saw the development of the infrastructure of a modern capitalist economy. In 1941, Reza Khan abdicated in favour of his son Mohammed Reza. In the late 1940s America became closely involved in Iran's internal political development, in part motivated by a desire to forestall Soviet acquisition of Iran's oil assets and any possible advance by them through Iran toward the warm waters of the Persian Gulf. The Americans advised the Iranian government on economic policy, organized Iran's police and army, and supplied it with military aid.

British control of Iranian oil production through the Anglo-Persian Oil Company aroused intense hostility, and in 1951 Prime Minister Mosaddeq pushed a bill through parliament to nationalize Iran's oil assets. In 1953 the CIA, strongly encouraged by Britain, helped the army to attempt to overthrow Mosaddeq. The effort initially appeared to have failed, and the Shah fled the country. However, within a few days Mossadeq was overthrown and the Shah returned. In 1954 the Iranian National Oil Company was formed; it operated the oilfields jointly with a consortium of international companies, including the Anglo-Persian Oil Company (renamed British Petroleum) and several American oil companies.

The Shah ruled with absolute powers. Throughout these years America was preoccupied with the possibility that Iran's vast oil resources might fall into the hands of the Soviet Union. Following state-led, inward-looking economic policies, and with the benefit of large oil revenues, Iran made substantial economic progress, accompanied by far-reaching improvements in education and health. The Shah controlled the army, the secret police (SAVAK), and the intelligence agency. He appointed the ministers, selected half of the senate, and manipulated parliamentary elections. A small elite dominated Iran's political life. Iran was closely allied to America and was dependent on American military assistance and financial support. It also maintained close relations with Israel. In 1977 Britain concluded a secret agreement to supply 20 nuclear reactors to Iran, recognizing that it was likely that by the end of the twentieth century Iran would have obtained the technology to build nuclear weapons. The Shah's authoritarian regime crushed the Communist Party (Tudeh) and the National Party, as well as bids for regional autonomy by Kurds, Arabs, and Baluchi minorities.

In the 1970s the Pahlavi regime became increasingly oppressive. Vast fortunes were earned from oil revenues, but they accrued to a tiny elite, and the government spent a large fraction of its income on armaments, mainly supplied by America. The fact that the regime was dependent on American political and military support contributed to popular anger against the Shah's regime. In 1979 this discontent spilled over to become the Iranian Revolution, which toppled the Shah and brought to power a new Islamic regime, in which Ayatollah Khomeini became the official head of government following his return from exile. In the early years, the new regime pursued a fiercely puritanical form of Islam. It carried out large-scale purges of national and religious minorities, as well as purges of liberal nationalists, Marxists, and the mujahideen. Large segments of the Westernized middle class fled into exile.

In 1980 Iraq attacked Iran in the hope of capturing the rich oilfields in the west of the country, close to the Iraqi border. The subsequent eight-year war was horrific, with truly dreadful human suffering, and during the 1980s the economy grew by less than one percent per annum. Saddam Hussein calculated correctly that America would not intervene on the side of revolutionary Iran, and from 1985 onward America tilted decisively in favor of Saddam Hussein's government in Iraq, supplying it with arms and intelligence information. Throughout the period since the 1979 revolution, America has attempted to destabilize the Iranian government. Its persistent hope has been that "regime change" will lead to the emergence of a pro-Western government that will be friendly to America and allow the large-scale involvement of Western oil companies in the development of the country's vast reserves of oil and gas.

For three decades since the Iranian Revolution of 1979, America has operated trade sanctions against Iran. The first American sanctions were ordered by the Carter administration in April 1980. In the years 1988–91 the trade restrictions were slightly relaxed, but after the First Gulf War of 1991 they intensified again. In 1993, the so called "dual containment" policy was initiated by the Clinton administration. This focused on the "dual threats" from Iran and Iraq. This was followed by the Iran–Libya investment sanctions (1996–99), which aimed mainly at hampering the development of the Iranian and Libyan oil industries. Non-American firms investing more than $20 million in any one-year period were subject to a series of sanctions from the American government, continuation of which was endorsed by the administration of George W. Bush.

After the puritanism of the early post-revolutionary years, the centre of gravity in Iranian politics shifted. Between 1989 and 1997 the Iranian president was the pragmatic and conservative Akbar Hashemi Rafsanjani, who favored a market-based economy and détente with America. Rafsanjani was succeeded as president by Mohammad Khatami, who governed from 1997 to 2005. Khatami also followed a reformist agenda, which advocated "religious democracy" at home and détente with the West. At the end of the 1990s the Iranian government undertook extensive economic liberalization, including privatization of state-owned enterprises, reduction of import controls, reduction of food and energy subsidies, unification of the exchange rate system, and the establishment of an oil stabilization fund, alongside further expansion of the higher education system. The rate of growth of GDP accelerated to around six percent per annum.

Instead of responding positively to Iran's moves toward economic and social liberalization and détente with the West, however, President Clinton intensified American sanctions against Iran. President George W. Bush, when he came to power, responded even more aggressively to Iran's tentative suggestion of a "Grand Bargain," regarding Iran as he did as part of the "Axis of Evil." Iran was even designated by America (and the British Prime Minister Tony Blair) as the leading force in a "Crescent of Evil" in the Muslim world.

A major reason for Ahmadinejad's victory in the 2005 presidential election was popular anger at the American response to Iranian overtures for constructive engagement. The new president was more hostile to America and to Israel than his immediate predecessor, President Khatami. His populist commitment to the mass of poor Iranians was based on Islamic foundations, and was strongly appealing to large sections of the population. One important consequence of the rise in oil prices, itself driven in large part by the instability produced in the Middle East by American foreign policy, was that it provided resources for Ahmadinejad's populist regime to enhance its government-funded programs of social welfare, and to support international allies such as the Shi'ite Hizbollah movement in Lebanon.

The disintegration of Iraq and the success of Hizbollah in Lebanon intensified antagonism toward Iran among the policy-making circles around President Bush. From early in its existence, the Shi'ite Hizbollah movement in Lebanon has been supported in its battle with Israel by the revolutionary government in Iran. The Iranian government now announced that it was pressing ahead with a plan to enrich uranium, which could provide it with the capability at some point to produce nuclear weapons. In response, in 2006–7 American policy advisers floated the possibility of a major air attack on Iran, aimed at destroying the country's nuclear facilities and also achieving the goal of "regime change" that America had sought ever since the overthrow of the Shah. In order to ensure the success of this endeavor it was estimated that at least 400 targets would have to be hit. Moreover, in order to be sure of the destruction of the deeply buried alleged nuclear sites across Iran, it was argued that America would need to use tactical nuclear weapons. A former senior American intelligence official commented: "Every other option, in the view of the nuclear weapons experts, would leave a gap. It's a tough decision. But we made it in Japan." In autumn 2007 President Bush warned of the risk of World War III if there was not a common effort to prevent Iran from having the "knowledge necessary to make a nuclear weapon."

Israel was a key ally for America in the debate over Iran's nuclear program. Its leaders warned that any attempt by Iran to begin enriching uranium would be regarded as a point of no return. In a speech on March 20, 2006, President Bush described President Ahmadinejad's hostility to Israel as a serious threat: "It's a threat to world peace. I made it clear. I'll make it clear again that we will use military might to protect our ally Israel." However, one senior diplomat observed that there was much more at stake for America than simply the nuclear issue: "That's just a rallying point, and there is still time to fix it. But the [Bush] administration believes it cannot be fixed unless they control the hearts and minds of Iran. The real issue is who is going to control the Middle East and its oil in the next ten years." The possibility that America might attack Iran was being increasingly mooted in the wake of the disastrous campaign in Iraq. In December 2006 a *Financial Times* editorial said:

> The president [Bush] seems incapable of acknowledging the scale of the disaster in Iraq. He and his coterie blame the Iraqis and Iran for US failures. They persist in identifying the US national interest and Israeli hegemony as the same thing ... There is a terrifying possibility this administration will raise the stakes and compound the Iraq misadventure into a regional and international catastrophe by attacking Iran—or by acquiescing in an attack by Israel.

In 2005 the American National Intelligence Estimate concluded "with high confidence" that Iran "is currently determined to develop nuclear weapons" and that it was conducting a nuclear weapons development program. In December 2007 however, to the amazement of international experts, the American government produced a new National Intelligence estimate, which stated "with a high degree of confidence" that Iran had in fact frozen its nuclear weapons program in autumn 2003 and that the program had not been restarted by the autumn of 2007. This startling *volte-face* undermined radically the case for American or Israeli military action against Iran. Stephen Hadley, the White House national security adviser, said that the estimate "offers grounds that the problem can be solved diplomatically without the use of force." It seemed that America had replaced the military strike option with a decision to work with the international community to negotiate with Iran over the link between its civilian nuclear program and the possible future acquisition of nuclear weapons. Having looked into the abyss, it appeared that the American government had pulled back from the brink. However, the issue of a possible attack on Iran had not disappeared. In June 2008 the Israeli deputy prime minister and former defense minister, Shaul Mofaz, warned: "If Iran continues with its program for developing nuclear weapons, we will attack it. The sanctions are ineffective ... [A]ttacking Iran in order to stop its nuclear plans will be unavoidable."

Military presence During the era of capitalist globalization, America has constructed a network of major military bases in the Gulf region under the administration of a much-enlarged Central Command (Centcom). They include bases in Iraq and Kuwait (constructed during "Operation Iraqi Freedom"), Oman, Bahrain, Qatar, and the United Arab Emirates. The American armed forces in the Gulf region total around 200,000. In addition, Centcom controls American military bases in Afghanistan and Pakistan (constructed during "Operation Enduring Freedom"), and furthermore, European Command has large naval and air force bases in Turkey, which shares a border with Iraq. The American Fifth Fleet, with a complete carrier battle group, is stationed in Bahrain, and there are a total of six major American air force bases in the Gulf region (including two in Oman alone), and an air force base in Turkey, close at hand. In addition to America's own military capability, its Muslim allies in the region have their own large armed forces, most of which are supplied with American weaponry. Saudi Arabia alone has an air force which includes over 80 F-15s, while Bahrain and Kuwait together have a similar number of American-supplied F-15s, F-16s, and F-18s. In early 2008 the Gulf states were negotiating a ten-year $20 billion arms deal with America.

Britain has for many years been a major arms supplier to the Gulf states. The most important of the British arms deals in the Gulf was the so-called Al-Yamama deal, concluded in the mid-1980s between British Aerospace (now BAE Systems) and Saudi Arabia. The multi-billion-dollar program was described at the time as "the biggest sale of anything to anyone by anyone." Its core was the sale and maintenance of around 100 Tornado attack aircraft and over 40 Hawk trainer aircraft. This deal was followed by a further deal to sell to Saudi Arabia a large number of the next generation of British-made attack aircraft, the Eurofighter. France is also a major supplier of military equipment to the Gulf states; the UAE, for example, has around 70 French-supplied Mirage fighter aircraft. In February 2008 France announced that it was establishing a permanent military base in Abu Dhabi, the UAE capital. Its intention in establishing this base, which is directly opposite Iran across the Strait of Hormuz, was to "send a signal to defend its strategic interests in the region." France has also played an important military role in west and central Africa, including in several Muslim countries. Since decolonization in the 1960s, France has maintained military bases in many of these countries, and has frequently intervened to prop up rulers with whom it has close ties. The presence of massive American forces in the Middle East, alongside continued British and French military activities in the region, is a source of deep resentment across the whole Muslim world. For America, France, and Britain to criticize China's foreign policy as "adventurist" takes hypocrisy in international relations to a new level.

America and Israel

In addition to its deep involvement in the critical oil-producing countries of the Middle East, America's relationship with the region, and with the Muslim world at large, has been shaped fundamentally by its support for Israel. This has had, and continues to have, profound consequences for the whole world.

In ancient times Palestine (Syria Palestina) was a province of the Roman Empire, and the home of the Jewish people. The years between AD 66 and AD 135 saw a series of revolts against Roman rule in Palestine. The last of these revolts was crushed, amid great slaughter of Jewish people, and the surviving Jews were expelled from Palestine. At the heart of Jewish culture are the five books of the Torah (the five "books of Moses" in the Old Testament). The Torah chronicles the Lord's promise to the Jewish people to provide them with their own land, the repeated exile of the Jews from that land, and its violent reconquest with the support of the Lord:

> When the Lord thy God shall bring thee into the land whither thou goest to possess it, and hath cast out many nations before thee … nations greater and mightier than thee … and when the Lord thy God shall deliver them before thee; thou shalt smite them, and utterly destroy them; and thou shalt make no covenant with them, nor show mercy unto them … But thus shall ye deal with them; ye shall destroy their altars, and break down their images, and cut down their groves, and burn their graven images with fire. For thou art an holy people unto the Lord thy God: the Lord thy God hath chosen thee to be a special people unto himself, above all people on the face of the earth … And thou shalt consume all the people which the Lord thy God shall deliver thee; thine eyes shall have no pity upon them … and the Lord thy God will put out those nations before thee by little and little … [T]he Lord thy God shall deliver them unto thee, and shall destroy them with a mighty destruction, until they be destroyed.
>
> Deuteronomy 7

The Israeli people's close identification with the Torah was shown in striking fashion after the Six Day War in 1967, which led to a large expansion of Israel's boundaries. At the end of the war Israelis were intoxicated at being able to visit all the places they had read about in the Old Testament. In her book *Israel: Promised Land to Modern State* Rinna Samuel recalls: "Israelis toured all the new territories. With unquenchable excitement and interest they stood in line to enter the Tomb of Rachel in Bethlehem and the burial place of the Patriarchs of Hebron. They drove through Nablus and Jericho; went on long, uncomfortable trips through the wilderness of the Sinai Peninsula; and picnicked amid the formidable fortifications on the Golan Heights. Everywhere, families took the Bible along as a guidebook, showing enthralled children the places from which they had been barred for so long." Israelis felt that they were "the natural heirs to the land of their forefathers, living threads in a historic tapestry first woven in this same Land some four thousand years ago." In these people "flickered a flame of love for Israel which had first been lit when Abraham, obeying the word of the Lord, led his people into the Promised Land."

For 2,000 years only a tiny number of Jews lived in Palestine. In the late nineteenth century it was part of the Ottoman Empire, which included most of present-day Iraq, Syria, Lebanon, Jordan, and Israel. In 1878 a small group of Hungarian Jews established a pioneering village at Petach Tikvah, and within a few years around 1,000 Jewish farming families had settled in Palestine. A wider Zionist movement was sparked by the publication in 1896 of Theodor Herzl's book *The Jewish State*. The first Zionist Congress was held in Basle in 1897. It called for the colonization of Palestine by Jewish people, and by 1914 around 85,000 Jews had settled there. However, Palestine was not "a land without a people." Despite the large influx of Jews, at that time they made up only around one-tenth of the total population.

During World War I Britain had publicly supported Arab nationalist aspirations. However, on November 10, 1917, the new revolutionary government in Russia began to publish the secret treaties and agreements that had been entered into by the Tsarist government. The first, and most sensational, of these was the Sykes–Picot Agreement of March 1915, under which Russia would assume control of Constantinople after the defeat of Germany and its ally Turkey, while Britain and France between them were to take control of a large part of the Middle East. Within a few days the British government issued the Balfour Declaration, which stated: "Her Majesty's Government view with favour the establishment in Palestine of a national home for the Jewish people, and will use their best endeavours to facilitate the achievement of this object." Arthur Balfour, the British Foreign Secretary, was a Christian Zionist, deeply versed in the Old Testament. He believed passionately that the Jews had a right to occupy the Holy Land, from which they had been expelled almost 2,000 years previously.

In March 1919, in the midst of the deliberations of the Paris Peace Conference in Versailles, President Wilson recommended the establishment of an Inter-Allied Commission to investigate conditions in "Syria." This remit was interpreted broadly, to include the territories formerly ruled by Turkey in "Greater Syria," which includes most of today's Syria, Jordan, Israel, Lebanon, and the West Bank and Gaza. Wilson intended that the commission should prepare a report for consideration by the League of Nations, which the conference had agreed to establish. The British and French, however, both refused to participate in the report. The American government instead decided to proceed with its own investigation, and appointed Henry King (a theologian who was president of Oberlin College) and Charles Crane (a prominent Democratic Party donor, who became American Ambassador to China in 1920–21) to head a small team of advisers, all of whom were "students of the problems of the Middle East" and had been connected with the Paris Peace Conference, to prepare the report. They worked at great speed, interviewing a wide range of people representing the different communities, in locations across the region, and completed their report by the end of August 1919.

The Commission concluded that establishing a "national home for the Jewish people" should not be equated with making Palestine into a Jewish state. They took the view that "the initial claim, often submitted by Zionist representatives, that they have a right to Palestine, based on occupation 2,000 years ago, can hardly be seriously considered." They warned that the "feeling against the Zionist program is not confined to Palestine, but shared very generally by the people throughout Syria." They reported that "the fact came out repeatedly in the Commission's conference with the Jewish representatives, that the Zionists looked forward to a practically complete dispossession of the present non-Jewish inhabitants of Palestine, by various forms of purchase." They emphasized that nearly nine-tenths of the population of Palestine itself were non-Jewish, and that these were "emphatically against the entire Zionist program." They considered that to "subject a people so minded to unlimited Jewish immigration and to steady financial and social pressure to surrender the land, would be a gross violation of [President Wilson's] principle [of free acceptance of settlement of any given question by the people immediately concerned] and of the people's rights, [even] though it kept within the forms of the law." They concluded that the Zionist program could only be realized by force of arms, with the "the gravest trespass upon the civil and religious rights of existing non-Jewish communities in Palestine." They recommended therefore that Jewish immigration should be "definitely limited," and that "the project for making Palestine distinctly a Jewish commonwealth should be given up."

Instead, they recommended that Palestine should be included in a united, federal Syrian state, which should include almost all of present-day Syria, Lebanon, Israel, the West Bank and Gaza, and Jordan. They reported that this was the view also of the "great majority of the people of Syria." They observed that the territory is "too limited, the population too small and the economic, geographic, racial, and language unity too manifest, to make the setting up of independent states within its boundaries desirable, if such division can possibly be avoided." They noted that the country was "very largely Arab in language, culture, traditions, and customs." The commission argued that "in general, to attempt complete separation [of different peoples] only accentuates the differences and increases the antagonism." They took the view that "[t]he whole lesson of the modern social consciousness points to the necessity of 'understanding the other half,' as it can be understood only by close and living relations." Today, these territories have a combined population of 35 million people, around the same as Malaysia, Poland, or Spain, and a land area of around 220,000 square kilometers, around the same as Britain.

Although they found that the Syrian people's first demand was for "absolute independence," the Commission concluded that the whole territory ought to be under a single international mandate for "a limited term," of around 20 years. They argued that such a mandate would be best exercised by America, "which had no colonial or territorial ambitions" and would "willingly withdraw when the Syrian state had been established," rather than by Britain or France, which were deeply distrusted in the region for their colonial ambitions.

The decision about whether or not to pursue a federal state rather than separate, smaller states, one of which was to become Israel, was a fateful one for twentieth-century history. It was fateful especially for America's international relations. If the recommendations of the King-Crane Commission had been followed, America might have cemented a position at the forefront of "soft power" in the twentieth century, both within the Middle East and among the world's Muslim population.

President Wilson had been the guiding spirit behind the establishment of the commission. On his return to America he became preoccupied with obtaining passage of the Treaty of Versailles through the Senate, in which he was ultimately unsuccessful, and in the midst of these strenuous efforts he suffered an incapacitating stroke. The King-Crane Report was ignored both by the American government and by the British and French, and was finally published only in 1922. At the end of the King-Crane investigation the British Foreign Secretary, Lord Balfour, commented: "In Palestine we do not propose even to go through the form of consulting the wishes of the present inhabitants of the country ... Zionism, be it right or wrong, good or bad, is rooted in age-long traditions, in present needs, in future hopes, of far profounder import than the desires and prejudices of the 700,000 Arabs who now inhabit that ancient land." Wilson's illness and American withdrawal from world affairs was "one of the great tragedies of our time." Instead, Europeans took over the area and failed: "When the United States re-entered the region a quarter of a century later, they did so for oil and, shortly thereafter, as an almost unquestioning supporter and funder of Israel" (Robert Fisk, *The Great War for Civilisation*).

In 1920, Britain was given the Mandate for Palestine by the League of Nations. Even though the Jewish population constituted only a small fraction of the total population of Palestine, a British Jew, Sir Herbert Samuel, was appointed to be the first British High Commissioner for Palestine. The Jewish population in Palestine were jubilant: "For the first time in 1,850 years, a Jew ruled over the Land of Israel." The Arab inhabitants, who composed nine-tenths of the total population, were enraged, but in 1922 the American Congress placed on record that "the United States favors the establishment in Palestine of a national home for the Jewish people." From 1919 to 1925, around 50,000 Jewish migrants arrived in Palestine.

In 1925 the former British Foreign Secretary, Lord Balfour, paid an historic visit to Palestine. He came to lay the foundation stone of the newly established Hebrew University, whose campus is on Mount Scopus, on the Mount of Olives. On the day of the ceremony the open amphitheatre was crowded with around 8,000 spectators. Jewish hawkers sold "Balfour biscuits," "Balfour *keftas*" (rissoles), and "Balfour chocolate." The proceedings were begun by Grand Rabbi Abraham Kuk, after which Dr Chaim Weitzmann, President of the World Zionist Organization, declared the university open. Sir Herbert Samuel conveyed the good wishes of the British government. Then Lord Balfour rose. As he did so, "16,000 feet kept time to some 16,000 gesticulating arms waved by their cheering owners." Only after several minutes could Balfour speak. He did so in his best Eton and Trinity College,

Cambridge manner: "A new epoch has begun within the Palestine which came to an end so many hundreds of years ago."

There was intense opposition to Jewish immigration from the indigenous people of Palestine, both from Arabs and from Greek Orthodox Christians. By the mid-1930s these feelings had erupted into full-blown revolts against Jewish settlement. The conflict between the Jewish colonists and the indigenous Palestinians rose to a crescendo in the Great Revolt of 1936–9. During this violent struggle, the Stern Gang, a Jewish self-defense force, committed some of the most appalling atrocities in modern Palestine, including extensive reprisal bombings in Arab markets. The British imported a special force of 20,000 troops, which worked in tandem with Zionist "special night squads." The British and their Zionist counterparts used the usual tactics of counter-insurgency (the "first way of war"), including the collective punishment of entire villages, targeted assassinations, mass arrests, deportation, and dynamiting of homes of suspected guerrillas and sympathizers. It is estimated that upwards of ten percent of the male population of Palestine was killed, wounded, imprisoned, or exiled. Long after its brutal suppression, the Great Revolt continued, and continues today, to provide a symbol of national resistance for Palestine.

As Hitler's persecution of the Jews intensified in the 1930s, the number of Jewish people migrating to Palestine from Germany and elsewhere in Europe increased. By 1944 Palestine contained 529,000 Jews (30 percent of the total population) and 1.06 million Muslims (61 percent of the total). During the interwar period, nationalist sentiment among the Palestinian community grew stronger. The most politically vocal part of the community demanded independence for a united Palestine from British rule, and rejected proposals to divide Palestine between Jews and Arabs. Nationalist sentiments among both the Jewish and Palestinian communities was fueled by use of vocabulary from the Jewish and Islamic religions respectively.

The New York World's Fair of 1939–40 provided a vivid insight into the nationalist aspirations of Zionism. The World's Fair was based around pavilions constructed by each of the participating nations, except for the "Jewish Palestine Pavilion," which represented a community, namely the Yishuv colonists in Palestine, rather than a nation. The dioramas in the pavilion portrayed Palestine as an empty wilderness which had been fructified by the arrival of Jewish colonists: "For centuries this ancient land lay barren and neglected, ravaged by wars fought over its holy sites … A primitive population lived a semi-nomadic life in this land, which could barely provide them with a meager sustenance … Into this land came Jewish settlers, inspired by the hope of establishing there a new home for the oppressed." The pavilion was designed in the form of a tower and stockade, which had become a key symbol for the Jewish settlers. It was designed to present the settlers as an outpost of civilization in a savage land, as heroic frontiersmen. The American director described the effect the pavilion would have on young visitors. He imagined they would say to themselves: "That's just like American history. Those pioneers defending their stockades against the howling Arab terrorists are no different from our ancestors fighting off the howling Indians."

With the onset of World War II, following the path that it had followed in World War I, Britain shifted its policy in order to placate the Arabs and gain their support in the struggle against Germany. Jewish immigration was restricted, and there followed intense struggles by Jewish settlers against the British, including many acts of terrorist violence committed against the British forces by the Zionist militia, the Irgun, and the Stern Gang.

After the war the appalling facts of Hitler's death camps for the Jewish people came to light. The genocide against the Jews stands out among the many horrific crimes of the twentieth century, and it helped greatly to increase international sympathy for the idea of establishing a Jewish national home. The revelation of the genocide also greatly intensified the determination of the Zionists to establish an independent homeland in Palestine. In mid-November 1945 the leader of the Jewish people in Palestine, David Ben-Gurion, returned from a mission to Germany. He gave a speech on his findings to the Representative Assembly of the Jews in Palestine, a recording of which remains in the archives of Kol Yisrael, the Israeli state radio station. In his speech Ben-Gurion recalled what he had seen: "I was in Dachau and Belsen. I saw the gas chambers, where every day they poisoned thousands of Jews, men and women, the aged and the elderly, infants and children, led them naked as if they were going to take showers. The gas chambers are really built as if they are shower rooms, and the Nazis could peep in from the outside to see the Jews writhe and struggle in their death throes." Ben-Gurion's voice is restrained. From time to time, someone in the audience can be heard sobbing, or emitting a sigh of pain.

The mingling of the unimaginable horrors of the Holocaust with the future of the Middle East was to be a fateful one for modern history.

The establishment of the state of Israel was a politically convenient solution for European governments, as it meant that they did not have to deal with the resettlement of millions of displaced Jews. It was expedient also for the American government, which would avoid having to face pressure to support large-scale Jewish immigration. In 1945 President Harry Truman announced that he would support both the partition of Palestine and the establishment of an independent Jewish state. His advisers argued that America had a moral commitment to the victims of the Holocaust, and that the Jewish vote was crucial to his political security. In addition Truman's advisers pointed out that with American support, Israel could become a "Western outpost in a potentially hostile region."

In 1947 Britain announced that it would relinquish the mandate to govern Palestine and would withdraw its troops by May 1948. The British government passed over to the newly founded United Nations the question of how to resolve the Palestinian issue. At this point the UN had just 51 member nations; a large number of countries, containing much of the world's population, were not represented because they were still ruled by the colonial powers. The United Nations

Special Commission on Palestine (UNSCOP), set up to resolve the Palestinian issue, produced two reports. The minority report recommended the establishment of a single federal state containing both Jews and Arabs. However, the majority report recommended the partition of Palestine into two states, one Jewish (Israel) and one Arab (Palestine). This partition drastically shrank the territory of Palestine. The UN decision to establish an independent state of Israel was forcibly resisted by the Arab League, and a violent war followed. From the outset, Israel received strong backing from the American government and fervent support from the American Jewish community, who supplied the foundation of Israeli armaments capacity through their financial aid. The Israelis were at a significant disadvantage; they had to fight both the indigenous Palestinians and the surrounding Arab states. However, the Arab states were divided; they had conflicting objectives, and failed to fight as a single army. The war ended in May 1948 in defeat for the Arabs and the establishment of the state of Israel. At the same time, the state of Transjordan absorbed the portions of Palestine west of the River Jordan, while Egypt took control of the Gaza Strip. Israel remained in a state of war with Egypt until 1979, and with Jordan until 1994. The war became known by the Israelis as the War of Independence and by the Palestinians as "the disaster" (nakba).

In the first 18 months of its existence some 341,000 Jews arrived in Israel. During the war an estimated 750,000 Palestinians from within the territory over which Israel claimed sovereignty became refugees, scattered on the West Bank of the River Jordan, or exiled into Transjordan, Lebanon, Syria, and other Arab states. Between 65 and 85 percent of Palestinians living within the boundaries of Israel fled into permanent exile, while another 15–25 percent were uprooted and became internal refuges within Israel. Around 1.3 million Palestinian refugees still live in camps run by UNRWA (United Nations Relief and Works Agency). Meanwhile the Israeli government took over an estimated 94 percent of the property abandoned by the Palestinians who had fled, distributing it to Jewish Israelis. More than 500 Palestinian villages disappeared completely. In an infamous campaign known as Operation Hiram, a wholesale transfer of population took place in the Galilee region, in which Zionist forces executed substantial numbers of those who resisted. A total of 24 incidents of terror or massacre have been identified, the worst of them involving the killing of hundreds of people. The Palestinians who remained within Israel were subject to martial law until 1966. Former Israeli Prime Minister Ehud Barak, who became Israel's defense minister, acknowledged the scale of what had happened: "It was the shattering of a whole society, accompanied by thousands of deaths and the wholesale destruction of hundreds of villages." Barak is reported to have said that if he were a Palestinian he would join a terrorist organization. Israel's constitution affirms the "right of return" to Israel for Jews from any country, while the Israeli government argued that the refugees, as Arabs, could find homes in the Arab states. The masses of Palestinians in exile nevertheless remain in refugee camps, and Israel still refuses to countenance their repatriation.

A decade of border clashes culminated in the Second Arab–Israeli War in June 1967. In 1964 Israel unilaterally diverted the River Jordan away from Syria. The resulting dispute flared up in May 1967, when Israel massed troops on Syria's border. Egypt was informed by the Soviet Union that Israel was preparing to attack Syria, and Nasser sent the Egyptian army into Sinai. At the same time he ordered the closure of the Straits of Tiran, thereby denying Israel access to the Red Sea. This produced a massively disproportionate response from Israel: in the first few hours of the Six Day War, Israeli air strikes destroyed almost the entire air force of Egypt, Jordan, and Syria, whose aircraft were on the ground in their bases, entirely unprepared for the violent onslaught.

The war ended in complete victory for Israel, which took possession of the Gaza Strip and Sinai from Egypt, the West Bank from Jordan (as it had then become), and the Golan Heights from Syria. Israel also won control over the whole of Jerusalem. Over the following years, powerful movements developed within Israel calling for the colonization of the West Bank, and for the annexation of the West Bank and Gaza. Israel expropriated land and water resources, and during the 1990s the number of settlers in the occupied territory of the West Bank grew by 50 percent, four times the rate of growth of population inside Israel proper. By the late 1990s, there were over 140 Israeli settlements in the West Bank and Gaza. East Jerusalem was now encircled and enclosed by four big blocks of settlements, while housing and zoning restrictions inside the city helped ensure a Jewish majority. In the famous words of Ariel Sharon, "In Jerusalem we built and created facts that can no longer be changed." In June 2008, during the presidential election campaign, Barack Obama spoke to an audience of 7,000 people attending the annual meeting of the American Israel Public Affairs Committee, promising his audience, "Jerusalem will remain the capital of Israel, and it must remain undivided." His remarks were greeted with rapturous applause.

America has provided unstinting, uncritical support for Israel since the earliest days of its existence as an independent state. In 1973, Senator William Fulbright said in a CBS interview: "The Israelis control policy in Congress and in the Senate … Our colleagues in the Senate, about 70 percent of them, make up their minds more under pressure of a lobby than from their own vision of what they consider to be the principles of liberty and justice." In the next election, Fulbright lost his seat in the Senate. A large segment of American public opinion views America and Israel as almost one country. When President Bush visited Israel in May 2008 he said: "Some people suggest that if the United States would just break ties with Israel, all our problems in the Middle East would go away. This is a tired argument that buys into the propaganda of our enemies, and America rejects it utterly. Israel's population may be just over seven million. But when you confront evil, you are 307 million strong, because America stands with you." The way in which the Jewish state was established has strong similarities with the origins of America. In both cases the myth of the colonizers was that they were taking possession of an empty land

and liberating its productive potentialities. In both cases those who resisted the colonists' aggressive territorial occupation were regarded as "terrorists" against whom it was legitimate to wage the "first way of war."

Both the Zionist lobby and much of the Christian fundamentalist right believe that Israel has a right to occupy a large tract of Palestine, because the Jewish people did so in ancient times, and it was a God-given right. This view has been held at the highest level of the American government. President Johnson, for example, was brought up as a Christadelphian. The Christadelphians are certain that at the End of Days, when the Jews are gathered in the land of Israel, the Second Coming of the Messiah will take place. In his family album Lyndon Johnson's grandfather had written on a picture of himself that he gave to LBJ: "Take care of the Jews, God's chosen people. Consider them your friends and help them in any way you can." Lyndon Johnson repeatedly told Jewish groups of the depth of his feelings for Jewish people and for Israel. He felt that there was a special bond between Israel and America. "Our society," he once said, "is illuminated by the spiritual insights of the Hebrew prophets. America and Israel have a common love of human freedom and they have a common faith in a democratic way of life."

In a 1996 policy paper, Richard Perle and Douglas Feith, who both became senior figures in the Bush administration, advised the Israeli government to abandon the Oslo peace process in favor of permanent occupation of the Occupied Territories. Their report stated: "Our claim to the land—to which we have clung for hope for 2000 years—is legitimate and noble ... Only the unconditional acceptance by the Arabs of *our rights*, especially in the territorial dimension ... is a solid basis for the future." On the Christian right it is commonplace to find the view that "Israel alone is entitled to possess the Holy Land" (Senator James Inhofe, speech in the American Senate, March 2002). In May 2002, Dick Armey, the House Majority Leader, called for the deportation of the Palestinians from the Occupied Territories. He argued that Israel's right to occupy the whole of the Holy Land is based on God's command: "The Bible says that Abram removed his tent and came and dwelt in the plain of Mamre, which is Hebron, and built an altar there before the Lord. Hebron is in the West Bank. It is this place where God appeared to Abram and said: 'I am giving you this land'—the West Bank. This is not a political battle at all. It is a contest over the word of God." Many of the millenarian Christians in America believe that the restoration of Israeli rule over the whole of the kingdom of David is an essential precondition of the Apocalypse.

For the past quarter of a century, the American government has contributed around $3 billion a year in direct aid to Israel, along with a further $3 billion in indirect aid (including loan write-offs and special grants). In 2004 Israel received more than one-quarter of the entire American foreign aid budget, totaling around six times the amount of American aid for the whole of Africa. In July 2007 America announced an agreement to provide Israel with $30 billion worth of military assistance over the coming decade. The financial and military support received by

Hamas and Hizbollah from their external supporters are minuscule and primitive compared with that supplied to Israel by America.

Israel's military is vastly stronger than that of any other country in the region. From the late 1960s onward America has supplied Israel with its most advanced conventional weapons. Israel's air force has over 400 American-supplied combat aircraft, including 320 F-15s and F-16s, which means that it is more powerful than the air forces of all the countries in the Gulf region combined. It has almost 4,000 modern, mainly American-supplied, battle tanks and over 10,000 armored personnel carriers. However, far more significant is the fact that it is the only country in the region that possesses nuclear weapons. Although Israel officially denies that it possesses nuclear weapons, the International Institute for Strategic Studies estimates that Israel has around 200 nuclear warheads. America abhors any attempt made by other Middle Eastern countries to acquire nuclear weapons, but it makes no reference to, or criticism of, the widely accepted fact that Israel possesses a large stock of nuclear weapons, and it tacitly supported their acquisition.

Israel's nuclear weapons capability resulted from the secret agreement which it reached with France in 1956. The context of this was that France believed Egypt was a critically important force behind the Algerian liberation movement. Senior French political leaders believed that Israel and France faced a common problem: "In Israel a million Jews were besieged by Arabs, and, in Algeria, a million Frenchmen were in the same situation." Israel in return pledged to support France in any action against Egypt, "no matter how far France may go." The task that France assigned to Israel was to provide France with the pretext for a war against Egypt: "Give us the pretext to go to war," they said in effect, "and you'll get a nuclear reactor." Israel subsequently invaded Egypt, thereby precipitating the Suez Crisis. Israel's scientists also provided key support for the final stages of France's efforts to develop its own atomic bomb; France produced its first nuclear weapon in 1960.

The most significant part of the French assistance to Israel consisted of the supply of a 150-megawatt nuclear reactor, from which Israel produced the plutonium that enabled it to make its own atomic bombs. In addition, France agreed to supply Israel with enriched uranium and a plant for the extraction of plutonium. Work on the reactor began at the end of 1957, and just ten years later Israel produced its first nuclear weapons. It is estimated that each year the reactor complex produces around 40 kilograms of plutonium, and that Israel manufactures ten atomic bombs annually.

From soon after the explosion of atomic bombs in Japan, America was publicly committed to nuclear non-proliferation. However, in practice, in the late 1950s and early 1960s it turned a blind eye to the fact that Israel was acquiring the requisite technologies from France. America regarded Israel as a strategic asset in achieving its goals in the Middle East, the most significant of which was, and is, ensuring the stability of oil supplies from the region. In 1958 John Foster Dulles, the American Secretary of State, said: "The critical situation in the Middle East today gives Israel manifest opportunities to contribute, from its resources of spiritual strength and determination of purpose, to a stable international order." The former Deputy Assistant Secretary of Defense, Paul Warnke, wrote: "Both Kennedy and Johnson waxed eloquent about the dangers of an increase in the nuclear club, but key officials appear to have been either indifferent or ready to accept an Israeli bomb."

Israel has the capability to deliver nuclear weapons by means of both land-based missiles and aircraft. It has acquired three Dolphin-class submarines from Germany, and has armed them with nuclear missiles. One of these submarines regularly cruises the Indian Ocean. On October 9, 1973, Egypt and Syria launched a surprise attack on Israel (the so-called Yom Kippur War). That evening, Israel's Minister of Defense ordered that nuclear bombs be loaded onto fighter planes and that nuclear warheads be fitted to Jericho missiles. In the event it turned out that Egypt's main goal was not to invade Israel, but instead to seize control of the territory within close range of the east bank of the Suez Canal.

In the mid-1970s Iraq began to acquire the capability of building nuclear weapons, and in 1981 Israel launched an attack in which it destroyed Iraq's nuclear reactor. Immediately afterwards, Prime Minister Begin said: "Israel will not tolerate any nuclear weapons in the region." This policy is still in force today. Shortly after the attack, American Secretary of State Alexander Haig said: "The United States recognizes the gaps in Western military capabilities in the region, and the fundamental strategic value of Israel, the strongest and most stable friend and ally the United States has in the Mideast ... [W]e share a fundamental understanding that a strong, secure, and vibrant Israel serves Western interests in the Middle East."

One reason for America's unconditional support for Israel is the fact that Israel follows the "American Creed." It is regarded as the only democracy in the Middle East and deserving of American support for that reason alone. Israel is widely regarded in America as the sole bastion of American values in the midst of "a sea of savagery." Increasingly Israel has come to be regarded in America as the front line in the "global battle against terrorism," a view that was powerfully reinforced by the events of September 11, 2001. The balance of American political opinion on the Israel–Palestine issue can be gauged from the vote in the American Senate on May 6 2002, at the height of Israeli–Palestinian violence. The Senate resolution attacked Palestinian terrorism and declared that the "Senate stands in solidarity with Israel, a frontline state in the war against terrorism, as it takes the steps necessary to provide security to its people by dismantling the terrorist infrastructure in Palestinian areas." The resolution passed by 92 votes to 2. It contained no hint of any criticism of Israel.

America has been fatefully involved in Israel's struggle against Hamas. Following the Israeli victory in 1967, the Palestine Liberation Organization (PLO) came into being, with the main goal of reclaiming the Palestinian homeland for the Palestinians. Palestinians' sense of national identity became increasingly strong, and unrest culminated at the end of the 1980s in the so-called *intifada* campaigns of protest against the Israeli occupation, and the demand for the formation of a Palestinian state. Palestinian opinion, however, was divided. On the one hand there were those who favored compromise with Israel and the establishment of a secular state on the West Bank. On the other hand were those, mainly the Islamists, who favored a continuing struggle for the liberation of all of Palestine. Hamas emerged from the latter group as a distinct organization.

The defeat of Saddam Hussein in the First Gulf War and the collapse of the Soviet Union meant that America had become the unchallenged hegemonic power in the Middle East, and it used the opportunity to broker the Oslo accords in September 1993. These accords provided for the election of a Palestinian Authority on the West Bank, which would take control of local matters such as education, culture, welfare, tourism and the police, but which left Israel in control of military affairs. The PLO (led by Yassar Arafat) favored the accords, because they provided the chance to form a Palestinian administrative entity within which they were the dominant political force. The PLO was under tremendous pressure from America and Israel to suppress violence against Israel as the condition for implementing the Oslo accords.

The Palestinian opposition, led by Hamas, denounced the accords, because they failed to provide assurances about the eventual status of Jerusalem or to guarantee the return of Palestinian refugees, and they left Israel in control of military affairs. The Palestinian Authority has evolved into a checkerboard of fragmented "bantustan-style" Palestinian settlements amid a sea of Israeli settlements within the territory that the Palestinians consider to be their own. By 2006 there were almost half a million Jewish settlers in the occupied territories of the West Bank. They were connected to East Jerusalem by a network of dedicated road and rail links. The patchwork of areas occupied by the Palestinians resembled small-scale versions of the reservations set aside for North American indigenous people in the nineteenth century.

Hamas has carried out numerous acts of violence within Israel, and Israel has carried out mass arrests and assassinations of Hamas leaders. In 1995 America declared Hamas to be a terrorist organization, and following the bombing of an Israeli bus in September 2003, in which 23 people were killed, the EU also declared Hamas to be a terrorist organization. Despite its continued attacks within Israel, from the late 1990s onward Hamas moved increasingly into the mainstream of politics in the Occupied Territories, in a fashion similar to that of Hizbollah in Lebanon. Hamas participated in the Authority's institutions alongside the secular Fatah party, which had evolved out of the PLO. Initially, Hamas confined its political participation to the local, municipal level, and like Hizbollah in Lebanon, Hamas built up its own social and educational services among the Palestinians in the Palestinian Authority. It called for the formation of an Islamic state, with the stated goal of a social model along the lines of the AKP in Turkey, with Islamic values operating as the ethical guidelines for regulating a market economy. In 2006, despite considerable American aid to Fatah, Hamas was elected as the ruling party of the Palestinian Authority, winning 74 out of 132 seats on the Palestinian Legislative Council. Hamas is routinely castigated in the mainstream of the Western media as having a "repulsive" terrorist ideology, and after its triumph in the elections, America refused to negotiate with Hamas on the grounds that it was a terrorist organization. America persuaded the EU to join it in withholding foreign aid from Hamas, and together, they strongly supported Israel in withholding tax revenues from the Hamas government and in the arrest of many of the Hamas government officials. The Israeli secret service also continued its assassinations of the Hamas leadership, while in 2007, around 10,000 Palestinians were held in Israeli jails.

In 2007 the crisis erupted into violent conflict, which ended with Hamas taking control of Gaza and with Fatah, supported by Israel, America, and the EU, in control of the areas of the West Bank controlled by the Palestinian Authority. Gaza was cut off from the outside world by an Israeli blockade intended to throttle and destroy Hamas. Conditions deteriorated drastically.

Over the course of several years Hamas had been firing rockets into southern Israel, but the accuracy, level of sophistication, and explosive power of the weapons was low. It is estimated that over a period of seven years prior to December 2008, an average of around three to four Israelis were killed each year in rocket attacks from Gaza. In the twelve months between June 2007 and June 2008 Israeli airstrikes killed an estimated 560 people in Gaza. During his visit to Israel in July 2008, Barack Obama said: "If somebody was sending rockets into my house where my two daughters sleep at night, I'm going to do everything in my power to stop them. And I would expect Israel to do something." During the presidential campaign he stressed his "unshakeable commitment to Israel's security."

Although a six-month truce in the fighting was agreed in mid-2008, Israel refused to abide by its agreement to lift the blockade of Gaza, resulting in even further deterioration in the conditions of daily life. Meanwhile, the secular Fatah-led government on the West Bank was given extensive aid from America and the EU. President Bush urged the Palestinian Authority on the West Bank to "arrest terrorists, confiscate illegal weapons, and work to stop attacks on Israel." He linked the struggle in Palestine to the broader turmoil in the Middle East, saying it was part of the same struggle against extremists faced by Lebanon, Iraq, and Afghanistan: "Conceding any of these struggles to extremists would have deadly consequences for the world." Toward the conclusion of the six-month ceasefire in the second half of 2008, Israel intensified its blockade of Gaza, causing further deterioration in conditions for ordinary people there. An estimated 50,000 children were reported to be malnourished. By late 2008 the infrastructure in Gaza had been drastically damaged by eight years of Israeli restrictions on the Gaza economy, which culminated in the full-scale blockade from June 2007. According to a World Bank report in September 2008, 98 percent of industry in Gaza had shut down due to lack of raw materials and electricity, and an inability to export their products.

In December 2008 Hamas resumed its rocket attacks on southern Israel, and Israel responded with a ferocious, all-out aerial assault on the territory. Opinion polls suggested that 70–80 percent of Israelis supported the bombing. After a week of ferocious air attacks Israel's ground forces entered Gaza, and fighting continued for another two weeks. Opinion polls in Israel showed support from around 70 percent of the population for the land invasion. Israel's attack took place in the three-week period immediately preceding the inauguration of President Obama, when American political life was almost paralyzed. The incoming president was confronted with a *fait accompli.*

During the three-week attack on the tiny territory, Israel carried out more than 2,500 air strikes, in addition to the constant day and night barrage of naval, tank, and artillery fire. Thirteen Israelis died during the attack. It has been estimated that the attack resulted in a total of 1,300 deaths, including around 700 civilians, of whom around one-half were children, and more than 5,000 people wounded. The psychological impact on Gaza's population can only be imagined. The total damage to the infrastructure has been estimated to be around $1.4 billion, or around $1,000 per head of the population of the tiny impoverished territory. After the conclusion of the attack, Israel still refused to open Gaza's borders.

America gave Israel its full support. In the midst of the violent Israeli assault on Gaza, a spokesman for President Bush's National Security Council said: "These people are nothing but thugs, so Israel is going to defend its people against terrorists like Hamas that indiscriminately kill their own people." America blocked a UN Security Council resolution calling for an immediate ceasefire, and abstained from a second Security Council resolution calling for a ceasefire. In January 2009, in the midst of the attack, the American Senate unanimously supported a resolution declaring that it "stands with Israel," and the House of Representatives backed a similar measure.

America has also been deeply involved in Israel's checkered relationship with Lebanon. Under French control, the Mandate constitution of 1926 divided power between the different religious communities in Lebanon. Maronite Christians, Syrians, and Shi'ites each had their own political parties, schools, and networks of power. At last, in 1943, Lebanon became an independent state, but the divisions that had been nurtured during French rule persisted. In 1958, Arab nationalists tried to seize power, but were suppressed by American intervention. In the 1960s and 1970s, Lebanon was divided. On the one hand were those who wanted to use the country as a base for the Palestinian struggle against Israel. These were mainly left-wing groups, who favored a socialist path of development. On the other hand were those who wanted to restrict Palestinian activity in Lebanon and avoid confrontation with Israel. These groups largely favored a free-enterprise economy. Their main political force was the Christian Kataeb (Phalangist) movement. In August 1975 these tensions erupted into a civil war.

In June 1982, with American acquiescence, Israel invaded Lebanon in the hope of driving the Palestine Liberation Organization (PLO) out of south Lebanon, from where it had been mounting attacks on Israel, and from its headquarters in Beirut. Israel hoped that, freed from effective Palestinian resistance, it could pursue its policy of settlement and annexation of occupied Palestine. Defeated by the Israeli attack and now under siege, the PLO agreed to withdraw from its stronghold in West Beirut, which was inhabited mainly by Muslims. The agreement was brokered by the Americans, who jointly, along with the Lebanese government, guaranteed the safety of the thousands of Palestinian refugees in the city. The assassination of the Christian Phalangist leader, the head of the Kataeb political party, precipitated the Israeli occupation of West Beirut. Under the protection of the Israeli occupation, the Kataeb massacred thousands of Palestinians in the refugee camps of Sabra and Shatila. In all, it is estimated that around 19,000 people were killed during Israel's two-month siege of Beirut. An agreement was finally struck with Israel under which its forces would withdraw from the country, in return for supporting the Kataeb's assumption of effective political and strategic control of the country. The Americans gave both military and diplomatic support to the Kataeb and their Israeli backers.

Israel's occupation of South Lebanon stimulated the rise of new forces, notably Hizbollah (Party of God). In 2006, the *Financial Times* observed: "[Hizbollah's] parents were Israel and a US that declined to restrain its ally until it had nearly razed Muslim West Beirut." Hizbollah's roots were among the poor Shi'ite population of south Lebanon. It was backed by Iran, and its goal was to establish an Islamic republic in Lebanon. It took the lead in the struggle against Israel and constructed a network of popular social services, including schools and clinics. In 1991 Syria intervened to enforce cooperation between the warring factions. From then up until 2006, Lebanon enjoyed a period of peaceful capitalist development under Syrian overlordship. During this period, Hizbollah became increasingly integrated into mainstream Lebanese politics. In parliament, the party's slogans shifted from condemnation of Israel to the fight against corruption and the pursuit of social justice. By 2006, Hizbollah had won 14 seats in the Lebanese parliament, out of a total of 128 seats, joining the government as a minority partner. It was the best organized of the Lebanese parties, but its total number of seats was restricted by the system of sectarian allocation of quotas to the parliament.

This period of sustained and peaceful development was shattered by the Israeli invasion of 2006. Angered by cross-border attacks by Hizbollah, Israel seized upon the capture of two of its soldiers by Hizbollah as the justification for a massive assault on southern Lebanon in order to destroy Hizbollah's fighting capability.

The Israeli attack on southern Lebanon in July and August 2006 had the full support of the American government. In the early stages of the crisis, American Secretary of State, Condoleezza Rice, declared that the upsurge of violence legitimated the American vision of "a different kind of Middle East" and demonstrated that the "sponsors are in Tehran and in Damascus." She said: "Things are clarified now. We know where the lines are drawn." While most of the world called for a ceasefire in late July, shocked at the Israeli violence in southern Lebanon, Condoleezza Rice ruled out "temporary solutions," saying: "A durable solution will be one that strengthens the forces of peace and democracy in the region." With full

American support, Israel continued its violent offensive in Lebanon for a further three weeks. Condoleezza Rice's reference to the need to construct a "new Middle East" aroused massive anger across the Middle East, where the statement was widely perceived as concealing a plan to impose American–Israeli hegemony through the destruction of the Palestinian and Lebanese resistance movements.

Senior American government officials reported that President George W. Bush felt more strongly and was more engaged in his support for Israel's attack on Hizbollah than on any other issue. The officials said that the president "feels passionately that the US should support Israel in what he sees as the frontline in the global battle between democracy and terrorism." During the first month of the Israeli invasion of Lebanon, President Bush's language toughened from talking about the "war on terror" to stronger terminology, when he referred to the war against "Islamic fascists," and "Islamofascism," terms long in currency among the neo-conservatives. One former senior Bush administration official said: "People should not underestimate just how strongly [President Bush] feels in support of Israel and in his anger toward Iran and Syria [because of their sponsorship of Hizbollah]." The observers around President Bush said that he possessed a "visceral instinct to support Israel against its enemies, which he sees in terms of democracy versus totalitarianism." Across almost the whole Arab world, Israel, in its ferocious attack on Hizbollah, was widely perceived as acting as a proxy for America in its "war against international terrorism." President Bush himself was said by government officials in his administration to have considered that fighting between Israel and Hizbollah was a "proxy war between the US and Iran's theocratic regime."

The Democrats dare not criticize Israel for fear of losing support among the powerful Jewish lobby, especially its members in powerful positions in business and the media. In July 2006, the House of Representatives endorsed a resolution supporting Israel's military response to the cross-border raid by Hizbollah. Only eight out of the 418 votes cast opposed the resolution. In August 2006, Hillary Clinton scolded Nouri al-Malaki, the Iraqi Prime Minister, during his visit to America, for having criticized Israel: "His refusal to denounce Hizbollah and his condemnation of Israel sends exactly the wrong message about the importance of fighting terrorism and bringing stability to the Middle East. He should recognize that Israel has the right to defend itself against the terrorist aggression." In January 2009 Hillary Clinton took up her position as American Secretary of State, at the helm of American foreign policy.

Outside America, Israel's attack was almost universally condemned as grotesquely disproportionate. It is estimated that in just three weeks' fighting, nearly a million people were displaced, over 1,000 killed, and 3,500 wounded. It is estimated that the Israeli attack killed nine Lebanese civilians—three of them children—for every one combatant. The Lebanese economy, which had grown strongly over the previous decade, was devastated. The Israeli attack, however, had almost universal support in Israel. In a poll conducted on July 29 2006, 17 days after the Israeli invasion began, four out of five Israelis wanted the military to use more force to eliminate Hizbollah or remove it from the border. The mass-circulation newspaper *Yedioth Aharanoth* headlined a quote from a military commander, saying: "Every village from which a Katyusha rocket is fired must be destroyed." Most Israelis were reported to believe that the attack against Hizbollah was morally justified.

CONCLUSION

The widespread anger in the Muslim world against the West is a consequence of a set of interrelated historical factors that have little to do with religion, let alone class struggle. However, the fact that Muslims have an identity that transcends national boundaries has contributed to an anger and resentment which is international, and which unites much of the world's Muslim population. Naturally, the form in which this anger is expressed employs language and imagery from the Koran and its surrounding belief system, but it does not follow that the conflict has religious origins.

Islam is not opposed to capitalism. The medieval and early modern Muslim world constituted a vast unified free trade area, with all the dynamic benefits of specialization, division of labor, and diffusion of knowledge that flowed from this. From the late nineteenth until the middle of the twentieth century, from Indonesia through to North Africa, the modern Muslim world was mostly ruled by the colonial powers, and international capital penetrated most Muslim countries. In addition, a national capitalist class that invested in modern businesses emerged. Despite widespread anger at the long period of rule by foreign powers, the late nineteenth and early twentieth century saw a significant advance of modern industrial capitalism across the Muslim countries. In the wake of colonialism the main body of Muslim countries pursued some form of socialist planning, within the overall context of a mixed economy. From the late 1960s onward, however, most of the non-oil exporting countries began to implement some form of *infitah*, or opening up to international trade and capital flows, alongside the privatization of nationalized industries. A broad swathe of non-oil producing Muslim countries achieved quite rapid growth of output from the 1970s onward under different forms of modern capitalism, and experienced wide-ranging improvements in health, education, and women's position in society.

Since the earliest days, capitalist development in the Muslim world has been characterized by broadly similar inequalities in wealth, income, and power as have characterized capitalism in other parts of the developing world. In both the medieval and modern Muslim world, revolutionary social and political movements have from time to time arisen with the aim of overthrowing capitalism. As in other parts of the world, such movements have sought to establish communist societies based on collective ownership and egalitarian income distribution. Like Christianity, Islam can be used as the basis for a fundamental and often violent opposition to the injustice, inequality, individualism, and commercialization that is inherent in capitalism. In the Muslim world, these millenarian movements have used the language of Islam to express their protests at the injustice of capitalist development. However, they have rarely, if ever, been able to topple the existing socio-political structures. Violent attempts to overthrow societies based on private property and to establish a form of communism have almost always remained at the margins of the Muslim world, both physically and intellectually. The notion that there is a fundamental "clash of civilizations" between an anti-capitalist Islam and the capitalist West is refuted by over 1,300 years of Muslim history.

Both in the Muslim Middle Ages and in the world of modern Muslim capitalist development, there has been an intense debate about how best to ensure that Muslim societies can peacefully produce social harmony. The critical discussion of capitalist injustice has centered on the ways in which private property and material incentives can be constrained to serve the collective social interest, while allowing society to benefit from the explicitly recognized dynamic character of market competition and private property. The main body of Muslim critical thought has been preoccupied with achieving harmonious development between different social interests. It has emphasized finding a mean between the extremes of individual rights and social duties, and between the pursuit of profit and using the usufruct from capital to serve the social interest. It has recognized the benefit to society of competitive markets, while wishing to constrain commercial behavior through laws and individual conscience, acquired through education, in such a way as to serve the interests of society.

By far the largest oil reserves in the world are located within the national boundaries of the country that was the birthplace of the Prophet Muhammad and which is where the Islamic religion arose. It is where the key sites of the Islamic religion are located, including Mecca, which all Muslims wish to visit at least once in their life. A large fraction of the remaining oil reserves are located in the surrounding territories that formed the early core of Islam. The governments of the leading high-income countries have intervened unceasingly in the political evolution of the oil-producing countries of the Middle East in order to ensure the satisfaction of their national energy needs. These relentless geopolitical and military interventions, right through to the invasion of Iraq, in the pursuit of oil supplies from the region that is the core of the Islamic religion, have resulted in common sentiments of hostility among Muslims toward Western governments, and in particular toward America.

Since the 1940s the Middle East has been a focal point of American international relations, alongside its Cold War struggle with the Soviet Union, and the still unresolved relationship with China. America has unceasingly and extensively intervened in the region, and its relentless pursuit of oil and energy security, combined with its deeply ideological goals, and its unstinting support for Israel, have undermined capitalist development in the Middle East. Its activities have also nurtured the most important source of instability in the world today, namely the attacks upon America by Islamic groups.

It was America which helped to bring about the downfall of the democratically elected Mossadeq government in Iran in 1953 and the installation of the Shah in its place. Since the overthrow of the Shah, the Americans have tried ceaselessly to bring about the overthrow of the Iranian regime. They supported Iraq in its war with Iran, and have imposed a long-term and intensifying economic blockade of Iran. For many years in the latter phase of Saddam Hussein's rule they imposed an economic blockade of Iraq, causing serious damage to the welfare of the Iraqi people. Having long supported undemocratic regimes in the interests of *realpolitik*, the Americans belatedly attempted to implement a policy of establishing a so-called "new Middle East," to be based on democratic institutions in the region. This was widely perceived in the Muslim world (and, indeed, in the world at large) as a fig leaf to disguise the attempt to put into place regimes sympathetic to American interests in the region, including access to oil for American oil companies. Despite widespread dislike of the Saddam Hussein regime, the American invasion of Iraq was greatly resented by a large body of opinion throughout the Muslim world. The invasion brought chaos to Iraq, and still threatens to engulf the surrounding regimes. This caused still further resentment among Muslims worldwide. America has consistently supported authoritarian, pro-American governments in the oil-producing Muslim countries. There is widespread anger against America in the Muslim world for bolstering these corrupt and highly unequal systems of political economy. The fact that America stations a massive military force in the Middle East is widely resented in the Muslim world as an intrusion upon the region's sovereignty.

The attack on the World Trade Center was not perpetrated in the pursuit of class struggle. It was perpetrated by 19 Arab hijackers, of whom 15 were from Saudi Arabia. The Al Qaeda network is funded and presided over by the Saudi dissident, Osama Bin Laden. Al Qaeda was founded with the explicit purpose of attacking America (Al Qaeda, 1998). Al Qaeda's hatred of America is a result of the American presence in the Middle East, particularly in Saudi Arabia, and America's support for Israel. Al Qaeda's founding statement in 1998 pronounced:

[F]or over seven years the United States has been occupying the lands of Islam in the holiest places, the Arabian Peninsula, plundering its riches, dictating to its rulers, humiliating its people, terrorizing its neighbors, and turning its bases in the Peninsula into a spearhead through which to fight the neighboring Muslim peoples ... The best proof of this is the Americans' continuing aggression against the Iraqi people, using the Peninsula as a staging post ... [D]espite the great devastation inflicted on the Iraqi people by the crusader–Zionist alliance, and despite the huge number of those killed ... the Americans are once again trying to repeat the horrific massacres ... [I]f the American aims behind these wars are religious and economic, the aim is also to serve the Jews' petty state and divert

attention from its occupation of Jerusalem and the murder of Muslims there ...
The ruling to kill the Americans and their allies—civilians and military—is an
individual duty for every Muslim, who can do it in any country in which it is
possible to do it, in order to liberate the Al-Aqsa Mosque and the Holy Mosque
[in Mecca] from their grip, and in order for their armies to move out of all the
lands of Islam, defeated and unable to threaten any Muslim.

The colonization of Palestine by Jewish immigrants and the subsequent
establishment of the separate Jewish state of Israel is a festering sore at the heart of
relations between the Muslim world and the West. Instead of migrating to the region
to become part of a larger Middle East state (a "Greater Syria") to which they might
have made an invaluable contribution, the Jewish immigrants set out to build a
separate state in which people of the Jewish religion would constitute the
overwhelming majority. The colonization of Palestine was conducted in the face of
ferocious opposition from the native population. The Jewish colonists angered
Muslims by their propagation of the myth of an empty "Promised Land," that God
had always intended should be re-occupied by the Jews, his "Chosen People." The
fact that it was able to construct an immensely powerful military machine capable
of defeating its Arab neighbors in a succession of military conflicts intensified
hostility toward Israel. Muslims were greatly angered by the fact that Israel
relentlessly pushed its boundaries beyond those initially established, including the
territories seized after the 1948 War and those seized after the Six Day War. They
were angered by its refusal to countenance the return of East Jerusalem and the
return of Palestinian refugees to Israel. They have been angered by the fact that Israel
has strongly resisted the return of the Occupied Territories on the West Bank, Gaza,
and the Golan Heights, and that it has settled a large number of Jewish people in the
Occupied Territories. They have been angered by the fact that Israel has received
powerful diplomatic, financial, and military support from the Western powers,
including Britain and France, but especially from America. They have been angered
by Israel's invasion of Lebanon and its cruel treatment of the Palestinians in Gaza,
culminating in all-out military attack.

America has failed comprehensively over the long term in its policies toward the
Muslim world. It was already widely unpopular among Muslims prior to the attack
on Iraq. Since the attack, perceptions of America among wide sections of the world's
Muslim population have sunk to a new low. The Pew Global Attitudes Survey of
2007 shows that across much of the Middle East, a large majority of the population
(60–90 percent) holds an unfavorable view of America. Such views are not confined
to Muslims in the Middle East; they are held widely across the Muslim world. In
Indonesia, Pakistan, and Malaysia, 70–90 percent of the population holds an
unfavorable view of America. Moreover, the Pew survey does not include some key
countries, such as Iraq, Iran, Algeria, and Libya, in which it is likely that attitudes
toward America are likely to be even more unfavorable.

According to the 2007 Pew survey, overwhelming majorities of the population across the Muslim world consider that America "favors Israel too much." If the poll were held in early 2009, in the wake of the Israeli violence unleashed on Gaza, one can imagine how much more intense the anti-American sentiments would be. In America itself only 11 percent of the population in the Pew survey sympathize with the Palestinians in the Israel–Palestinian dispute, but in every single Muslim country an overwhelming majority of people sympathize with the Palestinians. A majority of people in almost all countries (not just Muslim ones) believe that America promotes democracy mostly where it serves its own interests. An overwhelming majority (60–80 percent) of people in Muslim countries "oppose American-led efforts to fight terrorism." However, there is little evidence of support for so-called "Islamic fundamentalism." A substantial majority of people in most Muslim countries have little or no confidence in Osama Bin Laden as a leader who will "do the right thing in world affairs." The vast majority of people in both America and Europe hold unfavorable views of Iran and its leader, President Ahmadinejad. However, in several Muslim countries, including Bangladesh, Pakistan, Indonesia, and Malaysia, a substantial majority of people hold a positive view of Iran, and a significant proportion (from 39 percent in Malaysia to 64 percent in Bangladesh) hold a positive view of President Ahmadinejad.

If America wishes to rebuild its global leadership role it has no choice. It must comprehensively reassess its relationship with the Muslim world and work patiently to establish a long-term constructive engagement. It must fundamentally reassess its whole strategy, away from the pursuit of ideological goals, unquestioning support for Israel, and the use of military force to achieve energy security. Instead it must develop consistent policies for long-term, non-ideological, constructive engagement with the diversity of Muslim tradition and its current reality.

Conclusion

Beyond Wild Capitalism

America's most difficult task, but historically the most critical, will be to embody to the world at large an idea whose time has come

Zbigniew Brzezinski, 2007, *Second Chance*

I have faith we can mature. Stranger things have happened. Maybe America, maybe the world is in its adolescence. Maybe we're driving home from the prom, drunk, and nobody knows whether we're going to survive or not. Maybe we'll survive and maybe we'll be a pretty smart old person, well-adjusted and mellow.

Lloyd King, in Studs Terkel, *My American Century*

We were inclined to think of the psychological crisis of the waking worlds as being the difficult passage from adolescence to maturity; for in essence it was an outgrowing of juvenile interests, a discarding of toys and childish games, and a discovery of the interests of adult life. Tribal prestige, individual dominance, military glory, industrial triumphs lost their obsessive glamor, and instead the happy creatures delighted in civilized social intercourse, in cultural activities, and in the common enterprise of world-building.

Olaf Stapledon, *Star Maker*, 1937

If everyone really desired a "world-state" or "collective security" (and meant the same thing by those terms) it would be easily attained … [N]o progress is likely to be made along this path, and no political utopia will achieve even the most limited success unless it grows out of political reality.

E. H. Carr, *The Twenty Year Crisis*, 1939

If feeling fails you, vain will be your course,
And idle what you plan unless your art
Springs from the soul with elemental force,
To hold its sway in every listening heart …
[W]hat is uttered from the heart alone
Will win the hearts of others to your own.

Goethe, *Faust*, Part 1

Introduction

As the world enters the early phase of the new millennium, humanity stands at a crossroads. The era of wild capitalist globalization has drawn to a close, hastened by the global financial crisis. The contradictions of capitalism in the early twenty-first century are, for the first time, global in nature. In the search for solutions to the multiple threats to the sustainability of life for the human species, there is no alternative other than to work together across national frontiers, cultures, and levels of development, to find a pragmatic, non-ideological, cooperative way to overcome these threats. The threats derive from the nature of capitalist globalization itself. The solutions also are inherent within the universal tendencies of capitalism. The path taken by America at this crossroads in its own history and in that of the human race will determine the outcome for the whole human species. This is a mighty new frontier in American history.

Capitalist globalization has provided immense benefits, liberating human beings from the tyranny of nature, achieving large declines in the real costs of goods and services, and lifting a large fraction of the world's population out of poverty. However, it has a Faustian duality to its nature, producing profound threats to sustainable development in relation to inequality, ecology, and financial stability, and, ultimately, posing a threat of violent international conflict.

The solution to the challenges produced by the nature of capitalist globalization is inherent within capitalism itself. Capitalist globalization has produced unprecedented technological progress, which can be harnessed to meet the needs of all human beings. Capitalism has become truly global, and global institutions are slowly emerging to meet the global challenges. Even before the financial crisis it was increasingly widely understood that market forces needed to be heavily guided, and powerfully restrained globally in the common social interest, in order to contain socio-economic inequality, ensure an ecologically sustainable future, prevent a global financial crisis, and avoid violent international conflict. More and more people, from a wide variety of backgrounds, had already realized that strict global rules and comprehensive international cooperation were needed to constrain global capitalism in order to build a sustainable future. People from different perspectives had come independently to the realization that humanity is at a crossroads. The sense of urgency was reinforced dramatically by the financial crisis that began to unfold in mid-2007 and exploded in terrifying fashion in a few weeks in the early autumn of 2008. The world was now decisively changed. The era of wild capitalism was over.

Raw, unconstrained capitalism does not exist anywhere. Even present-day America would appear to nineteenth-century economists and social thinkers as a highly regulated economy and society. However, the extent and nature of regulation of markets that is required today in order to serve the interests of society globally would alter capitalism radically. Previous efforts to solve the challenges posed by the internal contradictions of the capitalist system have included attempts to obliterate the market mechanism altogether, but few people now advocate a return to such a system. There has also been a wide range of attempts in individual countries to regulate the market mechanism, including Arab and Nordic socialism, America under the New Deal, and post-war state capitalism in western Europe. However, the new phase in the era of modern global capitalism poses greater challenges and requires more profound answers than any attempted in the past, answers that are essential to our survival as a species. They require cooperation and collective action on a scale that has not so far been attempted, but which exists in potential in the nature of human beings, as has been shown by other successful attempts at cooperation on a smaller scale to solve common problems. This is the Darwinian challenge facing our species in the twenty-first century. The fact that the survival of the whole species in anything like its present form is under threat increases greatly the possibility of a cooperative, collective response.

The contradictions of capitalist globalization

The full incorporation of 2.5 billion workers from low and middle-income countries into the global workforce has been a central force in drastic changes in the labor markets of both rich and poor countries in the period of capitalist globalization. In low and middle-income countries, incorporation into global capitalism has not only stimulated rising average incomes, but has also contributed to greatly increased inequality. It will be several decades before the seemingly unlimited supplies of underemployed labor in developing countries are exhausted, and these countries have finally passed through the "Lewis phase" of development. In high-income countries, capitalist globalization has helped to lower the price of most goods and services. Simultaneously, it has contributed to the stagnation of median wages and the deterioration of conditions of employment, alongside a dramatic increase in incomes for the global elite. This process needs careful international coordination between rich and poor countries, in order to avoid international conflict resulting from the destabilizing effect of capitalist globalization upon the social structures of both rich and poor countries.

The global business revolution has unleashed to the full the potential within capitalism for industrial concentration. Leading global firms benefit from superior technologies and systems integration capabilities, as well as from global marketing and global procurement. Through organic growth and through explosive merger and acquisition, global leaders in each sector have come to occupy dominant oligopolistic positions in global markets. Moreover, through the cascade effect they have stimulated high-speed industrial concentration far down into the supply chain, in the invisible segments hidden beneath the water of the icebergs of industrial structures. The lion's share of the world's globally dominant firms is headquartered in the high-income countries, with America at the core. On the one hand, this presents an immense challenge for firms from developing countries, in both international markets and their own domestic markets, as leading global firms build oligopolistic positions within developing countries at both the level of systems integrators and far down into the supply chain. On the other hand, the explosive growth of global firms' international operations is fast weakening their relationship with their home nations. This explosive process requires careful international coordination in order to avoid conflict. Business leaders, answerable to their shareholders and focused firmly on success in their respective segments of the world market, cannot be expected collectively to lead this coordination process.

The ecological consequences of raw unconstrained capitalist globalization have become dramatically evident in recent years. The destruction of flora and fauna is accelerating, alongside rising global population and economic activity. The list of endangered species grows ever longer, not only in the world's land masses, but even more seriously in the global commons of the world's seas and all that they contain. The most dramatic tragedy of the global commons, however, is that of the earth's atmosphere, with uncontrollable natural forces swirling across the skies, without regard to international boundaries.

Human ingenuity has produced the triumph of the internal combustion engine and its continuous technological improvement, and the ever-expanding supply of fossil fuels, including almost limitless supplies of oil from coal, from tar sands, and from shale, in order to meet the ever-expanding global stock of automobiles and aircraft. The costs of transport have fallen dramatically thanks to the power of technological progress driven by competition between global capitalist firms. Alternative fuels such as wind, wave, and solar power are a long way from commercial viability, as are commercially viable techniques to sequester carbon dioxide in underground deposits. For several decades to come the possibility remains of violent international conflict over tensions caused by global warming from carbon dioxide emissions produced by burning fossil fuels. There is, even, a threat to the very existence of the human race. Global warming, the ultimate externality, has done more than any other issue to impress upon people across boundaries, cultures, and income levels, that global cooperation is essential: it is a "choice of no choice" for human survival. However, the huge differences between countries in levels of economic development and per capita emissions of carbon dioxide make international cooperation especially difficult to achieve. This difficulty is increased by the highly uneven expected distribution of the impact of global warming across different parts of the world.

For the foreseeable future oil will be the critical source of primary energy for the internal combustion engine, which will remain the key source of motive power for several decades to come, until close to the point at which global population stabilizes. The Middle East dominates global oil reserves, and will increasingly dominate global oil production and trade. There is a high potential for international conflict over access to this finite resource, both directly, but also through the indirect impact of intervention in the region by America. Unraveling the damaging consequences of past American foreign policy in the region will take a long time.

The international financial system made enormous progress during the era of capitalist globalization. Financial firms from high-income countries brought their high standards of corporate governance and sophisticated techniques for risk management to developing countries. Dramatic advances took place in financial risk management through improved risk modeling, the securitization of bank loans, and the proliferation of instruments to hedge risk, especially the huge array of derivatives, covering every conceivable area of financial activity.

However, there were profound system risks embedded in the global financial system, which in recent decades witnessed ever greater liberalization of financial markets, with America taking the lead through its central role in the Washington Consensus. A small number of dissenting voices pointed out these dangers, but their warnings went unheeded in the face of the enormous profits earned by giant financial firms as a result of the liberalized financial system. Their warnings were also ignored by ordinary citizens in the high-income countries who had benefited over many years from their ever-increasing "wealth" and their access to ever-increasing debt. There developed an ever-widening "scissors" between the falling real price of most goods and services on the one hand, and on the other the unprecedented speculative bubble affecting every conceivable asset, including stock markets, property, commodities, and works of art. A vast speculative derivatives market emerged and swelled to monstrous proportions, growing in step with the surging asset price bubble. There was no central regulatory body to ensure order in the global financial system, and a profound imbalance developed between on the one hand the trade surplus and foreign exchange reserves of East Asia and the oil-producing countries, and on the other the yawning American trade deficit. There developed an ever-growing level of personal debt in high-income countries, intertwined with the speculative bubble in asset prices, especially property.

From the 1980s onward the liberalized global financial system encountered a succession of financial crises, including the Mexican "Tequila" crisis, the Asian financial crisis, the Russian financial crisis, the crisis at Long-Term Capital Management, and the Argentine financial crisis. However, none of these was global in scale, and the global financial system successfully weathered each of them. In 2007–08, however, a comprehensive global financial crisis unfolded, with at its core a collapse in asset prices. The "great unraveling" was set in motion as credit and asset prices plummeted, following each other downward in tandem, just as they had followed each other upward in the preceding decades. International financial markets have become so deeply integrated that the current financial crisis has profound consequences for the whole global political economy. The global financial system is flying blind, with no one at the controls, and it is of the utmost urgency that global coordination mechanisms are established in order to contain the crisis. It is unclear, however, whether international coordination is feasible. Even if it were feasible, it is not certain that it could contain the crisis and catch the falling knife of global asset prices. Already in early 2009 official interest rates were at almost zero across the high-income countries, but the economic crisis continued to gather momentum. If global coordinated action proves impossible or ineffective, then the resulting crisis will be cataclysmic. The interaction of the financial crisis with other destabilizing aspects of capitalist globalization is extraordinarily dangerous for international relations.

It is an extraordinary paradox of the era of capitalist globalization that nuclear weapons still exist in large quantities, with vast stocks held by the world's dominant power, America, as well as those held by Russia, Britain, and France. Nuclear weapons technology has progressed enormously, so that their explosive power is many multiples of the bombs that destroyed Hiroshima and Nagasaki. A growing number of countries have acquired nuclear weapons since the early 1960s, including Israel, China, Pakistan, India, and North Korea. America turned a blind eye to Israel's acquisition of nuclear weapons, though America and Britain justified their invasion of Iraq with the claim, later proved to be false, that it was capable of producing weapons of mass destruction within a month or so. Japan is capable of producing nuclear weapons within a few weeks, while the Gulf states announced in late 2006 that they would coordinate a program for the acquisition of civilian nuclear technology in the region. Iran is pressing ahead with plans to build nuclear reactors and process uranium. America has agreed to increase its support for India's civilian nuclear program, while agreeing to exclude India's military nuclear program from international inspection. The threat of global warming is likely to lead to a proliferation of civilian nuclear technology, which, other things being equal, greatly increases the likelihood of the proliferation of nuclear weapons. In the eyes of an increasingly wide spectrum of commentators, including Robert McNamara, the former American Secretary of Defense, there has never been a more dangerous moment in human history. America literally holds the fate of the species in its hands. In the era of capitalist globalization the American government spends only a few tens of millions of dollars each year on research into renewable energy, but it has simultaneously increased its military spending to a level of around $2 billion per day.

Nationalism, culture, and globalization

Few human beings regard "global" as their framework of reference or their source of identity. Only a tiny fraction of the world's population systematically roam around the world as a regular part of their life. A much larger number, but still a tiny minority of the world's population, participate in global tourism. A large absolute number, but still a small minority of the global population, migrate in search of long-term employment. For most people, the nation is the primary source of identity, after the family and religion, and the nation is the main forum within which they have a political voice. The forces of capitalist globalization, however, are increasingly international. The markets, employees, production facilities, and supply chains of leading international firms are global. The outlook of their leaders is increasingly global, and divorced from considerations of the national interest of any given country. While the identity of leading firms is increasingly global, the national interest of citizens and national governments remains an immensely potent force.

Capitalist modernization has almost always been associated with the creation and reinforcement of a sense of national identity. People within the same national borders, often with different dialects, and even different languages and histories, are welded together into a single entity through a central state, which employs unified national taxation and legal systems, constructs unified national transport, telecommunication, and broadcasting systems, and builds unified national education systems using a common national language. In the early phase of industrialization an increasingly urbanized population experiences a high degree of socio-economic inequality, while at the same time losing touch with their original local identity. Because of this, the construction a unified national identity has been a crucially important means of creating a socially harmonious society amid the conflicts and strains of capitalist modernization.

Nationalism was a powerful force in the rise of Britain in the late eighteenth and early nineteenth centuries, as well as in Continental Europe and the Far East at a later date. Trade and financial capital were international, but people, governments, the mass media, education systems, and firms were deeply rooted within given industrialized nations. The dominance of each industrialized nation's sense of its own national interest was inseparable from feelings of national superiority and intense national rivalry. The intense nationalism of advanced industrial capitalism contributed directly to the violent intrusion of rich countries into the less industrialized regions, whose population was viewed as backward and in need of the civilizing benefits of being ruled by the colonial powers. The intense nationalism of the advanced industrial nations contributed also to their violent struggle with each other. Militarism and nationalism went hand in hand in the industrialized capitalist countries. Teeming millions of dead soldiers littered the battlefields of the twentieth century, and teeming millions of civilians were killed in the century's war-torn cities. In the late nineteenth century it would have seemed unimaginable that, in the civilized era of advanced capitalism, human beings fighting to fulfill their patriotic duty to their respective nations could inflict such devastating violence on each other, using the most sophisticated products of industrial civilization, culminating in the atom bomb.

Nationalism is also central to the history of America. In the Gilded Age in the late nineteenth century, not only was America a melting pot of different national cultures, but it was also a massively unequal society. The large scale of immigration today, especially from Central America, means that America continues to face serious challenges to its cultural unity. The fact that it is a highly unequal society increases the incentive to mobilize strong nationalist sentiments as a unifying force. America retains a profound sense of its national interest, with intense debate at all levels of society about the challenges posed to the country's dominant position by the economic rise of a new generation of "latecomer" countries.

Humanity's attempt to grope its way forward in this extraordinarily dangerous time hinges on the relationship between the world's dominant power, America, and the two most powerful unified cultures, China and Islam, which between them embrace two-fifths of the world's population. Our ability to cooperate in order to ensure a sustainable future will stand or fall on these relationships. If the engagement is confrontational rather than constructive, the prospects for humanity are bleak. Many people within each of these cultures believe that there is an unavoidable "clash of civilizations" between the West on the one hand, and China and Islam on the other. They believe that it is utopian to imagine that a confrontation can be avoided, and that the central task of national policy is to prepare for the inevitable clash in order to ensure victory. Some even believe that mutual destruction would be preferable to defeat. It is impossible to measure the probability of such a confrontation, but even if the chances are indeed low, all possible efforts must be made to avoid such a disaster from taking place.

There is in reality no fundamental clash between Western capitalism and the civilizations of China and Islam. Despite their differences in culture, political structure, and belief systems, it is the common elements of the socio-economic systems of China, Islam, and the West that are most significant when viewed from the perspective of the early twenty-first century and the swelling tide of globalization. In both the East and the West, in both the medieval and the modern world, private property, extension of the market, and pursuit of profit have been the central forces stimulating human ingenuity to achieve technological progress. In the era of capitalist globalization, the unleashing of this force has been central to accelerated growth in China and in important parts of the Muslim world.

For more than 1,000 years, capitalism has demonstrated its uniquely dynamic force in these different contexts. It has also demonstrated its contradictory character. In each of these contexts, social forces have arisen which have attempted to rectify the inequality, the damaging psychological and interpersonal impact, the economic instability, and the environmental impact of raw capitalism. These have sometimes taken the form of revolutionary attempts to overthrow the existing social order entirely and establish egalitarian communist societies based on common ownership of property. However, up until the twentieth century, revolutionary communist movements were rarely able to seize power, whether in China, Europe, or the Muslim world. Almost always the revolutionary movements used religious or quasi-religious language as their ethical foundation. The anti-capitalist era of common ownership in the Soviet Union (from the late 1920s until the mid-1980s) and in China (from the mid-1950s until the mid-1970s) appears increasingly as a relatively brief interlude in the long span of the history of capitalism.

In both China and the Muslim world, the main focus of responses to the contradictory character of capitalism has been to try to find a "mean" or "middle way," which recognizes capitalism's unique dynamic power, while constraining the way in which it operates in order to meet the needs of diverse social groups. These constraints have operated through ethics, conscience, and self-motivated social behavior, conveyed through education, religion, and common traditional value systems. They have also operated through the law and through state action to provide public goods and regulate the economy. Both in China and in the Muslim world, in both medieval and modern times, intellectuals and political leaders have wrestled with the conundrum of attempting to "civilize" capitalism and establish a harmonious, stable society. In China this has taken the form of Confucianism and, more recently, the attempt since the 1980s to construct a form of Chinese socialism that builds a "harmonious society" which "learns from the past in order to serve the present." In the Islamic world, in both medieval and modern times, the dominant discourse for taming and civilizing the market has been the Islamic faith, based on the Koran. Both China and the Muslim world have a rich contribution to make to resolving the contradictions inherent in the nature of capitalist globalization. The Western world, for its part, has a great deal to learn from both China and Islam about ways in which to ensure that market forces are harnessed for the collective social good.

Sustainable global development in the early twenty-first century necessitates that America engages with both China and the Muslim world in a non-ideological fashion. It has become increasingly clear that America cannot hope to create a global economy and society that is a replica of its own Social Darwinist political economy. It cannot continue to nurture "progressive" forces within China and the Muslim world that support such a vision. It cannot seek to isolate as "hardliners," "fundamentalists" or "terrorists" the people in these societies who do not subscribe to such a vision, since these terms encompass a large fraction of their population. America has no choice but to accept that the nature of capitalism in these parts of the world is likely to be very different from its nature in America at the start of the twenty-first century. America itself is engaged in deep soul-searching about its own path of political economy, in the face of the profound contradictions that have emerged in the era of wild capitalism, culminating in the terrific shock of the global financial crisis. In the search for solutions to its own difficulties America may look back at its own history, and the great historic swings that have taken place in its public policy. It may also find that the Chinese Confucian traditions and the Chinese Communist Party, along with the Koranic tradition of the Muslim world, can each contribute to a world in which capitalist markets are more tightly and intelligently regulated in the interests of all than has been the case during the era of capitalist globalization.

America's constructive engagement with both China and the Muslim world would greatly benefit the economic rise of those parts of the world, regions which contain over two-fifths of the world's population, each with its own identity and belief systems. Such engagement would bring great benefits to American firms, and many advantages for the American people. However, China's rise already poses large economic, cultural, and military adjustment challenges for America. China is still a developing country, with a long way to go in terms of its potential growth of per capita output. Despite widespread capitalist development in Muslim countries in recent decades, they have underperformed their potential, due in no small part to the destructive engagement of America. Its positive, constructive engagement, on the other hand, would be likely to stimulate accelerated growth in these countries, which would itself pose further adjustment challenges for America.

Conclusion: our final hour?

The period of capitalist globalization, with America at its core, has liberated human productive capabilities in ways that were formerly unimaginable, to the benefit of the whole world. However, the destructive aspects of capitalism have intensified, in terms of inequality and injustice within both rich and poor countries, ecological damage, the battle for scarce resources, and potential global financial instability. In the era of capitalist globalization these problems can only be solved at a global level. However, despite some progress in the construction of global institutions of social control, these institutions remain weak. They are overshadowed by the immense power of profit-seeking global firms, which have little incentive, either individually or collectively, to resolve the contradictions of globalization.

The internationalization of business activity stands in striking contrast to the predominantly national basis of politics. Even regional political groupings of countries, whether in the Far East, the Muslim world, Africa, Latin America, or Europe, have encountered large barriers to political integration. Nationalism remains a powerful political force. Having been created in the process of capitalist modernization, the genie of nationalism has proved hard to put back into the bottle. The intensification of nationalism in the rising "latecomer" countries of the early twenty-first century sits uneasily alongside the widespread fear among the populations of the high-income countries of the damaging effects of capitalist globalization.

Since ancient times the exercise of individual freedoms has been inseparable from the expansion of the market, driven by the search for profit. This force, namely capitalism, has stimulated human creativity in ways that have produced immense benefits. As capitalism has broadened its scope in the era of globalization, so these benefits have become even greater. Human beings have been liberated to an even greater degree from the tyranny of nature, from control by others, from poverty, and from war. The advances achieved by the globalization of capitalism have appeared all the more striking when set against the failure of non-capitalist systems of economic organization.

However, capitalist freedom is a two-edged sword. In the era of capitalist globalization, its contradictions have intensified. They comprehensively threaten the natural environment. They have intensified global inequality. They have stimulated a high degree of instability in global finance. The world's dominant economic, political, and cultural power refuses to dismantle its vast stock of nuclear arms, sufficient to obliterate the entire global civilization. It benefits in numerous ways from global capitalism, but it also feels under intense threat, both internally and externally, from those same forces.

The present stage of development of global capitalism has produced in even more intense form the contradictions latent within the system. As human beings have taken to new heights their ability to free themselves from fundamental constraints through the market mechanism, so they have also plumbed new depths in terms of the uncontrollability of the structures they have created. Global capitalism has created uniquely grave threats to the very existence of the human species, at the same time as it has liberated humanity more than ever before from fundamental constraints. The British Astronomer Royal, Lord Rees, believes that "the odds are no better than fifty-fifty that our present civilization on earth will survive to the end of the present century." (Martin Rees, *Our Final Hour*)

Modern capitalist globalization began in the 1970s, and since then the removal of constraints on the operation of the market mechanism has proceeded unceasingly across the whole world. The first, wild phase of modern capitalist globalization has drawn to a close, as the intensifying and multiple contradictions have become ever more apparent. The resolution of these multiple contradictions necessitates globally coordinated regulation of the capitalist system. As the wild animal of global capitalism becomes ever larger and more powerful, it becomes ever more important that human beings, who have given birth to and nurtured this animal, establish a moral framework to regulate its activity, and thereby prevent it from devouring its creator, humanity.

The capitalist system is the product of the collective exercise of human intelligence. The way in which people choose collectively to exercise that intelligence is governed by their ethics. Ethics are the pole star which guides humanity on its journey through history. The possibilities for a sustainable future for human beings are, in turn, intimately related to our psychological needs. There have, since ancient times, been sharply polarized views of the fundamental human needs and the ethical systems corresponding to those needs.

Capitalist globalization creates unprecedented challenges that can only be resolved at a global level through international cooperation, but nationalism among both old industrialized and newly industrializing countries stands in the way of achieving the requisite cooperation. Human beings face a race against time.

The contradictory character of human psychology has been recognized since ancient times. One may interpret Homer's great works, *The Iliad* and *The Odyssey*, as concerned respectively with the "life instinct" and the "death instinct." The former book is a joyous celebration of human creativity and the pleasures of the human voyage of discovery. The latter is a remorseless catalogue of horror and mutual destruction by men motivated by patriotic heroism. Having witnessed the horrors of World War I, Sigmund Freud reluctantly concluded that human beings contained two contending forces: "Our views have from the very first been dualistic, and today they are even more definitely dualistic than before—now that we describe the opposition as being, not between ego-instincts and sexual instincts, but between life instincts and death instincts." (Sigmund Freud, *Civilization and its Discontents*) The life instinct (Eros) came from man's sense of his place within an infinite realm of being. The death instinct (Thanatos) came from man's most profound fears, especially the fear of death itself. The death instinct inclined people to distrust and compete with others, while the life instinct inclined people to trust and cooperate. In the wake of the horrors of World War I, Sigmund Freud posed the question of the survival of the human species in stark terms:

> The fateful question for the human species seems to me to be whether, and to what extent, their cultural development will succeed in mastering the disturbance of their communal life by the human instinct of aggression and self-destruction … Men have gained control of the forces of nature to such an extent that with their help they would have no difficulty in exterminating one another to the last man. They know this, and hence comes a large part of their current unrest, their unhappiness and their mood of anxiety. And now it is to be expected that the other of the two "Heavenly Powers," eternal Eros, will make an effort to assert himself in the struggle with his equally immortal adversary. But who can foresee with what success and with what result? (Sigmund Freud, *Civilization and its Discontents*)

If humanity cannot find a "mean," its prospects for survival are bleak. The destruction of human civilization may arise either from the internal self-destructiveness of extreme free market individualism, or from the nihilistic response of those excluded and angered by the globalization of the free market.

The challenges that confront human beings are the product of people's own activities, expressed mainly through the economic system. It is within their collective power to resolve the contradictions. The very depth of the challenges they now face may shock them into the action necessary to ensure the survival of the species. Alongside human beings' competitive and destructive instincts are their instincts for survival of the species through cooperation. However great the challenge may be, human beings have the capability of solving the contradictions that are of their own making. It may be only the approach of the final hour which finally forces human beings to grope their way toward globally cooperative solutions. The falling of the dusk, as humanity looks into the abyss, may be the final impulse to produce the cooperative solution that exists within the unfolding of global capitalism. "The owl of Minerva spreads its wings only with the falling of the dusk" (G. F. Hegel, *The Philosophy of Right*).

Epilogue

NONE of us escapes our upbringing. As I wrote this book, I thought a great deal about my father. He greatly admired George Orwell, especially his futuristic novel *1984*, which Orwell wrote as a warning about the dangers of totalitarianism. By an odd coincidence, my father died in 1984, the year in which Orwell's novel was set.

My father was born in Dublin, one hundred years ago, in 1908. He experienced British colonial rule at close quarters. His house was in Clonliffe Road, Dublin, next door to the Croke Park Stadium. As a young child in 1916 he was taken by his father to the center of Dublin and saw the occupation of the General Post Office by the anti-British rebel forces during the Easter Rising. Over 1,000 people were killed or seriously wounded in the violence, and 16 leaders of the rebellion were executed. My father kneeled outside Mountjoy Prison praying while the young anti-British hero, Kevin Barry, was executed. My father had vivid memories of the occasion when the so-called Black and Tans rode their horses into Croke Park on the day of the All-Ireland hurling final, and turned their machine guns on the crowd, who streamed out in terror past his family's home. Later in his life, while doing the washing up he liked to sing the patriotic song that was composed about Kevin Barry, who "gave his young life for the cause of liberty." He also liked to sing "Speed bonny boat, like a bird on a wing, 'Onward,' the sailors cry, Carry the lad who's born to be king, over the seas to Skye."

He and his three siblings were orphaned when he was 12 years old, and they went to live with their aunt and uncle, who owned a hotel in Bournemouth, a seaside resort on the south coast of England. They drove a huge Hispano Suiza motor car. Auntie had an armchair fitted specially in the front of the vehicle, and she insisted that the only safe place to drive was in the middle of the road. Auntie and Uncle died within a short time of each other, and my father went to work in London, where he lived in relative poverty during the Great Depression in the 1930s.

At the outbreak of World War II, he and his brothers could have chosen to return to the country of their birth. Ireland was neutral, and the brothers could have had a peaceful war. Instead, like so many Irish people in Britain, they volunteered to fight in the British armed forces. One brother volunteered to join the air force, one the navy, and my father volunteered to join the army. The brother who joined the air force became a navigator in Blenheim bombers stationed in Malta. He was badly injured. At the relatively old age of 32, my father became a gunner in the Royal Artillery, in the Fourth Indian Division (we still have his red eagle cap badge, of which he was immensely proud). The division saw fierce action in the battle of Monte Cassino in southern Italy, the most ferocious and bloody battle on the western front. The months-long engagement witnessed great bravery by German soldiers; the German cemetery at Cassino contains over 20,000 graves, and small, white crosses dot the hillside where German bodies are buried, three to a grave.

They fought against an army of British, American, South Asian, French, Algerian, Moroccan, and Polish soldiers. Like all the soldiers who fought at Cassino, my father considered that "it's better to fight than to run."

Scenes from the battle recall the horror of Homer's *Iliad*. In January 1944, during the early phase of the battle, the American 141st and 143rd regiments attempted over two days to break through German lines on the far side of the Rapido River. The German position proved to be impregnable. Over 1,300 American soldiers were killed or wounded in the repeated assaults across the freezing cold, fast-flowing river. In an interrogation after the battle, a junior officer said: "When I saw my regimental commander standing with tears in his eyes as we moved up to start the crossing, I knew something was wrong. I started out commanding a company of 184 men. Forty-eight hours later, 17 of us were left."

As for so many people of his generation, the horrors of the war never left him. To the end of his life, he walked close to the wall in any street, an instinctive reaction to years spent fearing snipers' bullets. Among his innumerable scorching memories from the war was the experience of picking up his friend, both of whose legs had been blown off. The incomprehensible violence of war ripples through subsequent generations in ways we hardly comprehend.

Despite the horrors of the war, my father returned with positive memories. He remembered the deep peace of Arezzo, where his regiment stayed to recuperate after Cassino. Years later, my mother and I visited Arezzo, which nestles in the Tuscan countryside. We ate tagliatelli with butter and fresh basil, and drank a pitcher of white wine, in an open café overlooking the main square. Afterwards, we wondered at Piero della Francesca's frescos of the True Story of the Cross on the walls of the church of San Francesco. My father was deeply influenced by the comradeship and mutual trust among ordinary soldiers. Having lived for five years in "a hole in the ground," as he put it, he derived great pleasure from simple things, such as "a roof over my head," a cup of tea, and home-made bread and cakes. He was deeply affected by the kindness of ordinary people in the countries in which he fought—North Africa, Italy, and Greece. During lulls in the fighting, he taught himself basic Arabic and a great deal of everyday Italian and Greek. He loved to read Greek poetry. When he died there were two books on his desk: one was a collection of poems in Greek by George Seferis, the Nobel Prize winner, and the other was a Hebrew language textbook. In the last years of his life he was teaching himself Hebrew. He used to pore over a book that provided detailed accounts, including maps and pictures, of the locations of the key passages in the Bible, from both the Old and New Testaments. He had visited many of these places during the war.

He loved to write short stories. His most successful story, published in the magazine *John Bull*, was set in an unidentified Middle Eastern city, and its hero was a young Arab boy, wrongly accused of theft. He also wrote fantasy stories for us, his children, with heroes called Jumpity and Pinkie.

We must find someone to help us. How about Bill the Old Soldierman? They walked along to Bill's camping place. He had pitched his tent on a level grassy spot. The guy ropes were neatly coiled close to the tent pegs. All his blankets carefully folded were outside the tent and his pots and pans too, shining like silver, were placed outside in the sun. Bill was glad to see them "Hello there Jumpity and Pinkie, you're just in time for a brew of tea." He had a pot of water boiling on his fire. Into it he dropped a handful of tea; then some milk and sugar. He stirred it with a stick and laughed saying, "There you are, me lads, a real soldier brew for you" as he poured out a mug for each.

For many years he taught a course on "Money and banking" at the local technological college. His bible for the course was the Radcliffe Report on the British monetary system, as relevant today as when it was first published.

I don't think my father had read Henry Thoreau's *Walden*, but his life was lived very much in the *Walden* style—"Most of the luxuries, and many of the so-called comforts of life, are not only not indispensable, but positive hindrances to the elevation of mankind. With respect to luxuries and comforts, the wisest have ever lived a more simple and meager life than the poor. The ancient philosophers, Chinese, Hindoo, Persian, and Greek, were a class than which none has been poorer in outward riches, none so rich in inward."

My father cultivated an allotment close to our house, from which most of our vegetables came. It had also an abundance of blackberries, from which he used to make blackberry wine. The wine was decanted into old soft drink bottles, with screw-on tops, and left in the coal shed to mature. He only gave up the attempt after several years of disastrous failures. In winter, he used to warm his bed with a brick heated in the oven. He used to prevent our dog from leaping onto his bed by means of branches of holly piled onto it. Unlike Pavlov's dog, ours never learned, always leaping up, and always leaping off with the same anguished surprise at his daily encounter with the holly. My father's advice to newly married couples at weddings was unvarying—"Don't get a dog."

When we were children, my father bought a wooden cabin in the small seaside hamlet of Wembury, near Plymouth. It was in a wood which had several other cabins. Glow-worms used to shine in the dark as one passed through the woods, which each spring were filled with a carpet of bluebells. The small feeding table outside the window was always full of birds, and swallows used to wheel across the valley in front of the cabin. Wembury's ancient church of St Werburgh looks out at the sea from a cliff-top vantage point: "No other south Devon church faces the open sea so squarely. The visual contrast between the square tower and the triangular outline of Great Mew Stone, the island off Wembury point, is singularly moving." (Nikolaus Pevsner, *The Buildings of England: South Devon.*) In AD 785 Wembury beach witnessed the battle of Wickenboerg, between marauding Vikings and local inhabitants. It is famous today for its rich marine life. We used to climb down a steep cliff path and fish from the rocks, the waves surging around us, the sea teeming with fish. We were hopelessly unsuccessful, but around us the experienced fishermen used to haul in enormous gleaming catches. Our wooden cabin was built in the clinker style, with wide, roughly-cut pine boards overlapping each other. In the winter months, at the weekends my father frequently used to walk the ten miles or so to the cabin and stay the night there. He would put creosote on the boards, and go down to walk by the beach to the sound of crashing waves. Like Thoreau, he was essentially a mystic, enthralled by the immensity of existence—"The stars are the apexes of what wonderful triangles! What distant and different mansions of the universe are contemplating the same one at the same moment!"

He was proud of Ireland's history. The Easter Rising against the British was a key part of his personal history. However, the extreme violence of World War II left him with an abiding hostility for militant nationalism. He had no trace of hostility toward ordinary German people. He was a fervent supporter of the attempt to build a European community in order to avoid future wars. He believed in the ethical foundation provided by religion and in the intrinsic importance of education. He considered that having too much money was almost as bad as having too little. One of the happiest periods in his life was when he retired from a long working life as a bank employee and ran a small one-room shop selling ancient and medieval coins. Much of the pleasure from running the shop came from his interaction with people who came there to "talk coins." In mid-morning he used to go out of the shop leaving a hand-written sign in the window—"Gone for coffee (not cocoa)."

Notes

[1] Unless otherwise indicated, "dollars" refers to "US dollars" throughout this book.

[2] Unless otherwise indicated, the term "developing countries" in this book is taken to mean low and middle income countries.

[3] This term was coined by the late Alfred Chandler, of Harvard Business School, who pioneered research on the large modern firm.

[4] The ecological footprint measures humanity's demands on the biosphere in terms of the area of biologically productive land and sea required to provide the resources we use and to absorb our waste. People consume resources and ecological services from all over the world, so their footprint is the sum of all these areas, wherever they may be on the planet. A "global hectare" is a hectare of world average productivity taking into account national differences in biological productivity and among different land types.

[5] The PPP, or "purchasing power parity" exchange rate in principle adopts a common set of prices by which to measure the output of goods and services in each country. However, there are immense difficulties with this apparently simple procedure. In practice, the prices used have been based on those of America. Hence, America's national income in "PPP dollars" is little different from its national income at the official exchange rate. For developing countries, adopting the prices of America results in a huge increase in their national income. In the case of China, for example, the World Bank estimated that its gross national income in PPP dollars in 2004 was $7,634 billion, or 65 percent of that of America, whereas at the official rate of exchange, the World Bank estimated that in 2004 China's gross national income was $1,938 billion, or a mere 16 percent of that of America. Those who wished to argue for China's rapid catch-up with America naturally emphasized the PPP figure for China's national income. Using the World Bank's PPP estimate of China's national income, China in 2002 was as energy efficient (in terms of national product per unit of energy use) as America, a result that few people consider is consistent with the real picture. In 2007, the World Bank announced that it had greatly overestimated China's national income in PPP terms. Their new calculations concluded that China's PPP national income was 40 percent less than their previous estimate had suggested.

[6] These include foreign exchange holdings under the control of the monetary authorities, as well as gold, special drawing rights, and IMF reserves.

⁷ For a different view of this process see my book *China's Rise, Russia's Fall* (1994), as well as various of my articles on the "transition" in Russia and China that preceded this book, all of which were written in the midst of intense debate about these issues.

⁸ For an extended analysis of these challenges see my book *China at the Crossroads* (Polity Press, 2004).

⁹ For an analysis of the interaction between Chinese economic reform and the global business revolution see my books *China and the Global Business Revolution* (Palgrave, 2001) and *China and the Global Economy* (Palgrave, 2001).

¹⁰ *Yellow Peril* was recently published in English under the title *China Tidal Wave*.

¹¹ There is a striking contrast between Condoleezza Rice's article in *Foreign Affairs* in 2000 and her valedictory article in the same journal in 2008. The former brims with self-confidence at the forthcoming transformation of the world under American leadership. The latter reflects complete bewilderment at the disintegration of this grand project.

¹² Huntington was closely involved in American foreign policy. He served in the White House in 1977 and 1978 under President Carter as coordinator for security planning for the National Security Council. He died on 28 December 2008 at the age of 81.

¹³ For example, the books that have won the Pulitzer Prize for Literature over the last two decades deal almost exclusively with domestic American issues.

¹⁴ Due to accounting anomalies, the world's total current account surplus and deficit do not balance.

Index

A

Abbasid Caliphate 194–5, 196, 208
Abu Dhabi 199, 229
Abu Dharr al-Ghifari 207, 208, 211
acid rain 134, 135
Ackerman, Joseph 82
advertising 57–8, 110, 169
aerospace industry 28, 54–6
Afghanistan
  American invasion of 222
  conflict in 206
  exchange economy 202
  military presence in 229
  struggle against extremism 242
  "system disintegration" 166
Africa
  agricultural output 68
  famine 36
  incomes in 61
  number of Muslims in 190–1
  oil assets 157
  pre-modern trade 11
  Sahel region 61, 198, 200–1
  trade with Muslim world 195, 198
African Americans 153–4
Africanus, Leo 198
aggression 6, 7, 105, 265
agriculture
  China 128, 133–4, 158, 171
  deforestation 43, 47
  Muslim world 195
  Sahel region 201
  technological progress 16, 35–6
  value-added 68
Ahmadinejad, Mahmood 224, 227, 250
AIG 83–4
air pollution 33, 134–5, 137
Airbus 55
al-Azhar university 211
al-Malaki, Nouri 245
al-Mawardi 210
Al Qaeda 206, 213, 224, 248–9
Algeria
  attitudes towards America 249
  conflict in 206
  Egyptian support for 239

French control over 218, 219
  number of Muslims in 190
America 1, 5–6, 7, 104–19, 254
  agricultural output 68
  arrogance of 102, 157
  attitudes towards 249–50
  carbon dioxide emissions 51, 113,
    114–15
  China's relationship with 98, 102–4, 114,
    120–23, 149–52, 156–66, 186–8, 261–3
  cultural introversion 155–6
  distribution of wealth 64
  dominant role of 97–8
  energy consumption 46, 49, 114–15, 136
  energy contest with China 157–8
  energy technology 174–5
  environmental issues 112–15, 158–9
  Federal Reserve 23, 72, 81, 83, 84, 90, 117
  financial crisis 79, 81–5, 89, 91, 93–4,
    116–19, 169–70, 172, 175–9
  financial sector profits 78
  fiscal policies 73–4
  foreign exchange reserves 73
  foreign policy 107, 114, 151, 156–7, 165,
    219–45, 258
  Gilded Age 166–8, 260
  global firms 140
  globalization 4, 104–5, 169
  government borrowing 92
  hedge funds 75
  income inequalities 65–6, 166–7
  interest rates 90
  international institutions 38
  Islamic terrorism 205
  Kyoto Protocol rejection 49, 51, 115
  labor market changes 65
  manufacturing decline 65
  military power 97, 161–4, 228–9
  modern firms 17
  Muslim world's relationship with 98,
    102–4, 114, 156, 188–90, 219–45,
    247–50, 261–3
  nationalism 260–1
  need for enemies 152–7
  New Deal 256
  nuclear weapons 97, 162–3, 164, 259

America (*cont.*)
  number of Muslims in 190
  oil in the Middle East 188, 219–28, 248,
    257–8
  Progressive Era 168
  protectionism 141, 160, 166
  purchasing power parity 271n5
  recession 91
  religious beliefs 152–3, 189
  resistance to financial regulation 79–80
  social capital 168–9
  social contradictions 107–10
  Social Darwinist ideology 105–7
  soft power 119, 233
  support for Israel 229–30, 231–3, 235–6,
    237–45, 248–9, 250
  support for Saudi Arabia 200
  technology 173–5
  tertiary education 173
  trade and finance 159–61
  violence 110–11
  "war against terrorism" 103, 107, 240,
    245
American Economics Association 167–8
Angola 199
APEC *see* Asia-Pacific Economic
  Cooperation
Arab League 215
Arab nationalism 216–17, 231, 243
Arab socialism 211, 246, 256
Argentina 22, 23, 77, 258
Aristotle 95, 184, 196
Armey, Dick 238
ASEAN *see* Association of Southeast Asian
  Nations
Asia-Pacific Economic Cooperation
  (APEC) 37
Asia-Pacific region
  agricultural output 68
  America/China relations 152
  distribution of wealth 64
  oil demand 46
Asian financial crisis 5, 23, 74, 77, 258
  American soft power 119
  impact on China 144, 177
  spread of 96
  Washington Consensus 161
asset prices 78, 116, 145, 259
  credit expansion 71

decline in 81, 89, 90, 117
inflation 73
speculative boom 48, 94
Association of Southeast Asian Nations
(ASEAN) 37
Australia 49, 111
automobile industry 48, 51

B
Baghdad 194–5, 197
Bahrain 200, 215, 218, 229
Baker, James 221
Balfour, Arthur 231, 233–4
Balfour Declaration (1917) 218, 231
Banco Santander 86
Bangladesh 191, 202, 203, 250
Bank of America 21, 89, 91, 144, 178
Bank of Canada 81
Bank of England 72, 81, 90
Bank of Japan 90
Bank of New York 89
banking 19, 21–2, 76–7
  China 144–6, 176–7
  deregulation 176
  financial crisis 81–2, 83–90, 91, 93, 178
  informal sector 68
  Muslim world 203
  resistance to regulation 95
  Washington Consensus 178–9
  see also finance
Barak, Ehud 236
Barclays 88
Barma, Mustansir 204
Barry, Kevin 267
Bear Stearns 81–2, 83, 178
Belgium 80, 86
Bellamy, Edward 167
Ben-Gurion, David 235
benevolence 183, 184, 185
beverage industry 28, 54, 56–8
Bin Laden, Osama 248, 250
biofuels 31, 44
Blair, Tony 227
BNP Paribas 21, 86, 178
Boeing 55
bourgeoisie 36–7, 53
BP (British Petroleum) 39, 222, 225
Bradford and Bingley 86, 88
Braudel, Fernand 198

Brazil
  biofuels 44
  economic growth 72
  foreign banks 22
  inequality 67
  multinational firms 20
  research and development 27
Brown, Gordon 94
Brzezinski, Zbigniew 73–4, 102, 224, 254
bubbles 71–2, 77–8, 82, 91, 116, 145,
  160, 258
Bulgaria 22
Bursa 197
Bush, George W.
  "Axis of Evil" speech 227
  financial crisis 94
  foreign policy 151–2
  global warming 115, 175
  Iraq war 222, 223, 225, 228
  religious belief 189
  sanctions against Iran 226
  Sino-American relations 103, 156, 162
  Social Darwinism 106–7, 170
  support for Israel 228, 237, 242, 245
business power 2–3, 5, 25–9, 53–60, 96, 263
  aerospace industry 54–6
  beverage industry 56–8
  cascade effect 29, 54–8, 59–60, 256
  China 119, 140–2, 186
  external firm 18, 58–9
  see also large firms; multinational firms;
transnational corporations

C
Cairo 196, 211
Canada 65, 111
capital flows 12, 13, 19–21, 38, 39
  America 117
  derivative products 75–6
  developing countries 92
  global production 64
  inequality 69
capital punishment 111, 220
capitalism
  automobile industry 48
  China 119, 124–9, 261–2
  competition 23–4, 26–7
  contradictions of 2, 7, 41, 96–7, 120, 255,
  256–9, 261–2, 263–5

external firm 18
Faustian pact 41
finance 19
growth of 10–14
inequality 69
injustices 61
"invisible hand" 14–17, 18
large firms 17–18
Muslim world 190, 193–205, 206–9, 211,
  213–14, 246–7, 261–2
nationalism 260
regulation of 3–4
speculation 95
universal impulse of 121, 186
urbanization 34
"wild" 1, 2–3, 7, 41
  see also free market economics
carbon dioxide emissions 32, 33, 48,
  49–52, 257
  America 113, 114–15, 175
  China 135, 136, 158, 175
  see also pollution
carbon sequestration 33, 48, 50, 137,
  174, 257
carbon trading 49–50
Carlucci, Frank 221
Carr, E. H. 254
Carson, Rachel 42, 45, 112–13
Catlin, George 112
CCP see Chinese Communist Party
central banks 72–3, 78, 79, 81
Chavez, Hugo 118, 224
Cheney, Dick 151, 222
Chile 22
China 4, 5, 6, 120–48
  agricultural output 68
  America's relationship with 98, 102–4,
  114, 120–23, 149–52, 156–66, 186–8,
  261–3
  coal use 50
  comparison with high-income countries
  147, 148
  Confucianism 183–5
  currency 118
  distribution of wealth 64
  ecological implosion 133–5
  economic growth 72
  embryonic capitalism 124–9
  energy issues 32, 46, 135–6, 157–8, 174–5

China (*cont.*)
  environmental issues 45–6, 133–5, 136–7, 158–9
  financial crisis 171–2, 173, 175–9
  financial institutions 19, 144–6
  foreign direct investment 20, 202
  foreign exchange reserves 73, 175–6
  global business revolution 140–2
  global warming 136–7
  "harmonious society" 121, 166, 170–3, 185, 188, 262
  inequality 63, 67, 138–40, 166
  informal labor 66, 139
  International Monetary Fund 80
  market coordination 14–15
  military power 161–4
  nuclear weapons 97, 259
  number of Muslims in 190
  "peaceful rise" of 165, 166, 188
  poverty 138–40
  purchasing power parity 271n5
  reforms 13, 25, 120, 130, 138, 170, 187
  research and development 27
  responses to capitalism 261–2
  rise of 130–3
  role of the state 142–4
  technology 16, 173–5
  tertiary education 173
  trade and finance 11, 159–61
  unbalanced growth 137–8
  war in 12
  western critique of foreign policy 229
Chinese Communist Party (CCP)
  bureaucratic structure 131
  corruption 142
  Mao's leadership 128
  national flag 123
  "peaceful rise" of China 166
  political stability 120, 142, 186
  reforms 13, 120, 130
Christadelphians 238
Christian right 238
Christianity 189, 192, 208, 216
Churchill, Winston 217
Citigroup 21, 89, 91, 144, 177
Civil War, American (1961–65) 110, 154
civilian casualties 153, 154–5, 234
"clash of civilizations" 102, 188, 190, 193, 213, 247, 261

class struggle 69, 143, 167, 181, 183, 193
climate change *see* global warming
Clinton, Bill 51, 226, 227
Clinton, Hillary 245
coal 30–1, 46, 47, 50
  China 135–6, 137, 158, 175
  Sino-American relations 174, 175
Cold War 193
colonialism 201, 216, 246
communism 12, 72, 193, 261
  Abu Dharr 207
  China 128–9, 156
  collapse of 13, 94, 130, 165
  Muslim world 210, 211, 246, 247
  see also Chinese Communist Party
competition 23–4, 26–7, 30
  flat 54–5, 59
  labor market 64–5
  oligopolistic 18, 29, 65, 78
  Social Darwinism 105
  uneven 60
concentration 24, 26, 28–9, 59–60, 256–7
  advertising and communication industry 58
  aerospace industry 55–6
  beverage industry 56–7
  developing countries 53
  see also mergers and acquisitions
conflict 5–6, 52–3, 255
  America/China 120, 150, 164, 187
  nationalism 260
  see also war
Confucianism 125, 128, 183–5, 262
Constantinople 197, 231
constructive engagement 104, 187, 250, 262–3
  see also cooperation
consumer goods 34, 38–9, 107, 129
consumer price inflation 72–3
consumption 48, 52, 182, 183
  America 104, 159
  asset price bubble 78
  China 129, 159, 174
  global 53–4
  happiness relationship 109, 185
  recession impact on 90
cooperation 7, 97, 103, 255, 256, 265
  America/China 120, 121, 123, 164–5, 172–3, 174–5, 179, 188

American global leadership 98
  global warming 257
  Ibn Khaldun 210–11
  nationalism as barrier to 264
  see also constructive engagement
corporate governance 21, 38, 144, 145, 258
corruption 120, 142–3, 145, 186
cosmopolitanism 36–7
Crane, Charles 231
credit 23, 71–2, 76, 78, 79, 90, 198–9
Credit Agricole 21
cultural globalization 40
currencies 117–19, 177
Czech Republic 22, 27

D
D'Amato, C. Richard 160
Daoism 184, 192, 193
Darwin, Charles 6, 105, 167
Davos Economic Forum 72
Dawkins, Richard 189
death instinct 7, 264–5
death penalty 111, 220
debt
  America 116, 160, 166
  financial crisis 75, 76, 77, 78, 79, 91
  growth in personal 48, 177, 258
Defense Planning Guidance (DPG) 151,
  152
deflation 90–1
deforestation 43–4, 134, 158–9
democracy
  American foreign policy 107
  China 143
  global governance 69–70
  Pew Global Attitudes Survey 250
Deng Xiaoping 130, 142
Denmark 118
deregulation
  Iceland 86
  Social Darwinism 105
  Washington Consensus 38, 132, 176
  see also liberalization; privatization
derivatives 23, 75–6, 77, 83, 258
Deutsche Bank 21, 82
developing countries
  agriculture 35–6
  air pollution 33
  capital flows 92

carbon dioxide emissions 50–2
consumption 54, 183
deforestation 44
economic reform 25
energy consumption 32, 48–9
environmental transition 45
equity funds 21
financial crisis 178
financial institutions 21, 176
financial liberalization 5, 19–20, 22, 93
foreign banks 22
foreign direct investment 20
GDP growth 35, 132
global recession 91–2
global warming 96, 115
globalization impact on 5, 256
IMF/World Bank 80–1, 95
industrial concentration 53
inequality 66–8
integration into capitalist economy 13,
  14
international cooperation 97
labor markets 64–5
large firms 24, 59, 60, 256–7
"lumpen labor" 183
post-war economic policies 12–13
standard of living 35
telecommunications 34
tourism 40
transport 48, 50, 51–2
urbanization 34
Dewey, John 168
Diamond, Jared 158–9
Dickens, Charles 10
division of labor
  China 124–5
  global production 38
  Ibn Khaldun 210–11
  Smith on 14, 15, 36, 179, 180–1
Dodge, David 81
dollar 117, 118–19
Donne, John 1
DPG see Defense Planning Guidance
Dulles, John Foster 239–40
Dylan, Bob 149

E
East Asia
  agricultural output 68

East Asia (*cont.*)
  financial crisis 74
  foreign direct investment 20
  foreign exchange reserves 73, 160, 258
  inequality 67
  see also Southeast Asia
Eastern Europe
  collapse of communism 13, 94
  foreign banks 22
  personal debt 177
ECB see European Central Bank
ecological footprint 49, 113, 271n4
ecology 42–5, 96, 255
  America 112–13
  China 133–5, 188
  globalization impact on 257
  Sino-American relations 158–9, 165
  see also environmental issues
economic crisis 52, 89–92, 96, 148, 179
  see also financial crisis; recession
economic growth
  China 45, 121, 129, 131–3, 137–9, 146–7,
    170–2, 263
  financial liberalization 19
  Iran 225
  Muslim world 201, 203–4
  oil-producing countries 199
  optimism 72
  stock market capitalization 20–1
economic integration 165–6, 187
education
  China 129, 143, 171, 188
  Confucius/Adam Smith comparison 185
  developing countries 68
  Muslim world 204, 212
  religious belief relationship 189
  tertiary 173, 204
Egypt
  Arab socialism 211
  British occupation 217–18
  capitalism 201, 213–14
  conflict in 206
  education 204
  Fatimid Caliphate 196
  foreign direct investment 202
  French/Israeli coalition against 219, 239
  infant mortality 204
  Isma'ilis 208
  Israeli War of Independence 236

Muslim Brotherhood 214–15
  number of Muslims in 190, 191
  private sector 202
  Six Day War 237
  trade 202
  Yom Kippur War 240
elites 61–3, 67–8, 69
Ely, Richard T. 168
Emerson, Ralph Waldo 192–3
"end of history" 1
energy 30–3, 41, 46–7, 96, 257
  America 114–15, 121, 174–5, 187
  China 135–6, 172, 174–5, 188
  global warming 47–8
  increase in consumption 48–9
  oil in the Middle East 188, 219–28, 247,
    248, 257–8
  Sino-American relations 157–8, 165,
    174–5
  see also coal; oil
Engels, Friedrich 2, 29–30, 36–7, 39, 53
environmental issues 2, 5, 41, 42–53, 263
  air pollution 33, 134–5, 137
  America 112–13, 114–15, 121, 187
  China 120, 133–5, 136–7, 186
  energy 30–3, 46–7, 96
  environmental transition 45–6
  globalization 257
  regulation 4
  Sino-American relations 158–9, 165
  see also ecology; global warming
equity funds 21
Erzan, Ayse 204
Estonia 22
ethics 4, 6–7, 179, 264
  China 170–1
  Confucius 183–5
  Smith 180–3, 185
  Social Darwinism 106
  Washington Consensus 20
Ethiopia 190
ethnicity 155
euro currency 117–18
Europe
  agricultural output 68
  carbon dioxide emissions 51
  distribution of wealth 64
  energy consumption 49
  euro currency 117–18

financial crisis 85–7, 88–9
financial institutions 19
government borrowing 92
industrial policy 60
interest rates 90
Islam and 216–19
labor market changes 65
modern firms 17
pre-modern trade 11
privatization 13
recession 91
religion 188–9
Scientific Revolution 15–16
state capitalism 256
see also Eastern Europe; European Union
European Central Bank (ECB) 72, 81, 90, 94
European Union (EU)
carbon dioxide emissions 51
ecological footprint 113
overfishing 43
political unity 37
view of Hamas 241, 242
see also Europe
external firm 58–9

F
famine 36, 42
China 127, 129
Ireland 147
Fannie Mae 83
FAO see Food and Agriculture
Organization
farming see agriculture
fascism 97
Fatimid Caliphate 196, 208
Faust 41–2, 70
FDI see foreign direct investment
Federal Reserve 23, 72, 81, 83, 84, 90, 117
Feith, Douglas 238
fertility rates 35, 143–4
finance 4, 19–23, 41, 70–96, 97, 255
America 116–19, 121, 187
China 120, 186, 188
global financial risk 22–3, 77, 258
instability 3, 5, 121, 263–4
Islamic 198–9, 203
liberalization 5, 13, 19–22, 39, 77, 88, 93, 161
Muslim world 202–3

Sino-American relations 160, 175–9
financial crisis 3, 5, 41, 79–89, 97, 255, 258–9
America 116–19, 169–70, 172
build-up to 71–9
call for greater regulation 93–5
China 171–2, 173
end of wild capitalism 7
implications for global warming 52
shift to economic crisis 89–92
Sino-American relations 175–9
see also Asian financial crisis; recession
financial institutions 10, 13, 19, 21–2
China 144–6
government bail-outs 81
Muslim world 202–3
proliferation of 75
see also banking
Financial Times 82, 84, 87, 88, 89, 92, 228
"first way of war" 153, 154–5, 234, 238
fishing industry 43
Fisk, Robert 233
FitzGerald, Edward 193
flags 121, 123
Food and Agriculture Organization (FAO) 37
food industry 42, 109–10
foreign direct investment (FDI) 13, 20
China 132–3, 138, 140, 142, 166
decline in 92
Muslim world 202
foreign exchange reserves 73, 76, 118, 160, 175–6, 258
Fortis 21, 86, 178
fossil fuels 30–1, 32, 46, 47, 49–50, 158, 257
see also coal; oil
France
arms supply to Gulf states 229
financial crisis 88–9
government borrowing 92
Israel/Palestine 231, 232, 233
nuclear weapons 97, 259
role in the Middle East 216–19
Suez Crisis 218
support for Israel 219, 239
Freddie Mac 83
free market economics 1, 25, 72
American foreign policy 151–2

free market economics (*cont.*)
  financial crisis 84, 87
  Smith's influence 179
  Social Darwinist ideology 105–7
  Washington Consensus 97, 104
  see also capitalism; liberalization
free trade 107, 151
freedom 29–40, 96
  America 167, 168
  China 170–1
  from control by others 34–5
  from nature 29–34
  from poverty 35–6
  Social Darwinism 105, 106, 107
  trade 37–9
  from war 36–7, 40
Freud, Sigmund 7, 264–5
Friedman, Milton 105, 106
Friedman, Thomas 23, 24
Frisch, Otto 162–3
Fukuyama, Francis 222
Fulbright, J. William 102, 156–7, 237

G
Gaia hypothesis 47
Galbraith, J. K. 71, 74, 77–8, 93–4
gas 30, 31
GATT *see* General Agreement on Tariffs
  and Trade
Gaza 232, 237, 242–3, 249
GDE (Guangdong Enterprises) 144
GDP *see* gross domestic product
General Agreement on Tariffs and Trade
  (GATT) 37
genocide 153
Germany
  fascism 97
  financial crisis 87, 88
  government borrowing 92
  trade surplus 161
  World War II 205, 235, 267–8
Gini coefficient 35, 63–4, 67, 140
GITIC (Guangdong International Trust
  and Investment Corp.) 144
"Global 1250" companies 26, 27, 60, 104–5,
  147
global warming 3, 32–3, 45, 47–52, 96, 257
  American impact on 114–15
  China 136–7

impact on fishing 43
nuclear energy 259
sea level rises 71
Sino-American cooperation 175
globalization 1, 2, 4–5
  American attitudes towards 5, 108, 169
  American dominance 104–5
  China 120, 133
  commonality between civilizations 261
  contradictions of 107, 255, 256–9, 263–5
  cultural 40
  driving forces of 52
  financial crisis 71, 72
  financial risk 22–3
  growth of capitalism 10–14
  inequalities 61, 63, 64, 67
  labor markets 108
  market size 24
  non-zero-sum games 17
Goethe, Johann Wolfgang von 41–2, 70, 254
Golan Heights 237, 249
Goldman Sachs 80, 82, 83, 89
Gorbachev, Mikhail 25, 130–1
Gore, Al 189
Great Britain
  arms supply to Gulf states 229
  economic cycles 147
  euro currency 118
  financial crisis 81, 85–6, 88
  government borrowing 92
  gun-related homicides 111
  incomes 65
  industrial policy 60
  Industrial Revolution 11, 69
  interest rates 90
  Israel/Palestine 231, 232, 233–4, 235
  mergers and acquisitions 39
  nationalism 260
  nuclear weapons 97, 259
  oil in the Middle East 220, 221, 225
  recession 91
  role in the Middle East 216–18
  Suez Crisis 218
  World War II 205
Great Depression 12, 79, 96, 105, 110, 167,
  168, 172
Green, T. H. 168
Greenspan, Alan 23, 72, 223
Grime's Graves 1–2

gross domestic product (GDP)
America 116, 117
China 46, 132, 137, 138, 166
developing countries 13, 35
energy use 32
government borrowing 92
Indonesia 204
international trade 38
Iran 227
Muslim world 203
guerrilla warfare 153
Gulf Cooperation Council 200
Gulf War (1990–91) 221, 223, 226

H
Hadley, Stephen 228
Haig, Alexander 240
Hamas 238–9, 240–3
Hamilton, Alexander 141
happiness 109, 182–3, 185
harmony 127, 184, 185
Hayek, Friedrich von 105
HBOS 85–6, 88, 178
health issues
American obesity 109–10
China 129, 143, 171, 188
developing countries 35, 68
hedge funds 23, 75
Hegel, G. F. 265
Herzl, Theodor 231
high-income countries
air pollution 33
anti-Western violence 205–6
banking 21, 22, 176
carbon dioxide emissions 50–1
class struggle 69
comparison with China 147, 148
consumption 53–4
distribution of wealth 64
energy consumption 48–9
environmental regulation 45
financial crisis 77, 79, 93, 178, 258
financial liberalization 13
forests 44
GDP growth 35, 132
"Global 1250" companies 26
globalization impact on 256
government borrowing 92
imports of consumer goods 38–9

industrial concentration 54
inequality 64–6
interest rates 73
international cooperation 97
large firms 5, 17, 18, 60, 256
personal debt 177
tourism 40
trade protection 12
wildlife populations 43
Hiroshima 154, 162–3, 259
Hizbollah 227, 238–9, 241, 244, 245–6
Hobsbawm, Eric 40
Hollings, Ernest 141
Holocaust 235
Homer 264, 268
Hong Kong 142, 144, 145–6, 160, 203–4
HRE see Hypo Real Estate
HSBC 21, 144
Hu Jintao 172
human nature 6, 7
Hungary 22, 27, 118
Huntington, Samuel 152, 155, 156, 189,
190, 193, 272n12
Hurricane Katrina 71, 111
Hymer, Stephen 24
Hypo Real Estate (HRE) 87

I
Ibn Battuta 196
Ibn Khaldun 210–11
Ibn Rushd (Averroës) 196
Iceland 86
ILO see International Labor Organization
IMF see International Monetary Fund
immigration 159, 260
see also migration
import-substituting industrialization
12–13
income distribution 3, 5, 35, 41, 61–4, 96
America 109, 166–7, 169
China 140, 170, 171, 188
global governance 70
high-income countries 65–6
regulation 4
see also inequality
India
agricultural output 68
coal use 50
distribution of wealth 64

India (*cont.*)
economic growth 72
  energy issues 32
  Hindu-Muslim violence 206, 218
  International Monetary Fund 80
  inward investment 166
  manufacturing 125
  nuclear weapons 97, 259
  number of Muslims in 190, 191
  regional trading bloc 118
  tertiary education 173
  trade with Muslim world 195, 196
indigenous peoples 153
individualism 1, 105–6, 114, 153, 169,
  246–7, 265
Indonesia
  Asian financial crisis 74
  attitudes towards America 249
  attitudes towards Iran 250
  capitalist modernization 213–14
  conflict in 206
  GDP growth 203–4
  number of Muslims in 191
  trade 202
industrial concentration 24, 26, 28–9,
  59–60, 256–7
  advertising and communication industry
    58
  aerospace industry 55–6
  beverage industry 56–7
  developing countries 53
  see also mergers and acquisitions
industrial growth 135, 137
industrial policy
  China 140, 142
  high-income countries 60
Industrial Revolution 11, 16, 17, 29, 69
  China 124
  coal use 47
  finance 19
  Second and Third 18
industrialization 36, 45, 66, 69, 143
  American protectionism 141
  import-substituting 12–13
  Muslim world 202
  national identity 260
inequality 3, 5, 41, 61–70, 96, 255, 263
  America 109, 120, 153, 166–7, 169, 187
  business power 60

capitalism 246–7
China 120, 138–40, 166, 170, 186
developing countries 66–8
Egypt 214
Gini coefficient 35, 63–4, 67, 140
global 61–4
globalization impact on 256
Gulf states 200
high-income countries 64–6
industrialization 260
Muslim world 205, 206–7, 210, 246
Sino-American relations 164–5
Smith on 181
Social Darwinism 106
usury 213
infant mortality 35, 133, 204
inflation 72–3
informal labor 66, 68, 139
information technology (IT) 2, 24, 27, 72
  American dominance 104–5
  China 140, 166
  impact on labor 65
  Sino-American relations 173
  see also technological progress
interest rates 73, 90, 116, 160, 259
Intergovernmental Panel on Climate
  Change (IPCC) 3, 49
International Labor Organization (ILO) 37
International Monetary Fund (IMF) 13, 19,
  23, 37, 176
  American influence 73–4, 93, 95
  Asian financial crisis 74
  Chinese votes 147, 176
  financial crisis 80–1, 82, 90, 94, 178
  global recession 91
  objectives 38
  resistance to financial regulation 79
international relations 96, 97, 150–1, 155,
  216, 259
International Telecommunications Union
  (ITU) 37
internationalization 39
investment 2, 137
  see also foreign direct investment
"invisible hand" 14–17, 18, 180
IPCC *see* Intergovernmental Panel on Climate Change
Iran
  America's drive for regime change 227, 248

attitudes towards 250
attitudes towards America 249
capitalism 201, 202, 213–14
education 204
infant mortality 204
Iranian Revolution 226
Kurds 215
nuclear weapons 225–6, 259
number of Muslims in 191
oil 74, 219, 220, 224, 225–8
private sector 202
rebellions 207
Shari'ati 208–9
support for Hizbollah 244, 245
"system disintegration" 166
Iraq
American invasion of 74, 119, 222–5,
  228, 247, 248, 259
attitudes towards America 249
British control over 217, 218, 221
capitalism 202, 213–14
conflict in 206
Israeli bombing of 240
Kurds 215
military presence in 229
oil 219, 220, 221–5, 247
Ottoman Empire 216, 230–1
private sector 202
rebellions 207–8
sanctions against 221–2, 248
struggle against extremism 242
"system disintegration" 166
Ireland 86–7, 147, 267, 270
Irgun 235
Islam 191–2, 246–7
Europe and 216–19
Golden Age of 196–7
Iran 226
modern capitalism 199–205
Muslim unity 215–16
pre-modern capitalism 193–9
"Third Way" 209–15
see also Muslim world
Islamic fundamentalism 206, 212, 213, 214,
  215, 250
Isma'ilis 208
Israel 119, 206, 209, 229–46, 248–9, 250
assault on Gaza (2008) 242–3, 249
British control over 217

Christian support for 238
creation of the state of 235–6, 249
financial and military support 238–9,
  249
French support for 219, 239
Great Revolt 234
Hamas 240–3
Iran's relationship with 225, 228
Jewish immigration to 233–5, 236, 249
King-Crane Commission 231–3
Lebanon conflict 243–6, 249
misperceptions of 188
nuclear weapons 97, 239–40, 259
Ottoman Empire 216, 230–1
settlements 237, 241, 249
Six Day War 230, 237, 249
as source of anti-Western hostility 216
Suez Crisis 218
Yom Kippur War 240
Zionist lobby 193
see also Palestine
IT see information technology
Italy 65, 67, 92
ITU see International Telecommunications
  Union

J
J. P. Morgan 21, 82, 85, 89, 144, 178
Japan
American bombing of 154
American cooperation with 152, 162
asset bubble 91
distribution of wealth 64
fascism 97
foreign exchange reserves 73, 160
gun-related homicides 111
industrial policy 60
interest rates 90
inward investment 166
nuclear weapons 259
recession 91
trade surplus 161
Jerusalem 194, 197–8, 237, 241, 249
Jevons, Stanley 30
Jews 230–1, 232
Christian support for 238
immigration to Palestine 218, 233–5,
236, 249
settlements in Israel 237, 241, 249

Johnson, Lyndon B. 238, 240
Jordan
  British control over 217
  Israeli War of Independence 236
  King-Crane Commission 232
  Ottoman Empire 216, 230–1
  Six Day War 237
  trade 202
justice 183, 210, 212

K
Kalam, Abdul 204
Kant, Immanuel 36
Kataeb movement 243, 244
Kennedy, John F. 110, 240
Keynes, John Maynard 71, 74–5, 176
Khatami, Mohammad 226–7
Kindleberger, C. P. 71, 74, 77–8
King-Crane Commission (1919) 231–3
King, Henry 231
King, Lloyd 254
King, Malcolm 78
King, Martin Luther 110
King, Mervyn 81
Kissinger, Henry 156
Köhler, Horst 94
Koran 191–2, 193–4, 201, 206–7, 210, 215,
246, 262
Korea see South Korea
Korean War (1950–53) 155
Kurds 215
Kuwait
  British control over 218
  Iraqi invasion of 221
  military presence in 229
  national identity 215
  oil 200, 219
Kyoto Protocol 32, 49–50, 115, 175

L
labor markets 64–5, 68–9, 183
  China 133, 139
  developing countries 66–7
  globalization impact on 108
large firms 5, 17–18, 24, 41, 96, 256–7
  China 133, 140–2
  ownership 39
  power of 263
  Sino-American relations 164

systems integrators 53–4
  see also business power; multinational
firms; transnational corporations
Latin America
  foreign banks 22
  foreign direct investment 20
  inequality 67
League of Nations 217, 231, 233
Lebanon
  capitalism 202
  French control over 217, 218
  Hizbollah 227, 241, 244, 245–6
  Israel conflict 206, 243–6, 249
  King-Crane Commission 232
  Ottoman Empire 216, 230–1
  Palestinian refugees 236
  struggle against extremism 242
Lehman Brothers 83, 87, 178
LeMay, Curtis 154
Lewis, Arthur 66
Lewis, Bernard 190
"Lewis phase" 138–9, 148, 205, 256
liberalization
  American foreign policy 151–2
  Asian financial crisis 74
  capital markets 108
  capitalist development 25
  China 177
  financial 5, 13, 19–22, 39, 77, 88, 93, 161
  Iran 227
  labor markets 64
  Muslim world 211
  Washington Consensus 161, 178, 258
  see also deregulation; privatization
Libya 202, 226, 249
life expectancy 35, 133, 201, 204
life instinct 7, 264–5
literacy 40
Lithuania 22
Lloyds TSB 85–6, 88, 178
Locke, John 153
love 6, 7, 167
Lovelock, James 31, 47
Lugar, Richard 174
Luxembourg 86

M
Malaysia
  attitudes towards America 249

attitudes towards Iran 250
   biofuels 44
   capitalist modernization 213–14
   foreign direct investment 202
   foreign exchange reserves 160
   trade 202
Mali 198, 201
Malthus, Thomas Robert 125
"Manifest Destiny" 153
manufacturing
   America 65, 104, 141
   China 11, 125, 132, 165
   outsourcing 25, 108
   Second Industrial Revolution 18
Mao Tse-tung 128–9, 130
market coordination
   "invisible hand" 14–17, 180
   "visible hand" 17–18, 58
Marshall, Alfred 23–4
Marx, Karl 2, 24, 29–30, 36–7, 39, 53
Marxism 208
Maslow, Abraham 109
materialism 106, 169, 213
McCarthy, Cormac 1, 150, 156
McNamara, Robert 163, 164, 259
McVeigh, Timothy 110–11
Mecca 194, 197, 220, 247, 249
media 34, 40, 52, 58, 183
Meeks, Geoff 24
Melville, Herman 112
mercantilism 36, 74
mergers and acquisitions 24, 25–6, 39, 53, 59–60
   advertising and communication industry 57–8
   aerospace industry 55
   beverage industry 57
   China 140
   financial firms 22, 88, 178
   stock markets 21
   truck industry 58
   see also industrial concentration
Merkel, Angela 51, 87, 94
Merrill Lynch 83, 178
Mexican War (1846–48) 154
Mexico
   financial crisis 23, 77, 258
   foreign banks 22
   oil 199

Middle Ages 11, 16, 19
middle class 14, 42, 50, 140, 226
   see also bourgeoisie
Middle East
   energy shock 32
   oil 46–7, 188, 199–200, 216, 219–28, 247, 248, 257–8
   pre-modern trade 11
   see also Muslim world
migration 14
   Chinese migrant workers 170, 171
   global labor markets 108
   rural-urban 66, 68–9, 139
   see also immigration
military power 97, 103
   Israel 239–40
   Muslim world 228–9
   Sino-American relations 161–4
   see also nuclear weapons; war
Mill, John Stuart 2, 29
Minsky, Hyman 71, 74
Mizuho Financial Group 21
Mofaz, Shaul 228
money
   China 126
   financial crisis 74–5, 76, 95
   Muslim world 198
moral hazard 81, 83, 93, 177
morality 167, 180–1
   see also ethics
Morgan Stanley 83, 89
Morocco 190, 202, 206, 218
Muhammad, Prophet 194, 210, 219, 247
mujahideen 208–9
multinational firms 20, 22, 24, 25
   American attitudes towards 108
   developing countries 66–7
   labor market changes 65
   see also business power; large firms;
transnational corporations
Muslim Brotherhood 214–15
Muslim world 4, 5, 6, 188–250
   American soft power 119
   America's relationship with 98, 102–4, 114, 156, 188–90, 247–50, 261–3
   anti-capitalist revolution 206–9
   anti-Western violence 205–6
   attitudes towards America 249
   energy security 174

financial institutions 19
Islamic "Third Way" 209–15
market coordination 14–15
military presence in 228–9
modern capitalism 199–205
oil 46–7, 188, 199–200, 216, 219–28, 247, 248, 257–8
pre-modern capitalism 193–9
responses to capitalism 205, 261–2
technological progress 16
unity 215–16

N
NAFTA see North American Free Trade Agreement
Nagasaki 154, 162, 259
Nasser, Gamal Abdel 202, 211, 214, 218, 219, 237
national flags 121, 123
national identity 259, 260
America 120, 152, 155, 156, 190
China 186
Muslim countries 215
Palestinians 240
National Security Strategy (2002) 151
nationalism 259–63
Arab 216–17, 231, 243
as barrier to cooperation 264
Palestinian 234
Zionist 234
nationalization
China 128
financial crisis 81, 84, 86, 88
Iran 225
Iraq 221
Muslim world 202
nature
control over 45, 52
freedom from 29–34
Needham, Joseph 124
Netherlands 80, 86
New Zealand 65, 111
Nigeria 190, 191
non-zero-sum games 16–17
North American Free Trade Agreement (NAFTA) 37
North Korea 259
Northern Rock 81, 88
nuclear energy 31, 48, 174, 225, 259

nuclear weapons 259, 264
America 97, 162–3, 164
China 163
Iran 225–6, 227–8
Israel 219, 239–40

O
Obama, Barack 169–70, 237, 242, 243
obesity 109–10
oil 46, 48, 257–8
American consumption 114–15, 175
Chinese consumption 135, 175
level of reserves 30–1
Muslim world 46–7, 188, 199–200, 216, 219–28, 247, 248
prices 30–1, 52, 74, 82, 109, 223–4, 227
Sino-American relations 157–8
Oklahoma City bombing (1995) 110–11
oligopolistic firms 17–18, 20, 26–7, 29, 256, 257
Oman 200, 218, 229
Oppenheimer, Robert 163
Orwell, George 267
Oslo accords (1993) 238, 241
Ottoman Empire 196–9, 216, 217, 230–1
outsourcing 25, 108, 166

P
Pakistan
attitudes towards America 249
attitudes towards Iran 250
capitalist modernization 213–14
GDP growth 203
handover of power 218
Islamic revival 214
military presence in 229
nuclear weapons 97, 259
number of Muslims in 191
Taliban's impact on 206
trade 202
Palestine
British control over 217, 218
conflict in 206
Hamas 240–3
Jewish immigration to 218, 233–5, 236, 249
King-Crane Commission 231–3
Ottoman Empire 230–1
soap industry 198

support for Palestinians 250
  UN Special Commission on 235–6
  see also Israel
Palestine Liberation Organization (PLO)
  240, 241, 243–4
Paulson, Hank 80, 84, 89, 177
Penrose, Edith 24
pensions 143, 171
Perle, Richard 222, 238
Persian Gulf
  Arab nationalism 216
  British control over 218
  military presence 228–9
  nuclear weapons 259
  oil 200, 219–20, 225
  see also Middle East; Muslim world
Peru 22
Pew Global Attitudes Survey 249–50
PLO see Palestine Liberation Organization
Poland 22, 118
Polanyi, Karl 69
politics
  China 125, 129, 130, 142–3, 146
  Hamas 241–2
  Iran 226–7
  Lebanon 244
  national basis of 263
  Ottoman Empire 197–8
  Turkey 214
  urbanization impact on 34
pollution
  China 46, 134–5, 137, 158
  high-income countries 33
  impact on fishing 43
  see also carbon dioxide emissions
Polo, Marco 126, 127
population growth 10, 35, 42
  Europe 15–16
  Sahel region 201
poverty 35–6, 54, 66
  America 168
  China 129, 132, 133, 138–40, 171
  Egypt 214
PPP see purchasing power parity
prices
  China 127
  financial crisis 82, 116, 117
  oil 30–1, 52, 74, 82, 109, 223–4, 227
  see also asset prices

privatization 13, 25, 38, 53, 93
  China 142
  Iceland 86
  Iran 227
  Muslim world 203, 246
  Soviet Union 131
  see also deregulation; liberalization
profit 29, 41, 78, 181, 261
Progressive Era 168
property
  China 125–6, 143
  commonality between civilizations 261
  free market economics 106
  Islam 210, 212, 215, 247
  Koran 193–4
  Smith on 181
protectionism 11, 12, 37, 38, 72
  America 141, 160, 166
  investment 172
  mergers and acquisitions 25
Protestantism 152–3
  see also Christianity
purchasing power parity (PPP) 32, 63–4,
  271n5
puritanism 153, 156–7
Putnam, Robert 168–9

Q
Qaissouni, Ibrahim 211
Qatar 218, 229
Qutb, Sayyid 191–2, 211–13, 214

R
R&D *see* research and development
racial segregation 154
Rafsanjani, Akbar Hashemi 226
Rato, Rodrigo 80, 118
RBS *see* Royal Bank of Scotland
Reagan, Ronald 130
recession 86, 87, 89–92, 96
  America 111, 116, 117, 166, 179, 187
  China 138, 145, 146, 179, 186
  Sino-American relations 161
  see also economic crisis; financial crisis
Rees, Martin 264
refugees 236
regulation 3–4, 97, 255, 262, 264
  carbon trading 49–50
  environmental 33, 38, 45, 113, 136

financial 76–7, 79, 80, 81, 93–6, 175–6
Sino-American relations 173
Reinsch, William 158
religion 152–3, 188–90
research and development (R&D)
  aerospace industry 54, 55
  America 173
  China 173
  external firm 59
  "Global 1250" companies 26, 27, 60
resources 2, 4, 5, 174
  see also energy; fossil fuels
"Ricardo effect" 92
Rice, Condoleezza 151, 152, 244–5, 272n11
risk 22–3, 77, 258
Rogoff, Kenneth 78, 118–19
Roosevelt, Franklin D. 168, 220
Roubini, Nouriel 82
Royal Bank of Scotland (RBS) 88
Rubin, Robert 80
Rumsfeld, Donald 222
rural-urban migration 66, 68–9, 139
Russia
  economic growth 72
  financial crisis 23, 77, 258
  nuclear weapons 97, 163, 259
  October Revolution 12
  Sykes-Picot Agreement 231
  tertiary education 173
  see also Soviet Union

S
Saddam Hussein 221, 223, 226, 241, 248
Sahel region 61, 191, 198, 200–1
Said, Edward 102
Salam, Abdus 204
Samuel, Herbert 233
Samuel, Rinna 230
sanctions 226, 227
Sarkozy, Nicolas 94
Saudi Arabia
  American presence in 248
  military power 229
  oil 200, 219, 220–1, 247
savings 137, 159
science 173–5, 196
Scientific Revolution 15–16
self-interest 6, 104, 105, 106, 150, 185
September 11th 2001 terrorist attacks 154,

193, 205, 248
  Iraq linked to 222, 223
  "war against terrorism" 103, 107, 240
Shari'ati, Ali 208–9, 211
Sharon, Ariel 237
Sinai 237
Singapore 160, 203–4
Six Day War (1967) 230, 237, 249
slavery 153–4
Slovakia 22
small firms 17, 24, 26
Smith, Adam 2, 14–15, 36, 61, 125, 179–83,
  184–5
soap industry 198
social capital 168–9
social cohesion 183, 184–5
Social Darwinism 1, 6, 104, 105–7, 167, 168,
  170, 172, 262
social instincts 167
social justice 185, 208, 213
social science 132
socialism
  Arab 211, 246, 256
  Chinese 262
  Nordic 256
soft power 119, 233
solar energy 31–2, 50
Soros, George 93
South Asia
  agricultural output 68
  financial institutions 19
  handover of power 218
  market coordination 14–15
  pre-modern trade 11
  see also Bangladesh; India; Pakistan
South Korea
  American cooperation with 152, 162
  foreign exchange reserves 160
  GDP growth 204
  global firms 140
  industrial policy 60
  inward investment 166
  regional trading bloc 118
Southeast Asia
  financial crisis 74
  foreign direct investment 20
  foreign exchange reserves 73
  pre-modern trade 11
  see also East Asia

Soviet Union
  Afghanistan 206
  American foreign policy 151, 165
  anti-capitalism 261
  collapse of communism 13, 106, 156, 165
  economic development 12
  foreign direct investment 202
  Gorbachev's reforms 25, 130–1
  personal debt 177
  "system disintegration" 166
  World War II 206
  see also Russia
species extinction 44
speculation 71–2, 74, 78, 82, 93–4, 95, 144,
  258
standard of living 35, 38–9, 44, 131
standardization 67
Stapledon, Olaf 254
state intervention 25, 38
  America 168, 172
  China 126, 127
  industrial policy 60
state-owned enterprises
  China 139, 140, 141, 142, 146, 174
  Europe 13
  Iran 227
State Street 89
Staunton, Sir George 125
Stern Gang 234, 235
stock markets
  American dominance 104
  capitalization 13, 20–1, 145
  China 146
  emerging markets 92
  financial crisis 87, 90
Strauss-Kahn, Dominique 80
"sub-prime" housing market 79
Sudan 190–1, 198, 206, 217
Suez Crisis (1956) 217–18, 219, 239
Sufism 192, 208
Sunyaev, Rashid 204
"survival of the fittest" 6, 105
  see also Social Darwinism
sustainable development 7, 103, 255, 262
  China 120, 186
  financial crisis impact on 172
  science and technology 173, 174
Swiss Central Bank 81
Switzerland 80

Sykes-Picot Agreement (1915) 231
Syria
  capitalism 202
  foreign direct investment 202
  French control over 217, 218
  King-Crane Commission 231–2
  Ottoman Empire 216, 230–1
  Palestinian refugees 236
  Six Day War 237
  soap industry 198
  support for Hizbollah 244, 245
  Yom Kippur War 240
systems integrators 26, 28, 53–4
  aerospace industry 55
  beverage industry 56
  external firm 18, 58–9

T
Taiwan 152, 160
Taliban 206, 213, 222
technological progress 2, 27–9, 30,
  255
  agriculture 35–6
  beverage industry 56–7
  capitalist development 10, 11, 12
  China 124, 126, 136, 137
  commonality between civilizations
    261
  consumer durables 34
  energy technology 31, 32, 33, 50, 257
  fishing industry 43
  impact on labor 108
  oligopolistic firms 17–18
  population growth 42
  research and development 27
  Scientific Revolution 15–16
  Sino-American relations 173–5
  Smith on 15
  transport 33, 257
  trucks 58
  see also information technology
telecommunications 34, 40
terrorism 103, 199, 205–6
  Al Qaeda 206, 213, 224, 248–9
  Hamas 241–2
  Israel 234, 235, 236, 238, 240
  "war against" 103, 107, 240, 245
  see also September 11th 2001 terrorist
    attacks

textile industry 125
Thailand 204
Thatcher, Margaret 130
"Third Way"
  Chinese 127–8
  Islamic 209–15
Thoreau, Henry 269, 270
Tiananmen Square 123, 130
Timbuktu 198, 201
Torah 230
tourism 40
trade 2, 11, 12, 37–9
  American foreign policy 151, 152
  China 124, 138, 142, 166, 172
  Muslim world 194, 195–6, 197, 198, 202, 246
  Sino-American relations 159–61, 165–6
transition economies 22
Transjordan 236
transnational corporations 39, 96, 132–3
  see also business power; large firms; multinational
firms
transport 12, 16, 27–8
  America 109, 114, 115
  automobile industry 48
  carbon dioxide emissions 50, 51–2
  China 135, 174
  costs of 257
  energy 46
  green technologies 33
  trucks 58
Trichet, Jean-Claude 78, 94
trucks 58
Truman, Harry S. 162, 220, 235
Tunisia 202, 206, 208, 218
Turkey
  capitalism 201–2, 213–14
  education 204
  GDP growth 203
  infant mortality 204
  Islamic revival 214
  Kurds 215
  military presence in 229
  number of Muslims in 191
  trade 202
  see also Ottoman Empire
Twain, Mark 1, 70

U
UAE see United Arab Emirates
UBS 21
UN see United Nations
UNCTAD see United Nations Conference on Trade and Development
underdevelopment 44
underemployment 68–9, 139, 204–5, 256
unemployment 116–17, 168
United Arab Emirates (UAE)
  British control over 218
  capitalism 199
  military presence in 229
  national identity 215
  oil 200, 219
United Kingdom see Great Britain
United Nations (UN) 37, 79, 235–6
United Nations Conference on Trade and Development (UNCTAD) 37, 92
United States of America see America
urbanization 34, 66
  China 133
  Egypt 214
  Muslim world 203
US-China Economic and Security Review Commission (USCESRC) 160
usury 198, 212–13

V
value chain 18, 28, 58, 59
values
  American 151, 153, 240
  Islamic 192, 215, 241
Venezuela 22, 199, 224
Vietnam War 155
violence
  America 110–11, 153
  anti-Western 205–6
  Hamas 241–2
  Muslim world 209
  see also conflict; terrorism; war
"visible hand" 17–18, 58
Vivat Bacchus restaurant 61, 62
Volcker, Paul 3, 93

W
Wachovia 83, 85, 178
Waco siege (1993) 110, 111
wages 65–6

Wang Lixiong 150
war 12, 163–4
   American Civil War 110, 154
   "first way of" 153, 154–5, 234, 238
   freedom from 36–7, 40
   Gulf War 221, 223, 226
   Iraq 74, 119, 222–5, 228, 247, 248, 259
   Korean War 155
   Mexican War 153
   nationalism 260
   Six Day War 230, 237, 249
   World War I 37, 193, 217, 264–5
   World War II 37, 154, 205–6, 235, 267–8,
      270
   Yom Kippur War 240
   see also conflict; military power; violence
"war against terrorism" 103, 107, 240, 245
Warnke, Paul 240
Washington Consensus 13, 19–20, 80, 178
   American dominance 93, 97, 104, 258
   Asian financial crisis 5, 74, 161
   Chinese resistance to 130, 131, 177
   deep integration 92
   deregulation 176
   financial firms 22
   international institutions 38, 73
   see also free market economics;
   liberalization
Washington Mutual 83, 85, 178
water control 126–7
water pollution 134
Watts, Alan 193
weapons of mass destruction 222, 223
   see also nuclear weapons
welfare systems
   China 143, 170, 171
   Islam 212
   Muslim Brotherhood 215
Wells Fargo 85, 89, 178
Wen Jiabao 102, 136, 170–1, 185, 187–8
West Bank 232, 236, 237, 238, 241, 242, 249
Whitman, Walt 33–4, 167
WHO see World Health Organization
"wild capitalism" 1, 2–3, 7, 41
Willoughby, William 168
Wilson, Edward 3, 43, 44, 45, 113
Wilson, Woodrow 231, 232, 233
Wolf, Martin 82
Wolfowitz, Paul 80, 222

World Bank 13, 19, 37
   American influence 73–4
   capital flows 92
   China 139
   Egypt 214
   financial crisis 80–1
   inequality 67
   objectives 38
   wages 65
World Health Organization (WHO) 37
World Trade Organization (WTO) 37–8,
   141, 142
World War I 37, 193, 217, 264–5
World War II 37, 154, 205–6, 235, 267–8,
   270
World Wildlife Fund (WWF) 43, 49, 113
Wright, Robert 17
WTO see World Trade Organization
WWF see World Wildlife Fund

Y
Yom Kippur War (1973) 240

Z
Zewali, Ahmed 204
Zionism 193, 231, 233, 238
   counter-insurgency 234
   French support for 219
   influence on American policy 220
   King-Crane Commission 231–2
   Operation Hiram 236
Zoellick, Robert 80, 165, 222

About the author

Peter Nolan has researched, written, and taught on a wide range of issues in economic development, globalization, and the transition of former planned economies.

He has undertaken research on many of the world's leading companies and has been closely involved in public policy in both China and the UK. He has testified before the US–China Economic and Security Review Commission in the US Congress. He also speaks each year at the China Development Forum, organised by the Chinese government.

Peter Nolan holds the Sinyi Chair in the Judge Business School, University of Cambridge, and is Chair of the University's Development Studies Committee. He is Director of the China Executive Leadership Programme, which brings together leaders of top Chinese and global companies.

He has written numerous books including: *The Political Economy of Collective Farms* (1987); *China's Rise, Russia's Fall* (1995); *Coca-Cola and the Global Business Revolution* (1999); *China and the Global Business Revolution* (2001); *China and the Global Economy* (2001); *China at the Crossroads* (2003); *Transforming China* (2004); *Integrating China* (2006); and *Capitalism and Freedom* (2006).

John Lloyd, of the *Financial Times*, said in January 2000: "Peter Nolan knows more about Chinese companies and their international competition than anyone else on earth, including in China."

In 2009 he was awarded a CBE for "services supporting China's integration into the global economy," and an honorary doctorate from the Copenhagen Business School, Denmark.